Few are guilty,
But everyone is responsible…

An Invitation to Reason:

A Collection of Observations, Meditations, Anecdotes, Stories, Quotes and Concerns about Religion and Judaism in Today's World

By

Nourallah (Norman) Gabay

An Invitation to Reason:

"Man, as nature's frail being, was endowed with two things that should make him the strongest amongst animals: Reason and Sociability."

Lucio AnnioSineca

"I do not want my house to be rounded by walls and my windows to be closed to other cultures. I wish to become familiar with the culture of lands as much as possible, but I will not permit them to affect me or shake me from my own status."

Mahatma Gandhi

The secret of the unparalleled growth of the United States has been her embrace of a wide array of diverse cultures allowing them to meet and to merge. Let's not close ourselves off in the name of "religious observance." No bird ever learned how to fly while inside a cage. The breadth of man's conscience is miles above the bitter narrowness of bigotry.

Norman Gabay

Introduction

In the three decades since the Jewish mass emigration from Iran, one would have expected our community to advance by learning from the progressive achievements of our host countries and stand in step with the rationalist and intellectual segments of world Jewry.

Instead, a small yet active group of superstitious extremists have been promulgating isolation and dogma in the guise of promoting the Jewish religion and in the name of protecting our youth from the corrupting taint of a contemporary culture they deem immoral. These extremists follow a series of conflicting ideas and use them to steer our youth away from the realities of our time. This group proselytizes for following our ancestors' way of life at the cost of tearing apart our families today. The Jewish culture of our ancestral tradition was never the collection of superstitions they preach. At the same time, they remain oblivious to the fact that a culture can only be won over by a more powerful and exalted one.

The Jewish religion was established with the express prohibition against the worship of another human being, the making of idols and the spreading of superstitions and falsehoods – it was not meant to further such actions. The secret to preventing the misfortunes of the past is not to repeat them. Instead success for our community lies in being in step with our time.

There is a well-known Persian saying that the strongest of storms can't cause the slightest ripple at the bottom of the well. Likewise, the great tragedies of our past, the mass murders of millions of our people, and the setting of our libraries on fire, have not succeeded in causing permanent damage to Jewish culture – or to any culture similarly threatened.

Throughout history, many wicked enemies of culture have set the libraries of many nations ablaze – not only that of the Jews but also the Egyptians, the Chinese and the Persians. Little did they know that although they might postpone the growth of a culture by violence and enforced regression, they could never destroy its long-term progress.

The evolution of culture is very much like giving birth: if a mother or doctor tries to stop the process, the child will be lost and the mother may suffer as well. In a similar fashion, no religion, ideology or power can stop the march of time –they must adapt or suffer the consequences. Contrary to the claims of extremists, remaining in step with modern times does not contradict the essence of any religion. Even if the religion remains constant, its adherents must come to terms in each generation with the world around them. Religion may be inherited but its believers and their world change over time and they need to understand their religion in the context of their times.

The extremists' position is not unlike that of the man who sold blocks of ice. Empty-handed, he was asked: "Have you sold all your ice?" "No," he replied, "It all melted away." Similarly, the irrational beliefs and nonsense spread by the extremists will melt away – nothing will remain. Yet we can neither ignore nor remain complacent to the falsehoods of these regressive traditionalists.

This writer's criticisms are not of the Jewish religion, or any religion, but against those who would contaminate religion with superstition and preach those ideas. The basic tenets of the religion, such as the Ten Commandments, remain eternal. It is how those traditions and commandments are applied to our modern life that is of concern. It is the belief of this writer that for our religion to remain vibrant, the first step to success is to remain up-to-date and adapt the commandments to our times.

Oriana Fallaci once wrote, "There are moments in life, when one's silence would be wrong, and her speaking out becomes a human duty, a moral fight, a necessity – escaping from which would be equal to evading responsibility."

This volume was not written out of some supernatural mission but rather a responsibility to do so. I believe emphatically that the secret to securing the survival of the Jewish religion is to rid it of the irrational nonsense and superstitions that many mistakenly attribute to the religion itself as well as to cast out those who promote such bogus thinking.

Having written over a hundred articles, I gather my thoughts in one volume for you, my respected reader. I first wrote this book in Farsi and the Farsi version of this book has been successful in our community that I decided to have it translated to English version so that the younger generation and other people will be able to read this book.

In writing these pages, I am aware that each individual has the right to his or her beliefs as long as they don't impinge on the rights of others – and that such rights are crucial and vital to our free society. Just as no two people have the same fingerprints, each person's perceptions are unique and no writer will be able to please everyone.

I have put down my thoughts to address the issues of our time. If I use the words of erudite poets and scientists, I also rely on the notion that "everyone understands an idea according to his own capacity." In addressing these issues, I do so for the betterment of society, and without any fantasy about the realities facing us. Indeed, it is my conviction that, in the long run, humanity always adapts itself to reality.

In this book, I reaffirm the need to preserve the many rational aspects of religion that benefit society and pays due respect to moderate, rational and logical religious persons. Such leaders have the author's approval: Instead of blindly imitating the past, they have led themselves and their children to the highest contemporary level of humane social thought.

By contrast, I have reserved my criticism for a regressive and superstitious group who use religion to obstruct the progress of society, even at the price of causing great rifts among families and within society itself. I will, with the support of various sources and documents, try to convince my reader that each generation needs to support an evolution in its thinking. If its logical beliefs are to survive, we cannot preach a rigid mindset and inflexible attitude.

I issue a warning: We need to stop the growth of regressive traditionalism in our religious schools and among our families by spreading knowledge and by providing accurate information. If we do not, our children will be denied their rightful place in contemporary society.

In writing this book I am aware of the various reactions and strong opposition I am inviting. I call upon my like-minded readers to help spread the ideas developed in this book, by examining its contents in private gatherings and fostering critical debates.

Norman (Nourallah) Gabay

Winter 2011, Los Angeles.

Foreword

By

Nourollah Kharrazi

Mr. Nourollah Kharrazi is widely recognized as one of the most beloved writers of the Iranian Jewish community. The following is an abridged adaption of his original introduction to the book in Persian.

My good friend, relative and namesake, Mr. Nourollah Gabay, has penned a book that deserves a standing ovation! The subject matter is bigotry, prejudice, short-sightedness and blind traditionalism. These evils can render meaningless whatever they infect. They may even affect a family, tearing it apart with hostilities. This is a grave matter, and its weight can be felt on each page of this book.

Mr. Gabay, who has studied the subject of traditionalists, or "antique-worshipers," at great length, has made a surgical analysis of the problem, and presents his findings in his typically sweet Persian prose. He doesn't hesitate to bring in appropriate quotations and anecdotes from a diverse array of sources, mixing up poetry and prose, in order to prove his point. How well he has succeeded in his goal! But as passionate as he is in his argument, he never offends the religious extremists, because his job has been to offer kind guidance not to present vehement complaints. Even when on occasion he is infuriated by the nonsense he sees in the words and deeds of some extremists, he simply asks the reader to put aside regressive traditionalism and to avoid hurting our youngsters and intellectuals with a religion contaminated with superstitious thought. He reminds me of the man who said, "Religion was born for people, not people for religion." Religion is generally a good counsel, that is, until it's mixed with superstition; then, it can become a means to mislead its followers.

Originally, the commandments of religion were meant to look forward; they were meant to be like a ladder, helping us to ascend and progress. But in the hands of these traditionalists, they have turned into a ladder that has missing rungs and that threatens to make trusting climbers fall. Mr. Gabay has done a laudable job of explaining this issue in a pleasant way. I highly recommend this book to you and your friends, because every word is genuine and heartfelt. Faith is a gift to us, and we shouldn't let it be infected by the illness of superstitions. It's our trusted compass, and shouldn't be allowed to fall into the hands of those who might break it; otherwise, once broken our compass won't guide us, it will mislead us, instead leaving the true lovers of the religion ashamed of, or even outraged, by the label of "religious."

The late Dr. Houshang Ebrami used to say that some of the best articles are those written with sincerity and in a familiar voice by the non-expert. This is such a book, and it's a key to solving the problem of prejudice in our society.

Nourollah Kharrazi

A Word of Truth…!

Foreword

By

Manouchehr Omidvar

Mr. Omidvar is one of most revered journalists and political analysts of the Iranian Jewish community. Currently, he continues to write as the editor in chief of the widely read Persian magazine Payam*, in New York. The following is an abridged adaptation of an original introduction in Persian.*

For a long time, I have read Mr. Nourollah Gabay's writings as published in the various Persian outlets. He is a writer who speaks the truth but masks its often bitter taste with a sugar coating for his readers. Needless to say, those who are after the naked truth wouldn't need such attractive devices; to these, only original logic and blunt expression is needed.

My dear friend, Mr. Gabay, feels the pain in his heart, and rightly lets his pain out on the page. No doubt others such as this critic have felt or observed the sting of superstition. But they often shun the responsibility to express their concern. They tend to sweep the trash under the rug allowing the pain to grow until it's too late for any remedies. Of course, even a layman can realize that in today's world, wealth alone cannot bring us pride. At the beginning of the 21st century, more than ever, no society can hold its head high without depending on modern knowledge and science. Any group or individual who wishes to steer society off the main road and onto the dead end that is superstition, keeping them in the dark, is a de facto traitor to the religion.

The success of the state of Israel is a good case in point. Israel is a small, young country, with a population of about 6 million. It's surrounded by many hostile neighbors, some of whom even call for its eradication. Yet, over the past 60 years, Israel has managed to defend herself successfully in five major wars, against much more populous and wealthier countries. Despite wars and a lack of mineral resources, such as oil fields, Israel has managed to raise its *per capita* income to the standards of advanced Western countries. If it were not for her strong secular and scientific foundations, how could Israel have survived the unceasing storms of opposition?

Today we live in a different world, where we need to understand the nature of change to prepare ourselves for life in the modern world. Of course, respect for traditions of the past, national identity, and ancient political beliefs should be encouraged; but in order to live in the modern world we need the means of science, industry, defense and the modern economy.

A careful and unbiased study of Mr. Gabay's thoughts in this collection is certainly "a pathway to the land of light." I recommend this book to those interested in exploring such themes further.

Manouchehr Omidvar

New York

A Special Word to Young Adults, Children and Grandchildren:

I am certainly older than you, but I cannot say that I am wiser. I have, nonetheless, seen something of life, and had insight about life experiences that I can share with you. I cannot force you to read this book, but I encourage you to consider it, its words, its meaning, and its intent.

The story is told about the boy who pondered how to eat an elephant. The older man answered: "One bite at a time." Try this book and see if, one bite at a time, it opens your mind to new ideas, or helps you to expand your horizons. For, in truth, this book is written not for me, but for you.

I apologize in advance if some of you have heard me say these words in public, at my grandchildren's bar-mitzvahs or on other occasions, but I feel they are worth repeating:

Children are a blessing unmatched by any other that God bestows. Our eyes can behold nothing finer or brighter than our children or grandchildren.

Most of life's difficulties come when they are least expected. In order to have a good life at age 80, you must start preparing for those events at age 13. You can only be as substantial as your determination and as significant as the limit of your imagination.

Maturity has much more to do with understanding than age. You must decide who you will become. You may appear one way to some, but confidence in your ability and self-worth together with life experience shall mold you into the person you are to be.

Do not judge people based on brief experiences with them just as you cannot judge a tree by only one season. Like a tree, the essence of anyone, that is the pleasure, joy, and love that comes from that life, can only be measured at the end of that life, when all the seasons have passed. Do not judge life by one difficult season. Persevere when it is difficult and you will be ready for better times when they come.

Making right decisions in your life comes from having relevant and correct information.

Fortunately for you, in this age and time, there are limitless sources for obtaining social, economic, and scientific information. Information is power and to advance in life, you need to be more up-to-date than the past generation. Otherwise you will be left behind. To get there, you will need more than those life rules learned from books. You will need to understand the experiences of your siblings and friends so that you are aware of the exceptions to those rules. The way you handle these exceptions is what makes or breaks the opportunities in your life. Remember "anybody who points out your fault is not your enemy; he is your best friend..." As the Talmud says,"*Vadilma Ipkha Ipkha Mistabra.*"

Discover who is wise and who is not. You will evaluate the past and present experiences of your friends and family so that as you, and eventually your children live your lives, you may draw upon these experiences while increasing your joy and happiness by sharing them with others.

Life is the sum of all events occurring during its span, be they both happy and sad. So to be successful, you must not take your shoulder out of responsibility, but rather build a stronger shoulder. As stated in a famous Proverb "An ounce of prevention is better than a pound of cure."

You obtain some of this prevention from the daily experience of your life.

Learning is not a process that takes place just in school. Utilizing what you learn in school is perhaps more important, and is a true art form. Success in life is not just piling up money and getting rich. Money cannot buy you experience, but being well informed and effective and helpful to members of your family and community are what determine success or failure in your life. Similarly, the beauty of a home is not in its architecture and decorations, but in the quality of the people entering and leaving it. Therefore, choose your friends well because they will have an enormous impact on your life and the life of your children and your spouse. Seek their advice often and remember no one is rich enough to do without advice, and no one is poor enough not to be able to seek advice.

People do not become just each other's friends. They become each other's partners in their success, happiness, and knowledge. You will be proud of your friendship when you become their trusted advisor, and they yours.

You are now directly responsible for your own actions. You and you alone are the hero of your life, the architect of your future and responsible for your family and siblings. Today's successful adults are yesterday's studious children. You cannot buy experience but you can learn from experienced people.

Life is not a rehearsal and man lives only once and that life is not long. Never wait for luck. Good luck does not go to those who are sitting and waiting for it to knock at their doors.

You must be prepared. Your family supports you but the only person who can make a success of your life is you. Parents, Grandparents, teachers and books cannot teach you everything you need but they will be able to point you to the right direction.

If you want to know what you will be, see what you are doing now. Understand what is harmful and what is not; who is your wise friend and who is not. From this day on, prepare yourself for a better tomorrow.

A Friendly Conversation

With the Respected Leaders of Traditional Schools

Concerning Religious Studies in the Era of Science

"The world is a dangerous place to live; not because of the people who are evil, but because of the people who don't do anything about it." (Albert Einstein)

"The pain of the patient can go away,
only after the doctor has found the cause."
(Persian Classical Poem)

Respected Leaders, dear Instructors,

I'm certain that you would agree that to cure society of the ills of narcissism, dogmatism and bigotry, we need constructive criticism followed by rational solutions. Not all men think the same way and not all people reach the summit of progress at the same time. We can only discover truth by relying on freedom of speech and by tolerating the expression of opposing views. Freedom of speech and tolerance are two of the most important privileges of civilized societies. Intelligent people may look for solutions to problems; but the true genius prevents such problems from happening. Let's join together to find such solutions.

I write these lines as a humble student in search of knowledge, admitting that I lack in information, well aware that others more erudite that I might better satisfy your doubts and concerns. Yet, as a concerned member of our community, I find it is my obligation to share my views with you. I hope my readers receive this with an open mind and a generous spirit, and that a critical dialogue might follow, resulting in positive changes in our thinking.

In writing these lines, it is my hope that religious teachers will join with parents to prevent the spread of backwards and anachronistic thinking within our community, an illness that is clearly not exclusive to any single religion or school of thought. It is urgent that we halt a backwards slide away from progress. This is why I ask you, please, to let me express my opinion, as well as I can, on the issue of excessive religious studies among our youth. Let me share not only my ideas, but particularly, the well-thought out and diverse answers that I have gathered from the writings of a variety of critics on religious factional topics.

The late Persian humorist, Abolghasem Halat, once noticed that "few books are published in the world that doesn't need any proof-reading and subsequent corrections." Given the immensity of my task, I will be happy if only the essence of the subject is communicated to my erudite readers, both you the educators as well as the thousands of students of religious schools.

The present book has been organized as a collection of diverse views and different critiques. The reader will find essays, thoughts, arguments, poems and quotations – each in its manner intending to highlight some of the weaknesses of today's traditional and extremist religious cultures; it hopes to find the causes behind the problems; and it aspires to invite everyone to find solutions to the internal issues of our small community, and by extension, those of the larger society.

The readers of this book are familiar, no doubt, with the ongoing problem of brainwashing by those whom I call "regressive traditionalists" or "regressors" -- those individuals belonging to the backwards looking and anachronistic factions who seek to continuously advance the promotion of superstitions and nonsense. At times I refer to their leaders as *mullahs* and their edicts as *fatwas* because they act as such. They are extremists who would have others believe they are our representatives, or have us believe they are the keepers or preservers of our faith, when, as I argue, they are nothing of the sort.

The arguments are presented herein not only by dry reasoning, but also through the use of appropriate, enjoyable and inspiring quotations, proverbs, poems and anecdotes, which have been selected not only from our Persian literary heritage, but also from the world's treasury of recorded ideas. These will hopefully encourage the reader's curiosity and persuade him to consider the arguments presented herein with an open mind. I ask for your generosity of spirit to forgive the shortcomings of this book, at the very least, in return for the sweetness of these anecdotes.

This humble writer would never claim to be either a guide or an advisor to scholars, or to other knowledgeable readers of this book. However, I have no doubt, that someone who has experienced first-hand the pain of what the regressive traditionalists has done to our community can attract curious minds to discuss these problems. It shouldn't matter that some see these problems as self-evident or others find this discussion redundant.

What matters is that an attempt be made to offer credible arguments and constructive suggestions to illuminate the general public's mind about the dangerous trends at large in our community. I do so to encourage a collective effort aimed at finding the causes behind these trends, and to fight against those who in the guise of religion try to blend truth with falsehood. I am stepping forward to present my thoughts because I believe it's no shame to make a mistake; but it *is* a shame if one never finds out about his mistakes; and still worse, if he goes on repeating those mistakes.

Winston Churchill once said, "I have benefited greatly from criticism, and I have never suffered for a lack of it."

A Persian poet once said, "It takes not only time, but talent, effects and disposition, persistence, pathos, and personal experience, to turn a child into a wise mind or into a charming poet." The majority of us can only try to do our share and hope that we have contributed something worthwhile to humankind.

My friends! Those who seek out truth are indeed desirable, regardless of their station in society. By contrast, those who support superstition and illusion-filled nonsense are doomed, even if they have a grip on power. The one who imagines that he knows the whole truth is simply wrong, because the entire truth can only be known to people as a whole.

However the sort of people who believe that they alone know how we should live and ask us to forsake modern ways, have been present throughout the history of mankind. The pain of regression is not a new ill.

Even the great Persian poet, Omar Khayyam (1048-1142, C.E.), complained about such human follies in his poetry, some 900 years ago, writing:

"Those yet unborn would never wish to be born,
If they'd only known of our suffering in the world."

The ancient Persian prophet, Zoroaster or Zarathustra, a.k.a.
Zartosht, wrote, "Listen to the best of words, and evaluate it with the clearest of thoughts. Only then one can find his own way freely."

Meanwhile, those passionate religious followers of today would do well to heed the wise advice of Al-Farabi (872-951, C.E.), offered more than 1000 years ago, that "Since we own some ancient words, we have everything." About those who just parrot age old sayings, repeating them, promoting them, and worse, teaching them out of context, and without critical thinking, Al-Farabi wrote:

"To be a good thinker, one who is able to formulate theories, we need to satisfy three conditions:

1) We should know and fully understand all the laws and the premises of the subject;

2) We should be able to make the necessary deductions and inductions from the laws of that particular science, so that we might come to the right conclusions;

3) We should be able to find the reasons behind regressions and mistakes; to answer the erroneous ideas; to analyze other people's thoughts and opinions; to distinguish between right and wrong; and to correct the errors."

Do those who think of themselves as "religious people" or even hold some religious rank or position, even satisfy the above basic qualifications? This humble writer, for one, admits that he doesn't meet all of the above requirements. Thus, I quote the French philosopher, René Descartes (1596-1650 C.E.):

"In studying a subject, we shouldn't look for what others think or what we ourselves imagine, to be true, but we should look for something that can be seen clearly, or else, something that we can prove through analogical or deductive reasoning. That is the only way to achieve scientific knowledge."

The works of those commentators, whose sayings have been rendered inaccurate or whose writings no longer agree with the proven facts of modern science, should be consigned to the library archives. Even Buddha (563-483 B.C.E.), the wise man of the East, wrote:

"We shouldn't believe in something, just because others have said it. We shouldn't accept the reports of others, just because they have come to us from the past. We shouldn't submit to the thoughts, sayings or writings of the wise men, without thinking for ourselves, just because those words belonged to a wise man. We shouldn't readily accept anything, just based on partial similarities and analogies. We shouldn't accept just everything that comes our way. We shouldn't take the master's words for anything, just because they are his words."

We should only accept any idea, regardless of what form it takes, whether spoken or written, if we are convinced of its truth as confirmed clearly and unequivocally, by independently relying on our own thought, knowledge and understanding.

The great Persian poet, Ferdowsi (935-1020 C.E.) wrote,

"My salutes go to the one whose very fabric is composed of justice and knowledge."

Let's remember the valuable words of General Douglas MacArthur (1880-1964), who once said, "There is no security on this earth; there is only opportunity." Let's not take away this unique opportunity for learning from our students in the name of religion. Let's not waste their one-time chance at life. No power will ever be able to permanently obstruct the path of humanity's progressive evolution.

Let's be realistic, because our reality, or our perception thereof, has continued to evolve and progress by staying in step with science and the scientific thought, not through prejudice and bigotry. That's all there is!

Surely, we have all run into people who have become aliens to logic, as a result of their unbending prejudice; who are trying to force the world to adapt to them, instead of trying to adapt themselves to the world. Let's ask ourselves if such people can ever succeed? Have they ever accomplished anything positive for humanity, or will they ever do so? On a larger note, has religion *per se* been of any use or success to the human society?

For successful people, life is an attempt to reconcile ideals with possibilities. By contrast, those who are indifferent to their own destiny and that of their society remain passive and see themselves as subject to the angry forces of fate. They see themselves as the grass in the green meadows, forced to bend and break by a forceful wind.

However, I ask you to do your part: School is our children's one-time golden opportunity for development: Don't waste their precious time by teaching them subjects that have no value in today's world.

You want to turn back the clock for our youngsters, compelling them to conform in appearance, thought and mind to the times when those very ancient laws and traditions were first established. But what are the real causes for doing so? And what are the effects of doing so? This we need to study.

In effect, you have deemed the whole society to be worth nothing by thinking of your own ways and beliefs as unique and the only way to live – **because for an extremist, by definition, nothing will ever be enough.**

After so many years, has your way of life accomplished anything other than making some people superstitious, and causing many more to flee religion entirely? Isn't the net result of all your teachings and efforts, a decrease in our population? As the poet wrote,

"Baseless claims won't be proved truthful just by talking about them! Wrong words won't be forced to be right just by the angry veins showing on your neck!"

There have been great people among the promulgators of religion who walked with wisdom, dignity and grace; who left behind good names because of their good deeds. Their actions, however, never trampled on other people's rights.

If you aspire to be as great as they were, take a hard look at their deeds and the reasons for which they were so admired – and then do the same.

Asking your students in the name of religion to follow ancient directives that conflict with today's knowledge and way of life is misleading. You imagine that by doing so, you are being faithful to the religion and keeping it alive, but your mistake will not only inure to your students' detriment but to society's.

Your mistake is that you honestly refer to sayings and writings that are no longer worthy of acceptance, certainly not in our time.

Just because you were once indoctrinated is no reason to mislead your students, by teaching them that rejecting a certain text equals repudiating the whole religion.

There is no obligation to observe many of the religious texts that are no longer practical. Entire communities have been put at risk for certain of these observances. Instead, I implore you to observe moderation.

The true faithful is one whose relationship is directly with God. A group of co-religious people who look at their religion from a common point of view see God as one of them.

Dogmatic people typically exhibit baseless trust and as a result their worldview is never realistic. Sadly, others generally pay for the mistakes of these bigots, and with all likelihood, will continue to pay. How anyone who is entrusted with the education of other people's children can just pray for good fortune to protect them, is unbelievable!

If we wish to remain as a people, we have to know our faults so that we can correct rectify them. Problems are never solved by sweeping them under the rug.

My friends! Let's not be afraid to point out the shortcomings we see! Even our own holy books point out the good and the bad, the positive and the negative, the merits and the faults for us to learn from.

Our goal is self-improvement so we can reach the pinnacle of modern civilization. Most of the world's advances have been achieved by those rational minded people who gave up needless slavish piety and religious rapture, and dared to say "No!" to baseless belief.

As I will try to explain in later pages, contrary to what the regressive traditionalists want us to believe such changes by no means necessitate a break with religion; if anything, they could even result in the advancement of the religion! God can be worshipped in any clothes and under any circumstances, and we can place our trust in him, because as the poet Hafez (1315-1390 C.E.) wrote, "The pious man might have thousands of arts and skills, yet he'll still need to trust."

Solving today's problems doesn't require the approval of a few hypocrites. Human beings have the right to choose their own way of life. To have others decide for you what group or sect to belong to, isn't guidance; it's meddling, and it smells of partisanship.

Earlier generations of religious Jews in Eastern Europe, as most of us know, observed and practiced all the traditions, marking themselves as well as their doorposts and those of their *kollels* and *yeshivot* (traditional Jewish seminaries), with religious symbols. Yet they failed to see the future.

It would be better to put faith outside of the realm of tradition so it won't be abused.

The commandments pose no problems in of themselves. The self-appointed leaders who claim to be religious authorities don't have the correct information. A rational person when faced with choosing between two alternatives will always make the choice that entails the lesser harm. However adherence to nonsense and superstition has never resulted in anything but creating turmoil. The religiosity of the faithful has no value if it fails to consider human nature.

Finally, let's hear this beautiful song from the book of the *Gathas*, i.e. "The Hymns of Zarathustra":

"Oh God of reason! May we be as your true friends, among those who want the world to be new, and life to be fresh. May it be the case that based on the laws of life and creation, as our thoughts converge, all doubts and ambivalence vanish as we migrate toward truth."

Over time, I have studied the religious schools and observed them up close for many months. There is a deep gap in what their students, who are under the control of religious authorities, know of today's science. Today's religious schools derive from several centuries of traditional religious schools in Europe, created in an era when there were few universities and fewer still that allowed Jews. In such a world, the traditional religious schools managed to protect and preserve Jewish customs and the Hebrew language by studying the *Torah*. No doubt, that was a major achievement in its own right, and for its time.

However, once Jews were allowed to attend secular universities, they began to demonstrate admirable talents and laudable merits: while world Jewry comprises less than 0.2% of the world's population, Jews have garnered more than 24% of the Nobel Prizes awarded. Although it may be argued that today's achievements would not have been possible without the foundation of centuries of traditional education, we have to ask ourselves whether such an education has outlived its purpose for today's world.

The best proof for any claim is its objective achievements. Have these traditional schools had the slightest share in the great scientific achievements of the past hundred years? If indeed true, that might be reason to continue with the long-term education of our youth in religious schools. But let's admit that's hardly the case.

Are these major achievements, which have made us all proud, the product of studying the sages of a bygone age in traditional religious schools? Or are they the results of the education provided by modern universities? We may compare the two as the difference between the dim light of a candle and the strength of sunlight.

The German philosopher, Friedrich Nietzsche (1844-1900) wrote, "What does not kill me makes me stronger."

I am convinced that the wit, intelligence, and success of the scientists mentioned above have nothing to do with their religion. It is about their tragic history. As the great Persian poet, Rumi (1207-1273 C.E.) wrote, "Even if you pour an ocean onto a vase, it can only hold the share of water for a day."

Throughout the ages, the Jewish people have been forced to constantly move from place to place, like a flower or a plant, often suffering arid climates or the breaking of a branch. Resilience and the ability to adapt to any environment have had to become second nature. We Jews have suffered much throughout our history, and yet we have gained experience as we learned how to find solutions in the face of closed doors; how to open gates at the heart of dead ends. As we went forward, we saved those keys for solving our future problems. We also benefited from interactions and a continuous dialogue within our own community and with the outside world. Any other nation that endured the same experiences would also exhibit the same high degree of intelligence, creativity and genius.

For example, consider that a farmer living next to an arid desert might be forced to get his water from the depth of the earth, perhaps by digging a well ninety meters deep, in order to irrigate his land. The challenges of such a difficult life make him a better farmer. By contrast, a farmer living next to the easy waters of a river might spend his days much more leisurely but produce less!

This has nothing to do with religion. Those who try to attribute every positive or negative outcome to religion, muddy the waters in a hypocritical way. It is a simple law of nature that depending on his environment, a person may become productive and successful; or lazy, oppressed and victimized. To quote another Persian poem, "You can't become famous without putting in some effort; Even the moon gets more attention when it has thinned herself into a crescent." The secret of survival is that every morning, the deer wakes up with the thought that he has to run faster than a lion, to save his life. Likewise, the lioness opens her eyes every morning planning to hunt the slower deer among the flock, if she is not to starve to death!

In short, both the deer and the lion observe the law of the jungle to survive. The Jewish people, for their part, have learned how to compensate for the brutality of this world's jungle by trying to achieve excellence through education, hard work and intelligence.

In 1994, genocide took place in Rwanda, Africa. It was during President Clinton's tenure, and occurred as world governments, the U.N., numerous human rights organizations, as well as his Holiness the Pope and other religious leaders, looked on. Within just 100 days, more than 800,000 members of the Tutsi tribe -- men and women, children and adults, the young and the old-- were all murdered in the most brutal of ways by the Hutu militias. The victims were not soldiers. Quite to the contrary, they were innocent civilians whose only crime was that they had been born on the wrong side of the fence, into the Tutsi tribe.

Today, hundreds of thousands of African Christians are being massacred in the Darfur region of Sudan. A force of 1000 troops might have stopped these murders. However, the United Nations, world governments and other powerful institutions have failed to take any strong action beyond expressing their regret and remorse!

Are those victims not human, like the rest of us? What happened to human rights? Where are the people in charge?

It's against this backdrop that you, our religious instructors, are teaching our beloved twelve-year old students that the Bible has a prayer that would protect them even from a wild beast in the jungle! Don't you realize how untruthful and possibly harmful that statement is?!

Faith is an alchemist's dream of producing hope from nothing. Yet, as we have seen over and over again, faith alone cannot save someone thrown into the whirlpool who doesn't know how to swim; nor can it save a soldier in his time of danger, if he's not adequately prepared. No, faith has never saved them, nor will it ever.

As a result of the nonsense you teach our religious youth either don't join the military or, if they do, they stop in the midst of danger to invoke the "guarding prayers" you teach them! Can such dangerous lies be called "faith"?

Teachers in these schools of backwards religious thought are being irresponsible, and history will hold them responsible for the social and cultural retardation of their charges. At the same time, those who might have stopped such intellectual hypocrisy and family discord by cutting off their financial support to these institutions, will be considered their accomplices.

One would think that after so many years of tragic and bitter experiences, you teachers would know that prayer can only give an internal sense of satisfaction. Prayer, by itself, has never been shown to be a cure, nor a defense. Isn't it time for all us to admit the truth? Isn't the Holocaust, that tragic and horrendous experiment done on six million innocent Jews, enough proof of the failure of faith and prayer?

What are the causes of our disappointments and the lessons from the past that we can use to root out the dangers to our community. Today, the world is in a worse position than it was in the years of WWII. Your continued negligence will make your responsibility that much greater.

No one here is against prayers, trusting a higher being, or asking for help from Him, within our hearts. But these have no place in the outside world which obeys the law of the jungle.

Let's not keep our children in the darkness, in the name of religion. The first victim of the jungle of human societies is the runner who has fallen behind the caravan. Let's not keep our children from running ahead as fast as they can.

Even today, hundreds of millions of people, many of whom are intelligent, continue to worship cows as part of their tradition! Can we expect any more from the hundreds of millions of others, who are not nearly as intelligent or educated as the people of India? How can you claim that a prayer can actually protect you from harm! This reminds me of a story in the Persian magazine *Payam of New York* (No. 591, p. 39), about a certain episode in Middle-East history,

"Once the Brigadier General Derakhshan asked the leader and guru of the Esmailieh cult, namely Aga-khan Mahallati, 'How is it that in the twentieth century, you claim to be a prophet, and some people are offering you the equivalent of your weight in gold and valuable stones?'

Without a frown, or any sign of anger in the tone, Prince Aga-khan replied, 'I am surprised that this question is coming from a wise young man like you.' Then he smiled and said, 'In a country where hundreds of millions worship cows, what's the problem if a few million of them instead worship me? Do you think of me any less than a cow?!'"

In such a crazy, crazy world, can one depend on anything less than the power of human intellect and science? A wrong lesson, regardless of the intention behind it, is still wrong. Well-intended goals don't excuse wrongful deeds.

If our common goal is having everyone study and observe the teachings of the *Torah* then the unhealthy and ugly divisiveness of the religious sects only defeats that purpose. We need to ask whether our current practice of dividing the Jewish community into Orthodox, Reform, and other sects has had any other result than weakening our community.

The mission of Judaism, its main moral commitment, has been *tikkun olam*, i.e. "healing the world," improving people's lives and expanding their freedom. This is a moral imperative, not a religious issue. It's an obligation upon every generation to take a step toward this goal, in good faith.

A free person, who admires freedom, cannot support a version of religion that imprisons its adherents with illusions and superstitions. Each generation must build on the accomplishments of the past generation to progress. However, they can't just imitate past practices or remain slaves to the literal pronouncements or writings of the past.

Consider that even Judaism, like many other religions, once condoned slavery. The laws to regulate this abomination have long been abandoned.

Let's ask ourselves what caused those laws to become obsolete: Was it hewing to tradition, or changing to keep pace with contemporary civilization?

The traditionalists explain that they are obligated by their religious beliefs to observe the commandments. But they are wrong – neither God nor the religion requires strict adherence of each commandment (otherwise we would still have slaves). Nor is there an obligation to be pretentious and artificial about observance or to follow those dictates that modern science has rendered unnecessary or obsolete. Furthermore, you shouldn't mislead others to believe as you do, to observe in manner that is an incomprehensible shadow of those original commands by parroting the habits of ancient practitioners. Doing so puts the whole of our tradition and religion at risk.

Your mistaken way of observance has fostered a superficial approach to religion imitated by your followers. This approach will only result in the gradual decline of our culture. Instead of misleading our children, we should instead observe our religious commandments proudly, but in a manner consistent with our time.

If we were obligated to follow all of our ancient customs then we would still have to follow the explicit and emphatic Biblical instructions concerning animal sacrifice. But we have abandoned – or even forbidden – those practices – so why do you cling to so many others that are equally impractical and out-of-date?

Dear Teachers,

Realistically – and rationally – no one will descend from the heavens to allow us or forbid us to do one thing or another. We must use our gift of human thought and intellect to decide how to observe our religion.

Prejudice and bigotry only blind us to the world. Narrow-minded people imagine bigotry as a reason for observing religion, but that's plain wrong. Fanatic adherence to a subject can only lead to destruction, not survival. I call upon you: Please stop the fanatics! As they say, a small flourishing village is better than hundred cities in ruins.

You will not be able to make today's civilization adapt to you, by dressing up in old-fashioned clothes and indulging in ancient superstitions. Instead, you should adapt tradition to be in step with modern science, and thus, create a living religion.

One can't learn to drive or swim by just reading a self-help volume on the subject!

The history of the Jewish people is filled with sorrow. Jews have been the pressure gauge for each civilization they've inhabited. Yes, "Let's cry out loud against the cruelties of this old, ruthless and baseless world."

Sir Muhammad Iqbal (Lahore) (1877-1938) said, "Fifty-three years of my life went on the wind, and nothing is left of them but sorrow and pain. It's as if I was watching a chaotic nightmare, or that I learned a lesson that was senseless to the core." Let's not teach others baseless lessons and illusions that have no foundation.

History has forced the Jewish people to become their own midwife and governors, self-made and self-sufficient. There is a saying that a bald person runs faster to grab his hat from the wind! Our weaknesses made us better runners, too.

The blunt criticisms in this volume are not meant to reject other people's ideas and beliefs but to improve our understanding of religion in keeping with our times; and to preserve cohesion within our families. Nowadays, the doors of all universities are open to everyone as is the internet, that endless ocean of information, to learn the most up-to-date knowledge and news. Despite this, many a healthy young man remains captive within the religious schools where old books by religious sages who lived centuries ago are taught by old-fashioned teachers.

I once read about the entrance exam to a religious seminary where they posed the following two questions, "Is the devil male or female?" and "Whether *manna*, the heavenly food has *talgeh* or not?" Is any comment about the relevance of these questions even necessary?

Are the knowledge, words and deeds of religious teachers ever sufficient to prepare students for living in today's world? Aren't these teachers harming not only these young men and women but also causing harm to future generations?

On another subject, let's talk about the place of women in our culture.

To follow an old patriarchal, misogynist culture that asks all women to strictly obey the rules of men, is tantamount to placing half of our priceless human resources, i.e. fifty percent of the very meritorious talents of human society, behind a dark curtain; and to isolating the other half in the religious schools and *ghettos*. This is nothing but an insult to justice and a senseless sacrifice of precious lives in our society? God created both man and woman equal, so why do these people expect women to obey men's wishes in deciding where to sit or what to wear?

A Jewish adage says, "God didn't create women by herself, lest they claim there were two Gods. He didn't create her from the head of man so that she would become his subject. He didn't make her of man's leg, either, so that she wouldn't become his slave. Instead, God created woman from the side of the man, so that they would always be next to each other's heart (even at the house of worship), and to know that they are both from one being, that they have only one God, and that they are at an equal rank, none above the other."

Long gone are the days when in Arab and Hindu society the parents of five children (four girls and one boy) would claim to have only one child! Is it fair to take a doll away from a 9- year old girl and make her a bride, all because of religious laws? Misery always enters from the door that has been left open for it, and ignorance is the main gate. Let's close the gate of ignorance!

In ancient times, man's taking a woman as wife was akin to holding a slave. The remnants of this attitude are still manifest in the symbolic custom of exchanging a coin at the time of engagement. In a time of equal rights between men and women, is this still appropriate?

Woman was considered to have been guilty by birth. She was supposed to remain quarantined so that no one could set eyes on her hair, long before today's seductive wigs. Why should anyone put their faith in traditions that promote such unacceptable standards?

Why should one fall back on those traditions that stand in opposition to freedom and equality -- just because a religious authority has written it or said so? Why should we be afraid of fighting wrongful traditions?

Nietzsche wrote that, "Life's true name is fight. What is truly needed is ability not altruism. What truly decides destinies is power and not justice."

For example, if Iranian Jewish parents had ignored their own dire predictions, and if they had not sent their children abroad before the 1979 Revolution, the lives of the Iranians in Europe and America would not have been nearly as prosperous as it is today. These parents relied on reasonable predictions based on acute observations. They acted wisely in a timely and efficient manner. Doing so provided their children with a better future. Instead of being content to sit on the sidelines and say prayers, they made judgments and took action. Hence, we see that true power lies in acquiring knowledge -- verifiable, scientific knowledge - based on the realities of life, and not from the commentary books of the *mullahs*.

Tomorrow, the generation being reared by today's anachronistic traditionalist will not question the mullahs' self-invented traditions. The cycle will continue, unless we break it.

Just look at the way some of our youngsters have accepted the baseless traditions of Eastern European Jewry, the likes of which were never known in our community. The beliefs of these Eastern European teachers are not part of our ancestral traditions. These traditions grew under social circumstances unique to their times and cultures, including the isolated life of the *ghettos*. Let's act now to keep our schools and families from such alien traditions. Tomorrow will be too late.

A society's value is measured by the merit of its minds. To hold the precious brains of our society captive in old-time schools, in the name of religion or tradition, is tantamount to sentencing them to prison. To preserve our identity we need to preserve our ancestral knowledge *along* with learning today's knowledge, and *not* to the exclusion of the latter.

Passing on to the next generation such nonsensical ideas and superstitions as the "evil eye" is a crime committed against this and future generations. Those who claim this has a religious basis are simply lying. There is absolutely nothing about the "evil eye" in the Holy *Torah.* Rather it's just that about 700 years ago, a religious authority, a *mullah,* expressed his personal opinion in a morning prayer that also revealed his low opinion of women's status. Given his own ignorance, his opinions should be abandoned rather than followed.

Today, in the first decade of the 21rst century, even in a progressive country such as France, the birthplace of modem ideas of democracy, hardly a week goes by that at least one woman is not injured, mutilated or murdered by a husband or another acquaintance for having broken some religious tradition or tribal custom. Yes, bigotry is very much still alive, all in the name of tradition.

To imagine man without woman is to imagine flowers in the absence of the soil....

As the greens grow out of the soil, man too springs out of woman. Man and woman are the two sides of one coin. They are the two wings of a single bird. They are the two eyes of one living entity. Woman's potential for motherhood alone should be a source of pride. A famed Persian poet and scholar, Malek-o-Shoara Bahar (1884-1951) wrote,

> "If a heart were ever to be the throne of God,
> It could've been only a mother's heart.
> What do you know of her heart,
> Of her love's breadth for you?
> Her love holds you and your name safe,
> And it's not just any kindness, but God's very love.
> Love's meaning is in her every element; indeed,
> If love had a face, it'd be in the shape of her heart."

There is a story about the young Bayazid Bastami (804-874 C.E.), a famed Persian Sufi and thinker, who once left the classroom, as the teacher began to talk about the greatness of God and the obligation to worship His name. The teacher scolded him and asked for the reason. Bayazid explained to his teacher, "Yesterday, you exalted the status of "mother" to such degree that I have no room left to worship any other being. Now, I am left to choose between worshiping God or mother!" The teacher smiled and said, "Each one of them has his or her own place ...."

Napoleon Bonaparte (1769-1821) said that "To know and measure the progress and civility of a nation, observe their women."

These are just a few quotations from vastly different cultures, appreciating the true status of woman. Many cultures continue to undermine the status of women based on religious beliefs. The promulgators and practitioners of religion historically have not placed women in worthy positions. Often, such villains are merely opportunists, taking advantage of the resilience and adaptability of women, looking upon them as "the shorter competition," deeming their humiliation a boost to their own presumed greatness. No wonder that religious authorities claim that men are the cause of 99% of all miracles! *Thank God people can't see the future; otherwise, no one would be in peace from another's noisy mind!*

Even today, these regressive traditionalists think so lightly of women as to say, "This book belongs to you, but you can't touch it!" A European thinker once said that, "a government should be just strong enough to protect the rights of its people. Anything stronger than that would become inclined to infringe upon those very rights itself." Now consider that in some countries, these backwards-thinking fanatics have taken hold of the governments, too. What women have to endure in those countries is beyond anyone's imagination.

Indeed, we know from experience that once self-appointed caretakers of religions have been granted more power than they deserve, and once they have received exaggerated respect from their flatterers, first they begin by humiliating others, particularly women.

The main exception is those who respect the "rights" of women because of the income they bring in, saying bluntly that in such difficult times one can't lead a family without the wife earning money!

Hillel the Elder (1rst century B.C.E.) said, **God created mothers because He needed their help.**

Let's put aside those commentaries that are no better than excuses for bad or unjust behavior. Our students' enlightenment and creativity are too valuable to let some old thoughts covered in the dust of centuries be the food of our daily lives. Let's instead enable our youth to make new dishes to nourish them. As for those who want to feed off our children – let's push them away from the table that is our community.

Some try to change the subject by saying that "it's better to become *religious* than an addict!" This fails to account for the damaging and disintegrating effect of such words on the lives of thousands of families and their children who end up in misery and agony because of this mistaken way of thinking. Are black and white the only two colors in the world?

Man left the Stone Age as his knowledge and innovation grew. He left behind the age of ignorance and stepped onto the roads of progress and evolution. We shouldn't abandon this advantage because of baseless doubts induced by superstition. Superstitions become even more dangerous when they become part of the national identity of an entire society. Superstitions are transient by nature. We should neither fear them nor remain silent about them - particularly in an era when economic opportunity and freedom of speech have provided the grounds for production, creativity and growth.

The Holy *Torah* provides some of its highest punishments for occultism, so-called psychic readings, wizardry and the like. Such superstitions have been prevalent in all cultures, and Judaism strongly reacted against them. Admittedly, they can be a source of amusement too. For example, some people in Iran considered an owl to be a jinx; but in America, it's considered to bring good luck! The fact that the owl is just a bird like any other, is what's most puzzling in all this, isn't it?!

Ignorant, superstitious people can be found anywhere. The "evil eye" is nothing but some people's envy for others who tend to flaunt their fortunes. One shouldn't do anything to raise the jealousy of the enemy. Admittedly, this is a reasonable conclusion and there is no need to fall into nonsensical superstitions to explain this very basic social and psychological principle. Let us remind ourselves that Moses rose to fight against superstition, not to promote it in the name of religion!

Together let's look at the living roots of our religion, so that its trees don't wither away. We need to repudiate those traditions and writings that are inconsistent with our modern times, whether concerning the status of women, or regarding superstitious nonsense. It doesn't matter who said it, or who says it. We should rise to stop this wrong from continuing. A Persian proverb states, "A sermon based on lies is of no use to the speaker himself, let alone his audience!"

Progressive thought, as well as regressive ideologies, have coexisted in all times and places. Just consider how progressively a man like Hillel was thinking more than 2000 years ago, and yet how today, at the start of the 21rst Century how some of our contemporary regressive traditionalists think! We might remember that Hillel was the same sage who told an impatient man standing on one foot that the essence of Judaism could be explained simply by this one commandment: "Do unto others as you would have them do unto you." The man was naturally surprised, because another contemporary sage, Shamai, had already refused to answer that very question.

A witty Persian poem reads,

"Unveiling the secrets isn't expedient. Otherwise, there isn't much really in the house of the hypocrites!"

It's easy to create a mess of a simple tie but hard to unknot it. Please, don't corrupt and ruin our innocent children with your misleading lessons. It's good to promote religion, but not with superstitions masked in hypocrisy. Our ideal house, i.e. *beit hamikdash,* is no further than one's own family. Please, don't ruin these holy houses in the name of religion. Let parents fulfill their obligations to fatherhood and motherhood and let them enjoy it, too.

Compassion and harmony are a nation's greatest assets, and they begin in the families. Disintegrating these cells of love and compassion in the name of promulgating religion is not a service but a treacherous act against those who have placed their trust in you. Rumi wrote,
"So many Hindus and Turks, who share hearts, but no word,
And so many Turks, who share all words, but no hearts.
Thus, two hearts in harmony have a language of their own,
And that's way above the common language of words."

My friends, how could you expect any better given the enormous support given to those who promote such a divisive culture ?

According to the census, the Jewish population of the world is declining at an alarming rate. Yet, you blame mixed marriages exclusively for this problem, instead of opening your eyes and realizing that many young Jews who listen to your nonsense choose to leave Judaism behind altogether. I say that you are responsible for such defections!

These anachronistic traditionalists try to grab attention by claiming that, "Were it not for our traditional schools and our religious students, Judaism wouldn't have survived, nor would it have any future."

I invite you all to assess the effect of their actions and the ideas that they have been disseminating. I can say firmly that their claims are not true; that the results have been nothing more than cultural retardation or even regression; and that many a Jew has come to despise Judaism because of their teachings. We've done enough sweeping the problem under the rug; let's now join together to find the solution.

Our society has a dire need for leaders and active lay members who are able to see the world realistically, and not through the lens of prejudice and religious superstition. The hypocrisies peddled by extremist religious cults will not end until we, as a global minority, make our own universal principles conform to modern times and science. We, the Jewish people, have a responsibility not just toward our own society but to the global community.

The Israeli newspaper, *Haaretz,* in its issue of 12/21/1999, included an article that addressed the ultra-religious groups of the country, partly known as the *Haredi* community. The article stated that these groups were the main producers of a most unique kind of poverty in Israel and the world, "ideological poverty," imposed on children by their teachers and parents as a result of their own intellectual poverty. The *Talmud* refers to those without a job as *moley olam,* destroyers of the world.

One of the most important of all ongoing debates in the world concerns the relationship between "church and state." The question is whether governments should remain secular and be based on human reason; or should they become theocracies and be run according to those man-made standards contained in religions?

We may also ask whether, on a smaller scale, the religious centers of a society should be run solely based on the religion, or else, according to the realities of time and religion. Theocracies base their decisions on the strict, unbending rules of their religion as interpreted by themselves. Likewise, traditionalist religious centers, too, wish to practice their faith and run their centers based on the laws of their religion, yet only do so according to their own interpretations! Over time such centers inevitably become like corporations, relying primarily on their annual income accumulated by expanding their membership, while paying salaries to their operators from the pockets of their naïve audience.

When a conflict arises in a theocratic society among various people's beliefs and between the wishes of the governments and the aims of the religious centers, each wants to go his own way. Inevitably, the opposing sentiments of the majority and the minorities collide. They begin to avoid each other and the doors are closed to constructive dialogue.

Meanwhile, secular governments, such as the United States, travel a century's road overnight, shining brightly like the sun. That's because they stand firmly against the threatening flood of religious thoughts intruding into government by maintaining that as important and exalted as the status of religion might be, religion belongs to the privacy of one's heart and home.

Considering mankind's experience over the past several millennia, adaptive laws and resilient practitioners are best qualified to govern the people. They recognize the differences between people and their ideologies and treat them equally under the law. Equality, when established in society as a matter of law, allows neither the government, nor religion, to turn into a means of oppression, partisanship and divisiveness. In such a society, the laws of the nation, as well as religious obligations, are practiced not with a rigid mindset, but according to the necessities of the time, and in accordance with civil law. To improve the function of these institutions, the free press plays a significant role in monitoring the better performance of government, as well as that of the religious organizations.

Thomas Jefferson (1743-1826), one of the Founding Fathers of the United States and its third president, famously affirmed that between "a government without a press" and "a press without a government," he would surely choose the latter. Jefferson believed that our liberty depends on the freedom of the press and that cannot be limited without being lost. The reason was clear: that knowledge of the facts is necessary for people to assess the performance of their government and to have an informed say in its direction.

With this in mind, I ask the instructors of traditional religious schools to help people
distinguish between right and wrong, rather than promote nonsense, superstitions and illusions. Superstitions only survive because people continue to believe in them; and as they say, "whatever you believe in, won't be a lie!"

More than 160 years ago, in 1850, Victor Hugo (1802-1885) famously addressed the Legislative Assembly of France, saying,

"Let us try to set the foundations of a society in which the government won't be able to defend itself anymore than a murderer, and when it acts like a wild beast, it will be treated as such.

"Let us create a society in which the priest and the government will each have their own place, and neither the state would interfere in the religious affairs of the church, nor the religion will have anything to do with the government's budget and policies.

"Let us create a society, in which last century's affirmation of the equality of all men will be matched by the present century's assertion and realization of the equality of all men and women.

"Let us create a society in which free public education, from the elementary schools to College de France, would be equally open to all talents; a society in which wherever there is a mind, there will be a book; where no village will be without a grade school, no town without a high school, and no city without a university; and all these be run and supervised directly by the government, without the influence of the religious sectors. Let us create a society in which there will be no room for that destructive plague called hunger. You, the legislators, take my word that poverty is not the plague of a class, but it's the illness of the whole society. The suffering of a poor person is not only her suffering, but it's the destruction of the whole society. It's the long and slow death of the poor that brings about the sudden and fearful death of the rich. Poverty is the worst enemy of law and order. Poverty, as ignorance, is like a dark night, which by necessity, requires to be followed by a bright day...."

My Iranian Jewish friends, on the day Hugo said those words, our Jewish ancestors were living as second class citizens among the third world society of Iran. In retrospect, we can better appreciate the living conditions of our ancestors in those days, compared to the equal status

44

that we now enjoy in the United States.

The Greek philosopher, Plato (428-348 B.C.E.) stated that, "Knowledge is the foundation of all other virtues." For centuries, religious instructors in the traditional schools have fed children the so-called laws of the commentators of *The Jewish Bible* as their daily bread, believing it will survive the test of time! They hardly realize that people have to be informed before becoming followers! It was said of the British, during WWII that they would bravely fight and resist in any battle until the last drop of their hired Indian soldiers! The traditionalist, too, if given the opportunity, would continue "doing good," propagating his lessons and earning his daily bread with the seasoning of *mitzvot,* until the last child has been fully separated from his family!

One can never accuse the traditionalists of "not understanding" reality. Their aims and beliefs are simply rotten to the core. They tell everyone what he or she expects or likes to hear, and thus, they entrap their audience. They support religion through an anachronistic and rigid traditionalism that is not based on freedom of thought. Unfortunately, these regressive traditionalists believe in and propagate the superstitious contents of their books, while the likes of this humble writer believe in their intellectual value.

Meanwhile, some call one group "religious" and the other one "anti-religious," debasing both to fighting in the mud. Instead consider the words of Rabbi Akiva (ca. 50-135 C.E.), one of the most prominent sages of his time who said, "If you have to, make your Sabbath a weekday, but do not depend on others," i.e. you can even work on Sabbath (if you need to), but don't beg. (Quoted from *Chashm-Andaaz Monthly.)*

A superficial interpretation of this very wise saying would cause an angry reaction among some fanatics. But rational-minded people whether they observe the Sabbath or not, would still have affection for such resilient intellectuals. That is because every thinking person can understand what Akiva meant, "Don't take it so far as to fall into poverty," or as we say in Persian, "don't heat the oven so much as to burn yourself with the pot!"

An American friend of mine, a rational religious person who observes all the Orthodox customs sent his two children to Catholic school to give them a better education. Today, they have both graduated and lead very comfortable and religious lives, without ever being dependent on others.

Indeed, a rational religious person is much different from a regressive traditionalist. Unlike the traditionalist, he doesn't dive into the abyss, taking others along with him, in the name of religion. Neither does he let religion get in his own way, his children's or that of the society. He always follows the rational, logical, even scientific content of the religion, instead of its superstitions. Moreover, they don't interfere in the lives of others. I feel ashamed to even quote some of the past and presents beliefs of these fanatics.

It's said that a mother once complained, "I have three children. One never lies, while the other one doesn't say anything but lies. I have no problems with these two. But I have lots of trouble with the third one, with whom you never know if he's telling a lie or the truth!" The same holds true for those religious groups that depending on their audience, approve or reject a person, or even a book. "Their true intent is a secret, revealed only in fleeting gestures." The true belief of such people is what they whisper in the privacy of each other's ears.

Oh, you who claim to be the guardians of the religion!
Preserving the culture of captivity from the *ghettos* doesn't mean

the preservation of Judaism, but the prolongation of captivity.

A Finnish proverb says, "One who slips twice off of the same stone, deserves to have both his legs broken!" I ask you please, once was already enough; don't make others slip as well!

The religious commitment of a family or a society should not be taken as an index of its stability. Instead, stability depends on the degree of intellectual sophistication and understanding in that family which automatically leads to religious balance. Miserable are those families, parents and instructors, who use every excuse to make their religion a hindrance to their children's scientific, academic, social and economic progress. They don't know that "growth" means "change."

Instructors need not take my word. They should evaluate the outcome of their years-long activities and study the statistical data that indicates a dwindling Jewish population. Then they will realize that one can't preserve our population with a world of superstitions.

Materialism can appear in many guises, including religion, and it only leads communities to spiritual destruction. An anachronistic and regressive traditionalism will only lead society and religion toward complete doom. Families and communities will first become divided and then separated to the point of disintegration. Just consider the state of Israel, with at least 22 political parties, each singing its own song, each calling out for a separate agenda. Some of these factions at times add a religious flavor to their messages, not for the love of God but to help the sale of their political products. You see, the underlying condition of their cooperation is money and hypocrisy and not the communal interests of the nation.

My friends, if the cohesion of families today is under threat from such hypocrites, then fending off these religious con men should be given a priority, as much as our primary goal should be to preserve harmony and peace within our families. This holds true even if we allow that there is even some shred of truth in their beliefs regarding men, women or religion. That is because no truth should ever be achieved at such a grave cost to the lives of our children.

Once you let anyone else interfere in your personal life in any way you have given away your freedom of thought! Even turning to these so-called learned men for answers to religious questions leads unwittingly to being under the umbrella of their nonsense. These graduates of traditional religious schools are already fully immersed in superstitions, wasting their intelligence on such nonsensical questions as whether to continue the use of electric speakers in our temples on the Sabbath and on the High Holidays. Better to check the actual sources ourselves, in the first place! We should not ask these mullahs to make decisions for us

It's said that a good question already contains half of a good answer. If so, a nonsensical question, too, would naturally carry half of its baseless answer within! Civilized societies no more deserve to wait for the *fatwas* from such sources. They deserve much more than such games and the entrapment of their innocent people. We are really in trouble, as a people, if the validity of a synagogue depended on allowing or forbidding the use of speakers on Holidays, or if the religiosity of its congregants is judged by the mere appearance or absence of a piece of cloth on their head.

I have been told that when someone went to ask one of the most prominent authorities among the traditionalists about this very issue of using speakers on the High Holidays, he was told that a congregation shouldn't be larger than 350 people! The second time he asked him, they requested a large sum of money to study and answer the question.

48

How can we consider such people "spiritual leaders"?

The gentleman is worried about the treasure chest, while the house is rotten to the core!

Truthfully, who voted to make these religious figure an authority? Judaism has no "supreme leaders," no "Pope," no "Ayatollah," or even a chosen "final arbiter"!

I am reminded of the story told about a quick-tempered athlete in Yazd, a central city of Iran, who rushed one early morning to a shrine of modest size, in order to ask the supposedly holy person buried there to heal his son. The caretaker overheard the man asking the dead, in an angry, depressed and agitated voice, to cure his son. The caretaker thought to himself, "If his son is not cured, he will take revenge by shutting down this place." So he went to the man and told him, "I'm sorry that your son is in such bad health. Our holy person only heals little illnesses, like a toothache, a cold or coughs. Given the condition of your son, you'd better go to those holy shrines with larger domes!" Likewise, it seems that to solve bigger problems like the issue of speakers, the shape of the facial hair, or the appropriate head gear, one should shun one's own responsibility, and just go to the bigger *mullah!*

We have long left behind those times and places when people, afflicted with illiteracy, would seek solutions to every problem, were it baldness or stomach ache, from a shrine, a priest or a psychic, and then wait for a miracle to happen. **The miracle of our time is the Internet.** There's no more need to fast, make a pledge, or seek the prayers of the *mullahs,* to find your answers. These days, everyone just Googles!

Once Hafez wrote,

"Until you've become familiar with this song, you can't hear the secrets of this melody. The ears of a stranger are meant to hear the message of the angel of reason."

The future has arrived. We should expel the enemies of free will from all our congregations. Independent free-thinking will continue to bring us all it has always offered us; but the regressive traditionalists will only preserve those very miseries that have always brought us to our knees.

Those people who pretend that it would be a sin to avoid their nonsense and superstitions, only demonstrate their own narrow vision. Our commandments are by no means as humble as they would have us believe. Let's learn the original tongue, and let's dive into the ocean of thoughts expressed directly by that language, to personally comprehend the secrets of the truth.

Dear educators, with official positions,

Our history was never pleasant, so why depend so much on nonsense and why continue to teach it? I warn you that left unheeded, historical faults will only come back to harm us with a vengeance. One of the many reasons behind anti-Semitism has been the ignorant mistakes of those who have made religion a source of income for themselves. You play right into their hands. Iranians have an old humorous saying, "The flaunting hypocrite has indeed no certainty in his faith. All his exhibitionism is a distraction, and it doesn't have anything to do with the religion!"

Max Weber (1864-1920), the great German sociologist, once wrote, "To explain any social phenomenon, one should be looking for the causes behind it, and we should also know how the operatives of the events view the events themselves." We should learn which group(s) benefit from the teaching of nonsense and superstitions. The extremists should note that, eventually, we always move forward and progress in the river of life. A better understanding of the world will be the most efficient solution to our problems. Making our youth dependent on the idea of fate, this empty and powerless concept, and other such superstitions can only result in holding us back, and consequently, building hatred toward our religion. A Persian poem states:

"A people achieved its goals through its efforts, While the other left its desires to fate.
No one knows where the ideal rests,
But it's close enough to hear the sound of the bells."
    The footsteps of science can be heard, striding forward every minute. While at the same time, backwards and anachronistic forces are sheltered by dens of secrecy in the name of God. Let them stay behind, if they wish. But we can't ignore our children. Instead of tying them down with chains of bigotry, let's light a torch to guide them through the unknown roads ahead.

It's said of the 13th century Iranian philosopher and scientist, Khajeh Nasir-al-Din Tusi (1201-1274 C.E.) that:

    "Once Khajeh had arrived at the city of Maragheh, he began to think of building an
observatory next to the city. He discussed the issue with the Mongol ruler, Hulegu-Khan, who governed the city at the time, asking for his help. Hulegu asked the Khajeh, "What's the point?" The Khajeh replied, "The observatory has this advantage that it allows the man to know what's going to happen." Hulegu commented indifferently, "What is the use of knowing about heavenly events?"

    The Khajeh thought for a moment and replied, "A little experiment will prove my point. Would you do as I ask, please?" Hulegu agreed.

The Khajeh said, "Unbeknownst to others but the two of us, order a servant to climb up to the roof, and suddenly throw a huge lead pot into the courtyard," where there was a crowd. The shocking impact scared everyone around; some even fainted! However, the Khajeh and Hulegu, aware of the proceedings, hardly even frowned.

Then the Khajeh explained, "This is the advantage of the science of astronomy, that through its knowledge, some people will learn about the cosmic events in advance. They'll inform the others of their predictions, and as a result, no one will be surprised when the unusual happens!" At this point, Hulegu agreed with the Khajeh, and he immediately ordered for an observatory to be built nearby the city of Maragheh, on the outskirts of a mountain known today as Rasad Daghi."

We need science to help us prepare for the unexpected events of the world rather than waiting for them to happen, and then calling what we can't explain a miracle caused by religious belief. The secrets of the world are so many that even today, despite all our scientific achievements, we have not yet discovered more than a mere fraction of the facts of the universe. Mankind is no more than a little particle within the vastness of the world.

The 12th century Persian poet, Attar Neyshabouri (1145-1221 C.E.), put it perfectly when he wrote,

"On the vastness of the blue skies,

The earth is like a poppy embedded on the ocean

Compare yourself to the size of the poppy,

And you'd see it fair to laugh at yourself!"

The most ignorant people in the world are those who do not learn from the changes of the world.

Nietzsche wrote, "Not only have we inherited the wisdom of the ages, accumulated through the millennia, but also the follies and superstitions of our ancestors."

Let's not give false witness against the truth to our children. The day will come when our grandchildren will remember us for what we taught them and they will see if we have been wise parents.

We have arrived at this point because we kept our personal religious beliefs hidden even from our children. Many people hold two contrasting types of beliefs - one within their hearts, another for the world to see! it would have been better to mix and reconcile these two opposing worlds, so that a balance could be achieved for us and our children. A main cause of the rebellion against religion amongst our youth is that they see the contradictions and hypocrisy of their counselors and preachers. Such hypocrisies make a conscientious mind react. Following intelligent advice and the path of progressive wisdom doesn't require pretentions, hypocrisy and divisive conflicts.

Thomas Jefferson considered ignorance to be worse than making a mistake. As he said, one who doesn't believe in anything is closer to the truth than the one who holds erroneous beliefs.

You can't accuse the regressive traditionalists of not understanding the truth. It's their very beliefs that are wrong.

Society will be harmed most by whoever has clung unwittingly to other people's mistakes, and then tries to convince others to accept those mistakes. We can't let our children be corrupted by the mistakes of others. Our children should be the first to learn that what their religious leaders say is often at odds with today's science and civilization.

The *Torah* says "Blessed be one who accepts criticism." *(Parashat Devarim)* Those afflicted with prejudice and bigotry can't agree to wake up from the dream of desires; but one has to wake up first, if a dream is to be lived at all!

My friends! We can learn from the mistakes of others - and these mistakes could make the best of teachers for us. Let's accept that societies need to improve ideas and not to become more rigid in their thinking. An idiot is excused from understanding the issues; but we can't ignore those erudite people who continue in their erroneous teachings. We should not give such people any power. Power entails corruption; and absolute power only yields absolute corruption!

The corrupting influence of nonsense and superstition grows faster and more persistently in the suffocating atmosphere of the so-called religious schools, where dissent is suppressed in the name of religion. Such dishonesty will be passed on from generation to generation like a hereditary disease. Having a correct understanding of the religion is more important than believing in the religion itself. Beliefs mixed with bigotry lead to turmoil, first in the families, and then in the world, since the bigot pulls out the tree just to pick an apple!

All around the world, the Jewish people believe in the holiness of *Torah,* and we are all proud of it. But the traditional fanatics don't just believe in the commandments of the *Torah.* They believe as much, if not more, in the writings and sayings of the religious commentators who profess such claims as the coming of the savior, etc. They are conspicuous in their widespread opposition to independent thinking, in contrast to the original Biblical stress on the freedom and independence of mankind. We can't take this issue lightly.

Sometimes, at the corner of a garden, an ant might carry a wingless louse upon a tree, setting off a long chain of reactions, spreading sickness and causing every tree to wither and die. This corruption of our religion, filled as it is with nonsense and superstitions, is not any less dangerous than the plant louse.

The secret of success is to remain in step with the world around us, and to adapt ourselves to the pace of time, and not to opt for separation and seclusion from the rest of the society, in the name of "religion observance." Success doesn't mean "being rich"; many a wealthy person continues to live in prejudice and bigotry. One can overcome financial shortcomings with effort. But it is near impossible to rectify the mental suffocation and the ideological retardation to which our children have been subjected. Like the plant louse, such plagues are persistent!

Humankind's intelligence is a gift of nature, a blessing of creation. All humans are endowed with this gift to a greater or lesser degree. It can be cultivated, sharpened and developed, but it cannot be acquired through science, wealth, or religion. Once we allow our intellect to function properly, we can understand things. Meanwhile, one who claims "I'm the only one who understands!" is exactly the one who doesn't understand anything!

Avicenna (ca. 980-1037 C.E.) said it best, that "One can't describe in words the story of wisdom and comprehension," or communicate it through explanations because no one can talk about that faculty other than by firsthand experience. Whoever wishes to attain knowledge has to attain it and experience it – and not just hear about it.

Exaggerating the merits of the commandments in public, while calling them empty in private, only disseminates hypocrisy, ambivalence, and furthers deception. The first step toward rationality and a proper education for our children is to be sincere with ourselves, as well as with others. The rational person doesn't advertise, and doesn't have anything for sale; thus, she doesn't find it necessary to adhere to hypocrisy. In contrast, the regressive traditionalist often spends much time and fortune to attract and recruit new members.

The French writer, Antoine de Saint-Exupery (1900-1944), best known for his short story, *The Little Prince,* said, "Humans have got used to buying everything already prepared. But since there are no stores where you can buy true friends, they have remained without friends."

Today's parents spend much less time with their children than the previous generations of parents did. They have little time to cook and they tend to feed their children prepared foods rather than home cooked meals. By extension, we have gotten used to buying everything ready-made and pre-packaged including religion, which we tend to buy from those religious figures who act like *mullahs* without much research or study on our own! This is why our cooperation with, or indifference to, the regressive traditionalists is the beginning of our widespread cultural retardation.

Instead of accepting a "brand" of religion, let's focus on the substance and the meaning of our teachings. The poet Rumi wrote,

"How long to remain in love with the face?
Change your way, instead, and desire the meaning!"

I believe our message should be: Stay committed to your religion, but remain flexible in your approach. To quote the great Rumi again,

"Once rid of hypocrisy, I saw both worlds were indeed only one; Now, I search for and read, speak and know, only one."

Today's extremist is a graduate of yesterday's traditionalist family, or the school of hatred where he studied. Some teachers have been promoting the books of such regressive commentators' and some parents have been passing on whatever wrong information they once learned to their children, all in the name of religious education. As long as this situation continues today's religions and their followers will continue to seem outdated. Alas, these educators won't even listen to the constructive suggestions and the criticisms of the more enlightened parents. Modem science won't stop at any frontier for the sake of religion. The droplet can only be saved if it joins the sea -- that is the sea of free-thinking and open-mindedness, and not the polluted lakes of bigotry and prejudice.

The dark lens which the fanatic parents and teachers hold before their children's eyes can only lead to damaging their vision for the rest of their lives. It's one thing to be religious another to treat religion as a means to other ends. Many of the preachers, who claim to be defending their religion, are in fact promoting their self-interest, rather than watching over the interests of their faith. Such so-called religious authorities paint a fuzzy future, full of ambiguities, instead of creating a bright, clear future for everyone.

Fyodor Dostoyevsky (1821-1881) said, "Man is a creature who can get used to anything, and I believe that is the very best way of defining him." But should we get used to something harmful, if it can be eliminated? Should we continue to put up with deception and superstition if indeed we can reject these harmful absurdities?

The problems in today's world are not religion or the clerical community in general; the real problem comes from a limited group of extremists and their continuous brainwashing of those who are susceptible to their claims. They disguise superstitions and outright lies in a shroud of holiness and teach empty ideas in their classrooms, supporting their claims by relying on the writings of like-minded propagandists of such superstitions. They don't realize that once a young person turns into a regressive fanatic, he or she could even see the faults of a society as its virtues. He won't be curable, nor will she ever learn to appreciate moderation.

In our time, the acceptance of religious commandments depends on a common understanding by the majority, one that does not include cutting off contact with the rest of the world. The family must be watchful of the dangers of superstitions and absurd thoughts, and be aware that such ideas can remain unnoticed in the cup of mind until it has become full, when their embarrassing content has already spilled all over the ground.

Parents must appreciate that regressive traditionalism is not only a headache within the family, but a cause of shame in the eyes of the outside world. What fanatics do in the name of religion resembles the story of a fisherman who drove the fish into the marsh, so deep in the mud that it couldn't get out! These people are throwing our youth into a quagmire, the exit from which could only be described as painfully difficult, if not impossible.

Dear reader, I know that it's unlikely that you agree with everything I say, but as long as you have found even one of my arguments convincing or close to your own convictions, I shall feel rewarded. I would be happy if only one single sentence has succeeded in bringing the members of my community closer, making their resolution stronger for seriously fighting the threat of those who promote divisions, separations and isolation.

To be blunt: If the extremist Orthodox factions ever became dominant in our society, there would no longer be a country for us, nor even a religion called Judaism. They would have brought down Judaism by their resistance to change. At best, they might still be in the *ghettos*, praying for miracles, waiting another 2000 years for the promised savior to show up! If today we have a thriving worldwide Jewish society and a country of our own, it's because of people whose belief in the Jewish cause did not make them abandon reason and common sense and whose contributions to civilization remained on a par or exceeded those of the rest of the world.

There is certainly no guarantee for a bright future. In the end, it's all in our hands. But one thing is certain: someone who refuses to accept facts and truths will end up paying a high price. We need to acquire knowledge to tell the difference between the safe road and the trap, to distinguish the wise from the misled, and to recognize our friends from our enemies. As a Persian saying goes,
"It's so hard to tell an enemy disguised as a friend.
After all, the wick rests at the heart of the candle,
Only to bring about its demise."

Winston Churchill (1874-1965) once quipped that *it would be better to worry first and rest later, than the other way around!*

Clinging to a backwards and old-fashioned view of religion is an escape from responsibility and does not excuse one from human responsibility in the name of God. Indeed, if societies only followed the empty thoughts, nonsensical writings, or baseless sayings of the fanatics of today or yesterday, society itself would disappear with the blow of the first warm breeze. A famous Persian historian, Zell-ol-Sultan, wrote in "Masoudi History" that,

"When the Persian king Nader conquered the Afghanis and the city of Isfahan, 70,000 students of the Islamic seminaries of the city (very much like the masses of the jobless *mullahs* in today's Israel) still received payments from the government treasury, and claimed that were it not for their prayers, the world would have already ended by then!

"Nader put an end to their salaries and alimonies. The heads of the seminaries went to him, pleading that 'These religious students are the army of God! Why should the King cut their alimonies and confiscate their belongings?' Nader replied, 'Years ago, when the Afghans had conquered us by a meager army of six thousands, what were these seventy thousand "prayer-sayers" doing? Where were they? Now, if they want any salaries, they should put on armors and join my victorious troops, because I need an army of swordsmen, not an army of idle worshipers!'"

Muhammad Iqbal (Lahore) wrote in *The Message of the East* (Pakistan, p. 235), that

"One can't measure the religious philosopher with the politician by the same stick;
One is blind with the sunlight, while the other can see things clearly;
One offers shaky arguments for the word of God,
While the other brings very strong reasons for very shaky words!"

Regressive traditionalists are a burden on the rest of the society. By appealing to people's sense of pity on the one hand, and proclaiming their "good deeds" on the other, they think they are receiving their "unemployment benefits" without realizing that to drink water for free, there needs to be a water source in the first place! How can people march in the name of religion against their own true interests, as well as their society's? Or even worse, brainwash others to join them?

To those trying to raise money by sentimental appeals that claim that without their prayers the religion would not survive, I ask: is there any religion in the world that has ever defended itself or any country by prayer alone? Why should the rest of us pay for the ignorant claims of a small and limited faction? If, in the name of religion, they wish to escape any responsibility to the rest of society, why should doing so come at the price of respect for religion in general or the security of the greater society?

Everyone can say prayers; but without the appropriate means, those prayers offer little defense. Of the six million Jews, one and a half million Armenians, and hundreds of millions of other helpless victims throughout history, many have prayed, but no prayer could defend against the unspeakable atrocities committed against them.

Despite this simple fact, it is often a fanatic who should be ridiculed for his superstitious beliefs who is given the power to decide the future of our children.

It's impossible to exaggerate the seriousness of the dangers that lurk behind regression, which can imperil the destiny of whole nations. A case in point is the historical fall of the Persian Sultan (King) Hussein that led to the rise of the Safavid Persian Empire (1501-1736). In *Rasm-ol-Tavarikh*, a historical chronicle by Muhammad Hashem Assef, we read that Mahmoud Afghan, a twenty-year old rebel and his army of bare-footed, hungry Afghan looters laid siege to the central Persian city of Isfahan. The city fell into a terrible famine. People were forced to eat tree leaves and roots, dogs and cats, and later, even dead human flesh. Children were dying every day. Bodagez Rodzinski, a Christian priest, witnessed people so desperate that they were cooking *kabob* out of the meat of dead human thighs.

Faced with such undeniable misery, Sultan Hussein heeded the counsel of his religious guide, Sheikh-ol -Eslam Majlesi, and decided to defend the city, and by extension, the country and his crown, by ordering the cooking of a "pledge soup of garbanzo beans." Accordingly, everyone in the palace and all other associates of the court, men and women, were ordered to hold a piece of garbanzo bean in their hand, form a sincere and pure intention, say a prayer, blow at the raw bean, and throw it into the pot of soup to be cooked.

Meanwhile, the king informed his subjects that "we are doing something extraordinary, which will wipe our enemies off of the face of the earth!"

Just imagine the situation for a moment; the city was burning in flames, thousands were dying of starvation, and this religious (!) king wished to defend his kingdom by cooking a pledge soup based the advice of his religious leader – clearly the outcome of years of brainwashing by the nations' *mullahs*.

The pledge soup was cooked and distributed, but it had no avail, and people continued to die. The *mullahs* explained to Sultan Hussein that the miraculous powers of the soup had been neutralized, because either "an evil eye" had beset the pot; or one single bean had slipped through without a prayer being said; or one of the maids had said the prayer without having taken a ritual bath. Thus, the soup had entered the stomachs, but the Afghan Army had yet to be destroyed.

The Sultan, faced with his imminent death, ordered another pot of the soup to be prepared, only to be informed that no garbanzo beans nor people to say the prayers could be found to fulfill his wish. Alas, what disasters have come because of superstitious beliefs!

The tragicomic element of this story becomes more evident when we learn that Prince Muhammad Ali Mirza, the heir apparent to the throne, was not faring much better. Having been brought up in the superstitious culture of Sultan Hussein's court, the prince decided to fight alongside his dad by ordering the women of the *harem* to recite prayers and repeat mantras over bread crumbs, and then feed them to the chickens and birds, which had been lucky enough to survive the raging hunger that ruled the city. Sadly, this young man could not think of a better technique to fend off the enemy. A Persian proverb could be aptly applied to him: "The son, who bears no sign of his father, is a stranger, not a son."

May I mention that this Sultan was the same, who besides thousands of soldiers, held an army of 70,000 praying religious students! Yet they had all become paralyzed with fear before the enemy, petrified like a mouse before a cobra, because their leadership had decided to heed his religious advisors and resort to prayers and two rounds of pledge soups, now guaranteed to be devoid of evil eyes or the words of un-bathed maids!

What stupidities have resulted from this widespread notion of "evil eye"! A child would fall ill in bed, dying from diphtheria, and the family and friends would blame her illness on the eyes of an auntie, who had visited them the day before...

Fortunately, we live in an era of science. Bacteria were first discovered in the 17th century by Antonie van Leeuwenhoek (1632-1723), and vaccinations and other effective remedies were discovered about 200 years ago by Louis Pasteur (1822-1895). Over the last century, the causes of diphtheria and so many other diseases have become well known and science has uncovered appropriate cures or treatments. Accordingly, isn't it a shame that even today, there are still superstitious people who believe in this absurd notion of "evil eye," fostering its very survival by passing the idea on to their children, and consequently, harming the intellectual health of their community?

This belief is all the more absurd when we recall that past and present religious leaders have further expanded this nonsense claiming it can even be caused from too much love and not just because of hatred, jealousy or a sense of hostility! The thought of "a bushy bald head" would have been more conceivable than this paradox.

We need to hold accountable the people who surrender themselves to such lies. Otherwise intelligent people who let themselves be fooled are even more to blame than those who soft-talk people into bloody crimes! I am reminded of the Greek philosopher Aristotle (384-322 B.C.E.), who wrote that, "People are of three types. The first are the wise, who learn from their own experiences. The second are the fortunate, who learn from other people's experiences. The third are the miserable, who neither learn from their own, nor from others' experiences." Let's be wise and fortunate, and let's not repeat the mistakes of the past.

Have our religious leaders ever taken an inventory of their records, examining their past to see what good or harm their actions have produced? If so, have they learned any lessons? On a smaller scale, have any of us studied ourselves, to see which of these three types could best describe us as individuals?

We should learn from our painful past experiences. Having our young people spend their days singing religious lamentations or spreading backwards ideas all in the name of religion cures nothing, and advances no cause and no religion. The best case in point is America, where the progress of its civilization has had nothing to do with the various religions of its people; but it has had much to do with the secular nature of the state. These regressive educators need to find another business!

A free-thinking man's ideal is not to recreate the past but to create a brighter future. Not everything that the previous generations wrote or said was correct, or should be blindly emulated.

An anecdote says that once, the head of the cardiac division of a French hospital rushed back to the morgue, and shouted in an agitated voice, "Please, pull out the body No.16 from the refrigerator! There has been a mistake: It wasn't his heart but my watch that stopped beating!"

The extremist fanatic doesn't realize that his own ability to discern has stopped functioning and not the unceasing beating of human civilization. This is all the worse when politicians, educators and religious authorities make a similar mistake.

An Arabic proverb says, "Once the scientists are corrupted, the whole world will follow suit." So many tragedies could have been prevented only if the world had understood the ramifications of this profound statement. Education matters; and what's being taught matters even more.

For years, on the hillsides of Afghanistan, lessons of hatred were being taught in the guise of religion to innocent children, both at home and at school. If only the world had truly understood that the outcome of those misleading lessons would eventually result in destruction and horrendous explosions in New York, Madrid, Iraq, London, Bali, and Beirut, etc. -- Unfortunately, those in charge of social policies often opt to tolerate such things, and as a result, the good and the bad end up sharing a common fate.

Wouldn't it be better if global organizations with the help of major religions instead did serious studies to root out and stop this corruption of religion! Will the United Nations someday achieve the comprehensive power to stop such hatred? Will the day come when humanity has reached such a degree of civilization that its members would autonomously act to prevent the promulgation of hatred, especially at schools?

The best way to become religious, in the best sense, is to uproot hatred and animosity from the hearts of mankind, and open it to love for our fellow human beings. If the world's religious school textbooks are not drastically revised, a most bleak future awaits the entire world.

Let's isolate those who like others only conditionally. Someone who chooses his friends and foes with a self-righteous attitude, only based on how closely they ape his own way of life, is a backward person. Those who bear an unconditional love for humanity are loved by all, and so they truly love God.

It's not too late to discard misleading ideas from our families and society. A rigid, prejudiced brain can't be a foreseeing mind. Delusions of grandeur makes solipsistic minds believe that they exclusively own the truth. If only they would heed this saying of the *Talmud*, that "**Greatness is something given to those who avoid it, not to those who are running after it.**"

There are those, who because of the prejudice of belonging to a certain group, consider religion to be a cause for their own superiority and domination over others, even over other members of their own group. One cannot expect such people to have a sense of responsibility and to respect the rights of the others.

I'd like to address our responsible educators, telling them that life is a collection of accidents, and accident is **just** another name for human destiny. Accidents can never be fully avoided but by learning the lessons of our past experiences, we could prevent certain possibilities from happening in the future. Someday, you'll be held responsible for what you are teaching today.

Think with an open mind, and act wisely. Consider that in our time, more than half of the 613 commandments of the *Torah* are fully impossible to be practiced, mainly due to the destruction of the Holy Temples. To be precise, only 90 of the 248 imperative, and 200 of the 365 inhibitive commands still have any practical application. In other words, the passage of time has made some 323 of the original commands no longer relevant.

Over the long centuries of the Jewish Diaspora, we have lived with the commandments in exile or captivity. Certain of the commands have been archived or deemed obsolete by religious authorities – let us also judge them by reason or science and modern society. Time is the most powerful ruler. Let's go along with it.

The famed contemporary Iranian Jewish scholar, Ms. Shirin-Dokht Daghighian has pointed out, these 613 commandments were not actually commandments *per se*, but mostly a series of principles, organized and edited by Maimonides (1135-1204 C.E.), which later came to be known as "commandments." Many of these had requirements related to a specific time and place, which after the destruction of the Temple, rendered them impractical. As such, by a unanimous consensus, it was decided that their practice would be thenceforth terminated. I ask, does this not signify the fact that by necessity, religion has to remain in sync with its times?

Humans are born to learn progress and evolve toward ideal perfection. Yet I'm surprised that nations, societies and the followers of religions continue to practice certain customs and traditions, passing them on to the next generation, even though they are fully aware that history has proved them wrong and found them to be a source of strife.

It's very much like those cigarette addicts who continue to smoke even though they are fully aware of smoking's harmful consequences. We can ask, who is to blame, the manufacturers and distributors of cigarettes and other addictive drugs, or the addicts themselves? The correct answer would be "both"!

Others have noted this analogy. The father of modern psychoanalysis, Sigmund Freud (1856-1939) was convinced that religion impeded the progress of civilization, and was a worldwide psychological illness. The Communists used to quote Karl Marx (1818-1883), saying, "Religion is the opium of the masses." Yet religion, if practiced and understood correctly, can be a most powerful, healthy medicine, and a much needed, most soothing comfort for all societies.

History has shown that religion by itself cannot invest human life with more meaning. It's the humans themselves, who are capable of giving meaning to religion. Our Jewish ancestors often lacked the proper place or position to justly introduce themselves and their religion to others, and this became a major cause of anti-Semitism. The only meaning that religion can have is the one we give to it. A better understanding of religion requires seeing above and beyond hereditary cultural limitations.

Every person has a unique dialogue with his faith according to his time and place. According to statistics, 28% of Americans at some point convert to another religion. Perhaps that's why unfortunately, close family ties, as seen in our Persian Jewish culture, do not exist in the wider American society.

We should appreciate our strong points and be grateful for them. Money, fortune, religion or even science cannot, by themselves, preserve family values. Only you and I can identify the causes that tear our families apart and heal them. Back in Iran, our community was a rather unified whole. It is only recently that some speculators created a divisive, partisan atmosphere.

The author of these essays is not so self-righteous or arrogant as to offer you direct advice on issues. But I don't hold back from expressing my opinions, hoping that this might affect some changes. I hope that as a result, we'll realize both our weaknesses and strengths, and we'll make an effort to improve ourselves. We have to offer our children the kind of information that we would have expected our parents to provide us with.

Understanding religious commands doesn't require us and our children to regress, either in thought or appearance, to the ancient times when those commands were decreed! Instead, we should try to adapt those old ways of thinking to our time. Doing so might even end

68

the sort of isolation that has historically led us to be envied or detested by other cultures.

Anti-Semitism was not the beginning of racial or ethnic discrimination; nor is it going to be the end of it. Anti-Semitism is only one of the many manifestations of humankind's capacity to hate one another.

Every day, in some corner of the world, a thug rises to power, promoting categorical hatred against some other group, whether it is religious hatred against the Jews, the Christians or the Hindus, or ethnic or racial hatred toward the Turks or the Kurds. Sadly, this has been a common pattern throughout history, one which continues to this day. The hatred goes on, until after much hardship, everyone has learned that all humanity is one and the same, and that the meaning of humanity only resides in being good to each other, regardless of color, language or ideologies. That is what makes us human.

During the Crusades (in many stages, from 1095-1272), the Jews and Christians of Jerusalem were forced into exile. In 1492, the Jews and Muslims of Spain were forced to leave the country in another round of expulsions. History has been full of such forced exiles and there seems to be no end in sight. The only remedy is to be alert and vigilant. Every individual can contribute something to improve his or her own future.

Yet individual contributions can go far beyond the perimeters of one's own life. Mohandas Gandhi (1869-1948) once said that the single reasonable vote of one man could become the vote of the majority. Sometimes just one person can redeem an entire nation.

As members of society, each of us has the responsibility to prevent the spread of ignorance, dark ideologies and hatred. These all begin at home and at our schools. There is an evolution to every idea whether it takes hold within a family or takes root in the larger society. The most destructive of such changes happen when ideas themselves start to veer off the main course, even though those who have inherited these religions, ideas or ways of life, haven't always had a choice in accepting or rejecting these notions.

A Persian proverb says, "One who keeps staring at the stars is bound to stumble and fall to the ground!" In other words, stay in touch with reality, no matter how grand or distant the ideals might look to you. Our youngsters are being led by their educators to glorify and admire the writings of the sages of the past, but they are oblivious to contemporary science. Our children's best learning years are being wasted on anachronistic ideas. Many become burdens to society, instead of being useful and productive, forming families of their own, living on donated allowances. Children raised in such a set-up can't be expected to fare any better than their parents. If they ever came to their senses, they'd realize that the blame is on none other than themselves.

Who can claim that our moderate and well-balanced young believers who study at universities and enjoy the comfort of their hard-earned Ph.D.s or other advanced degrees, have been misled? Whoever said that to be a knowledgeable person, to believe in truth, would require some pretentious labels and discrimination? Why these "color codes" and imprisoned intellect? A Persian poet once wrote, "I'm humbled before the one, who is free of all dependence."

The greatest enemy of human civilization has been such divisions, this variety of colors and labels, these differences in formal appearance. Do you truly think that human understanding has anything to do with how long one's facial hair has grown, or how large a hat one wears?

These different color hats and outfits lead to a fractured society. Those who in the name of tradition, accept the symbols, signs or colors of the *ghettos*, are those who submit to oppression and tyranny. In essence, they serve discrimination. They don't realize that throughout history, the very enemies of different religions, faiths, cults or life-styles, have taken advantage of these artificial social flaws to impose their malice, brutality and crimes.

A painful point in case is the example of Eastern European Jews, who lived in *ghettos*, and were forced to go to temple on foot. Today, certain Jews, continue to do so voluntarily, forming more or less closed neighborhoods, i.e. self-imposed *ghettos*! Superstitions, no matter what name they might take, are the cause of failure. A free mind is the beginning of all victories and freedoms.

Our ancestors simply didn't have the means to address the divisive and destructive issues among their communities. Today, we have no need to adopt or recreate the ghetto life-style, which has become so divisive in our community.

There is a beautiful saying that "you can wake someone who's asleep, but you can't wake someone who pretends to be so!" Every day, we learn of the beating or even the murder of innocent people, somewhere in the world – be it in the neighborhoods of London, Paris, Madrid, Rome or New York; in the Punjab province of India; or in Ireland – for reasons that stem from fanaticism and bigotry. Often, because these people had simply gathered in peace, or hadn't followed the strict dress codes of a religion, they were subjected to insults, harassment, and attacks and even murdered by a group of fanatics.

The regressive traditionalist should ask himself, what kind of a religion relies so heavily for its existence on appearances and symbols, such as a mark on the neck, a shawl around the waist, or a piece of cloth on the head? Why not try to gain even more "heavenly rewards" by asking everybody to crawl on their chests to the temple, as the members of a certain Tibetan cult are said to do?!

Let's stop this nonsense. No one ever became a pilot just by wearing the pilot's hat! It's not a shame not to wear a hat; the true shame is to have an empty mind! It's not a crime to walk, but the road is not paved! It's true that no one can or should judge or deem inferior other people's personal choices. But this doesn't apply to those whose choices affect other people's lives for the worse. Those who brainwash our children are infecting our entire community divisively and dragging us all down. We should fight against such people, because every member of the society and every family matters; otherwise the big ship of our society is doomed to sink.

The Jewish sage, Se'adia Ben Yousef (882-942 C.E.) said, "Religion and intellect complement each other." Yes, the survival of each depends on their other but it's the intellect that stays in tune with its time and allows us to practice our religion, rather than the words of an ancient book dictating what we are to think and act today.

Communities ought not to allow regressive groups to deceive others in the name of religion; and to perpetuate the ignorant habits of past generations, sowing discrimination, separation and seclusion and creating rifts among families. The word "religious" should bring to mind the most righteous members of all cultures, religions and societies, and not the current image of a fanatic.

When there is a talk of religion, it's not just about blind obedience or dogmatic faith. The main concern is the very essence of knowing and understanding. Any interpretation or commentary which is not based on reason, logic, and understanding of today's young men and women, is misleading. Past or present sages should be evaluated for what they said or wrote, and not based on the official positions, uniforms or the words of some contemporary promoters.

This writer is convinced that one reason for our past failures in the Diaspora has been not learning from our mistakes. Today, the Internet has provided the global community with unprecedented access to information. In such an age, one can't and shouldn't go on repeating and teaching our children what was written long ago, by men whose knowledge was limited by the *ghettos* and religious schools of their time. The people who continue to live by such ancient nonsense and superstition cannot be considered worthy of the position of teacher.

The Persian poet Hafez attacked religious hypocrisy in many of his poems. Once, he advised that the stink of hypocrisy should be washed off of a religious man's clothes by wine, a forbidden drink in Islam! He also advised that to see the truth, one has to clean up the mirror, since no flower ever grew on an iron surface.

Individual aptitude for understanding comes in different degrees, and humankind's perception of the world changes constantly. Those people and societies that have set themselves on the path of progressive change will be better off. As a poet once wrote, "Our heart changes with every breath, choosing another religion or a different path." Let's accept change as a fact of life, and not resist it by clinging to the past.

Dear Parents, drowning is the one experience, for obvious reasons, from which we cannot draw any useful lessons. Let's not drown our children by teaching them books of doubtful or harmful content, books that according to *Shofar Magazine* (No.269, p.47), are a mixture of moderate and humane words, put next to some very much superstitious, unfair and occasionally inhumane statements.

One of the more respected educators told me with regard to the harmful content of these books: "As we teach, once we get to such points, we pass over them quickly!" Won't such behavior (and such harmful content) cause a student to distance himself from both religion and the world around him? Or else, if he accepts these dictums, won't he live the rest of his life in the darkness of ignorance?

Leaders and educators cannot consider such books as reliable sources for your lessons. We won't get anywhere by presenting the facts and truths upside down. *One can't wash away the blackness of charcoal with soap!*

You will never be able to whitewash the words and deeds of educators, preachers or even extremist parents by forgiving their negligence. Although translations were not readily available to us in Iran, here, people can read these texts for themselves and question their meaning.

It may start in the privacy of a whisper, over a minor issue, then turn into an outcry putting the whole text in doubt. Communities would do better to act now to correct our understanding of these texts – if not time, will eventually do it for them albeit at a much higher cost. Let's not postpone the inevitable. The later we arrive at understanding, the longer we will have lived in ignorance.

The historical record is clear that societies that didn't act in time to prevent or solve their problems, fell victim to them. You may feel happy that you have provided your tidy and disciplined students with the best possible things. But you don't heed the song of the bird in cage, who says, "You only see the water and the seeds placed by you in my cage. But you don't realize the pain of captivity in this small confinement, which makes me forget how to fly."

Teaching ideas based on shaky logic only yields empty words and stasis, while rational science leads to positive action and success. It is said, "How good is the scent of the flowers, once we've got rid of a nasal congestion!" Don't hinder our youngsters' potential for a clear perception of the world; don't take away their one-time chance at living on the path of evolution and progress. Let them smell the beauty of truth.

74

Luck means to be prepared for opportunities, whenever they arrive.

Let's benefit from the golden opportunities of our time. As a first step, let's drive the traditionalist's culture of "antique-worship" out of our homes and schools.

Konrad Adenauer (1876-1967), former Chancellor of Germany, wrote that, "God kindly set a limit on human knowledge, but he left ignorance unlimited!"

We should learn the limits of knowledge and the extent of ignorance. Superstitions, such as prescribing the dirty water of the *mikveh,* i.e. the ritual bath, or the like, as cures for certain illnesses, are not a *mitzvah* – they constitute an act of treason. They're on par with psychic-readings or the occult, and constitute an abuse of people's trust.

By no means all people are like this or think like this. It's certainly wrong to dismiss all members of a group categorically, such as all the Orthodox or Reform Jews, or to reject all books of religious commentary. However, by contrast, not everything in the commentary books can be correct or worthy of being taught in our schools.

In our modern world, only some narrow-minded people remain inflexible. The teachers fear that they will be discharged once these ancient books are discredited. Communities the world over suffer because of fanatical religious groups; yet no society can cite religion as the reason for its good fortune. Tolerance and moderation is the key to success and the most trustworthy of schools is the school of home and family, especially if the parents themselves are open-minded and endowed with a broad perspective.

In this regard, our own Jewish community in Iran can be cited as a successful example. We didn't form opposing cults or religious schools among ourselves; we preserved our faith throughout the 2700 years of our history in Iran; and today, our moderate younger generation is considered among the most educated and successful groups in society. We can only hope that the "*mitzvah*-doers" let our youth be free, so they can remain in sync with the outside world without any prejudices, aware of the flaws and the harms of the larger world. A Persian poet once lamented that "In the vast fields of the East, no stone is clear from the smears of human tears and blood, and no place can be found where a heart is not anguished because of religion."

If children don't improve on their parents' example, they're doomed to be culturally backward.

"If we want to know who we are," they say, "We need to see who we were. If we want to see who we will be, we should examine what we are doing today."

The greatest good is not the possession of wealth, or the number of one's children, but it's about how we put our powers to use. Today's fanatics who are desperately looking to recruit and exploit lost souls should not be seen as an expression of a community's power, but of its decline. **Contributing to the sustenance of the wrong power is tantamount to aiding one's own demise.**

Iraj Mirza (1874-1926), the witty Persian poet, a prince of the Qajar dynasty, fluent in foreign languages, who spent some considerable time in Europe, had this to say about the use of modern knowledge by religious hypocrites:

"I'm stunned at the religious leader of the city, who learned the secrets of the hypnotism only to put the city to sleep!"

The French writer, Émile Zola (1840-1902), well known for his role in fighting anti-Semitism in France during the Dreyfus Case, said, "The writer is the voice of life. He's the heartbeat of a society, a vital sign of its health."

Let's protect our intelligent writers against the forces of deception and hypocrisy. To fight fanaticism and regression we should develop better muscles. How could anyone expect to fix the faults of the society by silencing those writers who point out its shortcomings with courage and clarity? Let the regressive traditionalist break the mirror because he can't tolerate to see the reflection of his flaws! This would only make for many smaller mirrors to show his faults, making it harder for him to deny the truth. *The breaking of the mirror was his very error....*

The regressive traditionalist is not concerned with interpretation, research or a deep philosophical view of the subject at hand. In contrast, a competent, motivated writer can examine the strengths and weaknesses of an idea without any bias or prejudice. An able writer will illuminate the mistakes of the past and help its readers pass safely through the mythical and story-like layers of religion arriving at a better judgment of good and bad.

The best book is the one which is devoid of lies and insults, as "the sweetest of hearts is the one which is devoid of any thought of hurting others." (Zoroaster) The regressive traditionalists and I do not differ about religion or life-styles. We differ in our perceptions of how to apply the laws and the commentaries that have been written over the past two millennia.

As a novice of the school of independent thought, well aware of my own shortcomings, I have repeatedly drawn on the words and ideas of a variety of enlightened writers, scholars and poets, to argue my case. I am most indebted to each and every one of these thinkers, as I am looking forward to the comments and critics of my friends and my readers, following the study of this book. I strongly believe that it's not just enough to repudiate the fanatic, if our aim is to rectify the problem. In the same way, it wouldn't be enough for a smoker to just acknowledge the harm of cigarettes, if the goal is to free him from his addiction.

One way to help the addict might be to offer him a healthier habit as a substitute. But to completely vanquish the problem, the addict should learn not to replace one addiction with another. He or she has to make a concentrated effort to cleanse his mind of the very thought of addiction.

Likewise, one should throw away religious nonsense and superstitions, in order to free one's mind from captivity. To arrive at independence of thought, one should first emancipate his intellect. To tell people, as some indeed do, that they will have to choose between "religion and addiction" is like trying to oust one illness by bringing in another! In such a situation, we all bear the responsibility to inform others, and to help them from becoming corrupted with such superstitions.

My friends, a chain is no stronger than its weakest link. Likewise, any society is as strong as its weakest building blocks, i.e. its families and schools. **We should fear the regression and ignorance of religious authorities and educators; their nonsense could be absorbed by our children along with their milk, and stay with them throughout their lives!**

Let's remain vigilant; modern man is concerned more with the future, than with the words of the past. The texts that have arrived in our hands, have changed and evolved over centuries in content, interpretation, and even the very meaning of their words. Only a clear mind, devoid of any prejudice, can comprehend the truth of these words and ideas.

We should value doubt among our youngsters, not discourage it. One who doubts a statement only wants to better understand it. One who is after the truth won't be content with mere imitation. She should evaluate the statement, understand it, and only if convinced of its accuracy, accept it as the truth.

In contrast, there are those who tend to blindly accept a variety of claims without ever understanding their true content. They get used to a habit, only to replace it with another. God help us if such people wear the frock of religious leadership! Then no one could dare question them anymore. There is as much chance of expecting them to provide effective leadership as there is of breaking an anvil with a fist!

The 1970 Soccer Games of Asia were supposed to take place in Iran, but the Israeli team was not invited. A famous humor magazine of the time, called *Tofigh,* explained that the Israelis had not been invited, because they never leave any land which they enter! (The main reason, of course, was the political considerations and strong anti-Israeli sentiments that existed even in the Shah's Iran.)

Nevertheless, there was some truth in this joke, if only it had been applied to some other groups! Once the under-qualified clerics have put on the frock of "religious leadership," they never let it go.

Eliezer Ben-Yehuda (1858-1922), born Eliezer Yitzhak Perlman, was a great linguist and historian, who was responsible for reviving Hebrew as a modern language. Ultra-Orthodox fanatics threatened him on many occasions, bringing him to the brink of death several times, all because he wanted to turn "the holy tongue" into a universal language! They wished the Hebrew language to remain a museum piece, much as they wish for so many other aspects of the Jewish religion.

Ben-Yehuda persisted, bringing new life to the ancient language of Hebrew and restoring the pride, freedom and identity of a self-alienated people.

In 1889, Ben-Yehuda founded the first academy for Hebrew culture, which today boasts of more than 50 scientist members. He stood up against the short-sighted fanatics, who went so far as killing his beloved dog, simply because he called it in Hebrew! In 1882, God blessed him with a son whom he named Ben Zion (son of Zion), and who, he announced, would be the first Jewish child since the Roman Empire to speak Hebrew as his mother language.

In 1883, he published the first Hebrew language newspaper in Jerusalem, under constant threats and insults of the Jewish *mullahs*. In 1909, he published the first dictionary of Hebrew language, which by 1959, would be expanded to 16 volumes. Ben-Yehuda's selfless efforts speak volumes about the innate love of a man for the moral, spiritual and cultural advancement of his people and society, without or even despite the influence of religion.

Despite fierce traditionalist opposition, his efforts were not lost to the larger Jewish society. When Ben-Yehuda died at the age of 64, more than 30,000 people gathered on the Mount of Olives in Jerusalem to pay homage to him; and today, in every Israeli town and city, there is a street named after him. If Jewish culture has been successful in establishing its modern identity, it was certainly not because of fanatical resistance to change from the ultra-traditionalists, but despite of it. Ben-Yehuda's resolve to oppose the forces of regression led to the revival of Hebrew as a modern language.

I emphasize: "A modern language." I ask my traditionalist readers to consider that out of more than 100,000 active words in modern Hebrew, only 12,000 belong to the original ancient language. Do you think one could communicate in the contemporary world with the limited vocabulary of the Jewish Bible? Instead, should we have all waited on the sidelines, until the promised messiah arrived?

To me, "the savior" means "hope", and you can't place your hopes on an inflexible single-minded person. It's said if it were not for hope, no mother would have even breast-fed her child! And a child is the best hope one could wish for. The "savior" won't be anyone but the intelligent and enlightened children of our society, who will live and improve on the ways of their parents. Societies need both change and cooperation in order to survive. The point is that those who want to remain intellectually sterile, let them do as they wish. But the others, who are still not contaminated with that dreadful disease, should become aware and watchful of the health of their mind.

This discussion reminds me of my childhood in 1940's Iran: whenever we saw a newspaper or magazine in Hebrew, we'd kiss the paper and keep it somewhere safe! We didn't know or heed its secular content; we were simply proud of its letters and words. But you shouldn't be harsh on us. Back then, we didn't know any better....

National Geographic Magazine (No. 112, October 2007) wrote that in our time, one language becomes fully extinct every other week and centuries of a people's unique culture and knowledge are buried along with it. This highlights the astonishing accomplishment of Ben-Yehuda, and his historic services to the Jewish people.

Those very people who wanted to prevent the revival of Hebrew language are still among us, with the same mentality, thinking that they are promoting and protecting the religion. Let us cry out loud for help!

Recently, I heard a story that, rising water threatened to sink a place called Garrabas (I'm not exactly sure of the correct name or its spelling), located somewhere between the Hawaiian Islands and Australia. A fanatical group there refused to leave the island, despite the clear and present danger everyone faced. They insisted that according to their holy book, Noah had said that "no city would ever go under water again." I guess that's some kind of faith, too, albeit an ignorant one.

How can anyone possibly be able to understand things, yet go on marching against his own and his society's interests, in the guise of religion?

The greatest question of our age is not whether religions will remain or disappear. It is whether science can vanquish prejudice and bigotry. We are fighting a battle between love and hatred, realism against myth, and truth versus lies.

We need to examine what benefit or harm the self-appointed religious leaders and their followers have brought to humanity. We need to do so in a way that makes clear whether such results occurred because of the religion itself, or from the actions of individual groups – which would certainly include the fanatics of Garrabas Island! -- as well as those Jews who harassed Eliezer Ben-Yehuda. I fear that as long as people remain afraid of the fanatical religious *mullahs* and their superstitions, nothing is going to change.

Plato warned the wise elite, the philosophers, that if they shunned undertaking leadership positions, some thugs would grab the chance and fill the gap.

Religion or the religious way of life is not the exclusive property of any one person or group. As such, one should be able to criticize it, and such criticism shouldn't have to hurt or excite any reasonable person. Superstitions, often ascribed to religion, become most dangerous when they partake in society's beliefs and identity. A love to fulfill the commandments is much more effective than a fear of certain things or certain people.

A fanatical Jewish *mullah* recently told a relative of mine that if he installed *mezuzahs* (the little boxes proscribed by the Torah) on the gates of his warehouses, he would have no more need for fire or theft

82

insurance! There is no difference between this *mullah* and those who attacked Ben-Yehuda, or the clergy of Garrabas. In effect, these so-called sages follow their emotions, not their intellect.

The good news, if there is any, is that regressive traditionalists can only mislead those people who are already of a mind to believe in superstitions. Let us prevent them from giving our children this handicap, in the name of religion, in their schools. The regressive traditionalists promote such nonsense thinking that they tread the path of piety. What they fail to realize is that when their beliefs, words and thoughts lack credibility they weaken the social side of their followers' personalities, and by extension, the communities in which they live.

We should admit that the fanatical bigots who opposed the revival of Hebrew language, just like their contemporary counterparts, didn't mean ill. They just wanted to defend their faith, and their way of life. They equate a scientific view with not being religious. Consider, however, China, the largest and most populous country on the planet, with its 5000 years of recorded history and a most unique and complex language, will soon turn into the largest English-speaking country in the world! One wonders if they could have arrived at their current success, had they been thinking as the fanatics have done.

If we don't get accustomed to speaking the naked truth, our children and grandchildren will fall prey to lies and superstitions. The ultra-Orthodox community who opposed Ben-Yehuda, didn't realize that their efforts, if successful, would have brought about the demise of the Hebrew language, consigning it to the dustbin of history with such other ancient tongues as Latin, Sanskrit, etc. As a result of their years of superstitious dogma, they so much believed in the holiness of the language that they could not see the reality of the situation before them. Ben-Yehuda's persistence, however, won the war. In 1922, for the first time in 2000 years, British Mandate Palestine in Jerusalem recognized Hebrew as one of the three official languages of the country.

Einstein once advised that before we trust anyone's words, we should admit that all of us, have said at different times, some right or false things. Let the regressive fanatics and their seasonal followers say and write whatever they wish. There will be more books like this volume and the voices of the learned majority of the society to counter them. We should also remember that the less-informed are looking forward to taking advantage of a chance while the wise person steps forward to create opportunities.

Einstein said that the pleasures of mathematics came from its absolute certainty, while other sciences were subject to debates, verification, evaluation of data, and constant revisions based on new findings. Two times two always equals four, while Newtonian mechanics doesn't hold true at all speeds. Change and innovation are inevitable, and the regressors shouldn't be allowed to manipulate and poison the minds and hearts of our children in the name of religion, plundering the greatest treasure of our families.

The safest place for religious instruction, this very private matter, is within the boundaries of family, combined with our conscientious judgment and moderation. Otherwise, there is no difference between the disintegration of a family or society for a lack of spirituality, and its more dangerous opposite, extreme religiosity.

The humanity of people is measured by their deeds, not by their particular faith or the strength of their beliefs.

Those disappointed by religion, wouldn't try to change it; instead, they opt for a life without religion. Ironically, the harbingers of this trend are the children of religious or anti-religious extremists, and not the moderates, who typically maintain a balance between reason and faith. Faith and conscience complement each other. If one of the two is contaminated with bigotry and prejudice, the result is a catastrophe. Indeed, we see this all the time in the modern world, where a learned man with no conscience makes the bombs, while the ignorant fanatic explodes them on the streets. By contrast, the conscientious philanthropist scientist spends a lifetime to discover a vaccine that could save the lives of the others.

Napoleon once said that history was the only true philosophy and psychological tool to understand nations.

History is an honest advisor to learned men. Look at the darkness of the past, to learn where the black-hearted men of today came from. As a Persian poem states, "What could you expect from the wine-seller or the drunkard? What could you expect to happen, when the king and the city are sound asleep, as the enemy is lurking around?"

In 1848 C.E., one of the most prominent historical figures of Iran, Prime Minister Amir Kabir (1807-1852) ordered the first vaccination program sponsored by the government, according to which, all Iranian youth were expected to be inoculated against small pox. A few days into the program, he was told that many people in the country refused to be vaccinated. Their fear was in no small part due to the rumors started by some psychics and talisman-writers who told them that vaccination would permit demons to enter the body and possess the person!

When the news arrived that five people had just died of small pox, Amir Kabir decided to increase the pressure. He announced that whoever would not agree to getting the vaccination would have to pay a fine of 5 *toumans*. But the words of the psychics and public ignorance overcame this order, too. Those, who could afford, paid the fine; others hid away in the water-reservoirs, until the officers had left the town.

Some time passed, before Amir was informed that in all of Iran only 330 people had been vaccinated. They brought to him a poor tailor, whose child had perished because of that dreadful disease. Amir Kabir looked at the corpse of the child, and asked the man, "Why, when we sent people to vaccinate and save your children?" The old man replied in a sorrowful tone, **"Your Highness, I was told if inoculated, my child would become possessed or suffer from the evil eye…"**

Amir Kabir shouted, "Such ignorance! Now, not only you lost your child, you should also pay the 5 *toumans* in fines." The old man implored Amir, "Believe me, I have no money to pay." Amir Kabir gave him 5 *toumans* from his own pocket, and said, "The order cannot be reversed. Pay this to the government treasury."

A few minutes later, they brought him a grocer who had also lost his son to the pox. Amir could bear it no more and sat down to cry. One of the court ministers, Mirza Agha-Khan Nouri, seeing this told Amir that it was beneath him to cry for the children of the poor whose death was caused by their refusal to be vaccinated. Amir replied that, "As long as I hold custody for these people, I'm also responsible for their deaths." The minister whispered, "But they refused vaccination because of their ignorance!"

At this point, Amir raised his voice and said, "We are responsible for their ignorance, too. If we build schools and libraries in every village, on every corner of our cities, the psychics and occultists would have no choice but to close down their shops. All Iranians are my true children, and I cry because I wonder why they should be so uninformed, as to die for refusing to do something so simple?" (Source: *Stories from the Life of Amir Kabir*, Hakimi, M.; Nashr Farhang, Tehran.)

Amir was an enlightened man in a dark time. The public
imagination was filled with stories of genies and demons, the evil eye
and magic talismans. It was a time when our Jewish forefathers were
living as second class citizens struggling to survive! But Amir was no
better than his times.

On January 11, 1852, while alone in a public bath, Amir Kabir was
assassinated by a group of royal conspirators, which possibly included
that very same Mirza Aghan Khan.

The Jewish tradition says, *kol yisrael arevim zeh la-zeh*, -- as
diverse as we are, we are all bound together, and we are responsible
for each other. As a community, we share in both the glory and the
blame. Responsibility doesn't know any compromise. All human-
beings are responsible for the safety and security of one another. We
should better say, *kol ha-**adam** arevim zeh la-zeh,* that is, all *humans*
are mixed and connected to each other. One should cry tears for
societies in which the regressive traditionalists are active, while the
intellectuals are silent. Today, we can better understand why Amir
Kabir cried. May the day never come, when others cry for us. The
world is a much more dangerous place than we think. A Persian poet
once observed, "Why the entire world quiet, and what is it waiting to
hear? Do I hallucinate from a fever, or is it the true face of the monster
of night?"

What we do defines our status. Napoleon used to say that to him,
people were like numbers; their value depended on where they stood
next to the other; much in the same way that the number "1", when
followed by six zeroes, turns into a million.

The regressive traditionalists prescribe, in the name of religion,
that we should consciously keep our youth away from the realities of
the global community and modern life. But this would only turn our
children into a community of third-rate citizens, instead of the proud,

productive and useful people they can be. We could boast at their talent at reciting prayers but what would they be contributing to the scientific progress of our civilization?

I say to the regressive traditionalists, your way offers nothing to civilization, and no incentive for the rest of the world to engage with us. Persistence in repeating our past mistakes is just another mistake in its own right.

Being religious doesn't mean that we know everything!

Parents should note that the writings or sayings of the so-called religious missionaries can only be effective if the psychological, social and family groundwork for their acceptance is already there. That's why your worldview and that of the religious educators is so critical to the success or failure of your children. The authenticity of religion and rational faith are too important to be based on empty or ambiguous beliefs. You should focus your attention on the authentic substance of constructive religious commands, devoid of any backwards fanatical beliefs.

The regressive traditionalist pretends that his meddling in other people's spiritual affairs is necessary to preserve the religion – an assumption that should be strongly questioned.

What we need to do is to marry religious beliefs and modern science, thus, transforming the commandments from rigid religiosity to a logical application for our lives. If everyone -- fathers, mothers, teachers or *mullahs* -- gives up logic and reason, why should any child ever accept any logical argument? And as we have seen, such families would be lost to us. Sadly, the regressive traditionalist is only concerned with furthering the interests of his own group, and not the interests of the whole society. He is thinking of defeating rationalism, and to this aim, he considers everything permissible, as long as it serves the cause of his own religious beliefs and the growth of his community.

On page 769 of *Dehkhoda Persian Dictionary*, named after the foremost Persian lexicographer, Ali-Akbar Dehkhoda (1879-1959), the word "bigotry" or "prejudice", has been defined as such: "Bigotry (*ta'assob*) means not to accept the word of truth in the face of compelling reason, because of side motives."

A prejudiced, bigoted person thinks of himself as the official legislator and executor of the law! Furthermore, in the name of *mitzvah*, he wishes to impose those "laws" on the others, even at the cost of fracturing families and society, or even worse, killing others and being killed.

The Persian mathematician, Professor Mohsen Hasht-roodi (1907-1976) wrote, **"Bigotry is the enemy of the free thought of man."** It's true. Blind belief, without morality, has no place in human intellect and conscience. It's almost impossible to change a fanatic traditionalist. But it's possible to prevent the spread of regression by disseminating knowledge, remaining current with modern science and civilization, and expelling regressive preachers from our homes and our schools. This can be achieved once people have put an end to their indifference. We cannot lay the blame for the appearance of such regressors among us solely on these uniformed, "color-coded" groups and their proselytizing efforts. The blame is also on those of us who could have rebuffed them from the outset – but didn't.

Indifference is the great culprit. The crucial moment for a society or family arrives when as a result of their indifference they permit the regressive traditionalists to pursue their mission. We do not debate the need to have faith along with morality and honor but we must be vigilant against the kind of blind, slavish submission which we have witnessed among many religious people of the world.

Too often, we have seen how fanatics commit massacres in the name of religion despite commandments prohibiting murder. Religious fanatics won't stop at anything, According to statistics, in the 20th century alone, more than one hundred million people have been killed, for different reasons and excuses, mostly rooted in religion, to promote certain ideologies, or because of a simple conflict of ideas.

Has mankind learned its lesson? Or does man continue to persist in committing evil in the guise of "religious good"? Alas, the tragedy continues!

Hate is conceived at that moment when religion becomes the standard by which human-beings are measured; when the leaders of religions or cults begin to imagine that humiliating others means elevating themselves. To paraphrase Motti -o-doleh Hejazi, "right" is the word, from which thousands of "wrongs" have been made! These people, at their best, aim for heaven, but instead, turn the earth into a hell.

Muhammad Iqbal (Lahore) said it so beautifully that, "Hell" is not about a physical place, but it's about certain conditions and dispositions, which ensnare human-beings. Or as a Persian poem states, "My friend, heaven is about comrades, whose hearts are in accord; and hell is nothing more than the meeting of two unfitting friends."

Religious superstition doesn't, in of itself, kill anyone. However, it has led followers to cry out, "Oh, death, come to us, because life is killing us!" Dr. Jalil Mahmoudi once said, "Oh, God, I am not afraid of your wrath, because you are kind. I'm not afraid of your hell, because you have no such place. But I'm afraid of myself, because I'm ignorant."

If I ever burn, I'd burn in the fire of my own ignorance, and not in the fires of hell of your wrath. I have no enemy worse than stupidity, and I find no abyss deeper than what lies for us beyond the cliff of ignorance. **Being religious doesn't mean that one knows everything about everything!** There are many secular poets or writers whose wise advice remains with us forever. It's not important who's the speaker; what truly matters is the content of what's been said.

Many people pay more attention to the history behind the books by religious sages than their actual content. Centuries ago, these books might have been the best of their time. Today they belong archived in libraries rather than being taught at our schools. Being boastful of the writings of the sages is fine, as long as what they said was correct, meaningful and a cause for pride. Beyond that, the writings that do not agree with today's sciences and the culture of our youth, are not worthy of our attention.

The contents of some religious books are often based on weak evidence, and they are devoid of any serious meaning. They are cause for alarm among the truly knowledgeable. Unfortunately, such writings are good material for those who wish to criticize our holy books. For them, any incomplete truth is a complete lie! Although all of the "Abrahamian" religions, i.e. the Judeo-Christian monotheistic religions, stem from a single source, they seek to repudiate our holy writings in their prejudiced books in order to reject everything altogether. Just take a look around to find out the truth for yourself. To paraphrase a Persian poem, "Alas, finding a cure for our hidden pain and distress has been left to those who imagine themselves thriving over our ruins."

Thus, these self-appointed critics, like termites, chew away at everything. They don't notice that such misplaced criticism is nothing more than gossip. They should be justly reminded that killing the ant doesn't punish the scorpion!

A speaker once held a hundred-dollar bill in the air, and asked his audience, "I wish to give this money to only one person. Any volunteers?" Everyone's hands went up. He crumbled the bill, threw it on the hall floor, rubbed it into the dust, then asked again, "Who wants it now?!" Once more, almost everybody shot their hands in the air. Why? Because these people well knew that nothing the man did could take away the true value of the bill. Sadly, over the centuries, time and again, the Jewish people have been kicked around. But happily, those with cruel intentions have never succeeded in taking away from Judaism its spiritual value along with its progressive laws and commandments.

Time after time, the Jewish people have reappeared from the heart of burning flames, like the mythical phoenix, their wings spread, or like the mythical Persian bird, *Simorgh*, flying high to create new reasons for pride and victory. Only we can help those progressive commandments to flourish by observing them with a better understanding of their meaning.

A "nation" or "society" as defined recently by sociologists is, "a collection of people, who amid the diversity of ideas and tastes, maintain an emotional bind among themselves." Such a group of people tend to have a shared history and a common language and culture. Their common roots lead to a shared collective memory, strengthening their ties, allowing them to continue as a nation, by remembering their joint past.

Many nations have a history of aggression and violence, waging wars, conquering other lands, murders and massacres, oppressing some people and discriminating against others. In contrast, while Jewish history is full of suffering and pain, tolerating anguish, it is also filled with trying to make the best of whatever chances the Jewish people were given, forgiving and forgetting those oppressions, patiently moving on to build and thrive, trusting time, and hoping that tomorrow would be a better day.

The Russian writer and philosopher, Leo Tolstoy (1828-1910) wrote that no two warriors were ever stronger than "time" and "patience." But he didn't clarify, what constitutes "patience"? How long will the world continue with unjust political trades, disguised as legitimate expectations of "kindness for kindness," or go on amassing fortunes in the name of religion?

Noosha, our precious contemporary poet, has composed a beautiful poem in Persian, praising the Jewish resolve for life, and our proud history of innovation and creativity, despite centuries-long pain and suffering. Here, I would like to present a paraphrase of his poem, hoping that its message and some of its imagery would be conveyed in English:

"Thousands of years have passed, and still,
This pained people are barred from a life of peace.
No mountain could've born such suffering,
For centuries, to cry tears of blood.
But they stand tall, still, against time's blows,
Never bent to failure, despite the weight of defeats.
Once, slaves of the Pharaoh,
Next, captives of other's demeaning prejudice,
And yet, their history remains
A proud record of wisdom, and of good deeds.
The tree of arts bears much of their fruit;
The land of science is nourished by their arts.
Einstein, the wise, marching for peace,
Proudly holds their gleaming, streaming flag.
Nowhere is the Nobel mentioned,
Without a Jew on the side.
They're small in size, but their feat is immense;

Insults endured were great, but
Stronger was their will to build.
Thrown into the flames of nations' cruelty, time and again,
They emerged like the phoenix, wings wide spread.
They've watered their fields, glass by glass;
They've built everything, with their own bare hands.
Word of God on the tongue,
They're true heirs to Moses, the man,
Before whom the sea parted,
And for whom the mountain's fire
Transformed into a cool breeze."
(Based on a poem by Noosha)

It might be instructive to compare the above to the following two poems, from the perspective of a wise gentile, protesting the cruelties of the world:

"Still captives of the first sin, we wage
Bloodshed, disasters, and wars.
Like Cain, after murdering our brothers,
Doing nothing to end the aged pus
Of this sizzling, infectious wound."

And:

"Angels are ashamed of our deeds,
So much blood we shed on the ground.
Oh, sun of peace! Dawn on us!
So that we'll no more shame the ground."

****

Today, we live in a different world.

The world has finally understood, the hard way, that evil, even thousands of miles away, can bring us fear and misery at home. The tragedy of that dreadful Tuesday, September 11, 2001, is a recent case in point. As civilization spreads, it seems that the boundaries of state, as well as religious autonomy are undergoing a profound change.

The Universal Declaration of Human Rights is essentially a code to protect the rights of others. It's a means to preserve freedom. It's a treasure chest of ages-long accumulated wisdom, one that says: No one should be compelled or coerced to accept a specific thought or idea; No one can be subjected to brainwashing; No one can be compelled to give up her freedom; No one can use his freedom to take away the freedom of another.

The Declaration of Human Rights is the vault where the essence of humanity's wisdom is preserved. Alas, the Declaration has not specified whether someone who disagrees with another person's right to live should still be called "human." Should such people, too, be granted the freedoms provided in the Declaration, as well as other progressive rights of civil society?

American president Theodore Roosevelt (1858-1919), said that "order without freedom" and "freedom without order" are equally damaging. Indeed, liberty and moral limitations complement each other.

A survey of The Declaration of Human Rights suggests that humanity is not limited to one's national or religious identity. Religion could comprise a fraction of one's identity, and may be a source of pride or of shame, but it cannot consist of one's entire identity.

You and I have had no say in choosing the faith into which we were born. Nonetheless, our religion shares more than a name with the faith of prejudiced ultra-Orthodox believers or even ignorant, treacherous fanatics. Like it or not, the world regards us all as one Jewish people. In truth, we are a highly diverse group, without a single, all-encompassing common belief. Some of us claim to be the true defenders of the religion, waiting for the savior to arrive; while others follow science and reason. Is there much, if anything, in common between these two groups? Can we say that they belong to the same faith?

There are those who would deprive an audience of two thousand from hearing the voice of the temple's speaker or cantor on Sabbaths and High Holidays because they follow a fanatic *mullah's* decree that the use of electrical speakers is forbidden on such holidays. In contrast, others regard this prohibition as a matter of superstition. Is there much in common between the former and the latter factions of the Jewish people?

It's sad that so many people take being religious to mean following the literal pronouncements of regressive traditionalists, instead of following the essence of the commandments of the *Torah*. The more we study and think for ourselves, the more we realize the depth and significance of those commandments. Our religion is not what a group of regressive traditionalists have been claiming it to be, those who have scared our youngsters, using them as shields to hide behind.

As is the case with all religions, being co-religionists doesn't mean sharing the exact same ideas. It's a major flaw to ignore such distinctions and to treat all members, good or bad, as one. Doing so is a sign of prejudice and should be rectified.

In my opinion, faith is a private issue between man and God. It's hypocrisy to maliciously criticize others for observing (or not observing) a custom about which they had no choice. True human identity shouldn't depend on one's color, religion, ethnicity, country or nationality.

Thus, it's sad that even today a whole group can be demonized or dismissed just for the mistakes of a minority of the group. The good deeds of thousands of scientists, writers, artists and intellectuals are dismissed in the eyes of the world because one murderer has come to represent that entire group or faith. This is a clear error in judgment, since many (even the overwhelming majority) of the group's members also repudiate the murderer's actions.

The Pakistani philanthropist, Dr. Abdul Sattar Edhi (b. 1928) put it best in a TV Interview, when he said, "I am a Muslim, but my religion is Human Rights." Will the day come when all of us are this civilized?

Religious abuse is a catastrophic problem of global scale. Humans have never fully appreciated the true reverence and significance of religion and never understood the difference between religion and material concerns. As such, mankind has continued to do so for the wrong means, as if to say: *"Oh, people of the world, I want to complain! I want to complain, even of God!"*

We will regret it if we waste any more time avoiding this issue. We need to take the initiative to evolve religious understanding that meshes with today's youth and their contemporary interests. Doing so would put an end to religion that is a blind imitation of the past, and to the influence of those who have long employed religion as a tool for their own aims. If not, we'll trail the rest of the world.

The best solution would be to offer a better alternative to disseminating hatred and superstitions. This writer believes that the (Jewish) extremists do not intend in principle to cause differences and divisions. But regardless of their intentions, that is the result of their actions – tearing apart families and causing rifts among entire communities.

Sowing the seeds of separation is tantamount to cultivating hatred. Yesterday's fanatics attacked by dagger; today's wealthier and more educated fanatic attacks using an airplane. That's because the fanatic's knowledge and wealth grew within the very rigid boundaries of his family's bigotry and his school's prejudiced teachings, not within the open air of free-thought, science, love and kindness. This fanatic simply graduated from the classrooms of the literature of hatred to the advanced schools of violent actions. As Rumi wrote, "Better give the sword to the hands of a drunken slave than to those with evil intents, because in their hands, knowledge, wealth or position, all turn into flames of rage and conspiracy."

Religious practice doesn't mean extreme observance. Instead, it should mean becoming better humans.

Mulla Sadra (c. 1571-1636 C.E.), a Persian theologian and philosopher, said that "God is infinite, timeless, and without any physical boundaries. But He would become as small as your understanding, and He would come down as low as your needs. He would spread to the extent of your dreams, and He would become as effective a key as your faith is."

Nature is such a bad teacher, because it gives us the exams first, then the lesson! To better understand what faith truly is, we might like to consider the following story:

As drought raged in the land, the people of a Jewish village decided to organize a communal prayer, asking for rain. The whole community gathered in one place on a Jewish festive Holiday, but only a child had brought an umbrella along! This is faith, in its true sense, full of hope and resolve. This is the jewel, a realistic vision which we need to cultivate and encourage in our children.

History has well demonstrated that no nation should ever depend on others for its very survival. Many a political or religious leader, including some powerful Popes passed over those vast fields, where millions of Jews or Armenians were being massacred without offering a word in protest. They witnessed as millions of innocent, helpless humans were being killed but they chose to remain silent. Some of the victims even belonged to their own religion but these so-called leaders opted to ignore their misery, saving their tears instead for the ritual sermons at the altar.

William Shakespeare (1564-1616) was supposedly so outraged by the treacherous acts of world's leaders that he suggested we should feed dog's milk to our children, to see if they might develop loyalty as adults! Who can trust such self-appointed caretakers, who pretend to be protecting our morality, after we discover that they have repeatedly lied and betrayed us? Nietzsche once quipped, "I'm not upset that you lied to me; I'm upset that from now on I can't believe you."

Sadly, the world has not changed: Just think of the hundreds of thousands of Christians being killed in Darfur, Sudan, or those of so many other faiths who are being killed elsewhere mainly for religious or ethnic reasons. Tragically, this is happening under the supervising but indifferent eyes of the world's major powers and the United Nations.

Let's remind ourselves of our own fanatic anti-Israel Rabbis of the *Neturei Karta* movement. A few years ago, members of this group travelled to Iran to meet with the Islamic leaders of that country to show their own enmity with the state of Israel! In Iran, they appeared in interviews, on national TV channels, and on newspaper headlines, to the delight of the anti-Israel Iranian hardliners and to the amusement of the public. As late as July 2009, they met in Gaza with the leaders of the terrorist group Hamas, only to re-iterate once more their anti-Israel agenda!

As you might know, *Neturei Karta*, "Guardians of the City" in Aramaic, was founded in 1935 by a group of so-called ultra-Orthodox *Haredi* Jews of Jerusalem. They insist on dismantling the Jewish State, because according to them, Jews were forbidden to have a country of their own until the coming of the Messiah! Today, they also go by their English name, "Jews United Against Zionism." Their agenda, which threatens the very existence of the Jewish people, is based they claim in Jewish belief. With such an enemy within, who needs an enemy without?!

The history of other religions and ideological cults has also often been filled with the spilling of their own people's blood for religious reasons. Such sectarian bloodsheds continue to our day. Thus, I ask, how successful has religion been in correcting the path of humanity? As the 13th century Persian poet Saadi (1184 – 1283 or 1291, C.E.) wrote:

"What difference betwixt friend and vicious foe,
If the friend too is to treat me like a brute?
Don't trust your emotions with your mind,
As the wise would never go near the vice.
Why should I care about someone,
Who doesn't care about my wellbeing?
One can't silence a jealous tongue or the enemy's mouth,
So just keep friends happy, and ignore the rest."

Can it be a *mitzvah*, or *savab*, i.e. "a religious act of good" to tear apart a family? This is a prescription that causes more pain not relief! What we truly need are compassionate religious people, not immature self-appointed practitioners.

Once I asked an academic scholar who had spent a lifetime studying the religions of the world about a particular religion. He asked me in return, "Which religion stands as its opposite?" I was perplexed, until he explained, "I can answer your question better, if I know about its opposing religion!"

It's not enough for us enumerate the faults of the ultra-Orthodox groups. We should also speak more about the strengths of the Reform communities with their more than 900 synagogues, 1.5 million-strong congregation, their support of Israel, as well as the world's sciences and economy. A comparative study of the two groups, one a burden on the society, the other a contributor to its advancement, can be very illuminating.

The narrow-minded traditionalists don't consider these 900 temples as being *kosher*, i.e. "religiously approved", because the Reform synagogues have ignored certain Orthodox bans on electrical speakers and other similar superstitions.

The late Mr. Eliahoo Ghodsian used to say about the Jewish Orthodoxy that "They consider wine produced and bottled by clean machines under utmost hygienic conditions to be non-*kosher*. But they imagine house-made wine also bottled and distributed by others, produced under open conditions, with grapes that have stomped by bare feet, while mosquitoes were flying around, to be *kosher*!"

The regressive traditionalist is not law-abiding, he's only an imitator – following whatever his mullah tells him. Every traditionalist group has its own *mullah,* none of whom agrees with the other, as each is looking to expand his own market. Often, one can get to know people better based on what they've said about others, than what others have said about them.

One reason that this writer keeps addressing the religious teachers and leaders is that "the eyes of the master are more effective than the hands of the student." What these teachers think and say is many times more crucial than the words of their followers.

If the teacher's instructions consist of clear and enlightened ideas, the student will also develop a clear and realistic vision. Otherwise, as we see today all over the world, we have religious extremist graduates from the schools that preach divisiveness and hypocrisy.

As Rabbi Yadidia Ezrahian wrote in the Persian *Shofar of New York* (No. 323, p.39), "Let's pray for the day to come, when there would be no more left of those who sell out their religion, and who advocate divisions among the society. Let us pray for the day to come, when the people of the earth will have all become unified as one. As we read in our daily prayers, *vehaya bayom ha-hu, yihyeh Adonai echad u-shmo echad*, that is, "There will come the day when all the people of the earth shall worship only one God, and they shall follow only one law. *Amen.*"

The Persian magazine *Payam* recently held a discussion about the *Kippa*, or *Yarmulke*, i.e. the symbolic Jewish skullcap that brought back some old memories that I'd like to share along with my own distinct view, which differs from the erudite participants of Payam's discussion.

Many years ago, during the first hundred days of my miserable stay in the religious neighborhood of Ramat Shlomo in Jerusalem, the residents, mostly ultra-orthodox Haredi Jews, would not return my greetings, simply because I did not wear a piece of cloth on my head!

In my opinion that's because their belief system relies primarily on appearances and not on meaning or substance – a trait which they share with the fanatics of all other religions. It's quite telling that the Persian people refer to their fanatics as *gheshri*, which literally means "superficial," because they look only at the surface of things. During my time there I asked several rabbis about the *kippa* on many occasions and received a variety of answers based on different explications, commentaries and interpretations. I must report that their answers were not in conflict with the opinions expressed in *Payam* by

Rabbi Ezrahian, Rabbi Parvaneh Sarraf, and Mr. Koushanfar. It was clear that **according to tradition**, we are obligated to wear a cap while practicing a religious ceremony.

However, **with all due respect** to those who believe we should wear a hat or a skullcap at all times, I pose the following question:

Is wearing the *kippa* in non-religious public places an obligation, too? Even more importantly, is it the most appropriate thing to do? After all, has it not been said in the holy *Torah* that we could pray anytime, any condition, anywhere?

Why is it necessary for us to employ certain headgear or dress a certain way to symbolize one's religion or beliefs, and do so at all times on the streets of this wild world, so full of hatred and brutality? When all dress alike, the mistakes of an individual can easily be blamed on a whole group, even a whole nation? What's the point of this exhibitionism?

Has the world changed that much since brutes forced Jews to a wear a badge patched on their chest of Jews, to make it easier to identify them and carry out some unspeakable act of cruelty? Are there less dangerous, violent fanatics in today's world? All things being equal, who would be more at risk – the innocent singled out on the virtue of his *kippa*, or those who don't carry such a symbol? (Needless to say, this applies to others who wear the garb of their religion).

After World War II, the ghettos were finally abandoned. This makes it all the more surprising that our religious fanatics didn't learn from that ages-long ordeal, and instead chose to create new closed communities. The founded *de facto* ghettos all around the world, all so that they can follow their irrational practices of avoiding using electricity or driving cars on certain days, so that they can walk to their synagogues? Which healthy mind would approve of this?

It's as if the little patch on the chest has now voluntarily moved to the most prominent position of our body, that is, to the top of our heads! But why? Based on which explicit commandment?

Do corrective lenses bring us knowledge?! Likewise, does the skullcap have anything to do with our brains?! Or is "religious observance" merely exhibitionism?

According to the religious, a rational opponent of the *kippa* is someone who's ashamed of his religion, a "self-hating Jew."

But that's nonsense! The fanatics indoctrinate their followers, especially our youth, with a false sense of guilt over the "sin" of not wearing the *kippa* – or the wig for women. This is not only an insult to the intelligence of our community but they also blind our youth from an accurate understanding of reality; and, in some cases, they act as impediments to successful marriages

Given the enormity of our current global problems and daily challenges, societies are in need of people who build bridges, bringing them together with the outside world. The last thing we need is greater division and discrimination.

Although none of us is responsible for another's member of our community's false interpretation of our religion, sometimes we must pay the price – be it by the consequences of their provocations, or by being judged (and even mocked) as if we endorse the ideas and actions of the most myopic preachers of the fanatic community.

Alas, the forgetful human never learns enough from past experience but we should make an effort to remember history. In the 18th century, **Mullah Reyhan o'Allah**, anticipated the 20th century Nazi Germany by requiring Persian Jews as well as Christians and Zoroastrians, to wear a badge on their chest, so that they'd be singled out, and harassed or persecuted with ease! History repeats itself, and we must endure the consequences!

To understand the false, philosophy behind the constant wearing of a skullcap, suffice it to say that every religious sect has its own unique requirements for the size, shape, color or even texture of their headgear. Whether this is done for sheer hypocrisy and exhibitionism or for recruitment purposes is debatable, but in essence they function as "identification cards" or "uniforms" distinguishing "friend" from "other." Such division make even less sense given the very low number of the entire Jewish population worldwide! Shouldn't we rather unite?

My friends! We ought not to remain indifferent before the promulgation of superstitions. **Saadi** once wrote,

'Though the wise deems silence polite,
Better try and speak out when expedient.

For two things diminish our intellect: To remain silent

When one ought to speak, and To speak at the time of quiet.

By observing reason and courteous manners, we can express any of our ideas freely in a discussion that allows for pro and cons, and where each individual is allowed to express their own opinions. Unfortunately, the reasonable people do so politely, while the irrational ones do so with insults!

If the famous German philosopher **Moses Mendelssohn**, the father of Jewish Reform, had feared the baseless insults of the religious sectors; had he not taken steps to teach German language in European ghettos; then Yiddish would be the only language of European Jews. Likewise, if **Eliezer Ben-Yehuda** didn't revive the Hebrew language, the state of Israel wouldn't have an official language. Prayers and curses are nothing more than a regressor's tool to stop the progress of others. Let's not allow them to spread false fears to our youth.

To struggle toward a better tomorrow is part of life. Humankind is in a constant state of change, so that he could survive; and to survive, we need to change. Let's not allow some charlatans to build ideological ghettos by irresponsibly interpreting scripture according to their wishes.

The fanatics see the preservation of our identity in enforcing a lack of change, and in a blind imitation of the past, generation after generation, over and over repeating the mistakes of their ancestors.

This is in direct contradiction to the true spirit of the Jewish religion and its philosophy.

We don't have any problem, whatsoever, with the rational laws and commandments of our religion. However, we do take serious issue with a variety of commentaries and interpretations which disagree with reason, logic and science — and of course, with those which promote such absurdities.

To tie our children's security, their fate, and the faith of a nation at large, to a piece of cloth worn over our head, or to other similar religious superstitions, is, as I said earlier, an insult to the community's intelligence.

Let us wake up, so that future generations could sleep better. To continue imitating things blindly is not to preserve our identity; rather, it's to continue in a state of slavery. It's said that children have to grow tall on their own, regardless of their father's height. Let's not tie down our children, and confine their natural growth with our own superstitions.

Human intellect is, or ought to be, the ultimate judge for any given deed. This is exactly what a religious imitator tries to avoid. Religion asks us to protect our lives — to protect life. What was written in some distant time or place, and the practice of certain religious rituals may not be worthy of our blind trust when measured against contemporary risks, or even modern knowledge. Let's put an end to such dangerous pretentions.

The Persian poetess, **Forough Farrokhzad,** once wrote, in reference to a similar act of exhibitionism among the Muslims, "Our forehead better be bruised by the brand of a sin, than from pressing it on the prayer stone, out of sheer hypocrisy." It's a great honor to be proud of our faith but not with pretensions, colors and signs.

If religion was only a matter of its signs and symbols then even our enemy could put on a skullcap and call themselves a member of our community!

Saeb, the famed Persian poet, once wrote, "Beware of the ceremonial washing of the mouth and the hands, for it could be more ruinous than floods."

My friends,

Once upon a time, we lived all as one, until the fanatics discovered the secret of our unity, and began to divide us up falsely into the "religious" and the "non-observant" and further segregate those who worship one way, and those that worship another, those that wear a skullcap and those who don't. This is what the greatest military minds would have done to their foes: Divide and conquer.

Instead our community should come together now to make our society whole.

The eminent British philosopher and Nobel laureate, **Bertrand Russell** (1872-1970) once wrote (I paraphrase), "**Better for the world to break into pieces, than I or anyone else to believe in lies.**"

Alas, we live in a world where the ignorant is confident in his work, but the wise is never sure of his deeds.

Indeed, no group or sect can absolutely claim that only *they* could be right (Yet they do!).

Moderation and balance, and a society based on moral and spiritual principles, combined with mutual respect, demands that we find a way to worship and practice our beliefs without interfering in one another's lives and affairs. It's our humane deeds that speak of our good intentions.

Bertrand Russell also wrote (and I paraphrase again) to effect that, **"Our happiness depends on providing for the happiness of others."**

There are some myopic individuals who wrongly claim that if the superstitions in our religion are not observed, then the religion itself will founder and disappear. History has proven different, faith that depends on reason and logic is what survives and what has preserved us these many centuries – not a piece of cloth — be it 10 centimeters long, as for the Jews; or 10 meters long, as for some other religions!

The greatest scientists and inventors, such as Thomas Edison, Henry Ford, or Albert Einstein, each made perhaps hundreds of inventions or discoveries, not all of which were successful, or worthy of attention. Each of these great men became primarily known for their most important contribution. Edison is remembered for his role in the production and application of electricity; Ford for his cars; Einstein for the Relativity Theory.

Likewise, the greatest moments of the scripture, those eternal, indestructible selections from religious texts, will live on forever. Those parts, however, that conflict with today's science and knowledge will gradually become obsolete. Let us relegate the superstitions promulgated by religion to the archives of history. If we don't, then those very superstitions would turn us into history!

We don't dress, eat or drink, as we did in the stone ages! Likewise, we need no longer think as we did in those ancient times. If we think

108

rationally and act according to reason, we should be fortunate enough to learn from each other, and from the world.

Lucky is the believer who understands the meaning of things, and who avoids meaningless imitation. As a Persian poet once wrote, "Don't seek logic from a blind follower, for he's just a void, only a name, a plain shirt, a turban, and nothing more."

Let us be with the world, so that the world shall be with us.

We can't expect all religious leaders, past or present, to have reasoned or acted according to the same criteria – so why should they expect our children today to do the same?

We live in an increasingly interconnected planet.

Observing the religion we received from our ancestors is an art that requires us to think correctly and with a free mind. **We must commit ourselves to those practical traditions essential to our unity, such as the principle commandments, rather than parsing the words of irresponsible religious figures.**

This writer believes that God sent two types of prophets to guide humankind; first, the prophets of "human intellect," and second, the "tangible prophets," as we know them. Human intellect makes the rational commands of the religion both possible and acceptable through our moral understanding and conscience. Otherwise, the dead cannot be expected to help us live! Centuries ago, the Chinese realized this simple fact, as they turned toward promoting such philosophical books as the writings of Confucius (551-479 B.C.E.), without calling it "religion."

Many of the Chinese population realized the vacuous content of religious books and their lack of logic and reasoning. They also noticed the cruelty done in the name of religion. They left the religious books and their preachers behind turning instead to ethics and books of philosophy. Among these, the enlightened notions of Confucius became the heart of their culture. As such, they found, as a nation, a new center of spiritual and moral gravity, which helped them become unified, while others were left behind.

In our country of birth, the victorious but primitive Arabs considered themselves to be superior to the civilized but defeated Persians, based on their religion! They called the Persians *mavâli*, that is, "emancipated slaves." To humiliate them, the Arabs said that "three things would void a prayer – dogs, donkeys, and Persians!" Needless to say, those claims proved outrageously false. The moral value of human-beings is not dependent on any given religion. It is a healthy intellect, knowledge and wisdom that are the ultimate cure for imposed religious prejudices.

Those who talk nonsense reap their rewards at the cost of our suffering. But we know that at the end of the day, piles of leaves are doomed to an early fall, withering into dust, while fruit will fall ripe, growing into a fresh new tree. Humanity and human intellect will survive beyond the regressions of traditionalism. If anything, without human intellect, there would be no way to understand and appreciate morality and religion in the first place!

In my opinion, constructive criticism of these self-appointed claimants of religion, or even the religion itself, is not wrong, but rather very useful; that is, as long as the critic remains loyal to the enlightened commandments of the *Torah*, and as long as his criticism remains devoid of lies and insults.

Convinced that the narrow confinement of religious prejudice is a major impediment to progress, harmony and peace for families and society, I stepped forward to do some research and to share my findings and ideas in this regard. I further believe that,

The tiniest point, which could help us toward rational and independent thinking, is preferred over the grandest idea, which would entrap us in slavish imitation and continued captivity.

This book is neither a novel, nor a memoir, a guide, nor a book of advice. It's rather like an American quilt, using *all* of these colors and shadings, hoping that perhaps the reader might find the answers for herself, according to her own beliefs.

I have been talking about the past but thinking about the future. In an attempt to communicate my thoughts I've often seemed to wander in my thinking, brought in expert witnesses, or drawn upon memories. My words seem to be in a constant motion: They can't rest, as they keep reiterating certain themes in a variety of formulations, styles or ideas, hoping that perhaps this might help convey the concerns of this writer to his readers.

For years, as a friend once put it, I was of the idea that some things would better be left unsaid, since after all, we all belonged to the greater Jewish society, and I feared that the shame of criticism would eventually be thrown back at us, just like a *boomerang*. Besides, I used to think that there was no point is discussing such basic issues, as I assumed no one would take seriously those parts of the religion that are nonsense. But sadly, as time has passed, I've been witness to many of our youngsters and families who have fallen under the sway of the preachers of nonsense.

Again, this writer is well aware that he is only one person, but he hopes to address the concerns of a variety of people who might hold different ideologies or convictions. I am trying to approach the subject of regressive traditionalism from different angles and points of view.

For me, it's a rather painful experience. If my memory serves me well, a scholar named Benecke once said that, "One better not talk, than talk about nothing!" In truth, I suffer more than anyone I know from discussions about nonsense and vacuous ideas. But as Muhammad Iqbal (Lahore) wrote, "I am, as long as I go; Once I stop, I'd be no more." I am, as long as I write; once I stop writing, it would be as if I were no more. Meanwhile, I'm fully aware that once an author has written, he's opened himself up to criticism. This is a doubly difficult task for me. Once you put anything on paper, you've created a document, which could be used against you. As such, it seems that a burn of the skin would be better than a slip of the tongue, or a trip of the pen!

An author uses words to leave behind a self-portrait and his true self is reflected among the lines of the text. I couldn't have freed myself from my inner calling, which stemmed from the depths of my being, except through writing. Perhaps it was a sense of responsibility, which gave me the courage to write or, as someone said, "to be prepared to take the bricks that are thrown at me, using them to make a stronger building!" I tell you, my friends, life is not about just playing a good hand, but playing the best game you can even though you've been dealt a bad hand. So far, I've been trying to do my best "with a bad hand," that is with an unpleasant subject that I feel a responsibility to address!

Let's hope that none of us will remain indifferent because "a heart devoid of caring flames is nothing more than some dust, water and the wind."

There's nothing more shameful for our community than allowing outsiders to believe that Judaism represents the ideas and values of a narrow group of fanatics – and then read our religion criticized as such! We have a duty to speak out and write against such fanatical nonsense; otherwise, the scar of their objectionable words will stick to our foreheads and remain for future generations.

One of the fundamental problems in addressing this issue, is that so many of the commentators' pronouncements are attributed to the holy *Torah* itself – when in fact they are just commentary. If only we can turn to the original text ourselves rather than being misled by these ignorant misinterpretations. **The scent of no extract is as good as the smell of the flower itself.**

Today, after centuries of Diaspora existence, the Jewish people worldwide have finally put the chaos of wandering years behind. If we intend to survive, we'd be well advised to adapt this colorful assortment of different cultures and traditions to the necessities of modern civilization.

At this point, I wish to share a fable with you:

Once upon a time, there was a beautiful island, where all human emotions, such as Joy, Sorrow, Pride, Love, and so on, lived with the other residents in peace. One day, they heard news that the island was going to sink into the ocean soon. So the inhabitants of the island prepared their boats to set out for sea to save their lives – all of them, except Love, because Love just loved the island.

Before long the day arrived when the water began to rise. Suddenly, Love realized the seriousness of the threat. She looked around and saw Wealth leaving on a most luxurious boat. Love asked if Wealth would take her along but Wealth said, "No, you can't come with me. My boat is filled with gold and other jewelry. There is simply no room for you." Then, Love asked Pride whether he would help her but Pride refused, saying, "I can't take you on my boat. Just look at yourself! You are all soaked and muddy. You'll make my boat dirty."

As the water kept rising, Love looked around and saw Sorrow a few steps away. "Would you take me on your boat?" – Love asked. "No, I'm truly sorry," said Sorrow. "I regret that I'm very sad. Unfortunately, I need to be alone for awhile."

Love began to shout at Joy, who stood farther away on the shore, but Joy, overwhelmed with happiness, couldn't hear her pleas.

The water was rising fast and Love was beginning to give up all hope when an aged voice whispered next to her, "Come on, Love. I will take you." Love was speechless! She was so happy that she even forgot to ask for the old man's name. She jumped onto the boat, and like everyone else, left the disappearing island behind to look for a new place.

Once their feet landed solidly on new soil, Love and the old man parted ways. Shortly afterwards, however, Love began to feel indebted to the old man for saving her life. She felt compelled to find him, to convey her sense of gratitude, but she knew nothing about him. Hence, Love went to see Knowledge.

"Who was that old man?" Love asked. Knowledge looked up, and replied, "That old man was Time."

"But why would Time, of all beings, have helped *me*?!" Love asked. With a kind smile, Knowledge explained, "Because only Time would be able to understand the grandeur of Love and righteous action…"

What a strange concept is Time. It solves all kinds of problems, though sometimes at the cost of human life! In practice, however, only the ever vigilant conscience of humankind can maintain a balance among nations and keep happiness, sorrow, pride and love in step with time, thus saving all of us from drowning into the oceans of doom.

We might call the interdependence of a collection of people with shared beliefs, history, book(s) and a prospective future, a "nationality." This is how I regard our Jewish people.

This book is my attempt to preserve and strengthen this aspect of the Jewish people. I only wish to be remembered as one "who tried to encourage people to understand better." Well-placed criticism can initiate evolutionary changes in morals, religion and society. I can only hope that my writings might contribute in some small way to such a change.

The *Talmud* is perhaps the only religious book in the world that actually encourages its students to doubt and to question the subject at hand. Let's not be afraid to say that angels and devils, heaven and hell are no more than metaphoric and symbolic expressions.

In the past, criticism was considered a crime. After all, it was a threat to the authorities. But today, criticism is widely accepted as a necessary means to better understanding.

Many decades ago, during a meeting of members of the Tudeh Party (the long-running Communist party of Iran) someone criticized the Party's apotheosis-like exaltation of Stalin. The leader of the session issued him a warning. But the fearless young man stood up and said, "I'm Jewish. I come from a culture that requires everyone of us, even a commoner, to point out the mistakes of our leaders, even as it might be just a little slip of the tongue or a pronunciation error, while reciting the *Torah* at the temple." He left the session and the party for good, and it was said that his departure ended up saving his life. (Today, the party has been officially disbanded.)

Several translations of our religious books are available in Persian, including a (partial) translation of the *Talmud* by Mr. Yehuda Hai, which was published in Iran. But these have proved to be largely incomprehensible, particularly as the original texts themselves are not easily understood.

Instead I read a translation of *The Essential Talmud* by Rabbi Adin Steinsaltz (b. 1937), which like the Persian translation of the *King James Bible*, was done from a gentile perspective. Admitting my own shortcomings, I realize that the *Talmud* discusses its subjects outside the boundaries of time, regardless of whether something was considered significant for its time or place and might be deemed useless or even meaningless in the future. In the *Talmud*, we observe a truth-seeker at work, one who follows the *credo* that states, "There is nothing in the world that you can't think about." It records long and detailed debates on many subjects which often include several contrasting, conflicting, or even opposing point of views.

In one sense, the *Talmud* is like the wine in one of Rumi's poems, where he explains that depending on the person, wine could bring out the best, or the worst of qualities or behavior! "The wise could become wiser, or the bad could turn into evil." Then he adds that since the majority of people were not good in essence, wine was banned for Muslims "to take the sword away from the looters."

As Rabbi Steinsaltz has explained, some of what is found in the *Talmud* is valuable, while others sections might be found inappropriate or outright useless. Nevertheless, or perhaps precisely because of this, the *Talmud* has played a fundamental role in the spiritual life of Judaism. Mr. Yousef Shaheri, the founding member of the Persian magazine, *Shofar of New York*, one of the most meritorious promoters and defenders of the Jewish culture, wrote that (*Shofar,* No. 321, p. 21) "The *Talmud* could neither be called a literary, nor a religious book. Generally, it's a collection of scholastic arguments, incongruous and unrelated [by nature of the subject and method], all of which have been reflected with utmost sincere fidelity." If a reader only _focused on the side of the argument which supported his own viewpoint – he would miss the point of the Talmud.

I ask the parents and educators of our community whether in times of scientific flourishing, such books are still worthy of our attention? You have made our children spend their school years studying them, treating them as textbooks, all for the sake of preserving our religion and identity. You teach these books beginning in the first grade, and you claim to be raising our children as religious people. In the name of identity preservation, you take our most talented and meritorious children to the *kollels*, i.e. traditional rabbinic schools, to spend their entire life studying one book, plus some centuries-old commentaries.

Each of these children could have become a great scientist; yet, you seem to prefer to keep them apart from the progressive evolution of their time. Teaching and studying the *Torah* is a regular obligation for any Jewish person, and it poses no conflict with studying modern science. So why should you deprive our children of a modern education, purporting that to do so is necessary for studying the *Torah*? My point is, let's give the students the opportunity to benefit from all available sources because doing so need not conflict with our religious books.

Plato said that "injustice" was not a mere trampling of one's rights; but that withholding equal opportunities from people also constitutes another form of injustice. Accordingly, let's give our children their equal opportunity to choose and to flourish.

I once read in a Persian scientific magazine about the strange custom of an African tribe who during the times of drought would have their wizard brutally sacrifice the wisest man among them, believing that his soul would take their message asking for rain to God, and thus, they'd all be saved! That, too, was a religion and there's no reason to think that they didn't believe in this horrible nonsense. This should put some of our own nonsense in perspective.

Certainly, one who has acquired modern knowledge can still understand the religious commandments! I have no doubt in the sincerity of my religious readers who mean well. But just look at what is happening to our community in terms of higher education. In the past, when the brightest students were taken to the *kollels,* perhaps no more than 2000 members of the whole community could read and write. The kollels were the highest form of learning available to them. Today, it's no exaggeration to claim that more than 80% of our youngsters have received an advanced academic degree. Is it still necessary to take our youngsters into the captivity of the *kollels*, making them repeat some useless words? Why should these beautiful souls, our children, be so limited?

How can every action that was appropriate for a bygone age still be right for our time? Why would we lock our poor students in a cage for religion's sake, one that deprives them of the modern sciences? Why confine them to the *kollels*, so that supposedly, they will discover some secrets and support the religion? The answer, my dear reader, is, No. We should not -- and need not -- do this to our children for the sake of religion.

We should teach all children as much as we can, and as well as possible. If anything, science facilitates a better understanding of religion, enabling more people to practice the best of it with more conviction, thus helping its preservation. We need to learn from the bitter experiences of our past and use our spiritual and monetary resources, as well as those of our community, for modern education.

I ask the religious educators to teach the commandments of the *Torah* in the language of modern science, so that your students can arrive at a deeper understanding of the commands and benefit from them.

It's good news that today people are paying more attention than ever to the meaning of the ancient religious texts. Sadly, however, there is still a less knowledgeable group, who read aloud the religious writings, day after day, without appreciating the meaning of what they articulate. Even if their actions run contrary to what they've been reading, they won't hesitate to call themselves religious!

There are many others who are convinced of the necessity of religious schools; but unlike me, they have not been alarmed by the regressive culture that is taught to our children in these schools. I believe it was Alexander Pushkin (1799-1837) who said, "Everyone is responsible for everything." Each one of us is responsible for the injustice that goes on in our community, in our society, all over the world. In this way, just as you are responsible for what you teach – so are we! Your lessons are often saturated with narrow-mindedness, inflexibility of thought, and brainwashing. Such dogmatic words and writings have led to one fanatic group flattering our enemies in the name of religion.

In one extreme case, these teachings produced a zealot such as Yigal Amir (b. 1970), who assassinated Yitzhak Rabin (1922-1995), the prime minister of Israel and a Nobel laureate, during a peace rally in Israel.

You bear a responsibility; and by extension, all of us do. Let's remind ourselves, *kol yisrael arevim zeh la-zeh*. This inter-dependence of the Jewish people is not only meant for times of joy; it also holds true for our good as well as our wrong acts. Like it or not, the world admires us as one people for our achievements; and blames us as one, for our blunders.

We should spare our youngsters from destructive indoctrination. A brainwashed person turns into a robot, easily manipulated into committing despicable acts in the name of religion. He may even seek to further his cause by asking for help from our enemies! The indoctrination that is widely practiced in religious schools all around the world disrupts the much needed balance in individuals. These schools tend to cultivate divisiveness and sectarianism in their followers, instead of kindness, love and harmony.

It's fitting for us to recall a story from the *Talmud*, the book which is largely relied upon by the self-appointed claimants of our religion, particularly those who choose to flatter our enemies! The *Talmud* says that "Once, a fox advised a flock of fish, trying to escape a fishing net, to leave the waters for a life on the riverbanks. As scared as they were, the fish told the fox, 'Contrary to the common belief, you seem to be the most stupid creature on the earth! When we live in such fear within our natural habitat, how greater our fear will be, if we were to face our sure death on the dry land!'"

Likewise, those sects that statistics show to be unemployed liabilities for society and the governments that shelter them should be reminded that even as they live in their own country they are faced with the constant threat of violent attacks from our joint enemies. Yet they go to that very enemy expressing their desire for the disintegration of the state of Israel! I ask them, what would happen, if your false dream were to come true, and you lost the umbrella of protection, which you've long taken for granted?! Please, either change your clothes, or match your deeds to the demands of your respected uniforms. Even a naïve person would realize that *one's humanity is not summed up by his beautiful clothes...*

If I rise, if you rise, everyone will rise;
If I sit, if you sit, who's going to rise?"
(Hamid Mossadeq, Persian Poet)

Who will fight ignorance? Prejudice begets discrimination, and discrimination begets hatred. No wonder, it's said that "the devil" enjoys the death of a single scientist more than the passing of seventy pious ascetics. No surprise as a rational person favors science at least seventy times more than parroting prayers!

Judaism attests to the precedence of mind over tradition, as the *Mishnah*, a collection of "the oral customs accompanying the *Torah*", states, "*derekh eretz kadmah le-torah*"; that is, "the way of the land precedes the *Torah*." "The way of the land" is taken to mean "earning a living," or more commonly as "ethical, courteous behavior," and speaks to individual considerations of time and place.

The author of "A study of the Talmud" *(The Essential Talmud)* points to an interesting aspect of the book which opens a window into the historical views of its scholars, past and present. In the *Talmud*, for many generations, the opinions of the students could not best those of their teachers. Later on, the sages, who supposedly had good reason to challenge their opponents in the debates of bygone times, prevailed. I find this strange: **Don't the natural laws of progress and evolution suggest that, in the long run, students of later generations would have better information and be able to best their masters from past generations? Isn't valuing the sages of the past tantamount to prescribing a perpetual stasis, if not an all out regression?!**

Regressive traditionalism is by definition afraid of any change or progress. It rises up against science and avoids any effort in adapting to the demands of the present. Meanwhile, it continues to regard religious observance as best practiced in parrot-like imitation.

According to the *Talmud*, the principle of *lifnim mishurat hadin*, that is, "going beyond the letter of the law" is not to be forced on everyone; rather, it's a compelling innate law, for those who aspire to higher spiritual achievements. However, "going beyond the letter of the law" can be taken to mean either "demanding to do extra work"; or instead it could be interpreted as "avoiding a literal reading of the law." Either interpretation endorses a flexible mind, along with promoting independent judgment rather than a rigid adherence to a one-sided interpretation of the law.

It's safe to claim that today's division of our Jewish society into factions such as the Orthodox, ultra-Orthodox, Reform, Conservative, each with its own numerous shadings, stems in part from individualized interpretations or even misreading of the texts of the important books of Judaism. Such sectarian divisions will continue until the adherents of each group stop trying to read these books only in the way that furthers their sect or their best interests. As long as religious educators do not make a serious attempt to convey the big picture of these books, the situation will not improve.

Steinsaltz suggests that perhaps the contents of the *Talmud* were left unfinished; and that to some extent, all of the subjects under discussion have ended in *veduk,* i.e. "pay attention", and *dilma epicha*, "perhaps the other party is right." To me, that signifies the importance of understanding the *Talmud* as an encouragement to think and debate, instead of an affirmation of the truth of every statement contained therein!

Yet, some fanatics consider even reliable quotations by the likes of me as heresy, ignoring the fact that the *Talmud* itself says, "Discussion about the religion is good and it strengthens belief."

I am convinced that what should be emphasized about the *Talmud* is its overall message, which is an invitation to doubt, to think, to heed the opposite point of view, and to consider a given subject from many different perspectives. By all accounts, the *Talmud* was not the end of Judaism, but only a stage in its long and dynamic evolution. A healthy approach to *Talmudic* statements requires interpretation based on our present understanding rather than a blind acceptance of each literal pronouncement. For the Talmud to be timeless, we can't let it become a prisoner of its literal words or the interpretations of our wise ancestors. Let us be inspired by their example, and let us improve on their efforts.

To illustrate this point, I urge those teaching in our religious schools to put their prejudice aside and to consider whether the laws

122

offered in the *Talmud* regarding, say, theft, pillage or piracy; cows, water wells and grazing; fire, stones; properties, taxation or confiscation; matters of hygiene, cleaning, and purity; etc., all clearly devised for their times, are still valid and still worth teaching? If one accepts them literally then the answer is clearly, "No." So please stop wasting your students' time and talents.

Consider the following: According to Rabbi Steinsaltz, the *Talmud* has dedicated a full page to the subject of a mouse which has carried bread crumbs into a Jewish home *after* the house had been fully cleared of *chametz*! (*chametz* or *hametz* is a kind of food, such as common wheat bread, the production of which requires fermentation of certain cereals. According to the *Torah*, no *chametz* should be eaten during the days of Passover.) The records of the debate show that the sages began to discuss in detail the number of bread crumbs inside the room, before and after the entrance of the mouse; whether a rat would enter the room after the mouse; and other possible factors. This long and detailed research on the rodents, covering almost a full page of the *Talmud*, contains some interesting ideas and first-hand observations, all of which have been offered to answer the question of the mouse and bread crumbs!

I question whether our students' time is best served studying such writings. No wonder that so many people have become lost and perplexed about their religion, abandoning the religious practice, altogether.

Dear educators, you are responsible for these defections from our faith because people regard you as the defenders of such nonsense, rather than as the protectors of the pillars of our religion, such as the *Ten Commandments*, principles which inspire pride in the religious and secular alike. Based on what you are teaching, you can be certain that many of today's religious children will someday come to detest and shun our religion altogether.

We need a vision of our religious texts that offers readers reasonable and practical solutions to their lives. By the way, those times are past when the religious *mullahs* could get away with some quick fixes, dismissing criticisms by resorting to some allegorical after-thoughts, claiming for instance that this story of the mouse was about someone who talked ill of others, and the bread crumbs stood for gossip! Today's audiences are way more intelligent than you seem willing to admit.

The *Talmud* proclaims that, "Every new discovery or invention is already contained within what Moses said at Sinai." Some have suggested that this statement is not meant to discourage the coming generations of intelligent men and women but rather to emphasize the depth of the *Torah*.

The religious instructors have used this claim to keep our youngsters in the *yeshivot* and *kollels*, i.e. the elementary to graduate Jewish seminaries, for years or even lifetimes. But unless they give them two lifetimes, one to study Torah, and the other to learn about modern science and apply current knowledge, how can they succeed? Perhaps they expect their students to live for 950 years, as it was said of Noah, or to own a big *harem* with hundreds of women, as King Solomon reportedly did.

The survival of any culture depends on understanding the demands of its time – and I can't possibly stress this too often. A harm coming from a friend is more painful than a strike coming from an enemy. As a Persian poet wrote,

"Sugar, this nourishment of the soul,
Could bring harm at the time of a fever.
The candle might light the room,

But thrown at the clothes,
It does the job for the enemy."

Remembering Nietzsche's dictum, "Let's stay awake to sleep well," in 1993, Professor Samuel Huntington (1927-2008) famously warned that in the coming years, wars would be no longer about territory but instead would be caused by a clash of cultures and civilizations.

We, the Jewish people, are heirs to one of the most ancient cultures of the world. We need to teach our children that as time progresses no culture can remain static, preaching imitation.

When the late Yitzhak Rabin was assassinated in 1995, a piece of paper was recovered from his side-pocket, stained with his blood. The paper contained lyrics to the Hebrew song *Shir ha Shalom*, "The Song of Peace." One of the lines read, "Don't say the day will come; *bring* the day." Or as he might have said himself, "Don't say peace will come; *bring* it about." The backwards attitudes in our community won't disappear by themselves; instead, we should actively try to correct the situation by encouraging rationality.

In our religious books, the devil or *Satan* has been introduced as "the guide toward the wrong path," and not an "anti-angel," as other faiths claim. Let's be better guides for our children and not mislead them onto a path that will only waste their lives. We also need to make the educators in our community aware of their mistakes. We can't spend all our time righting every wrong, but unless we take this challenge upon ourselves nothing will change, and what is bad will only get worse and spread even further.

Equality means receiving what you deserve, not just receiving the same as everyone else, regardless of merit.

Undeserved freedom could lead to a state of anarchy in the democratic societies of the world. Being equal should mean being treated without arbitrary discrimination. It doesn't mean that a healthy and unhealthy mind are the same, or that an erudite woman and an ignorant man should be deemed equal in all respects. To let the regressive traditionalists do as they wish will only lead to the detriment of future generations.

Allowing these dangerous educators complete freedom with our children is akin to entrusting a sword to a dangerous drunkard.

The more prejudiced we are, the more we base our thinking on stereotypes, the more difficult it becomes for us to comprehend other nations.

Prejudice is an innate human quality, and it can potentially grow inside anyone, including this writer. If we wish to live in a society devoid of religious and sectarian hatred, it's paramount to alert our children to the past bitter experiences of religious prejudice, both within and without our own religion.

Let us examine a part of our ancient history, contained in a rare thousand-year old historical document, to realize what our people suffered at the hands of prejudice.

Mr. Nasser Engheta, a contemporary Iranian journalist, writes that the oldest existing dated document in the Persian language is a Judeo-Persian manuscript recording the purchase of a house in the city of in the city of Ahvaz (Huramshir), in the south of Iran in 1030 C.E.. Today, this precious piece of history is preserved in the archives of the Bodleian Library of Oxford, England,

Indeed, our history in Iran goes back to much earlier times, to the age of Cyrus the Great (died 530 B.C.E.), the king of Persia, who in the 6th century B.C.E., freed the Jews from the captivity of Babylonia. For 2700 years we lived as compatriots in Iran, without being able to hold government positions.

126

By contrast, in today's America, once we become citizens we have the same rights as any other immigrant Americans citizens. Our children, if born here, even have the right to hold the highest offices in the nation, including the presidency. It's this mix of cultures living in a free environment that has irrigated the miraculous tree of freedom in this country, making it possible to produce the best of everything.

It's a marvel to behold, how a country such as the United States, stretches from coast to coast, with so many people of different backgrounds, ethnicities, who speak so many languages, can come together and recognize, for the most part, English as their official language. The language itself becomes a means to bind the people while the diversity of cultures continues to nourish the civilization.

Ignorance and prejudice are a recurring theme in the history of mankind, sometimes to tragicomic effect. It's said that Louis XIV (1638-1715), King of France, brought his treasury close to bankruptcy and drove the people of his country into poverty as a result of years of war with his neighboring countries, as well as extravagant night-long parties in the Palace of Versailles, and other excessive expenses of his court.

Things were so bad that one day, his Treasury minister announced that there was no money left, even for daily expenses! The Sun King summoned his court, ordering them to find an urgent solution. A couple of days later, they advised him to sell his pure-bred Royal horses. The sale proceeded as advised. However, a young 26-year old Voltaire (1694-1778), with his typical passion, wrote the King advising him that rather than sell his horses, he should rid himself of his donkeys, i.e. the members of the court, who wasted the nation's funds.

Our own Persian courts didn't fare much better in comparison. As an example of the prejudiced mentality of the past few centuries in Iran, consider the following abridged anecdote, taken from the memories of Senator Hussein Deha, a member of the Iranian Parliament at the time of the Pahlavi Dynasty:

"A superstitious, hardly literate *akhond* fell badly ill. His acquaintances tried to convince him to choose a modern educated doctor over the exorcists, psychics or talisman-writers. Given the gravity of his situation, he reluctantly accepted. To buy his prescription, he visited a pharmacy run by an Armenian Iranian. Back then, pharmacists had to prepare or even make, measure and wrap the medicine themselves, right in the store, because today's ubiquitous pre-packaged drugs were not yet available. While in the store, the *akhond* noticed some large bottles on the shelves, which carried on their labels in Persian such names as "boric acid," "sulfuric acid," and the like. A few days later, having recuperated thanks to the medication, he gave a passionate sermon, in which he began to shout, "Oh, you, the Muslim people! We have reached to the point when right here in the capital of a Shiite country, a non-Muslim Armenian dares to insult our religion by naming his stinking drugs after our holy prophets! May God's damnation be on this treacherous man! We need to deliver his punishment today, breaking down his pharmacy, to give a good lesson to others!" A bunch of ignorant, gullible people, along with a group of stupid, Godless seminary students, clubs in hands, marched toward the store and shattered everything in pieces.

As for the cause behind that *akhond's* rage? Well, he had simply misread the labels! You see, in Iran, the Arabic-Persian word *seyyed* is generally reserved for those believed to be descendants of the Muslim prophet Muhammad. Unfortunately, the Persian word for "acid" shares a similar spelling – and…you get the picture…

Dear educators,

A prejudiced person is not more religious; he's simply more narrow-minded! The mind of the fanatic is as stiff as a stone, while the mind of a free-thinking man flows as smoothly as water.

Coming down the slope, a stone might stop at the first large obstruction; but water won't stop at anything. Water would first try to take the stone along. If not possible, it would try to find a way around it, to flow over it. If none of this works, water would patiently drill through the stone.

Therefore, water proves to be more persistent and efficient than stone in reaching its goals. Much like how rational people behave.

Although the intellectual, rational Jews were not generally considered to be "religious," they were in effect more religious than the isolated, supposedly "religious" Jews. Their rational will was stronger, too, as the will of water over stone is. Today, while the stones are still held behind the barriers, the river is flowing toward the delta, welcomed by the seas. And once there, each drop becomes indistinguishable from the ocean.

Being as fluid as water; absorbing knowledge as a sponge: these are the skills that will assist our children on the road of progress. As such, they will learn to be tolerant, to live in harmony, and to form calm and powerful oceans, composed of individual members of their society.

Stones wouldn't join hands, but resilient droplets merge together, until they have formed themselves into the sea....

David Ben Gurion (1886-1973), the first Prime Minister of Israel, and his party, stood up to the fanatics. He fought for and achieved the establishment of the independent state of Israel, fighting his opposition at home. What he did was the difference between a mechanic who changes the valve of a car's engine while it's stopped; as compared to the surgeon, who fixes a heart while it's at work! Ben Gurion didn't let superstitions slow his progress.

Let us not be afraid of blunt criticism and sincere expressions of opinions. The one who points out our individual, family or social flaws, is a true friend – not an enemy.

Rational educated members of our community ought not to remain silent. They should join in fighting the regressive traditionalists and in rejecting backward ideas, without disapproving of our religion. Otherwise, the fanatic's mediaeval ideas will swallow and sink the whole society.

Trying to keep both sides happy, and not taking a stand, won't have much effect. They remind me of how the Justice Ministry in Iran decided on the design of its logo.

In 1925, Reza Shah Pahlavi (1878-1944) overthrew the Qajar Dynasty (1794-1925), and established the new Pahlavi Dynasty (1925-1979). One of his first major initiatives was the establishment of the Ministry of Justice in Iran.

Mr. Davar was appointed Justice Minister and tasked with creating the new Ministry of Justice, based on the model of the Belgian government. Following the initial stages of the process, Mr. Davar suggested to the Shah that he allow him to choose a logo for the newly founded ministry. The Shah decreed a public contest to be held with entries from within Iran and abroad to choose the best design.

The Shah was especially pleased with the work of a Belgian artist. He received the artist, commended him for his effort and approved of his design and then asked him, "I have mostly understood the meaning of your design: an angel, blindfolded, holding a two sided scale in hand, fully balanced. However, I am still puzzled as to why one of the strings of the scale is broken?"

The painter explained, "As we can observe, the Angel of Justice is judging both the plaintiff as well as the defendant, and she is about to issue the verdict. She does this while being blindfolded, which suggests her decision based on absolute equality, exercising full justice. The broken string of the scale, however, signifies the fact that although the scale is in balance, one of the parties of the case would inevitably end up dissatisfied with the result. That's because no just person can ever keep all parties equally happy, until they have realized their mistakes by themselves."

The late **Chacham Yedidiya Shofet** used to say that he followed the way of his ancestors but didn't imitate any one particular rabbi. Eventually, the leaders of the extremist Jewish groups left him alone because the Chacham was a beloved intellectual, and remained so to the end.

"One of the gifts of the Jewish culture to Christianity is that it has taught Christians to think like Jews, and any modern man who has not learned to think as though he were a Jew can hardly be said to have learned to think at all." – *William Rees-Mogg, former Editor-in-Chief for The Times of London and a member of the House of Lords*

If we don't halt the regressive traditionalists from interfering in other people's affairs in the name of religion, they will continue trespassing into the boundaries of our families – and yours won't be an exception.

All parents and religious leaders have a duty to make everyone understand that although we might have different ways of life, we are all equal in principle. We are all involuntary heirs to the ways and the traditions of the world's religions. However, now is the time to eliminate those parts of the religion that have been shown to be baseless superstitions.

Don't dissuade me of God's kind grace, as no one knows what is hidden behind the curtain of creation.

World peace will never be possible *without* peace between the world's religions.

Mankind doesn't hate fellow humans by nature, and we don't inherently see the differences between one and another. But that doesn't mean that over time certain philosophies, traditions or ways of dress don't become outdated. After all, in our lifetime we have seen how such superpowers as the former Soviet Union or Communist China, a.k.a. "The Yellow Dragon," despite their strength and stability, and military arsenals of nuclear weapons, still found it necessary to adapt to the modern era and shed some of their past convictions.

Throughout history, Jews have been attacked and tyrannized, repeatedly, but our Book has not been affected by such changes. The sages of old prohibited us from proselytizing for our religion. Is this why our numbers continue to shrink? Why, although we continue to observe the spiritual values of our holy book that has inspired so many other religions, are we still the subject of attack?

Compared to the history of the universe, which is thought to be 14 billion years old, "The age of religions" is an extremely short period. Still we should remain eager to choose the best among different traditions and life-styles, casting aside those words and ideas that are utterly unreasonable and that don't fit our times. Consider that even the Catholic Church has changed over the last few decades, for example by finally denouncing false, damaging, yet long-standing accusations against the Jewish people.

"If there is any honor in all the world that I should like, it would be to be an honorary Jewish citizen." – *A.L Rowse, authority on Shakespeare*

For almost two thousand years, much suffering was inflicted upon Jews, and millions of us were killed, based on the simply false claim that "Jews had killed Jesus." Never mind that this false accusation went against the sayings of the Christian books, including the *Gospels of Matthew* (chapters 26 and 27), *Luke* (22 and 24), and *Mark* (14 and 15), all of which stated that the Romans murdered Jesus – and not the Jews. It was as if some ignorant leaders had got their subjects drunk, making them believe in this false and dangerous accusation.

But eventually, the sun re-emerged from behind the dark clouds. In 1965, after centuries of prosecution, **Pope John XIII** (1881-1963) said the following prayer, which would mark one of the greatest shifts in the history of Catholic Church:

"We are conscious today that many, many centuries of blindness have cloaked our eyes, so that we can no longer see the beauty of Thy Chosen People, nor recognize in their faces the features of our privileged brethren. We realize that the mark of Cain stands upon our foreheads. Across the centuries our brother Abel has lain in the blood which we drew, or shed tears we caused by forgetting Thy Love. Forgive us for crucifying thee a second time in their flesh. For we know not what we did."

This was followed a few years later by **Pope John Paul II** (1920-2005), who left a folded piece of paper, containing the following prayer, between the stones of The Western Wall in Jerusalem, also known as The Wailing Wall:

"God of our fathers,
You chose Abraham and his descendants to bring your Name to the Nations.
We are deeply saddened by the behavior of those, who in the course of history,
have caused these children of yours to suffer, and asking your

forgiveness,
we wish to commit ourselves to genuine brotherhood with the
people of the Covenant.
Jerusalem 26, March 2000
Signed: John Paul II"

During India's tumultuous battle for independence, one of her leaders declared that, "If it were not for the powerful impact of the reports of Gandhi's fasting for days, India's *fatwa* could have resulted in the murder of 400,000 Muslims at one time." Gandhi single-handedly did for the Muslims what the Pope and other self-appointed preachers of kindness never did for the Jews during WWII, or for the Armenians just a few decades earlier. One realizes why Nietzsche thought that the world has only known one Christian – and he was the one crucified long ago.

As the utterly despicable **Adolf Hitler** (1889-1945) was ordering the mass murder of the Jewish people, one of his colleagues told him that the world would not stand for this genocide. The monster replied by asking, "What did the world do when one million and five hundred Armenian Christians were massacred? What is there for us to fear?" Religious or ideological catastrophes are commonplace throughout human history, and, in all likelihood, they will not cease unless people make an effort to stop them.

Let's not forget the tragedy in Darfur, Sudan, where the Christians are being massacred by the Muslims. Until individual security for all people, regardless of our differences has been established, collective security for our global society cannot be achieved.

Religious bigotry has never been able to make us into better humans.

Tyranny goes on every day, in some corner of the world, by one religious group against another. The good news is that in the

end, truth has always prevailed and the perpetrators have been left to their own shame.

The story is told of a Christian priest who walked a Jewish person through a beautiful garden explaining that, "this is the garden of different Faiths. The beautiful roses represent Catholicism. The pretty lilies represent Protestantism. The iris flowers represent Buddhism," and so forth. The Jewish man asked, "What about the cactus?" The priest answered, "We believe that the cactus is the symbol of truth." The man thought for a moment, and then said, "You're right, and I think the reason is rather self-evident. Cactus is known for its endurance in heat and cold. People can stomp over the rest of the plants and ruin them all, but one can't just step over a cactus to destroy it. Perhaps that's why those who have been born in the Israel are called *zabraim*, which in Hebrew means 'cactus'."

"Some people like the Jews, and some do not. But no thoughtful man can deny the fact that they are, beyond any question, the most formidable and the most remarkable race which has appeared in the world." – *Winston Churchill*

Facts and truths will eventually be revealed, as they did to the kind Pope John XIII, and in the end, the obstructers of truth will find themselves the losers. We humans are no more than a passing audience, the involuntary guests of the phenomenon of life.

There is also the story of the rooster who caught a bad cold. Upset, he turned to the chicken, and said, "I am sad, not because I can't crow anymore, but because I'm afraid that without me singing, the sun won't be able to rise again!" The boastful claims of the religious extremists regarding the laws of nature and the survival of the species are no less funny than the claims of this rooster!

It is narrow-minded to hate someone and make them our enemy just because he or she doesn't agree with us. Faith is a gift granted by God to the faithful. However, once a belief is exploited as a means to other ends, as has been done by religious sects the world over, it can be used to have a person commit dangerous deeds. As such, faith without ethics and morality is no better than a lie.

Many ignorant people think of themselves as "believers." But what, we ask, exactly do they believe in?! Faith could be the crowning achievement of human intellect but when it's mixed with hatred, it's nothing more than a shortcut to superstition. That's one reason why intellect can't be measured based on the religion or ideological sect to which a person belongs. Both the wise and the ignorant may belong to the same faith.

The regressive traditionalists continue to call themselves "religious," as if this validates their beliefs. However, their actions stand apart from the religion they lay claim to. Our religion, Judaism, has certainly never asked us to sacrifice our young people and make them choose between dark-mindedness and rationalism. Our religion doesn't ask us to brainwash our youngsters to believe that defending their country is a sin, or to view the world through the lenses of prejudice and discrimination.

Don't we all believe that not even our prophets were devoid of faults? Are we indeed required to go on repeating the mistakes of past generations? To remind youngsters of our past mistakes in the name of "experience" doesn't clear our guilt. Our negligence in telling the truth is especially unforgivable at a time when bigotry and hatred are being cultivated in the seminaries of the religious extremists of all faiths, all over the world.

We can't stop the seeds of hatred by bullets or cannons, nor by imposing political and economic sanctions. Ultimately, we need to root out the prejudice and bigotry that exists in the classrooms of extremist religious schools.

International human rights organizations need to examine the textbooks of religious schools and their teachers before hatred spreads any further. Although the world's religious extremists are products of such schools, governments and individuals continue to support these centers of hatred, directly or indirectly, whether by financing them or by remaining oblivious to the serious dangers that they pose. Ironically, they do not realize that they are "enablers" allowing today's misguided children and students to turn into tomorrow's parents, teachers, and preachers of hate and extremism – and even in some unfortunate cases, terrorists.

I am reminded of a poem that asked, *What's this zealous madness in the name of religion, which has spread its evil all over the world? There's no more compassion between brother to brother, or between the father and the son.*

It's not enough to do good; we need to fight the wrong-doers. Humanity can't expect to sail through the storms of life by relying on religion. It has never happened, and it will never happen. Let us forbid senseless ideas to be taught by bigots in the name of religious observance. Instead let's foster a hate-free, loving environment. If anything, religion was introduced to the world to increase kindness; religion was meant to abolish superstition – not promote it!

"As long as the world lasts, all who want to make progress in righteousness will come to Israel for inspiration as to the people who had the sense for righteousness most glowing and strongest." – *Matthew Arnold, British poet and critic*

A student needs to be nourished with progressive thought, not rigid dogma. Knowing the difference between the two is the responsibility of parents and teachers, and not those with a stake in exploiting religion to their own advantage.

Health is not contagious, but sickness is! What better place for one who wishes to corrupt minds with backwards thinking than our schools? What better victims than our youth?

Whose development is more important to our future than that of our children? Over time, more often than not, rational people become more intelligent while the superstitious only grow more superstitious.

If you want examples, just study the extremists' writings and see what "nonsense" truly means! Truth requires that we neither ignore nor deny facts. I believe that truth will out even if it's forced to hide temporarily. But it's also true that some people find it easier to accept nonsense than understand reality.

Mark Twain (1935-1910) once quipped that *mankind could change the world or himself, although the latter was substantially more difficult!*

There is a Persian historical anecdote concerning the **King of Qajar, Nasser-al-Din Shah** (1848-1896) who had a soft spot for pomegranates. Once he asked his aides, "Is there anyone in this town who's never tasted pomegranates?" His minister, convinced the answer would be affirmative, searched the city until he found a poor villager who met the requirement perfectly. The poor man was brought to the king's presence and was given a bowl of pomegranate seeds. He stared at them for a moment then began to eat the delicious fruit voraciously. When asked if he knew what he had just eaten, the man said excitedly, "I don't know, but they say that the big city has very good public baths. So I imagine this to be a bath!" The minister told the king laughingly, "Your Highness! Not only has this lad never seen pomegranates, he's never taken a bath, either!"

Let's not be afraid of some preachers who appear to have never seen pomegranates! Recently, I heard of a fanatical groom who became angry with his relatives during the wedding days. Why? Because his guests had brought him baskets of flowers on the Sabbath when religious Jews believe that carrying objects is forbidden as they consider it doing work on the day of rest. Can we really call such ideas "religious"?

Anti-Semitism is not a new problem. However, it's sad to see that it continues to exist today partly because many people do not heed the experiences of the past (while many traditionalists believe that being religious requires continuing to make the mistakes of past generations!) As a Persian poet, **Adib Tousi,** once wrote, *The temple better be dismantled, once it became the cleric's shop in the name of God!* Alas, the task is not so easy. As the Persian poet **Attar** wrote about 700 years ago,

Secrets of this vast world we'll never know,
So don't blame the superficial pious man
For whatever he speaks of us,
As he, too, of our hearts does not know.

A German proverb says that, *a mirror is worth a thousand imagined pictures!* The proper, immediate understanding of a single commandment of the *Holy Torah* is more eloquent than volumes written by commentators. True vision lies in our independent insight and not in our blind obedience.

Pure and innocent faith, one that springs from human intellect and conscience, has never brought injustice or tyranny to people. The ignorant people who exploit religion for their own aims should be held responsible for those evils insomuch as their versions of religion leads to the disintegration of families

A great man once said, "Poverty leads to fear; Fear leads to obedience; Obedience brings regression and superstition; and superstition leads to the worship of another human." To this day, many communities continue to perpetuate this chain of poverty. Humanity's greatest misery is not knowing why we have failed.

Historically, one reason behind anti-Semitism was the involuntarily harsh conditions of Jewish life which kept us from joining larger society. But today, it's strange to see people voluntarily still living that way!

Choosing to look and act differently than the rest of society invites discrimination. Unfortunately, in the past, the surrounding communities were often more regressive than ours. But today we have joined the progressive global culture in which everyone can enjoy freedom of expression. As such, our continued isolation is unwise and unnecessary.

Social conditions and family circumstances have a major role in building our personalities. Today, all communities can, and do deserve to benefit from the social and economic advancements of our time.

To gain a better idea of the nature of the world's official religions, consider some of the actions of rich religious organizations, large or small, around the world. The wealth of some of these organizations exceeds those of international banks and corporations. Yet when it came to the Armenian genocide by Turkey, or the Jewish Holocaust during WWII, such organizations including the Vatican, were passive or silent.

As **Rumi** wrote, *It's a sign of ignorance to offer prayers based on imitation; Kudos to the man who walks the path of God with knowledge.* Another Persian poet, **Saadi** wrote, *The true obedience of God doesn't depend on one's religious artifacts or dress, but on serving our fellow humans.*

140

To spend billions of dollars making sculptures and mausoleums is indeed tantamount to worshipping icons and the dead, even though most religions claim to have abandoned these practices long ago! They have no qualms about sacrificing their followers, or even the whole world, for their superstitious causes.

Let's neither imitate nor flatter these religious leaders. Otherwise, we will have to follow their advice and live with their backward mentality.

Judgments are based on intellect not wealth. Spending money to support superstition blindly, enabling regression and supporting fanaticism, will bring about nothing but trouble to our community. Only that faith which grows from one's knowledge is a constructive faith, not one rooted in prejudice and bigotry. Let's hope that someday we won't end up regretting our way of life for having spent it in bewilderment.

People who seek the advantages that religion offers view religious observance through the filter of their special interests and fail to see the damage caused by extremists. To these blind followers one should say, "A parent's favorite child is not necessarily the one who does everything that she wishes." Thoughtless submission is the same as being fully lost!

Today it is often the very submissive and obedient children who accept every nonsense that they hear. Only now they call themselves religious. They fail to listen to the rational voices who keep telling us to examine what's being taught in our schools. It's sad that despite the eloquent and passionate voice of modern enlightened science, some can only hear the loud and ugly noise of superstition.

Johann Wolfgang von Goethe (1749-1832) once wrote, *The man bestowed with knowledge and art would have religion, too. But for the man who has none of the first two, let him have the religion!* Many unfortunate people would simply opt for other forms of extremism, if they can't choose a form of *religious* extremism. Such people were no doubt deprived of having balanced and thoughtful guides and teachers. What they call "faith" are only the seeds of extremism that have grown their roots in the very fabric of their minds!

On March 20th, 1995, the typical calm of the country of Japan was shattered when a group of fanatical terrorists, members of a sect called *Aum Shinrikyo*, brutally attacked the crowded Tokyo subway stations with sarin gas. Their sole aim was to kill as many innocent strangers as possible. They killed 12 people, injured 50 more, and caused temporary vision problems for a thousand others.

It's a sad fact that much of the world's problems are collective, rooted in factional and sectarian conflicts, yet the pain is experienced by individuals. Until the larger society comes to feel such pain on a collective level, there will be no end to human suffering. This is best summed up by Father **Martin Niemöller** (1892-1984), the German anti-Nazi theologian's famous poem:

When the Nazis came for the communists,
I did not speak out;
As I was not a communist.

When they locked up the social democrats,
I did not speak out;
As I was not a social democrat.

When they came for the trade unionists,
I did not speak out;
As I was not a trade unionist.

When they came for the Jews,
I did not speak out;
As I was not a Jew.

142

When they came for me,
there was no one left to speak out.

Discrimination won't disappear by itself. It might begin by harming only "the other," but it will eventually find its way to the home of the perpetrators. Niemöller himself was initially a supporter of Hitler and it was only later that he began to protest against the Nazis. The Nazis arrested him and he remained in German prisons until the end of the war.

Faith doesn't have anything to do with one's particular brand of religion or way of life. True faith is about the relationship between a human being and his God. I salute those societies in which people's faith is based on intellect and not hearsay; knowledge and not sentimentalism; reason and not blind zeal toward the writings of this or that person! Faith is related to the human soul, and the soul is related to God.

The relation between the individual and faith is like that of a flower and its good scent. If there were no flowers, there would be no scents. Likewise, if there were no intelligent human beings, there would be no rational and logical faith. And without rational faith, the true knowledge of God would not be spread.

Every day, we hear news of cruelties inflicted upon innocent people in the name of God, caused by those who were brainwashed to hold irrational and inhumane beliefs. Faith that doesn't stem from a healthy mind and conscience can only lead to hatred. Irrational faith is what causes a person to explode himself in an act of terrorism, or another to feel self-righteous in assassinating his country's prime minister. Such people suffer from the delusion that their murderous acts will ensure a place for them in heaven. Others, albeit on a much smaller scale, preach division and cause families and the larger community great pain, even as they mistake their despicable acts for good deeds.

I believe, however, that religion was introduced to fight immorality and promote ethics; and not to promote hatred or to cause war. The world's safety hangs on peace between religions. There can be no hope for peace or progress until the language of hatred and discrimination against other religions and factions is fully eliminated from the lexicon of these cultures and religions, and from our schools and families.

Human history has been tarnished by the acts of those who used such writings to exploit their followers and deceive them into acts of hatred and sectarianism, all for their leader's personal gain. This the main reason for the blood-soaked pages of the history of religions.

The language of hatred can't be eradicated so we must rely on the discerning mind of readers. We need to appeal to the exalted human nature in each of us to fight against such divisions. We must begin with families, asking them to raise their children to see the truth of God and to immunize them against the deceptions of the extremists. This may sound idealistic but sometimes an optimistic theory is better than a depressing assumption.

The language of false accusations has a long history among almost all religions and ideologies. If we eliminated the language of hatred from the vocabulary of all religions, few if any would remain.

Everyone knows about the humiliating fate that the great Italian scientist **Galileo Galilei**, (1564-1642) suffered at the hands of the Church Inquisition, for having expressed the truth about the orientation of heavenly objects. Centuries ago, some religious fanatics accused the great Persian mathematician and scientist, **Al-Farabi**, of heresy because he had placed philosophy above prophecy. They accused **Avicenna** (ca. 980-1037 C.E.), the pride of every Iranian, of *zandighi*, or "blasphemy." They ordered his books burned, and insisted that because he denied miracles, he was as big a liar as the greatness of God! They considered **Al Beruni** (973-1048 C.E.) a "heretic", despised by his religion, only because about 500 years before **Copernicus** (1476-1543 C.E.), he declared that the earth revolved around the sun. The remains of the great Persian poet, **Ferdowsi** (935-1020 C.E.) were not allowed to be buried in the Muslim cemetery, because in his masterpiece, *Shah-Nameh*, he had praised the Zoroastrians. They called the priceless writings of another early Persian scientist, **Rhazes (Ibn Zakariya Razi,** 865-925 C.E.), one whose time is now known as "the period of Rhazes," sinful and forbidden because he questioned the authenticity of miracles. They hit him on the head with his own books until he died a blind person.

These are only a fraction of the offenses committed by fanatics. Today, we see them as mistaken believers of nonsense and superstition. Sadly, however, there are many like them among us today, whose bodies exist in the 21st century, while their minds remain frozen in ancient times!

We should be vigilant about these poisoners. Let us help our children understand that without humanity, there will be no religion. To be religious means to be a better human being. We should teach them that their worst enemies are their ignorant friends, those who make them drink hemlock instead of medicine, and absorb hatred instead of kindness and unity.

George Bernard Shaw (1856-1950) once put it justly, when he said, "There is only one religion, though there are a hundred versions of it." I am again reminded of Rumi, when he wrote of those who spent much of their life thinking that they could find God in the *Kaaba*. But when they arrived there and began to fulfill the ritual duties, they heard an admonishing voice which blamed them for worshipping some clay and stone, instead of searching for the house which the truly pious always desired.

Religions should complement each other, providing peace and security for their followers instead of antagonizing each other because of delusions of self-importance. Intelligent minorities should never have to resort to fables and similes to express their ideas, as the Persian **Ubaid Zakani** (died 1370 C.E.) did in his humorous poetry of *Cat and Mouse*, or as the Indian writers of *The Panchatantra* (better known to Iranians as *The Kalila and Damna*) did in their collection of Sanskrit poetry and prose.

My dear educators, a superficial knowledge can never result in a correct perception. Righteous knowledge consists of a proper understanding of the commandments adapted to contemporary civilization.

The diverse array of civilized families in the world share a common denominator, i.e. knowledge and factual information – and not a single religion! Let's raise our children as masters of knowledge and kindness. Let's examine the backgrounds of the great scientists of the world, these prides of their religions, to find out in what kind of families and within what ideological atmospheres they grew up in.

God has endowed us with eyes, but to look with insight is up to us. Religious commandments give us a general message, but time shows us the proper way to carry out those messages.

Those invested in fanatical traditionalism have ended in spiritual or even physical bankruptcy and humiliation.

Human nature revolves around self-interest, ambition and a desire for power. Almost no individual or group is exempt from this principle, except a parent who would forego her own good for her child. Thus, parents are responsible for guiding their children and shielding them from destructive propaganda. We need to teach our children to view things objectively and realistically.

Religions have survived only because of the respectful, intelligent and reasonable attitudes among the faithful. Today's regressive traditionalists are waging an ideological war that reaches into the classrooms and touches families but also infects our cultural centers and political institutions.

Like all other fundamentalists, they intend to preserve, preach and practice what they consider the trusted traditions of their ancestors, with no alterations, through a rigid, inflexible attitude. They fear that the fragile commandments will not withstand change or that modernity may cause their followers to flee. Yet they fail to examine the statistics that show that many religious members continue to exit the cults through "spiritual migrations." Have you ever wondered, why?

Discoveries and success stories have largely been the result of understanding the mistakes of the past. Pleasure is not given by life, but it gives life to mankind. Our own behavior largely decides the way we'll be treated by others. You just see the effect and you panic. You try harder, but your passionate faith in your religion doesn't allow you to see reality, or else, you don't wish to see it. The main reason for these "migrations" are your anachronistic ideas, teachings that fail to make sense for our time. You attempt at demagoguery, appealing to people's emotions in order to make their rational minds religious, instead of trying to make religion become more rational! These self-appointed care-takers of religions have never succeeded: instead of adapting religion to science, they use nonsense and superstition to fight science.

The regressive traditionalist bases human existence on prayers and miracles rooted in the past and that only alienates him from the present. The culture of imitation is all about acting, without any deep knowledge. Throughout history, the counterfeiters of ideas have found books, myths and legends to try and slow down the progress of mankind, but they have never succeeded. Their behavior is as ridiculous as the act of the man who sat on the tip of the branch, and began to saw it at the juncture!

Many of the religious fables, intended to teach morals to their followers, are merely the products of their writers' imagination and fantasies. Those writers made up certain characters, who probably never existed. Characters with life-spans of 900 years such as Noah or Methuselah are fictional protagonists, no less than **Don Quixote, Rostam, Uncle Tom, Jean Valjean, Ulysses, Sherlock Holmes, The Count of Monte Cristo, or Frankenstein**!

Each reader can interpret these characters, either taking them at their face value, and believe them to be extraordinary miracle-makers, or they can appreciate them for their message, for the moral of their stories.

Sadly, it's often those close to us who can hurt us most. After all, some regressive traditionalists still avoid modern calculators just because they once saw the *abacus* in the hands of their fathers, and they continue to think of it as a symbol of their identity!

It's in the interest of our children that we all become harbingers of a rational approach to religion. Otherwise, we'll all be responsible for the actions of the bigoted extremists among us.

Educators, if you wish to be responsible, admit the danger in the bigotry and prejudice of what you teach. Excusing these faults by referring to some old writings or sayings is "an excuse worse than the original sin." This kind of worldview can only take your poor followers back to antiquity, but it will never lead them to modern times. As someone mischievously said, in eighteen months, you can get pregnant twice, but you can't give birth as many times!

148

Consider treating religion like a fruit where we peel off its rigid shell of antiquity while keeping its core message. Do you think that progressive laws such as the ban on capital punishment that exists in modern countries, including the State of Israel, are tantamount to rejecting the Torah? Or is it an example of laws that are in keeping with Jewish Law and extend its principles to modern times?

Isn't it wiser to swim with the flow of the river and follow our times? Or do you recommend that if the *Torah* doesn't mention or sanction something that we should remain trapped in the past? Perhaps we should also be waiting for a savior to enlighten and rescue us all!

No! Life is not a rehearsal! We are born only once. Being against innovation and believing that the commandments are unchanging is a sure sign of oblivion for the very philosophy of religion. All over the world, the more ignorant people are, the more prejudiced and fanatical they will be.

Adapting the commandments to the modern world doesn't mean rejecting them; if anything, this will ensure their survival. Imagine if we only spoke in our mother tongue and only as it was spoken centuries ago, allowing no new words, and not learning a new language when living in a new country – sounds foolish, but that is how the regressive traditionalists would have us live. The worshippers of darkness lull their followers into a state of numbness and blind compliance, and lead some zealots toward an ignorance-filled mirage.

We need to break the silence! All the misery in the world arises from ignorance and misinformation. Our most important duty is to introduce the progressive commandments of the holy *Torah*, those accepted by all monotheistic religions, to the entire world and not preach superstition and sectarianism disguised as religion.

Bringing the religious commandments in line with our times is as important as the commandments themselves. Their true value is

revealed in their contemporary relevance and that is what makes the commandments eternal.

The Ten Commandments are the most famous of the eternal laws introduced by our holy *Torah*. Today, after more than three thousand years, the commandments still hold true. They apply equally to the castle or the hut, to the rich and the poor. These eternal principles will never erode.

The same could be said of the timeless teaching of the ancient Persian religion, known as Zoroastrianism, which consists of three elements, namely "Good words, Good Deeds, and Good thoughts." Such shining treasures of human ethics will never fade away, just as the sun cannot be covered by a fist of mud. Regardless of the braying of groups who might try to diminish their value by attributing them to "just the Jews" or "the Christians" or "the Zoroastrians," these commandments and enlightened ideas will survive the test of time.

Dear religious leaders and educators,

The reason-loving Jews of the world, secular humanists, who count themselves among the faithful, are many and their number includes notable and prominent scientists, economists, physicians, bankers, scholars, researches, politicians and some of the greatest financial investors of the world. These are the very people who might have contributed scholarships to cover the living expenses and educational costs of your students. Yet you dismiss them as "non-religious"!

Their understanding and practice of religion is modern and they have adapted, changed and even excised those laws that are no longer relevant or appropriate in ways that are in harmony with our modern times and in ways that appeal to our youngsters. Their ideas are indeed closer to the mindset of our ancestors than those of the narrow-minded faithful.

Which of these two groups I ask, have been of more benefit to the world? From which group are the Jewish Nobel Laureates? We need to see with a new clarity that the label of "religious" has become arbitrary and deceptive. What happens in the depths of the water is vastly different from the surface. Much truth has been compromised in the name of religion.

As a Persian poet once wrote, *Even if we do strange things in life, even if we live up to five hundred years, at the end, we become legends only because of our wisdom.* Let's make sure that we leave behind a good legend.

It's sad that today, in many places of the world, religion is run as a profitable enterprise replete with a stock of accessories for sale, such as special food or articles of clothing, books and the like! This is a far cry from the spiritual vision of our ancestors.

Jean-Paul Sartre (1905-1980), the famed French philosopher, said that *mankind doesn't want to be condemned to freedom, but he rather wants to **enjoy** freedom.* Indeed, people want to enjoy their religious beliefs, and to be proud of their religious affiliations and their dependence on it. They certainly don't wish to be ashamed of their beliefs – and if they hear their religion preaching superstition and nonsense, they certainly don't want to be compelled to submit to such nonsense! If only the sages of old had no record of their commentaries, we wouldn't have later generations dressing them in a shroud of holiness, using nonsense verses as sources, or worse yet, teaching them at schools without even the student's parents knowing about it.

I once talked to a very knowledgeable gentleman, about such aged books of ours as the *Mishnah* and the *Gemarah*, and their collection known as the *Talmud*, as well as works by other commentators, some dating back 1500 to 2000 years ago. These books contain the practical and interpretive aspects of our commandments, including *halachah*, or the "practical laws." This gentleman told me that without these commentaries, the commandments of the *Torah* would have no meaning; and that we can't ignore the contents of these books; and, most importantly, that we have to be eclectic in our approach to them.

I expressed my agreement, and explained that was exactly what I meant. First, we have to be eclectic in our approach to these books, choosing only the best in them. Second, we need to interpret these commandments according to modern language and knowledge. Simply put, no one will ever accept all these writings, but everyone will be able to practice them in a way that is more understandable and agreeable to modern science.

In the meantime, let's remember that quotations and recounted narratives are very vulnerable to alterations, often involuntarily. I remember a TV program, many years ago, in which the presenter randomly chose six people from the audience and told them a short story about one of his trips. Next, he brought them back to the room, one by one, and asked them on camera to recount the story they had just heard. As you may have guessed, not two of these people remembered the story in the same way, and some recalled it far differently from the original story, or from how others remembered it. Their recollections were false – for no good reason, without any bad intentions.

If different people offer different versions of a single article that they read in yesterday's papers, then imagine what happens when 2000 years have passed, and the original subject occurred many centuries before the printing press existed! Shouldn't we allow for a reasonable degree of doubt when it comes to writings from ancient times? This, of course, applies as much to the writings and commentaries of all other religions, and not just the three so-called Abrahamian Religions.

152

To put it concisely, religion can be the medicine, or the poison. Today's informed youngsters should seek their validation in modern science and technology and not in some extremist or superstitious ideas. What the extremists prescribe often generates more problems and is used as a justification by prejudiced people with malicious intentions.

We cannot remain silent in the face of such an outrageous outlook or postpone our protests just because we fear the truth may hurt the believers' feelings! It's unfortunate that today many of those who bear the duty of resolving differences and bringing harmony among people, have themselves become part of the problem of sectarianism. They have become like those drivers who signal to the right, yet turn to the left! **Hafiz** once wrote,

There are no walls between the lover and the beloved;
Just move out of the way,
As the barrier is none but yourself.

Truth is always with us. Let's not deprive ourselves of experiencing it clearly.

It's our responsibility to personally take reasonable and appropriate steps to solve the problems of society. "To wish" doesn't mean that "We'd able to." To wish means to make the doing possible and to stop continuing the mistakes. Of course, making mistakes is part of what makes us human, and the bigger the mistake, the greater the dangers associated with it. Yet to repeat the same mistakes is against reason.

Some say the world has had 124,000 prophets; and yet, the world has not yet achieved peace. Simply wishing for peace and harmony is not enough. We need to be active in bringing about peace in our families, in our small communities, in our larger society, and on our planet. Make no mistake: No one will arrive from heaven to save us!

We drink and make love to our heart's content, because we know that's the fate of the world.

My friends, you may ask: why is it that in the past, non-religious people would be criticized, but today, anyone who is religious is subjected to criticism? Does it mean that we should all give up on religion? Could it be that the problem doesn't lie with religion itself, but with the superstitious and fanatical religious person?

As I have repeatedly said, our discussion is not about the religion, but about our approach to it. We should also understand that taking away from the Orthodox, so to speak, won't add to the Reform. Whatever is lost is taken away from all of us, and the true winner may turn out to be a third party with malicious intent. I am reminded of a passage from "Searching the Truth," a book by the late **Dr. Houshang Ebrami,** one of the most prominent scholars of the Iranian Jewish community. From the original Persian, I paraphrase:

"The pure waters of the original spring [of Judaism] become contaminated over time, as they flow and branch out into the river bed. We can look for the reasons behind this distortion in the attitudes and the deeds of two groups of people. The first are the rigid-minded religious, who don't even realize that they are the greatest enemies of the religion. The second group consists of those who are oblivious to the vital need of human beings for religion. The latter often write or speak amateurishly against a religious book, within the intellectual circles, a book which is sometimes utterly unfamiliar to them."

We left our homes behind, not because we wanted to join some regressive traditional sects that civilized society has already practically expelled. We sent our children to Europe and the United States, hoping that they would be part of modern civilization.

If someone decides to remodel their old family house to make it safer and better equipped for his children, he is not insulting his parents, or being ungrateful! The house is perhaps centuries old, and such renovation is a simple fact of life, dictated by time. In other words, let us focus on the core values, even as we try to bring the traditions up to date. Otherwise, if left as it is, this old house of traditions might someday collapse on our poor children.

I am holding a booklet published by a fanatical group, and I am embarrassed to even recount some of its content. It discusses whether one is allowed to pit out the seed of the cherry or olive on Sabbath, i.e. "The Day of Rest." Even more shocking, the writer claims that this is the very foundation of Judaism!

You might say, "Let them speak as they wish; who really listens or cares?" My answer is, "Your brainwashed child!" We need to teach our children to be able to say "Yes" or "No," as necessary and appropriate, and we should understand that self-righteousness or a sense of self-importance is a kind of illness. A Persian poet once wrote,

My enlightened guru gave me two advices,
As he walked on the water,
First, don't be so full of yourself,
And second, have faith in people.

Religious indoctrinators, with their selfish ways, lead their followers to abandon independent thought. The success of these so-called leaders is just the beginning of their interference in a person's family life. As a Persian saying goes, *A smirk like this is to be expected from a beard like that!*

This group brings the worst to the sacred principles of our world's religions. They call themselves "religious," and claim that "it's no one else's business that we are making a hole underneath of our bench," while their action are sinking our communal ship! Meanwhile, they are happy to find fault in others. I'd like to offer a Persian poem to these people,

Thou, the well-meaning pious man! Don't look for others' faults,
And remember that you won't bear another man's guilt.
Mind your own being, and leave me alone, good or bad,
Since at the end, a man reaps only what he sowed.

Think of the multitudes of our innocent children who are being brainwashed in religious schools, the cost covered by simple members of our community. Tomorrow, these children can only bring thousands of more problems to the world. Yet, as we can see today, at every corner in town, a shop has been opened in the name of a temple!

A seed won't ever see the sunlight, until it breaks through to the surface of the soil. Let the students grow. Let them fly away from the artificially built cage of religion. Otherwise, they will remain in the shell of their prejudice, like a chicken inside an unhatched egg, doomed to remain earth-bound forever. Our students won't be able to soar in the skies, as long as they haven't left behind the nonsense and superstition being preached to them in the name of religion.

Is it possible for such ideas to be literally advertised in the name of *the Torah* or other holy books? For every religion we should be asking: Should one obey everything that they teach? Which subjects should be followed? Which person, with what degree of knowledge and qualifications deserves to be heeded? We should all be vigilant; *otherwise, how can I wake you up, if I'm sound asleep?*

About 60 years ago, when WWII ended, the Allied forces rounded up a group of rabbis among the very few surviving Jews of the European *ghettos*. Ordinary Jews began to shed tears and cry, asking the authorities to let the rabbis go free, telling them that they had been good people, and were their confidantes through times of unimaginable hardship. It was revealed that in fact these so-called rabbis had been spying on the Jewish communities for the Nazi Germans!

Let's not be fooled by appearances. Let us heed the essence, and let us live in the present.

Someone smoking cigarettes today is much guiltier than someone who did so 30 years ago. Why? Because back then, they didn't know how dangerous smoking was or even that it was a major cause of cancer. But today, everyone knows the facts of the matter.

The more we examine the words of the regressive traditionalists, the better we can evaluate them, because people's thoughts and actions are the best proof of the value of their beliefs. A famous Persian poem states it best,

Words are the key to the treasures hidden
Inside the artisan or the sage.
Until the man has not spoken,
None could know the peddler from the jeweler.

In other words, if someone has remained silent, his vices or virtues remain unknown.

Recently, on a recent trip to New York to attend a wedding, I learned that an old friend of mine, whom I had not seen in 65 years, lived in the Great Neck area. I dialed her number. We were both so moved that we began to cry on the phone. Given my tight schedule, I asked if she could come visit me in the synagogue on the coming Sabbath. To my surprise, I was told that she and her husband had sworn off attending a synagogue ever again, and that they had advised their successful children and grandchildren to do just the same! She explained that many years ago, they had visited a synagogue on a Sabbath, where a man, who held some position in the temple, had talked to them in an insulting manner. He chastised the couple for driving to the synagogue. This was even though her husband is handicapped, and could only walk with difficulty.

Dear religious leaders, don't you agree that encouraging this couple to attend the services would be better than their shunning the religion altogether, even if it means that they need to drive a car to get there? Or do you truly believe that such nonsensical practices, as that fanatical gentleman seemed to espouse, were indeed the true intent of the Lawmaker – rules that, in effect, make it so they won't attend services?

If a writer or speaker doesn't understand what he or she says, his words or prayers won't be worth a penny. Via their actions, people can best demonstrate the merits of their ideas, or demonstrate the falsehood of their superstitions.

You and I can distinguish between the exalted beliefs and ideas of Judaism, on the one hand, and their abuse and misinterpretation, on the other. Unfortunately the abuses of our religion have been used all too often to promote ignorance and superstition. Unlike what regressive traditionalists claim, to return to religion does not mean to return to some rotten superstition or to engage in "antique-worship" of some native or foreign nonsense.

Yes, we need to return to ourselves, to our roots, as the spirituality of the commandments dictates, and as the truth requires us to do. Religion is not a bad thing in itself. But we should focus on addressing the core issues, rather than trying to fix the decorations.

The Italian philosopher and founder of modern political science, **Niccolò Machiavelli** (1469-1527), best known for his book on politics, *The Prince*, wrote that, **"Better to treat an illness in its early stages. Otherwise, as it progresses, the easier the diagnosis becomes, and the more difficult the cure."**

If we close our eyes to the actions of the fanatics among us, if we remain silent despite their deeds, our progress will be set back even further, and this kind of regression will only continue to spread all over the globe. I am concerned that the honor and glory of our most important commandments is going to be lost to the fanatics and their divisive actions.

According to the religious traditionalist's interpretation, our ancestors who did not have Orthodox wedding ceremonies, are not truly married and their offspring are illegitimate! The irony of this story is that the speaker himself belonged to the same generation of "illegitimate" sons! A Persian poet put it just right, when he wrote that *in all the temples of worship he visited, be it Kaaba, the temples of infidels, synagogues or churches, he found nothing but doubtful words and deception.*

In the old China, when they wanted to destroy a scientist, they wouldn't execute him. Instead, they would put him in jail, in the same cell as a stupid person, so that the stress and frustration of conversation with an idiot would kill him.

When a family's children are contaminated with superstition, their parents suffer, finding their company almost like that "Chinese Torture"! The daughter of a friend of mine, against her parent's wishes, married a handsome young man belonging to the infamous Jewish sect of *Neturey Karta*, about which we talked before. He is unemployed yet every year, "with God's blessings," he delivers a new child to the family! (He reminds me of a Persian poem, *The isolated young man is the lion-heart of the path of God; once he gets old, he can't rise up from his seat.*) He thanks God for everything, and since he doesn't feel any responsibility, he makes God responsible for everything. When criticized, he told them they should be thankful that their daughter had not married a member of *Kanaim*, i.e. "Extremist Zealots", who don't even move a bit on the Sabbath! What narrowness of mind! This is a tragic example of how a flawed faith obstructs humanity's path to knowledge and enlightenment. *A small stomach can be filled with a piece of bread, but a narrow mind cannot be filled with all the blessings of the world.*

As the French writer **Anatole France** (1844-1924) once wrote, **even if a thousand people believed in a nonsensical idea, that idea still remains nonsense.**

Dear educators and school officials,

A person whose thoughts are confined to the old *ghetto*-bound commentators, who doesn't want to see today's realities, doesn't deserve to teach in our schools. He or she lives under a delusion, and their ideas are better removed from our society than taught at our schools.

Today's world is no longer a place to confine our children within the narrow frame of prejudices. Doing so is akin to their committing suicide, if only spiritually and intellectually. The issue of religion has such deep roots that we need to approach it wisely, and try to understand its positive aspects.

"It was in vain that we locked them up for several hundred years behind the walls of the Ghetto. No sooner were their prison gates unbarred than they easily caught up with us, even on those paths which we opened up without their aid." – *A. A. Leroy Beaulieu, French publicist, 1842*

There is a saying that, *the optimist builds the plane; the pessimist makes the parachute!* In a similar fashion, rational-minded people build universities, while regressors build traditional seminaries, and call them "universities"! The prophets may have once made some life-enhancing pronouncements but ever since, the commentators have been arguing over how to practice them. Sometimes, this has gone too far, and in any case, there is often little agreement among them.

I ask, how can we remain silent, when those who form "family peace meetings" at their schools, become the destroyers of families, as well? How can we not speak out about such problems?

Oh, you pious man, don't try to fool me:
The Hell has no fire!
And if it has any,
It must have been taken from the earth!

There is nothing holier than a unified family.

The anti-Humanism that we see today is born of the same old anti-Semitism. This problem can only be solved when the whole world sees it as such. Until a few years ago, the Soviet Union supported terrorists all over the world. Today, Russia is asking for international help to fight terrorism! A contagious disease doesn't discriminate against someone's race, religion or ideology; it simply takes over anyone who is susceptible! The seeds of hatred and decadent gossip are being sowed in the so-called classrooms, or at kitchen tables, by fanatical teachers or parents, and sooner or later, all vulnerable parties become infected by their words.

An unbiased examination of history tells us that "the law of the jungle" consists of the attack and domination of the strong over the weak. Throughout history, the tyranny of the victor over the conquered, the majority over the minority, has been an ongoing tragedy. Whenever one group had a chance or an interest to do so, their first goal was to bring the minority to its knees. Long ago, the Ottoman Bosnians killed the Serbs. After about a century, the Serbs found the chance, and given that abhorrent heritage of hatred, they began killing the Bosnians. One of the worst things about of mankind is that hatred has often seemed hereditary, passed on from father to son, from one generation to another.

Such vicious acts are manifestations of the general turmoil among mankind. The weaker minorities are often convenient means for the dominant figures to achieve their ends.

One living example are the wealthy Chinese minority who have great economic clout in the Far East, in countries such as Indonesia, Malaysia, Thailand, Sri Lanka, and the like. Whenever there is any problem in those societies, the Chinese are singled out and persecuted, as occurred recently in Indonesia when the houses of Chinese residents were ransacked by mobs. Quite tellingly, these Chinese are referred to as "the Oriental Jews"! After all, cruelty needs its own victims. When neither consciousness, nor a proper enemy is available, the evil people create their own prey! Targeting Jews, Chinese, Black or White, are all different manifestations of the same phenomenon.

Tyranny may begin with the weak, but it never ends there. Just look around and see how, over and over, those whose history of tyrannizing their own people is so great that one could almost say they invented it, eventually become themselves became the target of cruelty. A Persian saying says wisely, *If you try to dig a well for others, you'd be the first to find yourself in it!*

Although pain is caused by those who inflict it, those who put up with it mistaking this as religious observance, are also responsible. The terrorists begin by placing bombs in their neighbors' home, not knowing that someday soon they will have explosions in their own backyards. That's because the germs that are fanaticism don't know any boundaries, and attract blind followers as much as unqualified leaders.

A religious person who is unconscientious is like a blind person with a torch, a menace who could as easily set another's house on fire as set his own ablaze. If the ideological foundations of a traditionalist are not based on ethics and morality, he or she may be indoctrinated in ways that let them justify carrying out horribly cruel acts. Someone who is merely imitating others, rather than using their own healthy mind, can be led to acts for good or evil. This is the natural outcome of those systems that close their followers' minds to reality, all in the name of religion. Such a way of life doesn't provide its followers with anything but chains of captivity.

Prejudice is the product of ignorance. Let's avoid the ignorant people and let's remember that neither religion nor science alone helped humanity leave the Stone Age behind. It was conscientious people who brought about the growth of civilization by preventing hatred to pass from one generation to another. Instead, they promoted kindness within families and at schools.

There is nothing more sacred than family for any society. Hence, there is no betrayal worse than destroying the unity and harmony of families.

We might say that the greatest problem in today's societies is the crisis of marriage and family. The holy act of marriage is of such critical importance that many other traditions are secondary to it. For my daughter, for example, nothing is given priority over her marriage. There are no rituals or books to follow or debate – and those that exist are not commandments at all! I pity the families who obstruct the future of their children by reason of some superstitious nonsense. We'd be better off to focus our attention on leading better lives. **To be useful is the highest of all religious services, and kindness is the greatest prayer.**

There is a saying, "Life is a gift from God, but what we do with it, is our gift to God." Let's prevent religious dogma from leaching into our families or we will see lives wasted and destroyed.

How others view our community is part of our self-image. It's said that when **Albert Einstein** (1879-1955) was asked his race on an American immigration form, he replied, "Human Race." Our identity as human beings, precedes that of all religions, ideologies or life-styles of the world.

The fact that religion is inherited doesn't mean that we should close our eyes to the world or raise our children as intellectually blind people.

"The Jew gave us the Outside and the Inside - our outlook and our inner life. We can hardly get up in the morning or cross the street without being Jewish. We dream Jewish dreams and hope Jewish hopes. Most of our best words, in fact - new, adventure, surprise, unique, individual, person, vocation, time, history, future, freedom, progress, spirit, faith, hope, justice - are the gifts of the Jews." – Thomas Cahill, Irish Author

No evolution can occur in a culture of indifference and self deception. When parents and educators fail to fulfill their responsibilities, regression is inevitable. We often inherit our religion from our parents but we need not adopt their practice of it. There is no covenant to practice nonsense. Sometimes, if we are negligent great changes can occur in society. A case in point is the catastrophic events that have taken place in Iran over the past three decades! For a wise poet such as **Saadi,** not even one's nationality, this most inherited of all accidental identities, is a necessary cause to stay in one's homeland. As he wrote,

An old tale is, this love of the motherland,
Yet one can't go on living there in humiliation,
Just because that's where he was born.

In all communities, there are many informed and enlightened people who are fully aware that there are some religious writings that make no sense. Yet, despite this, they choose to remain silent out of indifference or for any number of reasons or excuses. They don't tell the community of its faults, even though censure is a major problem among them. The remnants of this problem can be seen today even within our own small Iranian Jewish community. We do live in a country where freedom of speech is cherished; yet, for a variety of reasons, we are still censoring ourselves from publishing our ideas freely in a variety of available media outlets!

It's an absurd habit, because in today's world, anyone virtually anywhere around the globe could simply press a few computer buttons to download, say, this file at my dedicated site, **www.babanouri.com** , and express their reactions to my writings. Unlike many others, I have put caution aside, and as such, I am asking my readers and other interested people to simply put the word out in such a way that people in all walks of life, including those who might not agree with my opinion, can read these pages and express their ideas about it.

Is there any writing that is fully devoid of conflict and contradictions? Ultimately, the content of any book depends on the interpretation of the reader, what he's looking for, his degree of perception, and the lens he views it. May the day never come, when it's all too late, when people have ignored reality for so long that the snows have already turned into flooding rivers, washing away all of humanity, religious or not, to their doom. Wasn't our experience in Iran enough to wake us up to the consequences of what can occur when parents and educators fail to fulfill their responsibilities?

To prevent regressive ideas from being presented as holy beliefs, we need courage supported by wisdom and knowledge. We need to devise solutions to bring about positive change. We can't fight darkness with darkness. To defeat darkness, one needs light -- human enlightenment. This is exactly what the extremists are afraid of.

The secret to the loving popularity of the free-thinkers, such as the late **Chacham Yedidiya Shofet**, the famed religious leader of the Iranian Jews, stemmed from their knowledge and open-mindedness, which should stand as an example to everyone. The power of a person's intellect and perception is incomparably more preferable than the power that comes with wealth or position. Perceptive people, such as Chacham Yedidiya, have always been able to read between the lines, and avoided interfering in the private lives of families, Instead, they obey those commandments that conform to our modern way of life. They know that blind obedience can only lead to the dungeons of captive minds.

Chacham Yedidya was so modest that he always signed his name with the prefix "Public Servant." By contrast, look at those, who in the name of religion, will stand in a long line to kiss the hand of a so-called religious leader.

Sadly, despite the bans on physical slavery, mental and intellectual servitude still continues. Chacham Yedidiya despised idolization of anyone or anything. The greatness of this man was appreciated by our people, all the more so when they compared him to those other preachers of deception, seeing the difference between the pure gold and contaminated metal. Indeed, the more informed and intelligent our teachers, religious leaders, and parents are, the more beloved of the Chacham Yedidiya they would be. My praise goes to those rational-minded and free-thinking people, for whom religion is nothing but kindness!

There is a story told about a defense lawyer who was busy studying a case. His little son asked him, "What are you reading, dad?" He replied, "The law." The child continued, "What is the law?" The lawyer pointed to the lines of the text and said, "These black lines are the law." The child asked again, "Then what are the white lines between the black lines?" The father smiled, "Those are the ways to evade the law!"

The self-appointed care-takers of our religion and its educators should abandon preaching regressive thoughts to make a living. Too often they have misinterpreted our precious religious writings, claiming some incomprehensible commentaries as holy, while at the same time making them the preferred source material for some hypocrites who pretend to be kind in order to receive kindness!

Educators in all societies have the right to preach as they wish. They should be reminded, however, that a "right" that shakes the foundations of families and disturbs the pillars of societies, one that leads to conflicts and divisions, would better be waived. Such thing is not a right but an act of cruelty! And I hold you educators responsible for it.

Christianity became a universal religion, not because of its type of religion, but because it kept up with the pace of modernity.

"The Jew is that sacred being who has brought down from heaven the everlasting fire, and has illumined with it the entire world. He is the religious source, spring, and fountain out of which all the rest of the peoples have drawn their beliefs and their religions."
–Leo Tolstoy

Judaism first offered the philosophy of monotheism to the world but not only did the infidel societies of the time remain ungrateful, but those religions which followed have only made the Jewish people suffer for their contribution. In the words of a Persian poet,

I saw a peacock pulling out his feathers.
I warned, 'Don't, please, because your plumage is so pretty!'
He cried and said, 'Oh, you the wise,
You don't know that this colorful plumage is my archenemy!

America is only 200 years old, while Egypt boasts a 6000 year history. Let's compare the two: the first sent man to the moon, while the second continues to span a desolate desert! One is basking in wealth, but the other is desperate for help. Even today, in the 21st century, about 67% of the population of Egypt remains illiterate. To situation is no better in other repressive regimes. Consider that in the United States, for every 100,000 births, 12 mothers die while under the extremist religious regime of the Taliban, that number is 6500 mothers for every 100,000 births! Should we cite more statistics about less than progressive countries, such as Bangladesh, Cambodia, Egypt, Sudan, or Ethiopia?

Human beings are not born with prejudice. But as they grow, they do develop all types of bias. Religious prejudice, which can arise even between members of the same religion, is one of the worst types of prejudice.

In his book, *The World of Tomorrow or the Spirit of History,* the late **Dr. Ezatollah Homayoon-far** wrote of the great Persian calligrapher, **Mir-Emad** (1554-1615 C.E.), who lived during the reign of the **Safavid King Abbas** (1571-1629). About Mir-Emad we learn that, "His penmanship was just a miracle, so beautiful it was. No one had ever seen anything like it." Mir-Emad belonged to the religious Islamic denomination known as the Sunni Tradition, while King Abbas was a Shiite Muslim. The cruel King Abbas ordered the murder of Mir-Emad at his own home. Yet the Sunni and Shiite traditions are merely two different schools of the same religion, known to its followers as the holy Islam.

Just imagine how far bigotry can take a man. The would-be assassin went to Mir-Emad's home on the pretense of having lunch with him. He ate the meal brought before him by his host, then murdered him on the spot. Blood gushed out, and the table-cloth turned red with blood. The assassin fully separated the calligrapher's head and took it to King Abbas, to quench the thirst of king's prejudice! In the meantime, the King of India had already sent a message to Iran, asking King Abbas to forgive Mir-Emad and allow him to leave for India. In return for Mir-Emad's freedom, the King of India had offered as much gold and jewelry as the weight of the artist. Alas, the message arrived too late….

On another occasion, this very "religious" King Abbas, notorious for his zeal in promoting his beliefs, became suspicious of one of his sons, **Safi Mirza** (1587-1615), thinking that his son was conspiring to unseat him. In a sudden rage of jealousy, King Abbas ordered the hangman to cut off his son's head! But as soon as his anger subsided, he realized what a terrible thing he had done. Too arrogant to take the blame, he transferred his anger to the hangman, now ordering the man to murder his own son. The hangman, wishing to become closer to "His Highness the King", did just that – and in return, he received the King's approval.

Another contemporary writer, **Dr. Masoud Asgari Sarvestani** writes that King Abbas, who carried the title *Kabir*, i.e. "Great", further blinded **Imam Gholi Mirza** and **Muhammad Mirza**, his two other sons, just to have them forget about the throne. Such unimaginable cruelty could only stem from a faith devoid of conscience.

Two other historical books in Persian, *The Social History of Kashan* and *The History of Iranian Jews*, by the late **Dr. Habibollah Levi**, recount yet another tragic atrocity that took place during the reign of King Abbas. This time, the infamous king ordered **Muhammad Beyk Etemad-al-Saltaneh**, his representative to the Iranian city of Kashan, to force the Jews of that city to convert to Islam.

The king's envoy arrived in the city, and in one single day, he ordered one-hundred and fifty Jewish heads severed from the neck. Not surprisingly, on that same occasion, about one thousand Jewish families converted to Islam. To this date, the neighborhood known as *Jadid-ha,* i.e. "The New Ones," remains a remnant of the old Jewish times, and the *Neo-Islam* cemetery of the city, which stands apart from the Jewish and Muslim cemeteries, continues to remind us of that terrible period of our history.

Could we expect any better from such bestial personalities? Didn't we see how **Saddam Hussein** (1937-2006) murdered his own son-in-law and grandchildren? Haven't we heard enough of cruelty being done in the name of religion? In such brutal people, dogmatic beliefs have taken over their conscience. If they can do such unspeakable things to their own children, their own flesh and blood, then we can only guess at what they would do to others. That's all the more true when hypocritical exhibitionism and murder in the name of their religion enters the equation.

The future of mankind is not written or inherited; it's what we create for us. Parents and teachers alike are responsible for shaping the future of our societies. Let's remind our educators that faith that's not based on human conscience, no matter how religious that person might be, can lead to imponderable cruelty of the likes of King Abbas or Saddam Hussein. Religious observance should always be based on conscience, deemed second to conscience, and ruled by conscience. Such faith, indeed, shall endure.

Misguided people have been indoctrinated with "absolutism" that leads to hatred. Instead, we should teach the followers of religions that faith and conscience complement each other. Absolutism must be rejected to allow conscience to wrest control of the minds of our children and students. Otherwise, if we fail to do so, the catastrophic chain of utopian absolutism can lead to such ideologies as Nazism, Fascism, or Communism. People all over the world continue to be victimized or even murdered without any sense of conscience, all in the name of furthering a religious or ideological doctrine.

Religion *per se* is not based on realism, as it deems an absolute self-conviction to be the first tool for its survival. Genocides, including the Holocaust, have had their roots in such ideological absolutist mentality. By contrast, thinking globally, and heeding to "wish for our neighbor what we'd wish for ourselves," would make it possible for human conscience to dominate religion.

The world has learned the hard way that any individual or society that takes the road of imitation loses all chances, even the merit to grow. Any absolutist ideology which shuts all doors to free-thinking only yields captivity of imitation. If so, humanity would be doomed, and science struck down in the name of religion. The Persian King Abbas, pretentiously modest, called himself "the dog in the presence of the religious figures"! Saddam showed his religious observance by building a mosque, then writing the holy verses of Islam on its walls – in the ink of his own blood! Yet, all such people, seemingly religious, seemed devoid of any conscience, and thus, they were doomed to infamy or failure. Can we call murderers truly religious, or even consider them human beings? Can we even pretend that what they did was acceptable by any ethical standard?

Self-deception, for the purpose of deceiving others, done in the name of sustaining a religion, is the most dangerous cause of regression among societies.

Acts of bigotry and prejudice have not been limited to the followers of Islam. The Christian faith offers a violent history all its own. When **Galileo Galilei** (1564-1642) announced that the earth was round and that it was not the center of the universe, he was subjected to the judgment of the Church's Inquisition. The priests put up a big fire outside the Church, preparing themselves to burn not just a man, but the science itself. After all, they had already done so to another great thinker, **Giordano Bruno** (1548-1600), who had refused to repudiate his scientific thoughts. But Galileo relented, and the Church let him live. It's said that his friends asked him, "Why did you speak against your convictions?" He replied that he had found it more expedient to live, so that he could continue his research and prove the truth about our planet beyond any doubt. They asked, "When you were leaving the Church, you seemed to talk to yourself. What were you thinking?" He replied that he had been telling himself, "I might not be able to convince the Church of the truth about the earth, but I know the truth for myself." A Persian poem captures this idea beautifully:

Oh, my soul!
Even if the ignorant people can't appreciate my intellect,
I won't be ashamed before your court,
Because I know that you know the truth.

But there is more to this story. It's said that as Galileo was being tried, an old woman inquired about the bonfire being prepared before the Church. Upon hearing the gruesome cause, she hurried to seize a piece of wood to feed to the bonfire. But as she saw Galileo coming out of the Church with a smile of relief, she angrily threw the lumber to a side, saying "What a pity! The wood stick was wasted!"

Mankind might have progressed in many fields but it has yet to make any considerable progress in the spiritual realm.

A Persian poem justly states that,

172

If people survived, it was for their morality.
Once any people lost that ground,
It faded away, lost for eternity.

Human beings are not born as good humans.
We are *raised* to become good humans.

A father once chopped a map of the world into pieces then asked his little son to put it back together. To his surprise, the child solved this seemingly impossible jigsaw within a few minutes! When the father expressed his amazement, the child explained that the difficult task became easy, once he had noticed the human face, which had been printed on the back of the map! The experienced man smiled and said thoughtfully, "Indeed, we could mend the whole world, if we could help mankind to correct its ways and unite." Let us all place promoting humanity before preaching religions, so that our world could boast of conscientious religious observers, instead of a bunch of hypocritical exhibitionists, who lack any sign of morality.

The majority of world's Christians succeeded in putting "the dark ages" behind them, the ugly periods of Inquisition, those centuries of discrimination, prejudice, burning of human bodies, and mass murders. Instead, they gradually arrived at a period of kindness, tolerance, while adapting ideas to the needs of modern time and the relentless pursuit of scientific truth.

They understood that if they failed to bring about this change by themselves, eventually time would do it for them!

Should we wait for the truth to be forced on us, by friend or foe – just for the sake of religion? Should we continue to place our children in those religious schools where they are being raised blind, so to speak, to prevent them from potential bitterness in the future? We can never dismiss the past entirely, yet we can't go forward on the same old path. The past can offer us useful lessons but we also need science and up-to-date information to walk safely on the road ahead. That is why it is said, "The past is the torch to light the road of the future" – and not the road itself!

Parents need to form supervisory boards at schools in order to exercise better control over teachers and the textbooks. There is a difference between enlightening people and making them stupid, between shaping an eyebrow and blinding the person! The only way to get out of the darkness of bigotry and prejudice is with the torch of science, accompanied by the light of morality.

All around the world, unbalanced extremists stand firmly against science and modernity. For example, there are many fanatic groups who find watching TV, going to a movie, or using the internet to be reprehensible acts, forbidden to their followers!

A few years ago, I resided among such a fanatic group for three months, and I learned that even as they lived in the 21st century, they still relied on live human "announcers" in their streets in order to be "religious"!

Charles Darwin (1809-1882) was spot on, when he said that dogmatism made humans arrogant while science made us humble.

Let us all cry out when a dogmatic mind is given the enormous responsibility of becoming a leader or a teacher! The dogmatic mind preaches imitation. Ignorance and neglect push mankind to close-mindedness, fanaticism, arrogance, and cultural poverty. It imagines that the better someone imitates, the more "religious" he or she is! Sadly, the dogmatic mind can't see that:

Without informed people, there would be no worthwhile religions around to have any worthy followers.

Dear educators, please heed the lessons of history! The calm of nations is only the calm between storms! We need to learn science and technology in order to lead a better life. And we should do this while we still have the chance. Thousands of evil-doers, with or without facial hair, have walked and galloped across the pages of history, burning and destroying both buildings and men.

Let's not repeat the mistakes of the past and call this "tradition." Let's ask ourselves what is a religious tradition in the first place?

The act of circumcision, for instance, has received the approval of modern science, even though it came to us as an old tradition, as a so-called *brit* or "covenant" between Abraham and God. This tradition, as wells as certain other traditions such as marriage, are shared by many communities. They are observed in each region according to the local customs, and both science and civil societies have accepted these as reasonable.

On page 647 of *Dehkhoda's Dictionary of Persian Language* we read that,

"Tradition is of three types –*sayings*, *deeds*, and *admissions*. The *sayings* are what the Books and prophets have said; the *deeds* are those that have reached us orally; the *admissions* are things done by the people, which were not criticized or rejected by the prophets."

Now, I ask you, respected educators, which category does what you teach as our tradition belong to? Are all your writings or sayings or quotations acceptable and practicable? The religious laws you follow such as those regarding the symbolic sale of food or land, and that you observe in a rather artificial and exhibitionistic manner – are all done so that these so-called traditions will survive. But what exactly are you trying to preserve by such pretentious, anachronistic and artificial acts?

I dare to say that your pretentious, artificial and forced ways, will give a bad name to the central aspects of our religion, and bring about its demise. Neither you nor I can validate those eternal commandments – only time can.

Responsible teachers and preachers are rather lonely people who sometimes erect walls, instead of building bridges. Please, bring down the walls of superstition; otherwise, we might become even more isolated as a group.

You can't go on forever preaching the truth upside down! You need to teach religion in a scientifically acceptable manner, and to preach the commandments in the language of modern knowledge. The Persian poet **Saeb Tabrizi** (1601-1667) put it so metaphorically,

I could never win over the autumn winds,
So I'd better shed my leaves and fruits,
Ever so calmly, before the fall arrives.

Just ask yourselves whether your centuries-long attempts, aimed at our survival, has resulted in anything but a reduction of our population? Personally, I can't see any benefits!

I once read a very interesting article by the renowned Iranian Jewish scholar, **Ms. Shirin-Dokht Daghighian**, in the Persian magazine *Shofar of New York* (No. 310, p. 30), under the title "How Could We Be Better Parents?" Ms. Daghighian wrote in part that contrary to what we have come to think, "the prominent figures of *The Torah*, as distinguished as they might seem in many respects, were not so good at fulfilling their duties as parents!" The writer begins with a discussion of Adam and Eve, who raised two sons, but one son ended up killing the other. "Next, it was the turn of Noah, who was ridiculed by his own son. Many don't consider Abraham, the father of the three "Abrahamian religions," to have been a good father to his own son(s). Also, Isaac and his wife, Rebecca, discriminated between their two

176

sons, Jacob and Esau, which resulted in fracturing their family. Jacob loved his young son, Joseph, with an almost obsessive quality, which provoked the jealousy of his other sons toward Joseph. Same goes with Moses, considered the greatest Jew, the great liberator, the prophet, the leader and the great law-maker, who was a good shepherd to his people, but not present for his sons when they needed him most. In short, all things considered, the ancient parents of the Jews were not such great parents.

King David, considered the ancestor of the Promised Savior, also discriminated between his sons. Thus, we can't just look at the great historical figures to learn from them the best way to be parents.

One of the greatest accomplishments of the *Holy Torah* is that is shows both the good and the bad, the sweet and the bitter, the pretty and the ugly, in its characters and events, so that the reader is provided with a chance to choose the best way.

The main goal of this book is to teach the reader more about the highs and lows of life, the road of righteousness and its pitfalls, and to help them choose the path of salvation. I emphasize that this book never aims for imitation. Contrary to many of our religious figures, it aims to inform, not just to tell a story. It wants the reader to be first informed and only then to choose to follow.

After all, don't we Jews believe that not even the prophets were devoid of mistakes? Do you believe that we should imitate the way people behave in those tales? Have we ever been required to do so? How can we claim that everything we read in the Book – from what Cain did to his brother Abel, or what Joseph's brothers did to him, to lying to a blind father, the wandering of a mother in the deserts – are worthy examples of behavior?

The famed contemporary poet, **Fereydoon Moshiri** (1926-2000), used the stories of Cain and Abel, and Joseph and his brothers, for a beautiful modern Persian poem in which he lamented the death of humanity in our time. Like all other poetry, it's next to impossible to render the full beauty of the original poem in another language. Yet, I think an abridged paraphrase is still worth the effort:

Poem by Fereydoon Moshiri

Ever since the day Cain spilled Abel's blood,
Ever since the day the Children of Adam
Felt the poison of enmity sparkle in their blood,
Humanity died, although Man was still alive…

Ever since his brothers threw Joseph into the well,
Ever since the Wall of China was erected by whips and blood,
Humanity had already died…

Then Humans went on to fill the world,
Centuries passed, since the first Man died,
Yet, alas, Humanity was never meant to return.

Our century is the age of Humanity's death:
World's chest is now void of all goodness.
It's foolish to speak of freedom, piety, generosity;
It's no more fit to talk of Moses, Jesus, or Muhammad –
This is the century of dictators, and their victims…

This is the age of Humanity's death:
I have a lump in my throat,
I have tears in my eyes —
Each time I touch a withering petal,
Every time I hear the silent cry of a sick child,
Even as I feel the sadness of the man in chains –
Or even the agony of a murderer at the gallows.
These days, it's as if my cup holds not wine but poison,
And my barrels are filled with my eye's tears and blood.

178

If so,
How can *I* believe that *he* or *she* died – a beloved of mine?

> It's not about the shriveling of a single leaf:
> For crying out loud,
> They are making forests into deserts!
> They are hiding bloodied hands before people's
> eyes!
> Beasts wouldn't do to one another
> What these inhumane men have done to Man's life.
>
> It's no more about the shriveling of a single leaf:
> Suppose that the canary's death in a cage didn't
> count,
> That a single flower never grew in the world,
> That all forests were deserts from the outset...
> Then, imagine, at the heart of a dark and cold
> desert,
> A people, for centuries patient with such sufferings,
> Now speak of the end of Kindness, the death of
> Love.
> Now, it's all about the death of Humanity...

Can we prevent the death of humanity by believing in superstitions? The answer is simple: No! Only those writings, ideas, commentaries or traditions that speak to the highest levels of human perception in our time are worthy of our study. Otherwise, only a shadow of the religion would be left. When some Jews "sell" their food or land in "make-believe trades" just to accommodate certain beliefs or traditions—they are imitating a dead religion, not observing a living one. The self-proclaimed caretakers of our religion do so in name only and nothing more, exploiting the situation to all of our detriment.

Our *Holy Torah* advises parents to choose proper and beautiful names for their children. Have we ever paid any attention to the common religious names among different faiths? They offer a precious window into the mind, perceptions, attitudes, intellectual aptitude and educational status of the followers of their respective religions. They give us a glimpse of old time parents and their world-views.

People invest their given names with virtue or vice, based on their good or bad deeds – and names have, it has been shown, a major impact on the success or failure of their children. That's because names can evoke the past, origins, and cultures of an entire nation.

Awhile ago, a Persian magazine explained the meaning of some names of Arabic origin, commonly used by the believers of Islam in Iran, which were rather mind boggling. While I admit that I can't verify the accuracy of the entire list, I find it useful to mention a few that seemed to be plausible translations:

Bagher: a fat cow; *Asghar*: smallest, most humble; *Zabih*: a four-legged animal that has been killed according to the Islamic religion; *Abbas*: a bitter-faced, angry person." (The magazine had also mentioned some strange translations for two Jewish names, but they were repudiated by a very knowledgeable friend of mine.)

We might ask whether those parents, when choosing such names for their children, had the meaning of the words in mind at all. Someday, our children will ask a similar question about us and pity that some of the so-called religious ideas of our time are devoid of any sense, if not downright despicable!

Today, many of the names and ideas, once fully appreciated, are now considered inappropriate, or perhaps worse. In some cases they can lead to discrimination. Do we know indeed the meaning of the prayers that we recite? Haven't we all found ourselves shocked, once in a while, when we learned about the meaning of some of those familiar passages? If we continue to pass on these words to the next generation without a critical approach to their content, won't we be responsible? Future generations will blame us for such faults, as much for outdated ideas, as for strange names. Choosing a good name is the least we can do for our children.

Albert Einstein once said, "We can't solve problems by using the same kind of thinking we used when we created them." We can't fix our nonsense by our old customs. To quote Einstein again, "Life is like riding a bicycle. To keep your balance you must keep moving." We should keep moving forward, if we don't want to fall.

Change requires time. It's said that Moses kept the Israelites wandering in the desert for 40 years, instead of taking them the short distance from Egypt straight to Canaan. Why? So that a full generation, one that had got used to a lifetime of obedience and slavery, would wither out and a new powerful and independent generation, could replace it. To learn from the past, and to walk the path of progress, first we need to rid ourselves of the regressive elements in our religion. And this might take some considerable time.

Religion is a tricky issue, because you can neither eliminate it as a whole, nor follow everything it says. The best is to understand its content as well as possible, to remain realistic, and to maintain moderation. Otherwise, religion can turn into a kind of genetically inherited disease!

Oh, Hafiz, seek a cup of water from the springs of wisdom,
So that ignorance would be wiped off of the tablet of your heart.

We need to inform our children of facts as much as possible, so that they won't follow any nonsense. Only the regressors are afraid of science, as we might hear a "religious" person claim, "Until there is a religious seminary, there is no need for a university!" They are like the man who didn't know how to swim, so he went on talking ill of the ocean! The rigid-minded person is like the man at the river bank, who kept staring at his own reflection in the water. The water flowed, but his image was still there. Likewise, the world is in constant change, but the fanatic has a fixation on his own unchanging reflection in the world's river. They only read and hear some old superstitions without paying attention to the times in which they live. The world has finally come to understand a basic fact, that **just because an idea is old, doesn't mean it's true!** We might add that "people hate science, because they don't know it, without realizing that it's the essence of religion."

The problem of religion is so important that even a prominent figure recently called it "a matter of life and death"! I have no doubt that sooner or later, the coming generations will see a major revision of religious texts; a major fight against unreasonable and anachronistic thoughts; the elimination of those ideas and religious commandments that run counter to basic human rights.

We are not alone in our protests against religious superstition -- the whole world, from Cairo to Tel Aviv, is raising its voice against such nonsense. We need to join the chorus of the rational-minded people; otherwise, the enemies of intellect will go on establishing more regressive centers everywhere in the name of teaching or preaching religious subjects.

Healthy intellectual nourishment is vitally important to the survival of societies. The meaningless writings of some commentators as well as their followers' deceptive propaganda constitute a fundamental social problem. It's especially troubling that fanatical writings often survive their writers, risking the potential of producing future generations of fanatics.

Voltaire (1694-1778) once addressed God and said, "I avoid church, to be closer to you!" Or as the 19th century Persian poet **Foroughi Bastami** wrote,

The myopic can't realize the beauty of the pine tree.
The dress of truth is not cut to fit everyone.
Seek the truth within the soul of the pious men,
Who only sought One from both worlds.

My cries are a mere invitation to avoid prejudice; to stop promoting hatred; to follow the core commandments of the *Torah*; "to see nothing but God," because **to believe in any religion or idea with zealous prejudice leads to neglecting reason and wisdom.**

Such zealous believers reject even some members of their own faith. They accept irrationally everything that is supposed to be a "religious" writing. Such people become so entrenched in the swamp of their empty thoughts that they'd rather commit suicide than change their direction. Instead of leaving the stage courageously, they try to recruit more members underneath their decayed ceiling.

The Communists, after almost seventy years of causing suffering of all kinds, gave up indoctrinating their people. They realized it would be better to distribute wealth than share together in poverty! *Only reason can lead us in the path of goodness; A mind, devoid of intellect, has no religion, either.* Would it not be better if enlightened teachers, too, chose to follow their healthy intellect? If we could find better jobs for regressive preachers and support free-thinking, perhaps we could stop spreading scientific poverty in the name of religion. With more factual knowledge couldn't they better convince our youth of the meaning of religion?

Although, we need to admit that at least for the time being, the new Russia seems better for today's world than the Communist Soviet Union, it is worth noting that once the Soviet Union was dismantled, the very first groups who arrived there were well-funded extremist religious groups looking to recruit. After 70 years of Russia's steady fight against superstitious religion, these groups raised the flags of orthodox religion in place of the former Soviet Union's "sickle and hammer"! It wasn't much different than those times when Europeans would send missionaries to colonize new countries. Despite all appearances, not much seems to have changed.

The commentary books that you are teaching were written at the time when the invention of a matchstick was considered a miracle! But today, **no one thinks much of a matchstick**. For centuries, some have repeated this mistaken notion that "without the rituals, the principles would be lost." But we can clearly see that the opposite is true. It seems that unreasonable traditions, and preaching superstition has posed the greater danger toward the core principles of our religion, causing some people to flee religion entirely. **Maimonides** (1135-1204) advised us that "only 10 Jewish clergymen would be enough for each town."

Do we really need every inexperienced youngster to become a cleric, thinking of himself as a professional *mullah,* and parroting the stories they learned? Do we need such clergymen to tell us those things that only benefit their own interest and not the good of humanity at large? Often, their words, deeds and behavior, and more importantly, their use of certain comical commentaries as their source material, is actually quite tragic! To call the regressive traditionalists "religious" is an insult to the religion, and to the people's common sense and intellect.

Yes, indeed everybody is made for a certain job,
And each heart is made for a certain thought.
If one not fit for the sea chose to sail,
He'd sink both the passengers and the ship!

It's a mistake to grant "religious diplomas" to inexperienced youngsters, based on their mere study of some old commentaries. Often, just listening to them for a minute or two is enough to realize the nonsense that they attribute to religion. Do they truly deserve the prestigious clerical diplomas, which entail so much responsibility? It begs the question: Who is issuing these diplomas in the first place, and what qualifies them to do so?!

"It is certain that in certain parts of the world we can see a peculiar people, separated from the other peoples of the world and this is called the Jewish people. This people is not only of remarkable antiquity but has also lasted for a singular long time... For whereas the people of Greece and Italy, of Sparta, Athens and Rome and others who came so much later have perished so long ago, these still exist, despite the efforts of so many powerful kings who have tried a hundred times to wipe them out, as their historians testify, and as can easily be judged by the natural order of things over such a long spell of years. They have always been preserved, however, and their preservation was foretold... My encounter with this people amazes me..."

– Blaise Pascal, French Mathematician

I share with our educators their sense of danger regarding the complicated issue of mixed marriages and assimilation. But I strongly disagree with the path they've chosen to answer the discrimination that we, the Jewish people, have suffered during the millennia of the Diaspora. It simply doesn't work for our time. Experience tells us that the more isolated the Jews made themselves, the more jealous their neighbors became.

If we smell a gas leak we open the window. So why should we close the window on this most vital of issues, i.e. our own social life? Every day, the penalties that we all pay for religious regressions is evident; yet you keep insisting on keeping the windows closed, instead of promoting freedom of thought. You are building walls instead of bridges.

"Indeed it is difficult for all other nations of the world to live in the presence of the Jews. It is irritating and most uncomfortable. The Jews embarrass the world as they have done things which are beyond the imaginable. They have become moral strangers since the day their forefather, Abraham, introduced the world to high ethical standards and to the fear of Heaven. They brought the world the Ten Commandments, which many nations prefer to defy. They violated the rules of history by staying alive, totally at odds with common sense and historical evidence. They outlived all their former enemies, including vast empires such as the Romans and the Greeks.. They angered the world with their return to their homeland after 2000 years of exile and after the murder of six million of their brothers and sisters. They aggravated mankind by building, in the wink of an eye, a democratic State which others were not able to create in even hundreds of years. They built living monuments such as the duty to be holy and the privilege to serve one's fellow men. They had their hands in every human progressive endeavor, whether in science, medicine, psychology or any other discipline, while totally out of proportion to their actual numbers. They gave the world the Bible and even their "savior." Jews taught the world not to accept the world as it is, but to transform it, yet only a few nations wanted to listen. Moreover, the Jews introduced the world to one God, yet only a minority wanted to draw the moral consequences. So the nations of the world realize that they would have been lost without the Jews.. And while their subconscious tries s to remind them of how much of Western civilization is framed in terms of concepts first articulated by the Jews, they do anything to suppress it.

"They deny that Jews remind them of a higher purpose of life and the need to be honorable, and do anything to escape its consequences. It is simply too much to handle for them, too embarrassing to admit, and above all, too difficult to live by. So the nations of the world decided once again to go out of 'their' way in order to find a stick to hit the Jews. The goal: to prove that Jews are as immoral and guilty of massacre and genocide as some of they themselves are. All this in order to hide and justify their own failure to even protest when six million Jews were brought to the slaughterhouses of Auschwitz and Dachau; so as to wipe out the moral conscience of which the Jews remind them, and they found a stick. Nothing could be more gratifying for them than to find the Jews in a struggle with another people (who are completely terrorized by their own leaders) against whom the Jews, against their best wishes, have to defend themselves in order to survive. With great satisfaction, the world allows and initiates the rewriting of history so as to fuel the rage of yet another people against the Jews. This in spite of the fact that the nations understand very well that peace between the parties could have come a long time ago, if only the Jews would have had a fair chance. Instead, they happily jumped on the wagon of hate so as to justify their jealousy of the Jews and their incompetence to deal with their own moral issues. When Jews look at the bizarre play taking place in The Hague, they can only smile as this artificial game once more proves how the world paradoxically admits the Jews uniqueness. It is in their need to undermine the Jews that they actually raise them. The study of history of Europe during the past centuries teaches us one uniform lesson: That the nations which received and in any way dealt fairly and mercifully with the Jew have prospered; and that the nations that have tortured and oppressed them have written out their own curse."

– Olive Schreiner, South African novelist and social activist

You are creating social burdens instead of innovators. It's said that Russians eat ice-cream to escape the cold! Fearing that youngsters will flee Judaism, you teach them the very superstitions that will drive them away! Do you really think that the fundamental principles of our religion truly need such nonsense to survive?

Just do some research, with no prejudice, and learn for yourselves how many unique talents are being wasted in the name of religion. These are students who might have otherwise turned into world-class scientists. This is true for all religions and societies. Traditionalists promote their version of religion to preserve their own identity. To them, they are "rewarding good deeds," but in effect, they are taking their students back in time and molding them in ancient ways. Instead they should try to adapt the ancient wisdom and commandments to our time! All the while naïve people offer them their support, imagining that doing so is a "rewarding deed."

So far, societies have not been able to devise legal punishments against certain vices. To simply lie, to be a miser or mean, to be misguided or ignorant, or just prejudiced, are not in most cases, crimes under the law. Instead, admonishing against such deeds is done, for the great part, by ridicule from other members of the community! The people who are subjected to such a wakeup call often feel worse, being more concerned about others' mockery than the opinion of a judge.

In the meantime, the media bear a special responsibility. For instance, if the print media acts wisely and without prejudice to uncover lies – writing by fanatics– they can have a positive impact on the future of society.

No ignorant person would dare call himself a "religious teacher or preacher" solely based on his seminary education. Many of these neo-clerics have no choice but to beg for *mitzvah,* i.e. "rewarding acts of goodness"! We can't even compare such myopic persons with the graduates of a prestigious institution like The Yeshiva University of New York, who leave the school with a command of modern sciences. The narrow-minded sects have produced no cause for our pride, yet every reason for our society's diminution. Still, they think that they are advancing the religion!

Throughout history, superstitions have spread everywhere, acting like some contagious disease, bringing all the core ethical principles to their demise. We shouldn't encourage the promoters of nonsense with any form of false respect, cooperation or support. Otherwise, they will just go on creating new superstitions. *You won't recognize him anymore, because of how much flattery he's received!* Kind friends and unkind pals have often remarked, *How can one lead, if he doesn't know the road?* How can such people make such big claims on religious issues, or interfere in people's personal choices, when they can hardly meet the necessary religious and educational qualifications? *One shouldn't say whatever he can, neither do whatever he could!*

Unfortunately, the world sees us as one group, even if this generalization is clearly wrong. Some of us might try to present themselves as "more Jewish" by wearing symbolic hats and other dress codes, or growing facial hair. This includes the members of the *Neturey Karta*, who as we already said, went as far as "kissing the hands" of our enemies! Yet we try to maintain our balance and still treat such fanatics among us with respect and consideration.

Moderation is necessary even in matters of religious observance. The insatiability of some religious groups in observing their traditions, as well as their ugly words and their interference in the affairs of others, cannot be considered reasonable. **Epicurus** (341-270 B.C.E.) said that *for those who find "enough" to be insignificant, nothing would be sufficient!* That's why none of the religious groups can accept one another, despite sharing in one belief, and they use religious identity as a means to their ends.

I'd be humble before two virtuous men,
If and when I find them.
First, the one who tells me of my mistakes
Second, the one who talks about his own faults.

Let me emphasize again that **while I don't think I have a right to sit in judgment of other people, I do reserve my right to express my opinions.**

We don't talk ill of others, and we don't wish to smear
Other people's dress, while washing off ours of our sins.
But the fault of a man, rich or poor, is equally undesirable,
And better not to turn mistakes into absolute examples.
Yet, Hafez, be forgiving toward our foe's wrong words,
And let's not fight with his just words.

The traditionalist often says, "We, as a group, have chosen our own path in life, so why don't you let us be?" But the problem is that *they* won't let us or our children be! They meddle in every aspect of our lives, and *they* constantly try to convince our children to join them! The Persian epic poet **Ferdowsi** put it best, when he wrote of religious zealots that, *They seek to harm others for their own sake. They turn fathers against sons, and sons against fathers.*

Freedom should be accompanied by accurate information. Otherwise, as the great President **Thomas Jefferson** said, a people that is free but ignorant of the surrounding world is doomed to disappear and be forgotten forever.

Throughout history the Jewish people have been thirsty for freedom, despite ages of persecution in the Diaspora. The Jewish people have learned expedience by virtue of a realistic world-view rather than personal interest. *One who can see things through the eyes of expedience, wouldn't step where he could not see first.*

May the day never come that the fanatic heads off the edge of the cliff and takes the entire community with him.

A backwards way of thinking and anachronistic lifestyle is not only harmful but it also ruins the children ensnared by it, barring them from any chance of progress that modern life offers. Indeed, it's the regressive traditionalist who abandons science for nonsense, preaches superstition, and under pressure, faints and resorts to prayers!

It's said, "Try to be old when you are young, so that you'll be young, when you grow old." *Act only to the best advice of the wise sage, not because of his wrinkles, but for his wisdom.* The world has seen enough of anti-Semitism and discrimination, so please don't add to the toll by reason of your self-grandeur and your program of brain-washing. You tend to teach our children things beyond their understanding, and then send them back home to break up their families, only to have them live in spiritual or even material poverty. For instance, a son was said to have made his mother cry by throwing away a full pot of food, because of some nonsense you had preached to him! These are your "mitzvahs" -- your "rewarding deeds."

Such unhappiness is the result of your ways, when you turn reasonable commandments of the *Torah,* such as *kashrut,* i.e. "the food regulations," or its hygienic laws, into a commodity sold and preached by the literal renderings of thousand-year old commentaries from your ilk.

We are to be blamed for our own misery. Still, another Persian poet put this so beautifully, using the metaphor of fire and ashes.

At dawn, the raging fire of the past night was no more
Than some small flicker under the ashes.
When I asked it, "What is it that covers you?"
It said, "This is the misery that I brought upon myself.

Orthodox brainwashing causes disappointed men and women to hide their extremist beliefs that are very different from the way of their ancestors, until they are already married. This often leads to conflict-ridden marriages and even divorce, sometimes resulting in troubled children. Is this another of your "mitzvahs"? Once, as I accompanied the former head of the Reconciliation Committee of the Iranian Jewish Federation, the late **Mr. Elias Ghodsian,** I saw a young woman who complained that, for her, the Jewish festivities had turned into days of grief! She explained that she and her husband who was a modern extremist, couldn't agree on how to observe the festivities! She wished to follow the ways of her mother and mother-in-law, while her husband tried to blindly imitate some rabbis.

Who is responsible for such dualities and conflicts? The blame falls squarely on *you,* our regressive educators! Back in Iran, we were all one, but here, you began to create these arbitrary divisions, under the umbrella of *mitzvah.* Your protégés mistake superstitions for religious observance. They imagine that just because they don't lie, they are telling the truth. But since they were only taught lies, they are simply repeating them.

Comrades, let's promise each other
Not to accept vice and disrepute on ourselves.
Either we'll sacrifice ourselves to save the truth,
Or we'd succeed to close the road on our enemies.

A love-sick person is kind to others, only because he or she wants to receive kindness. But a truly kind person is the one who acts selflessly and generously, because his or her conscience indicates that it's the right thing to do. I suspect the regressor's smile belongs to the first category, as it's only for his own interest!

Maimonides, sometimes referred to as "the Second Moses," agreed with **Hillel ha-Zaken** (110 B.C.E. -10 C.E.) that the entire *Torah* could be summed up in one of its commandments, "Do unto thy neighbor as you'd have them do unto you." Maimonides spent years trying to reconcile the writings of the Jewish rabbis up to that time with the Greek philosophical school of **Aristotle** (384-322 B.C.E.), incurring the rage of his contemporary rabbis! So much so that upon his death they burned his books, just as the Muslims did with the works of **Avicenna**. And this was done to Maimonides, who is universally known as one of the greatest Jewish thinkers of all time. Those rabbis were afraid that some of Maimonides' ideas might lead the Jews away from the *Talmud!*

"The Jewish vision became the prototype for many similar grand designs for humanity, both divine and man-made. The Jews, therefore, stand at the center of the perennial attempt to give human life the dignity of a purpose."

– Paul Johnson, American Historian

192

Regression is as old as religion itself. Sometimes, the zealots burned books in Iran, at other times in Egypt , where Maimonides spent his life.

Calling others ugly won't make you beautiful. You'd better examine yourself more carefully, and begin by pointing out your own faults. Prejudice is like a weed which grows whenever it finds fertile soil. Its noxious damage only becomes apparent once it's entered the garden, or once it has already found its way into your house and taken over your children. *My tears never smelled of truth, until my heart was touched. Not every drop of morning dew is a rose-water....*

We should evaluate ideas according to reason and not based on propaganda. We should look to the meaning of the words, and not to who the speaker is. Truth is what a healthy mind accepts and finds practical. Forcing ourselves to follow anachronistic nonsense in an artificial manner won't ever lead to our spiritual awakening, no matter how many times we repeat those rituals.

No matter how hard you try,
The willow won't grow flowers,
And a dark skin
Won't be washed off of its color.

All religions of the world, despite their diversity and the multitude of their followers, share one common denominator: prejudice and zealotry. About forty years ago, for a few days in Singapore, I had a rare chance of being in the company of six persons of three religions. I should note that while I knew their religions, they didn't know mine.

As I compared the beliefs of the Indonesian Muslim with the Yugoslavian Muslim; the Korean Christian with the European Christian; and the Chinese Buddhist with the Thai Buddhist; I realized more than ever that just because two people belong to the same faith or clan, doesn't mean that they agree about their beliefs. As these religions are dispersed over centuries in various parts of the world, evolving from their origins, they have little in common anymore. Yet strangely enough, in the Jewish community we suddenly learned about the Ethiopian Jews, called the Falasha, who claim their lineage from the reported trip of **Queen of Sheba** to the land of Israel some 3000 years ago! One wonders what happened to **King Solomon's** other children from his 700 other wives?

I saw a dream that I want to tell
But I'm dumb and the world is deaf:
One can't hear, and the other can't tell!

I am so concerned about the regressive traditionalist's propaganda that I hesitate to encourage my children to attend Hebrew classes. The *mullahs* have created a situation, in which even brothers might assume radically opposing ideological stances. To catch the fish, they have muddied up the waters, and now, there is no water to drink for anyone! **Rumi** once complained,

There are things to be said only with heart's tongue.
To speak those thoughts, I'd need another language
A whole different vocabulary.
Only then I can tell you about the story of
My pains, my failures and my miseries.

To mislead people, showing them the wrong path in the name of religion is a disservice to humanity, and our ancestors surely avoided such vice.

When are we going to give up our harmful ways,
these religious pretentions that have nothing for us but poverty?
Sadly, people of all walks seem to have become an enemy to themselves,
Bringing down a blow to this tree – of our culture and society.

194

As I said before, those who promote their irrational ideas and prefer them over reality will soon lose both their reason!

It's a credit to the Jewish Reform movement that amid their 900 temples and all their social and scientific capabilities, they have avoided doing anything forceful to change the ways of the Orthodox youth, lest it fracture Orthodox families from undue conflicts. The Reform movement doesn't believe such interference to be "rewarding acts of good," -- *mitzvot*. In this respect, they stand in marked contrast to the Orthodox philosophy, which deems it a duty to meddle in every aspect of other people's lives, aiming to bring everything under the control of their version of our religion.

It's also to the credit of the Iranian Jewish community that after the emergence of regressive traditionalism among our immigrant community, many notable figures spoke out against this harmful trend, among them the late Chacham Yedidya Shofet, Rabbi David Shofet, Rabbi Yedidya Ezrahian, the late Dr. Houshang Ebrami, Mr. Manouchehr Omidvar, Dr. Mitra Maghbouleh, Dr. Meshkin-pour, Mr. Khanbaba Rokhsar, Mr. Sion Ebrahimi, Dr. Kokhab, Dr. Babalavi, Dr. Mousa Kermani, and many others who represent the best of our small community.

As an example of such warnings by our leaders, I wish to offer my readers an adaptation of what **Rabbi Yedidya Ezrahian** wrote in *Shofar of New York,* No. 148, as he protested against uninformed sermons being given in the name of Judaism!

Mr. Ezrahian first writes of the difficult position he is in, as a conscientious and informed rabbi, since he's faced with an obligation to tell a difficult truth which could cause embarrassment to religious Jews. As he says, these words coming from a prominent rabbi could have also given fuel to the enemies of Judaism allowing them to use his words for their nefarious anti-Semitic purposes.

However, he was so convinced that the quoting or misquoting the *Talmud* out of context by these Rabbis was an even greater threat to our religion. Rabbi Ezrahian tells us that there were three incidents he heard about that pushed him over the edge; much as an article by this humble writer that supported his views gave him reason to speak out.

Mr. Ezrahian writes of a sermon at a memorial service, in which, as related to him by a trusted friend, one fledgling rabbi, a self-proclaimed wise man, told his well-educated audience to avoid *non-kosher* cookies because the dye used in their baking was made of cat's wool! The audience laughed out loud – not only at the rabbi but also at our faith. Courageously Rabbi Ezrahian writes that he doesn't see much difference between this so-called rabbi and the *mullahs* of the Iranian city of Qum! Instead of strange remarks, he recommends these rabbis offer more reasonable arguments, as for example, explaining that in order to maximize their profits, non-kosher bakers at times resort to using animal fat which can lead to certain diseases. "Wouldn't this argument be better than feeding people some stories wrongly attributed to the *Gemarah*, humbling the glory of Judaism?"

The second incident involves another of these mock-rabbis who told his audience that everyone should recite the *Shema Yisrael* prayer before going to bed otherwise, *Satan* would blow under the person's eyes and come morning their eyes would be puffy and contaminated and they'd look angry and tired! Rabbi Ezrahian finds this claim even worse than the ways of the fledgling *akhonds!* "At least they'd say such nonsense as quotations," he explains. He advises these young rabbis to educate themselves in the modern sciences to better argue their positions. For instance, they could explain that there are many benefits to reciting this prayer before bed, not the least of which is the comfort it brings that helps to push away anxieties and improve sleep – making the person happier in the morning.

The third incident involved a well-known deeply religious rabbi, so-called, who told his audience that it was necessary to wash our hands after using the restroom because it was where *genies* lived! Some members of the audience immediately laughed; while, sadly, others already brainwashed, nodded their heads in agreement Wouldn't it be better to point out the wisdom of our ancestors who knew, even before the discovery of microscopic germs, bacteria and viruses, that washing hands provided health benefits! Rabbi Ezrahian wonders why these so-called colleagues of his don't bother to read a bit more, and then offer more reasonable interpretations of the content of the *Gemarah* or the *Psalms*.

Rabbi Ezrahian warns in strong terms against any literal reading of the *Talmud*, or the *Mishnah and Gemarah,* both of which use highly symbolic language and asks us to consider them in the context of when they were written. He asks these neo-rabbis to pay attention to the message of the *Talmud;* not to confuse its metaphors with their true intent; and to avoid parroting like a robot what they learned in the seminaries. Else, he warns, they might bring humiliation to the *Talmud*, and to Judaism.

Our modern world marches on: humans landed on the moon; science and technology are advancing in all areas, from medicine to physics. At the same time, our religion is the most progressive of all, with its laws and commandments in keeping with the best of scientific, social, political and economic knowledge. That is, when it is not taken literally or salted with superstitions about *genies* and *Satan* and other such dross! Even the famed book of *Kabbalah*, known as the *Zohar,* which is full of such stories, is seen as a metaphor, as tales not meant literally.

Rabbi Ezrahian advises that new rabbis not be content with a few years of studying the *Talmud* in seminaries, but instead, devote their lives to learning, as the *Mishnah* says in *Pirkey Avot*, "The Chapters of the Sages": "One who doesn't add to his knowledge, renders his knowledge inefficient." And also: "One who doesn't want to learn, has surely signed his own demise." Rabbi Ezrahian advises his colleagues to expand their knowledge, for the sake of the *Torah* and Judaism; to avoid superstitious and irrational sayings; and to replace literal interpretation of the holy commentaries with rational interpretations based on modern knowledge. "Only then will you have fulfilled your mission," he says.

Isn't there a big difference between Rabbi Ezrahian and the rabbis who distribute their nonsensical, embarrassing teachings in print, or on tapes and CD's, and who, much to my distress, are being supported by naïve people seeking to honor their dead relatives?

There are many more examples of people who have found a modern way to live the commandments. Consider the brave and always ready-to-serve Jewish emergency services, known around the world as *Hatzolah*. They, too, believe in *mitzvah*, but unlike some others who become a burden to the society, they understand this term as "helping others." When natural disasters occur they are often the first to provide aid, such as when the Tsunami occurred in Indonesia or, more recently, after the earthquake in Haiti.

There is a stark contrast between the likes of **Rabbi Ian Pear**, or **Rabbi Howard Needleman**, and some hypocrites who call themselves rabbis. In the 1980's, I witnessed personally how these two, along with the late **Manouchehr Ghodsian,** selflessly tried to save the lives of young immigrants. In one sensitive situation, I witnessed how Rabbi Pear, not a rich man at all, in his devoted love to serve others, jeopardized his sole property, his own small house, by placing it as collateral for a loan to save the lives of the youngsters.

Rabbi Pear, and others like him, truly observe the command, "Do unto others as you would have them do for you." They strive to create comfort for humanity, not to fracture its harmony.

The true concept of "rewarding good deeds" has been a vital secret of Jewish survival through millennia of the Diaspora.

Over the years, we have seen suffering, humiliation, hunger and disease, and have discovered the most enduring cure against them – taking action selflessly. The new generation can only learn to do so, however, if we pass this tradition to them. Mending broken hearts, or building schools, synagogues and hospitals – these were all done through the ambitious efforts of our true believers. These are all different manifestations of our humanitarian services. We should not allow some hypocrites, spreading lies, to exploit these great achievements to their own advantage. We ought not to allow this proud concept of *mitzvah*, general good deeds for all mankind, to be tarnished by hypocrisy and deception.

It's sad that a group of ignorant fanatics have arrived in our community, preaching divisive superstitions instead of promoting true knowledge and the kindness of *mitzvot*. A Persian poet once asked,

What's the difference between the pious and sage?
The first saves his own rug from the waves,
While the second, tries to save the drowning man.

Rabbi Pear and the likes of the late Ghodsian were for saving drowning people, regardless of their hat or beard.

I am reminded of the story of a fearful hypocrite who accompanied a brave hunter in his search for a wolf that had been attacking their village. As they spotted the trail of the beast, the coward told his company, "Alright, you now follow the trail to find where it went, while I go back to see where it came from!" The likes of Rabbi Pear would never give up serving humanity when faced with danger, but those cowards would. People ought not to be deceived by hypocrites using the guise of religion.

The wise man, who hears this story,
He'd break with religion to join science.

A beautiful Chinese proverb says, "Many a bitter tear-drop is shed on the gravestones, which was a word left unsaid when due." Let us speak out about what ought to be said now.

Almost everyone can see, but people of true foresight, those who can see the solutions to problems before they have even occurred, are precious few. Past experience can surely help us to better prepare for the future. A Persian proverb says, "What the young man can only see in a clear mirror, the old sage can see in a brick!" Let us not silence the voice of the wise. If people had heeded the advice of our rational minded people and rejected the regressive traditionalists from the outset, much conflict within families, societies and the world at large would have been avoided. Sadly, our small community's circle of marital options has grown even narrower, over the years, mostly because of such undesired conflicts.

Hypocrisy is so dangerous that the Persian poet Saadi once wrote

Tell all the pious men to know that
Saadi has left the ways of piety.
I'm not as nearly afraid of wine or the poison
Or the bell, as I am of the hypocrisy of piety.

It's said that the great philosopher-scientist **Avicenna** (980-1037 C.E.) and the renowned *Sufi* mystic **Abu-Sa'id Abul-Khair** (967-1049 C.E.), once convened for a private debate. Afterwards, when asked by his students about the results of the closed-door dialogue, Avicenna humbly responded, "Whatever I know, Abu-Sa'id *sees*." In turn, Abu-Sa'id told his own students, "Whatever I see, Avicenna *knows*." These were two great minds and spirits, whose humility and sincerity helped

200

them see through their contrasting methods and differences. Can we try, as well, to see the truth beyond appearances, beyond prejudice and personal interests? Our sages of the past can be forgiven, based on the limits of their time and place; but there's no excuse for today's fledgling rabbis to continue offering us their literal interpretation of old time nonsense.

Make no mistake: **such superstitions have no inherent relation to our religious commitments.** I urge our young rabbis to do independent research and confirm what I am saying. I also call upon them to stop further fracturing our fragile families. A wise man once said that the oceans were filled with the tears of parents who shed them over the ignorance of their children! Every bit of nonsense that you teach becomes a tear, falling from the eyes of a child's mother.

Ignorance could cause us to hurt, even as we intend to help.

Once upon a time, a little boy received a rare gift from his father – a box of silkworms, dwelling over leaves of white mulberries. The child loved his new gift so much, attending to it every day, watching the worms eat and crawl inside the box. He began to wake up early, and go to bed late, just so that he could spend more time with his precious worms. Soon, the worms began to weave their threads, and they disappeared inside their white cocoons. The father explained that inside each cocoon, there was a moth in the making, but that in order to see it fly, his son had to wait until the metamorphosis was completed. The son waited for days, until he noticed that one of the cocoons began to shake. Eager to help, the little boy decided to crack open the cocoon and help the moth break free. But to his surprise, the beautiful moth died soon after leaving its cage. The boy ran to his father, crying, only to learn from him that his "kind help" had indeed caused the insect to die. Little did he know that the moths needed to wrestle with their cocoons to strengthen their muscles, as an exercise to prepare them for the life in the outside world.

Another well-known fable speaks of the friendship between a grateful bear and a young man. One day, the man was sleeping soundly in the forest, when a fly sat on his forehead. The bear, trying to help his dear friend have a good rest, seized a large stone and brought it down on the fly -- right where it had been sitting – on the young man's forehead!

The relationship between our religious educators and their students -- confining people's children in prisons of religiosity, in traditionalist schools, *yeshivot* and *kollels,* i.e. the Jewish seminaries – or those of other faiths, for that matter – is very much like the friendship of that little boy and the worms, or the bear and the young man!

Your misguided teachings are robbing these children of their best years when they should be preparing to face the wild, wild world outside the classrooms. Thus, like a bird with untrained muscles, they much more easily fall prey to a hunter's trap.

The effect of such a way of life is evident, as these religious students bring so many children into the world only to become burdens on society. To live well is an art, but they never learned how to swim in the ocean of life. The blame is squarely on their parents and teachers, who took away their inclination to think for themselves or to earn a living. Blessed be the father who told his sons, "Money has two main applications. First, to pay with it, so that they would help you out. Second, to spend it, so that they would leave you alone!"

The talented and renowned Persian Jewish writer, **Mr. Rouhollah Kharrazi,** once wrote an article in the Persian magazine *Payam (New York),* "Those Who Whip," in which he wrote eloquently about a painful worldwide phenomenon:

"What can we say of the sick pleasure which some fanatics take in humiliating women and bringing them to their knees, that it's a trick of their unconscious mind? Do these tyrants, deep inside, consider themselves to be beneath the status of women, and therefore, they try to compensate for their natural-born sense of humiliation by resorting to religious Sadism?"

He stresses that religion should stay out of government. In a society ruled by religion, he argued, freedom disappears, and once clerics become lawmakers and judges, we should fear for the lives of their citizens. In such a world, religion is the first to lose its true identity; "antique-worship" replaces the worship of God; and nothing has any true meaning: traditions are misinterpreted by evil and ignorant people. Once the religious rulers, hiding behind a mask of hypocrisy, take command no one is safe anymore.

Superstition and prejudice don't know any boundaries. They are the cancer of the soul. The pure flowing water of religion, once driven out of mosques, churches or synagogues, only turns into muddy swamps. That's when innocent people are stoned to death; petty thieves have their hands cut off by fanatics; women are forced to wear black shrouds; and free-thinking men are chained to the walls in dark and damp dungeons.

The situation in Afghanistan under the Taliban is of telling importance. Under their reign, women have suffered even more; men are being lashed and whipped, for example, if their facial hair is too short; taxi drivers face whipping and imprisonment, if they give a ride to a woman unaccompanied by a man. In Kabul, the country's capital, any house with women in it is required, according to the Taliban, to have pitch black panes so the women can't be seen by "non-intimate eyes." These are not houses, but cages and graves.

A few years back, when Afghanistan suffered from a major earthquake, killing 5000 and rendering tens of thousands homeless, international aid was sent to the country from all around the world. Yet the Taliban rejected a 15-ton cargo of food and medicine, because the

rumor was that this medicine had come from Israel! This is not
religion, but a religious Mafia! How many innocent lives were lost
because of this fanatical decision?!

In today's Iran, there have been calls to ban women's faces from
being printed in the public media. In Algeria, rebellious fanatics killed
everyone in a village, including children, in the most brutal fashion,
leaving their heads at the threshold of their doors. Elsewhere, the
extremists demand sick women to be examined only by female
doctors, no matter how dangerous their condition might be.

We share no pride in the actions of fanatics. Instead of promoting
brotherly love, they have turned brother against brother, and replaced
kindness of heart with cruelty. These hypocrites don't even leave their
own people in peace. What explains their fear of women's hair? Where
does the animosity of these "certifiable lunatics" toward women come
from? Why do these brainless nobodies wish to humiliate their own
mothers, sisters and wives, by minimizing the freedom of these poor
women? Why such a desire for dominance over women, at all? I doubt
whether even Sigmund Freud could explain this phenomenon!

Meanwhile, Mr. Kharrazi finds that there is also an excess of 'fear
of religion.' So for example, in the United States, the recitation of even
a non-denominational morning prayer in praise of God is forbidden at
public schools: or consider the case of a judge, who was ordered to
remove *The Ten Commandments* from his courtroom because it was
considered an intrusion of religion in a public space! On another
occasion, the defense jumped at an opportunity to call for a mistrial
because the judge had quoted the Bible before reading out the sentence
for the defendant. Indeed, a few years ago, a group of fanatic liberals
went so far as to call for the removal of the words "In God We Trust"
from our currency. In summation, Mr. Kharrazi quoted a humorous
teacher of his youth, who used to say, "Moderation is the best choice,
as the street is always at the middle!"

My friends, the "second-hand," home-grown fanatics have yet to give up their deeds; if anything, they have intensified their assaults on our values. Whenever any of them undeservedly grabs a position of power, it's always the same old story. It's the same with all fatal diseases; if neglected at first, they grow worse until they cause us inhumane pain. While these regressive elements claim they seek the "rewards of their good deeds," rational people are only concerned with harmony within families and offering constructive advice. The regressors will not end their ways, as long as some people continue naïvely to support them.

I say to the regressors: If you want to promote the true religion, then try to preach common sense and reject superstition. Let's do the right thing, before the next storm has arrived. Children have only one chance to learn and *as the cane keeps whispering to the old man, only in our dreams might we visit again the days of our youth.*

I write about our flaws, because I believe that to withhold the truth is even more dangerous than a momentary embarrassment for our community. I am glad to say that as a result of revelations by me and other similar writers, an increasing consensus has emerged in our community to seriously fight superstition. The common interests of our community are much stronger than the power of the regressors, who are trying to divide and conquer the community. We consist of a single unit, and amid our diversity of ideas, we all share one common ideal, that is, to follow our *Holy Torah.*

We view the *Torah* as a work that can be considered rationally and understand the term "the Chosen People" to mean having the duty, long ago among all nations to promote the worship of one God.

The Beloved, this healer of love,
Can bring back life in you, with a breath;

But how could she heal you,
If she doesn't see your pain?

We need to tear down the masks of self-importance and prejudice, in order to reveal the truth and to become one community. A rational person sees the past as a ladder, whose steps we climb to evolve and advance into the future. In the past, often one person, such as **Thomas Edison** (1847-1931), **Henry Ford** (1863-1947) or **Louis Pasteur**, could have been considered solely or mainly responsible for a single invention or discovery. But in today's world, especially with the advent of the Internet, innovation has become a shared communal or even global activity.

Similarly, the notion of a "savior" – be it the "Messiah" or anyone else – need not apply to an actual person, but to the progressive movements of the past and future, which have guided humankind toward a better world. The reward or punishment of all deeds is inherent in the act itself, divorced from religion or God. And the best guide for any person is his or her fundamental and individual perception – and not a book or a mediator.

The regressors are intent on recruiting an ever increasing number of our people for their "heaven," by brainwashing them to fulfill their own interests and "rewards"! Parents should stay vigilant against such deceptions, if we are to thwart their dangerous plans.

My intention is to speak out against the extremist regressors among us who in the guise of religion do not hesitate to break apart our families. The regressive traditionalist desires oneness only if it means joining their group. They view others, even other members of their own faith, not to be worthy.

By contrast the rational person, of whatever religion, doesn't think that humanity's problems can be solved by one specific religion or ideology; instead, by accepting fair and constructive criticism, they allow freedom of expression to take flight, liberated from prejudice and a one-sided way of thinking. Sadly, we can't think of prejudiced people without noticing the superstitions they espouse; and naturally, we come to think of all superstitious people as one group.

All their thousands are no more but one;
They're just some confined minds,
Able to think only within a limited perception.

As a blind person's perception becomes comparably limited, the faith of the bigot is confined, as well, to the boundaries of his prejudice – while the faith of the rational-minded person remains as vast as her knowledge and foresight.

Winston Churchill said that change is the first necessary step toward progress.

The most tragic event is not mere physical death; resisting change and failing to stay in synch with modern progress, in the name of this religion or that lifestyle – whether it's done voluntarily or under compulsion, by choice or birth – this is a gradual death. The regressor in effect takes away tomorrow from today's children. To fight darkness with darkness is a futile task.

Please, do not let any person manipulate your children's emotions and attempt to control their mind. Our children should learn from us that extremism is not the way to observe religion. It's simply a sign of ignorance.

Humanity's special status comes from bonding with each not and not from being separate. The guilt of a son who avoids family gatherings at his parent's home because of some religious belief, is all the more unfortunate when he does so because he has been brainwashed to believe magical thinking from the past such as caring more about whether we walk or drive on the Sabbath or whether we eat certain foods or keep *kashrut* (kosher) than about the importance of being with one's family.

The bigoted fanatic even falsely imagines that it's alright to tell lies, in order to promote religion. Our children should know that not everything round is a coin; the world is not supposed to be a place for punishment, but a place to be happy and to live happily.

We should support those who need help to learn a science so that they, in turn, can show others the light of knowledge. Our young people need to truly *understand* what they've seen, heard or read. Otherwise, books are just a pile of papers, and universities are just buildings of lumber and bricks. Once a person has been emancipated from the chains of superstition and fate-based ideologies, once he's taken over the control of his life, only then he can have an impact on his destiny and the future of society.

Let's preserve what's necessary to our religion and throw away whatever causes backwardness. Prayers, at best, are anesthetics; they should never be mistaken as a cure. It's our duty to preserve the exalted concepts of religion but it is also our obligation to follow our conscience and maintain moderation at all stages. One could say that we should even remain moderate in our moderation!

A knowledgeable person, with a kind heart toward his fellow human beings, is indeed much more religious than a single-minded religious person who sacrifices everything for his prejudice and doesn't show any sign of kindness toward others.

As the *Torah* says, "We should wish for others what we'd wish for ourselves." All mankind is responsible for each other's security. That goes for everyone, not just a single tribe, city or nation. Evolution dictates the world move toward thinking globally. Long ago, people would know each other as "fellow villagers"; later on, the circle expanded, and they began to think of their "compatriots." But once we begin to call each other genuinely as "fellow humans," we will have reached the pinnacle of civilization. That day is not so far off: already the nations of Europe consider their people, simply, as "Europeans," with a single currency and passport. This is all in evidence, on a smaller scale, in Israel where Iranian Jews know each other simply as "Persian," regardless of their distinct city of origin in Iran!

With a nod to Saadi, someday soon, people will come "to see only one God."

It's said that once a shoe company sent two salesmen to a Caribbean island that had a small population of about 150,000 residents. A few days later, the first salesman informed the headquarters that everyone in that island walked barefooted, so there was no way to sell any shoes there. The second salesman, however, saw things differently. He called his bosses, and told them in an excited voice, "This is a gold mine! No one here wears any shoes. We could easily sell them at least one hundred thousand pairs a year!" Two people, same goal, same place, but two very opposite conclusions: one thinking negatively, the other positively. It's people of such open-mindedness and foresight that can bring success and good reputation to their companies – and to the larger society.

Some parents, encouraged or brainwashed by a misguided group, rear their children in a world of superstition, placing them in seminaries where they learn hypocrisy and anachronistic ideas. All this time, they imagine this will keep them religious!

By contrast, there are those who opt for higher education for their children, encouraging them to study at universities, become knowledgeable and useful people both for their own good and also for their community. Are those children who went to the universities "non-religious"?!

Successful families and societies are never content with what they know. They strive to keep up-to-date, well aware that what we learn for ourselves will fade but what we leave for others will live after us.

My friends, we've had enough of indifference. Let us now do our part in advancing society.

A potential that has not been realized is that same as impotence.

We shouldn't waste our children's golden opportunity for learning by filling their heads with useless information. Discuss with your children their daily lessons, and judge for yourself.

What a waste to use the gold for the golden monument!
How can you make it work with a false-hearted lover?
Laughter doesn't look nice on a toothless mouth,
So why should one open an empty shop, with nothing to sell?

Science and technology are not enough in of themselves to maintain world peace. We need to teach spiritual matters, as well. The only light that never goes out is the light of spirituality – and the *Torah* is the torch-bearer of this light.

Peoples are alive because of their morality.
A people that lost its morals, would cease to be alive.

Human conscience spreads its light everywhere to illuminate reality. The generous and vast table of conscience is preferred over the bitter quagmire of prejudice. For civilized people, conscience takes the upper hand over religious bias. As long as religion is rife with sectarianism, it will lead to conflict and murderous crimes, and as a result, the world will not see peace. The more fanatics put forward their ideas, the better we can see the worthless nature of their empty superstitions.

210

Religious observance, at best, is like pure water – good to drink, as long as we don't drown in it! Pure faith has never betrayed anyone; only the misguided exploit faith to their advantage.

By the way, what does it take to be called a religious person? Does it mean anything but to be a better person, inside and out, and to serve humanity? Sadly,

Many a preacher who pretends something at the altar,
But goes on doing the opposite in private.
It seems that they don't believe in the judgment day,
That they do so much deception in the work of God.

To better understand the meaning of the above verses, just look around and see how many families are suffering because of religious hypocrisy. By its indifference, our community is responsible for enabling those promoting superstition.

Whenever you see a tyrant,
Know for sure that the wise men
Had first given up their control.

A scientist once remarked that a little knowledge might push us away from God, but more knowledge would bring mankind closer to God and to a conscientious faith. Those who visited the *Nezamieh School* of Baghdad (founded 1065 C.E.), one of the most accredited religious seminaries of its time, could see the following warning posted at its threshold:

"Rational sciences are not allowed in this place!"

It's sad that fanatical seminaries still think this way – but it only pains the rational-minded, or those who've already been stung by religious corruption. As the poet said,

Flower, with all that softness, has to drink from the mud,
And the wise man has to feel sad, over the plight of the ignorant.

Those who run such seminaries are well aware of what they're doing, but to distract others, they quote words of their colleagues that make no sense and when cornered, they bring in some even worse commentary. As a last resort they explain that such things are "secrets," implying that somehow they're the only "experts" who can understand such things so others will follow them blindly. This is what religion means to most people!

The likes of **John Wycliffe** (1320's-1384), **William Tyndale** (ca. 1494-1596), or **Thomas Pelham Dale** (1821-1892) were severely tortured and prosecuted by the Church for advocating translating the Bible into the common language of people so that it would no longer be the exclusive territory of the priests.

The fanatic favors ignorant people, while the rationalist favors the informed.

The fanatic intends to imprison all minds, while rational people wish to enlighten every mind. A fanatic is well-aware that an informed mind will leave him alone. That is why regression, and the fight against it, is as old as the history of religion. Yet, there are many who are afraid to speak out, afraid it might lead to some embarrassment to our community. But if we keep silent, it only leaves others to do the criticism for us, albeit for their own purposes.

Here are two examples.

Awhile ago, I read about an article published in the Islamic Republic of Iran's *Resalat* newspaper that claimed that, "the chief rabbi of the Western Jews in Israel had issued a *fatwa*, indicating that on the resting day of Sabbath, Jews were allowed to kill lice, but not mice! The rabbi said that based on Jewish teachings, head-lice could be killed to prevent them from reproducing. Still, combing remained forbidden. Thus, the lice should only be taken softly off of the clothes. Mice, however, could only be captured, and taken away by their tails."

Thanks to this newspaper's clever editor, even the least intelligent of its readers would no doubt think, "How sad that in our modern age with so many complicated dilemmas, a chief rabbi felt the obligation to address such a mundane issue?!" It makes me wonder how the rabbi didn't realize that speaking such nonsense could only lead to people mocking our religion.

This article reminds me of what "the pot told the kettle!" Perhaps this *fatwa*, or perhaps even the whole story, was untrue. But we believe it is possible given all the similarly ridiculous dictates of our fanatical clergy.

The five-word favorable commandment to observe a day of rest per week has over the millennia expanded into a 39-set of laws by our later clerical bodies, with many caveats and nuances added sometimes to the point of absurdity. Such *fatwas* cause rational people to avoid religion, while some malleable children continue to be brainwashed by nonsense that orders them to avoid their parents' meals. Shame on those who destroy families with such superstitions! I remind our educators that to learn from our mistakes is a sign of wisdom.

When it comes to humans, we'd rather seek better understanding than stronger reins. After all, bridles are only for animals.

Dear educators, your duty today is not to teach our religious commentaries literally and to avoid, please, *mullah-style fatwas!*

Let me give you another example to see how others view our flaws.

On September 28th, 2000, *Keyhan of London* published an article by **Mr. Sadr-al-din Elahi**, titled "The Chacham and the Cucumbers," an abridged translation of which I'd like to share with you.

Mr. Elahi wrote, "Don't think that Iran is the only place where religion interferes in the lives of people. Even in Israel, a country that boasts a full-fledged democracy and freedom of expression, the rabbis have such power that they interfere in all matters of Jewish life, including how people eat cucumbers! This year, eating cucumbers has been forbidden. The bearded rabbis have announced that this year's Israeli cucumbers are *non-kosher* for religious Jews, and why? While the Israeli government is a secular one, the country is 100% religious. [*Actually, the population has a wide spectrum of religious beliefs.*] To ensure that all things are done according to the Jewish religion, a kind of legitimacy *fatwa* should be issued, be it in matters of food, clothing or the like. This complicated, frightening set of laws of legitimacy for food is known to Jews as *kashrut*.

"One such religious law is known as *shemita*, according to which, a Jewish peasant should stop cultivating the land every seven years. This was originally valid for the earlier pastoral days of flocks and farms, and it's similar to the years of *aayesh* in Iranian culture. But given the difficulties of observing this law in modern Israel, long ago, the rabbis made up a religious loophole, according to which, the Jewish farmer 'sells' his land for one year at a set price to a non-Jew. As such, the product of the land is considered *kosher*, because it's produced by a non-Jewish farm-owner! This is a common practice in Israel, and so far, there haven't been any problems. But this year, the rabbis made a pact with the Lebanese and Jordanians, to circumvent the monopoly of one Israeli company on cucumber farms in Israel, and to generate some money for the religious treasuries. Now this has turned into a big debate in the Israeli media. Israeli cucumbers which are seen to have been produced by violating the *shemita* laws are not being certified as *kosher*, and the religious Jews avoid them, lest they end up in hell next to Yasser Arafat!"

Doesn't such an article bring shame on our people? This article was used by the so-called Iranian rabbi and his colleagues to corroborate the *fatwa* against buying Israeli products!

Do you still think we should deceive ourselves and remain silent? This "religious trick" of selling land during the year of *shemita* – or similar "tricks" devised for the *Passover* festivities – is a remnant of the Eastern European *ghettos*. If your true explanation for the *shemita* is a purposeful commandment, intended for the soil to recover its minerals and other nutrients – that, is no longer relevant to modern farming, then why go on deceiving yourselves and others with such lies as "pretend-sales"? If the land is still being used what does it matter that a non-Jew is the straw man owner? This sort of deception, and the teaching of deception, is no foundation on which to support our religion. Doesn't this s artificial way of observing outdated practices run counter to the true meaning of our commandments?

Let me tell you the heart-wrenching story of a group of proud Iranian Jews, who lived in the Islamic city of Mash-had, in the North--Eastern region of Iran. In March 1839 (C.E.) the Muslims of the city attacked the Mash-hadi Jews, burned down their houses and synagogues, murdered many of them, and coerced the rest to convert to Islam.

Those Jews of Mash-had that survived became, in effect, "under-cover Jews," adopting a compulsory Islam on the surface, yet continuing to remain Jews in private. Some families went on to lead a dual religious life for more than a century. I dare say that during those tumultuous years of hidden Jewish life, it was their true adherence to the core aspects of Jewish culture, and not some superstitious beliefs or traditions that kept Judaism alive among this tormented group. They simply could not afford to practice certain customs, or maintain certain superstitions, yet they succeeded in maintaining their rich Jewish culture with its values.

Speaking of their historical wars on Iran, an Arab warrior once said, "We were defeated by the Persian mothers, since they kept speaking Persian to their children at home, and thus, they never adopted the Arab culture!" Indeed, animals inherit the past through their bodies, but humans do so through culture, i.e. their mind. Culture is our true human heritage, as it constantly evolves and is passed on from one generation to another. This is why animal behavior remains unchanged over numerous generations, while no two humans can be found to be the same.

Humankind has a dynamic essence and nothing, including religion, can fully obstruct its unceasing evolution. Culture is the source of all intellectual, spiritual and behavioral dimensions of a nation and their secret of survival through intense hardship. It's a reflection of their culture that the Jews of Mash-had survived a century of historical ordeals. Today, they continue to be proud Jews with renewed energy. The same is true about many other social groups with similar histories.

To remain silent when one has to speak is nothing but cowardice.

The true man of truth sails on,
Especially through a vigorous storm,
We ended up taking the long road,
Because we kept our eyes fixed
Narrowly, on our steps.

We need to be inspired by the pragmatic ways of our ancestors, rather than following this or that person's opinion.

Rabbi Eric H. Yoffie is the President of the Union for Reform Judaism, the congregational arm of the Reform Jewish Movement in

North America. The Union represents 1.5 million Reform Jews in more than 900 synagogues across the United States and Canada. During a speech on August 31st, 2007, in Chicago, Rabbi Yoffie remarked that:

"[...] As a Jew I know that our sacred texts, including the Hebrew Bible, are filled with contradictory propositions, and these include passages that appear to promote violence and thus offend our ethical sensibilities. Such texts are to be found in all religions, including Christianity and Islam.

"The overwhelming majority of Jews reject violence by interpreting these texts in a constructive way, but a tiny, extremist minority chooses destructive interpretations instead, finding in the sacred words a vengeful, hateful God. Especially disturbing is the fact that the moderate majority, at least some of the time, decides to cower in the face of the fanatic minority — perhaps because they seem more authentic, or appear to have greater faith and greater commitment. When this happens, my task as a rabbi is to rally that reasonable, often-silent majority and encourage them to assert the moderate principles that define their beliefs and Judaism's highest ideals. [...] And you cannot get to heaven by creating hell on earth." *Excerpt from Address by Rabbi Eric Yoffie to Islamic Society of North America, Chicago, August 31st, 2007*

This is a wonderful example of civility, a soft yet unequivocal cry against egotistic minds, and a protest against opportunist fanatics whose beliefs and deeds will only lead to catastrophic consequences.

We are fortunate to live in a time where we no longer need to blindly follow the strictures of some fable or superstition. Mankind, by nature, is fascinated by stories. From our early childhood, we love to make up stories or listen to them. Religious books have long been aware of this basic human characteristic; hence, they widely employed the art of story-telling to better communicate certain concepts to their audiences in their time and place. But today we live in very different times.

Many of our current religious leaders, instead of elevating the understanding of their followers, try to rein them in with biblical stories. To that end, they even resort to re-enacting the characters and actions of these tales, so that their naïve followers are encouraged, via audio-visual means, to stay within the void circle of their artificial ideas.

No wonder so many people mistake the compulsory imitation of superstitious and nonsensical rituals as the way to keep the Jewish religion alive or, worse, as its true observance. What is most disheartening is that the real reason for the false importance they place on these rituals is that it helps the self-appointed Rabbis stay in power and fundraise for their self-serving enterprise. They call themselves "religious," and they label those who are against such nonsense as "non-religious." This defames the truly religious, our ancestors, and all those who kept Judaism alive through centuries of Diaspora existence, maintaining their identity within prejudiced societies. In this regard, the success of the Mash-hadi Jews amid mountains of persecution is a case in point. They didn't – and couldn't – observe some superficial nonsense; what gave them the strength were the progressive concepts of Jewish culture.

I encourage you to read and do your own research on this subject.

Rumi wrote,

Oh, my friends, hear this story,
It's the truth, an account of our condition!
We'll have both worlds,
If we just understand this story of ourselves…

Napoleon Bonaparte said that religion was the best way to keep the common people quiet!

Mark Twain quipped, ""It ain't the parts of the Bible that I can't understand that bother me; it is the parts that I do understand."

It's sad that the regressive clerics, in their unceasing pursuit of new recruits, exploit the general lack of information among ordinary people who pay no attention to the deeper meaning of what they read or hear. These are the kind of people who call themselves "religious." More reasonable people, in general, have kept silent about these hypocrites, that is, until their own family is stung by this poison – but by then, it might be too late.

It's an irreparable mistake to deny our children a love for personal and social progress; to alienate them from the extraordinary spiritual potential that hides inside each one of them; and to inculcate them forever with superstitious prayer-saying. This can only lead to a bitter fate, not only for them but for all humanity – as people flee the preaching of superstition. As the poet **Saeb of Tabriz** (1601-1677 C.E.) said,

I can't blame my miseries on others,
Because just like a bubble,
My house is at risk because of the air inside.

To turn the clock back on our children and make them think and act as if they were living in ancient times is unconscionable. It reminds me of the poem by Goethe, "The Sorcerer's Apprentice," in which a wizard's pupil, tired of bringing water to the workshop, enchants a broom to do the job for him. But it turns out to be a mistake because the apprentice doesn't know how to end the spell, so the broom keeps on repeating the task until the workshop becomes flooded! (There is a happy ending: Luckily, the master comes back in time to save the day.)

We need to ask whether our children, raised in such a regressive atmosphere, will ever be able to provide for their families (which are often large). It's the doctor's job to cure the patient, not to paralyze him. The freedom to worship is one of mankind's most basic freedoms. It is our task to promote a healthy form of worship and to raise young worshippers who won't confuse maintaining their beliefs with violating other's people's rights.

Believing in prayers and talismans; visiting the so-called holy shrines; or giving gifts to unemployed clerics or other religious care-takers -- these have been going on for ages. Some people even believe that a particular idea, or a supernatural guardian, can solve their problems for them.

I once read that there were 6400 *imam-zadeh* shrines officially registered in Iran. These are small and large shrines, all over the country, which are believed to have been built on the grave of a direct or indirect descendant of the prophet of Islam. But more informed people know that quite often these places are not what they claim to be. For example, some of them are remnants of ancient Zoroastrian Fire Temples, bearing architectural marks that could go back more than a thousand years before Islam. Even in Israel, it was recently discovered that a place believed for centuries to be a shrine of a saint was indeed nothing but the mausoleum of an Ottoman King!

The Mediaeval Christians believed in many Patron Saints, each of whom was to be "invoked" against a certain category of illnesses or was believed to protect a given place, profession, etc. An exhaustive list of these saints could contain as many as several hundreds of names! Here are a few examples:

- **Saint Apollonia: tooth-ache;**
- **Saint Augustine of Hippo: sore eyes;**
- **Saint Bernardino of Siena: lung problems, gambling addictions;**

- Saint Blaise: ailments of the throat;
- Saint Dymphna: sleepwalking, epilepsy, mental illness;
- Saint Leodegar: blindness;
- Saint Nonnosus: diseases of the kidneys, back pains, and school-related students' crises;
- Saint Rasso: stomach pains, especially in children;

This gentleman must have been a very busy fellow:

- Saint Erasmus of Formiae: stomach pain in children and other intestinal ailments and diseases, women's cramps at labor, and cattle pest. Besides, he was the Patron Saint of Sailors, as well a few locations – Gaeta, Formia, and Fort St. Elmo;

Hollywood might specially like this one:

- Saint Lawrence: Patron Saint of Comedians, as well as Butchers and Roasters;

And when everyone else failed, there was always in waiting:

- Saint Jude Thaddaeus: the Patron Saint of lost causes and desperate situations.

Even today, there are some Christians who continue to believe in such nonsense. They refuse to see a doctor, even if they are dying of pain! How can any modern human resort to such superstitions, relying on this holy talisman or that prayer, reading this book or that, or calling out to that saint, or even sacrificing a poor animal as a "cure" to their problems?

In the past, when a patient suffered from acute appendicitis, they would lay him on the floor and quickly recite several pages of prayers, in order that he should feel better. In old times, many patients died of a burst appendix. Today, of course, we know that acute appendicitis is a serious medical emergency which often requires immediate surgery – and which the great majority of patients survive without complications.

Still more frustrating is hearing some dubious people who "oblige the book" and sheepishly claim that perhaps there might have been some truth to some of these old remedies! In the ignorant past when the patient died, people would blame it on the "evil eye" of this or that poor person. Even today, there are some people who don't realize the only solution to certain medical problems is "the sharp knife"!

Dear educators, there are times when prayers can be useful to console or even cure the mind and spirit. But prayers alone are not enough to cure a patient; modern science and a skilled physician are also required. In other words, I agree with religion but not in the way the fanatics do.

I'm not from the earth, but a bird from the garden of Heaven,
Confined in this cage of a body for a few days.
Who's the one in my ears that hears my song?
Who's the one who puts words in my mouth?
Who's in my eyes that sees the outside world?
Or what's this life, to which I have become like a shirt?
I didn't come to this place, nor will I leave it, on my own –
The One who brought me here, He will take me back to my home.
You shouldn't think that I say these poems to myself,
Since as long as I am awake, I won't say a word.

Those who live for themselves will someday die – forever.
But those who die for others shall remain alive – for eternity.

I salute those people who choose humanity over color, race or religion. As the poet wrote,

A love based on colors and appearances
Would end not in love, but in shame.

Or as another poet stated, I already know about death, but only if you could just show me a shortcut to the home of a friend....

Mankind learned many of its discoveries and innovations from nature itself. Avian migration alone could be read as a textbook by itself. For instance, have you ever wondered why birds fly in groups, lining up behind each other? Scientists have found out that they do this because the bird in front is actually "breaking the air" for the rest of the flock. That's why a group of migrant birds can fly about 71% longer than a single bird. They hardly leave the line, and they always return to it promptly. To avoid exhaustion, the job of the harbinger, i.e., the leader of the pack, is a rotating job; at certain intervals, the bird in front flies to the end of the flock, while another bird takes its place. Meanwhile, the birds on the back of the flock make much noise to "cheer on" their harbingers!

As with migrant birds, whenever human beings and societies have joined together, they have accomplished much more. It's sad that we don't do this more. If only nature had taught us the secret of cooperation the way it did to geese, we would have become much better team players, and we would be living in a world of much more heart-felt cooperation.

Migrant birds could also teach us something about compassion. During this very long journey, if a member of the flock falls ill, two other geese will land alongside the bird and stay with it until it has recovered. If only mankind learned more from nature, instead of following superstitions, she could truly appreciate the beauty of God's creations.

The great German Jewish philosopher, **Ernest Cassirer** (1874-1945) once said that "the fate of a nation was decided by its myths," – and, I add, by its religions. Throughout history, people interpreted myths in accordance with their time. In ancient times, many people didn't have many options to gain information other than to listen to the *mullahs*. Still over time some people grew to become rational individuals, while others turned into ignorant, narrow-minded fanatics, who even in the absence of the *mullah*, would refuse to let go of their holy books!

Once, the philosopher **Immanuel Kant** (1724-1804) was asked how people became intellectuals. He replied that **mankind would reach its intellectual maturity on the day he gets rid of the need for a guide and relied on his own intellect.** On another occasion, he remarked that **people looked more like their leaders than their parents!**

Perhaps our Jewish community in Iran was so unified because we didn't have regressive clerics among us. We had a very enlightened and moderate religious leader who didn't take *fatwas* from another rabbi. Back in Iran, we didn't see much of the regressive nonsense that we see in today's Jewish community.

An "intellectual" is one whose rational perception of subjects takes precedence over prejudice and emotion. Such people don't feel any obligation to limit themselves to the study of a single idea or religion. They never refrain from doing research or investigating the facts and they never refuse to hear the truth. Intellectuals place clear thinking ahead of any superstition and prejudice, and they seek modern knowledge, rather than heeding someone's *fatwas!* They heed the words of Louis Pasteur – what we are today is a product of what we have learned before. The extremists, on the other hand, try to explain everything – except what goes on in their heads. Instead they rely on others to do their thinking for them; and they depend on some ancient biblical *fatwas* to make their decisions!

My friends, single-mindedness is as undesirable a quality in an intellectual as it is in a regressive traditionalist. Only where a healthy mind rules, can you see a winner. Even though the regressors have made mistakes, it doesn't mean that I am always right! I simply suggest that logic does not follow those who give in to their emotions.

The knowledge of God is based on reason, not emotion. We shouldn't misguide our youngsters by manipulating their emotions. We can solve rational problems with some effort, but multi-faceted emotional dilemmas are next to impossible to fix. I don't hope to change the traditional extremists but I intend to prevent the expansion of regression by spreading awareness.

Comte de Buffon (Georges-Louis Leclerc, 1707-1788) said that human will is potentially strong enough to rein in all our powers, but only if it is fortified by reason, not our emotions.

I hope someone hears my cries that society might someday forget the words and deeds of the regressors, but they will never forget our silence and indifference against them.

The story is told that one night, an idiot rode a bus for the first time in his life. At some point, he walked to the driver and whispered in his ears, "Sir, all the passengers are asleep, so why are you still driving?!" Likewise, some friends warn me, "Why do you keep on writing and preaching, when no one seems to listen?" You, my reader, will be the judge…

The Greek philosopher **Socrates** (469-399 B.C.E.) was speaking of knowledge, when someone protested that people won't accept such ideas. The wise thinker responded by saying that **a man should say what is true in essence**, and that he wasn't obligated to make people accept his words.

Aristotle said that to reason meant to choose the option that offers the lesser harm. Indeed, intellect was given to humans so that they

could weigh things in terms of their harm or benefit. Religious
followers often mistake obeying the nonsensical or dangerous *fatwas*
of some clerics, with piety. They never ask if it's a sin to avoid
nonsense?! In the end, everything depends on the reader's perception
and judgment, irrespective of what the author has offered.

Everyone takes as much from God's blessings as he can,
You can't blame the oceans, if your pot is too small…

The God of the wise people is wise, as the God of the ignorant people is ignorant!

Whether we like it or not, a human's thoughts stem from his
beliefs. Thus, a misplaced prejudice can act like a filter that prevents
us from seeing the world clearly. This is why a prejudiced person is
never interested in changing his ways or beliefs. He imagines
"flexibility" to be a sin and he can't accept that human beings can
indeed improve their individual and collective environments by
changing and adapting themselves to the world.

By now, you have surely noticed that I find these made-up laws for
our days of rest and festivities, including the Sabbath, particularly
troubling. These include prohibitions for using everything from
electricity and cars to TV and telephone – and yes, amplified speakers
in synagogues. Back in Iran, we were never concerned about such
things. For many years after we arrived in this country, neither
Chacham Yedidiya Shofet, nor his son, Rabbi David, as well as many
other religious leaders, had any problem with this issue. All
synagogues had speakers, and all people used phones and drove cars
on Sabbath and holidays.

I wondered why these prohibitions were suddenly of concern. I
soon learned that it was the Eastern European *mullahs* who sought to
prevent people from doing work or business on Sabbath. Rather than
examining the original meaning and purpose of these prohibitions,

they prefer to follow the ban blindly, literally and by rote. This seems to be no different than someone who decides to protect children from drowning by shutting down the swimming pool, instead of building protective fences around it. Frankly, I find it so sad that some Iranians have opted to follow these unreasonable rules.

Let us ask who are these authorities, in the first place? What rational legitimacy or reasonable argument is there to support their claims? What are the harms or benefits of such regulations? From where I stand, it's all harm, and no benefit. If someone wants to rest, he or she doesn't need to drive a car, etc. Indeed, contrary to the claims of these fanatics, often the very use of these tools, such as electricity, cars or elevators, is a means to help us rest and relax. In fact, the use of air conditioning or electric lights is not forbidden. As was the case with the "make-believe sales" of land or food during the years of *shemita* or the days of *Passover,* that I discussed earlier, such hypocritical bans are the product of misinterpretations, not commandments.

Just a few years ago, on a Sabbath, a middle-aged Jewish couple decided to walk the stairs to reach the upper floor of a high building. Needless to say, by the time they got to the apartment, they were out of breath. Some neighbors, who saw the couple in such distress, asked them, "Why didn't you take the elevator?" They explained that it was the day of rest, and that they were not permitted to use the elevator. The neighbors exclaimed in a surprised tone, "What kind of a rest is this, when you can't breathe anymore for having taking the stairs?!"

Even more ridiculous is riding the so-called *kosher* automatic elevators that stop on every floor on the Sabbath or Jewish holidays – just so the so-called "observant" Jews don't have to push the elevator button. This is nothing more than a pretentious hypocrisy, a *de facto* attempt at deceiving ourselves and our God! Such behavior is an insult to our intellect and to our heritage. Making up prohibitions will only lead to our being taken over by delusions.

Subjecting a group of naïve or otherwise susceptible people to harsh indoctrinations is nothing short of "brain-washing." These religious zealots alienate their followers from friends and family, "anesthetize" them, and see to it that they completely acquiesce to their beliefs, with no resistance. Soon, like the honey-bees who can see nothing but flowers in a garden, they too cannot see anything but these religious beliefs, even though their eyes are fully open and imagine this senseless, illogical submission to be a "virtue" that will bring them "heavenly rewards."

I have seen this first hand. A so-called religious friend of mine, who is quite rational and normal in business and most social settings, becomes a completely different person when a religious issue comes up. Then he suddenly turns into one of those old time (non-Jewish) fanatics we used to see in Iran and I can hardly recognize my old friend anymore.

One recent Sabbath, when his wife, who is nine months pregnant, suddenly began to cry out in pain, she asked her family to get her to the hospital, as soon as possible. As their car waited in the garage, this rigid-minded husband stopped to consider the laws of the Sabbath and tried to recall what the *mullahs* had said about driving on a Jewish holiday. Fearing that he might commit a sin, he asked a man who worked in a neighborhood shop to drive his wife to the hospital, while the "religious" husband walked several miles to get there!

He should have known very well that during emergencies, especially in life and death situations, violating a prohibition, including some of these made-up laws, or even major commandments, would not only be alright, but even required – even under the strictest interpretation of Jewish law. We should pity the person who is more concerned about his Rabbi's approval than his wife's well-being, and so blinded by his devotion to his Rabbi that he can't reason for himself the obvious and essential elements of Jewish law that always favor preserving life. We should despise those preachers who instill so much fear in this gullible group that they can no more think for themselves and do the right thing.

The traditionalists would have you believe that the commandments are immutable, as are all the rules and regulation under which they suffer – and with which they make others suffer! But this is not so. The commandments have always been subject to interpretation –in accordance with their times. Rather than worrying that change will invalidate the commandments, to the contrary, it makes them relevant to our lives. When someone claims that religious laws are "unchanging," he is in fact projecting the rigidity of his own mind.

Our regressive traditionalists have demonstrated that they have no problem changing their laws when it suits them such as with the *Shemita* or "make-believe sales" that originated in the Eastern European ghettos. No, it is only the ideas that their own *mullah* didn't come up with that they disapprove. Does it make sense that God Almighty would give human beings the gift of intellect to come up with ways to fool themselves? Or did he grant them wisdom so that they might improve and make easier their lives and the lives of others?

In truth, they care more about who said something, than what he said! To them, the truth of the words, or whether they are reasonable, is not important. **Ralph Waldo Emerson** (1803-1882) put it so succinctly when he said that the only problem with truth was its frightening face! No wonder the regressors are so afraid of the truth that they try to scare other people of it, as well.

George Bernard Shaw once said, "Experience is a great teacher, but its fee is too expensive!" Can humanity still afford to pay for

Religion's mistakes? I was present at a meeting when a high ranking Orthodox cleric told a patient with an incurable disease, who had already given them all he had, that "If you donate 500,000 dollars to us, we and 4000 students of the *yeshiva* will pray for your health!" What worth can prayers motivated by financial incentives, have? Can we call such people "spiritual leaders"? **Not everyone is like them. But all of them have known behavior like this!**

If the night bird can't see well during the day,
Don't be surprised, because its vision is imperfect.

I am convinced that as a result of their religious brainwashing and its consequences, in the near future a strong global movement against religion will rise. I suspect this movement will be of such sweeping dimension that we cannot yet predict its good or bad consequences. This rather natural, self-initiated movement won't be against any particular religion, but against religion in its broader sense. It might not happen in our lifetime, but I'm certain that our grandchildren, if not our children, will benefit from it. The more religious nonsense is promulgated by the regressive extremists, the sooner this movement will arrive. In a way, we already see the vanguard of this movement among those who continue to call themselves the followers of their ancestral religions, even though they no more believe in them. However, in a few generations, they won't even remember know their former religion's name.

If we intend to survive, we'd better maintain our intellectual moderation, rather than repeating the outdated deeds and thoughts of ancient times. It doesn't hurt to repeat the words of Nietzsche: "Let's stay awake to sleep well!"

Just consider the catastrophe that has occurred in Algeria to understand the dangerous power of religious and ideological indoctrination. In the 1980's alone, more than 200,000 innocent

Muslims were murdered by other Muslims who considered themselves more religious. They were murdered for no reason – other than as a by-product of their indoctrination. A brainwashed man has no will of himself, as he remains a dummy in the hands of the puppeteers.

When the famed Persian poet **Naser Khosrow** (1004-1088 C.E.) pondered the massacres committed by History's God-worshipping murderers, he wrote,

God, I am right when I say it's all your fault,
But I just keep silent out of fear!
If you didn't have a problem,
Why did you create murderers?
You warn the poor dear to run,
Yet to spur the hunter to run after her!

D. H. Lawrence (1885-1930) wrote that every failure has at least this advantage: that we learn about one road that leads to failure. May I ask, after so many years of tragedy, what more do we need to learn from these historical roads that lead to failure?! Why do these so-called leaders keep repeating the mistakes of the past in the name of religion?

Wasn't the tragedy of Yigal Amir enough for us? I say *tragedy*, because Yigal Amir, who assassinated the Israeli PM Yitzchak Rabin, was a product of brainwashing.

Religious indoctrination is one of the most dangerous and horrifying powers the world has ever known. The examples are many: It's said that a convoluted reading of a single religious verse caused the wild and brutal Mongolian attacks on Iran, in about 1219 C.E.

One of the first, and best known innovator of religious brainwashing was the Persian **Hassan Sabbah** (1050-1124 C.E.), the founder of the *Hash-shashin* sect. They lived in the mountains, in the Castle of Alamut and were known for murdering their enemies. (The word "assassin" is a Latinized version of the name of this sect.) Sabbah exerted incredible mental and psychological control over his followers by the use of indoctrination and drugs (most notably *hashish*, hence their name), so much so, that they wouldn't hesitate to throw themselves off the cliffs of Alamut, if he ordered them to do so.

During the Inquisition, the Christian Church literally burned innocent human beings in the name of their religion. As the victim cried, the priests would tell the ignorant crowd to look at the raging flames, and see how "the sinful souls of the victims" were trying to reach up to the heavens!

It's up to us to live as our humanity demands us to. We are responsible for making sure that our species deserves its name. Certainly, anyone who doesn't heed life, his own or others, cannot be called a human.

If I've any share of faith, I just know that I'm a human.
I also think that there's only one God, and that I'm humbled before sincere men.
And that I know nothing outside the circle of love, kindness and friendship.

Scientists tell us that modern man, despite thousands of years of evolution, still uses a mere 5% of his brain capacity. At the same time, today it is said that the pace of scientific progress doubles every year. In this light, how can we expect that every notion conceived or expressed by the commentators of the past be taught verbatim?

Human beings are born to evolve and excel, and not to merely ape the past.

It's no sin to refuse to follow every religious code and commandment – or not to do so literally. The true sin is to prefer blind imitation of the past over rational understanding of the present. Not everything is worth being taught or obeyed.

The key to happiness lies in constantly learning new things; but it's also necessary to let go of wrong ideas from the past. Mankind is designed to evolve and make progress. The opportunities before us today are as never before. The negative beliefs of a group of people, who've gone through a long and bitter history of pain and suffering, are an outcome of their tragic experiences. However, there is no advantage in repeating the problems of the past – instead we must let go of the past to move on and reconsider the immense possibilities that the modern world has to offer.

Every society shows signs of the world-view, culture, and environment in which it grew. The beliefs and ideas of the Eastern European *ghettos* have little in common with Iranian Jewish culture, if anything.

The freedom to worship remains one of the most fundamental rights. Nonetheless a religion and its followers are only worthy of respect if they observe their beliefs reasonably without interfering in other people's lives in the name of some *mitzvah* or *savab*, i.e. some "rewarding good deed." According to **Rumi**,

"What a huge difference between a curious, inquisitive mind and an imitator!
The former is like the Judge, while the latter is just an empty sound.
The voice of the former comes from a sincere heart, which has known suffering,
While the imitator repeats whatever worn out ideas he learned.
Both the blasphemer and the pious man mention God, but
There is a sharp difference between the two:

That poor man speaks of God to earn his bread,
While the believer mentions God in fear of his life."

Goethe went so far as to place individual thinking and understanding above the law. In his opinion, law was reserved only for when there was no room left for individual thought and perception.

The true sin is "not to understand" the consequences of sin. To put the guise of religion on some superstitions, in the name of fearing sins and Hell, is itself a sin. Sin means promoting imitation. One who sins is one who has not understood truth. Moreover, he misleads others into his ways, via imitation.

The American **President Franklin. D. Roosevelt** (1882-1945) famously said, "The only thing we have to fear is fear itself." The forces of regression take advantage of this human weakness. Much of the reasoning offered by the fanatic religious ideologies is based on unfounded fear. Day after day, in the name of "rewarding deeds," which are supposed to be the opposite of "sins," they are spreading tyranny, hatred and hostilities, both within families, as well as throughout society at large.

"Thou, the chief of the caravan of pilgrims!
You don't flaunt your arrogance or piety before my eyes!
Because where you see a house, I see the house of God.

Dear responsible educators who hold office,

If you continue to ignore the dignity and the true rank and place of the Jewish people and its religion by propagating nonsense and superstition, then it will be by your standards that the world will judge us. They will consider us as fanatics and judge us as a backwards group of hypocrites ruled by superstition — and you will be responsible for that catastrophe.

Truth is above faith. If there is no truth in my belief or yours, our faith is worthless. No vegetable can grow in a salty desert. Faith is not attained from a *mullah* or a book, no matter how holy; it's gained from understanding the truth of the commandments. The love for observing the commandments can only arrive when the beloved has understood the love.

Is there any reasonable person, who could deny the *Ten Commandments*, which apply universally to all times?

"I'm just a particle within the essence of creation, and thus, I'm eternal.
I'm a ray from the sun of love, and thus, I'll shine forever."

My friends, we should agree that in order for our religion to continue, we must accept change. Nature is constant, yet always changing and evolving. Nature is a great source of education, and full of inspiring stories of birth and transformation such as the fable, "The Rebirth of an Eagle." According to this story, an eagle decided to fight the weakening signs of ageing and so never get old. Accordingly, when his beak became soft, his wings heavy and his talons bent, he first broke the beak, then pulled out the talons, and last plucked the feathers, and each time waited for months till fresh new parts grew. Hence, he was able to hunt again, to survive, and to live long beyond his peers, because of this painful transformation.

Although this is a fable whose veracity can't be ascertained it has gained a certain currency recently (See: http://wiki.answers.com/Q/Do_eagles_lose_talons_and_beak_during_a_rejuvenation_process_during_their_lifetime ;http://www.snopes.com/critters/wild/eaglerebirth.asp).

Change is a necessary fact of life. Nature demands we choose between death, on the one hand, and accepting change, on the other. To survive, we have no choice but to improve and update our texts, beliefs and traditions, without changing their essence. It's very much like the myth of the eagle that had to endure pain to live beyond its natural age. Without change and rejuvenation, the powerful becomes the weak, and fades away.

Let's recognize our weaknesses, so that like that mythical eagle, we'll be able to overcome our limitations amid the pain. One of those limitations is regression. As **Hafez** put it,

"Oh, thou, the cupbearer!
We're waiting at the brink of the sea of death.
Hurry up! Be mindful of our chance, which is
Shorter than wine's trip from the lips into the mouth."

It's the law of nature that one day, all of us will become silent, but our words, writings, and the consequences of our actions or inactions will remain. It's a law of nature that a two-day old lamb can already tell the difference between a poisonous grass and a nutritious one, among all the greens in a meadow. We humans are no less than a sheep: Before any commands, we should listen to the voice of our conscience. **Following another person's distinction between good and bad is imitation not independent thinking.**

The criticisms offered in this book can be applied to the regressive beliefs of all religions. Regression grows from arbitrary divisions, it thrives in the "I *vs.* Thou" and the dual oppositions of religions; and it grows by imitation. They try to recruit others "with the softness of the water, yet with its power of penetration," to borrow a phrase from the Chinese philosopher **Lao Tse** (600 B.C.E. – 470 B.C.E., i.e. 130 years!). For instance, they might begin by luring our youth with the warmth and comfort of practicing the *Sabbath,* i.e. by putting aside one day of the week for rest; then they'll go on to completely enslave him, through a fear of sins never committed and its consequences.

My friends, sometimes a proper reminder can be like rainfall in an arid desert. Let's not hold back ourselves from talking and writing; our silence, our indifference might be perceived, or pretended, as our approval.

"They don't know the why, so they wonder at my roaming eyes!
I'm what I showed you, but it's up to them how they wish to take it."

I think...

The greatest misery is, not knowing the cause behind the miseries...

...one of which is anti-Semitism.

Speaking, writing and hearing constructive criticism helps communities understand the reason behind their miseries. One example is the movement that has emerged against superstition in which the majority of our community has participated. This self-initiated popular movement is bound to succeed in removing ignorant beliefs of those who cause divisions among our people.

Victor Hugo once said that misery was a good teacher! No doubt, the Jewish people have learned much as a result of the enormous suffering they've endured through the ages. **Hafez** put it just right:

"Not every tree can tolerate the cruelty of the autumn:
I bring my hats down to the evergreen pine,
For its ability to do just that!"

No stone could be transformed into a priceless antique if it couldn't bear the blows of the master's chisel.

Yes, I'm humbled before the faith of my people who continue to bear such a deep love.

"The pen lacks the tongue needed to tell the secrets of love;
God's attributes go far beyond the limits of writing."

Jewish people are guilty of having offered monotheism to the world, and to date, they have stood by this idea, even at the cost of their lives, because they believe:

"The word can be revealed in full,
Only through a pure mouth:
A droplet of water could turn into a pearl,
Only if it fell between the shells of a clam."

[(*) This refers to an ancient belief that a pearl would begin to form after the clam closed its valves on a droplet of rain.]

From the beginning, the Jewish people have risked their lives, on the road of monotheism. As a scholar put it, as long as the name of God exists in the world, the Jewish people will continue to be persecuted by the Godless!

The renowned contemporary Persian poet, **Forough Farrokhzad** wrote in one of her poems,

"The road begins with "to know" and "to love".
Though its end isn't nearly in sight,
I no more think of the destination:
Just this "knowing", just this "loving", are beautiful."

Those who think only of their own interests or those of their religious group and who are guided by egotism, are confined in prisons of their own selfishness. While we can't save these condemned people, we should try to prevent them from contaminating others.

No issue has been more afflicted by rumors, gossip, expedient interpretations or commentaries than religion. There are also few other causes that have been as exploited to foster malice or prejudice, while providing a way to earn a living. We should cry out when a vulnerable wife or another member of a large family falls prey to the advances of these religious regressors!

238

The late **Muhammad Reza Shah Pahlavi**, the last king of Iran, gave support to religious regressive elements during his reign – this was in keeping with the policies of the West, and as a bulwark against Communism. Little did they know that this "cure" would prove far more dangerous than the "illness."

Similarly, The United States in its battles against Communism pumped too much water into "the houses on fire," in Afghanistan, Iran and many other corners of the world. In the end, although the houses were saved from fire, they were washed away by the flood!

Our own so-called religious friends, too, should learn to maintain a balance in their support of those who claim to keep our Jewish identity alive, and be fearful of those who would replace love and kindness with hatred.

I repeat,

Those who assist a wrong cause, only bring about their own doom.

The regressive traditionalists have never been, and will never be, the guardians of our identity. The regressive traditionalist, in order to promote his own so-called religious ideas, justifies his means, however despicable, by his ends. Such means can include creating rifts among friends and families, or even separating family members, all for their perceived cause. Instead of providing rational justifications, they substitute quotations from their like-minded clerics. For example, they claim that because a certain *mullah* once said such and such in a certain book, no matter how impractical it might be, we should accept it. No matter that reason tells us otherwise, we should still practice it, like a parrot, or by forcing ourselves! They would like us to believe that because they adhere to impractical anachronistic nonsense; it must be divinely inspired and religiously commanded. Nothing could be further from the truth.

The regressors imagine anyone who is a better imitator to be more religious. Their sham observances are thought by the indifferent members of our community to be a way of keeping our tradition alive – and they grant them support.

Meanwhile, when the more rational and serious members of our community cry out that, "We are not the followers of this negligible minority of regressors! We don't share their beliefs!" — no one believes them.

No one will believe us, or think us any different than those regressors, until we fix this flaw of ours. I'm sorry that I can't bring myself to even quote some of the more absurd points of the *halacha*, i.e. "the Jewish law of practices"; but readers can study for themselves, and see whether all of these laws are justified.

The *Talmud* says that, "Whoever is not skeptical, he or she could not study the *Talmud*." A "skeptic" is "curious," "inquisitive," in constant pursuit of truth. Alas, the walls of prejudice hinder the light of truth, and some speculators have kept their communities behind these walls. As **Saadi** wrote,

*"We're victims of our 'self'. Come the Judgment day, and
We'll cry sighs of regret, for not having killed the 'self'.
Alas, this priceless life passed by,
Yet we didn't abandon our mistakes and sins.
Youth came and old age arrived, as when
Night went away and the day arrived; but we didn't wake.
May the Providence help us in His grace; else, don't ever think
That we could get to Heaven, by these acts of the Hellish guys."*

240

Enough of self-deception in the guise of religion! If just you and I join together, even if we are just two among a thousand, we could bring change, we could make science cast its shadow on religion, and we could destroy the dry face of prejudice.

You ask, "To what religion do you belong?" I am the wandering Jew, the traveler of the world. I was raised in sadness and pain. Look at the world's map; cross the borders; and you'll find no land where my people don't live and share in my pain. There are so many who live away from their motherland, yet feel as if they are still there; and so many who live in the motherland, yet feel far from her. But these are not the people called "religious." The so-called observant consider themselves religious but their true characteristics are hypocrisy and bigotry – they will flatter someone while in their presence, but gossip about them in their absence, and exploit their religion as a means to indoctrinate others and to earn their living.

"The wise guru's first sermon is,
'Avoid a the company of a crook. '"

Anti-Semites consider the Jewish people a tribe apart and force them to be separate from others. So it is not without some irony that the zealot Jews, in their own right, consider themselves different from other people. Our enemies considered us different, to impose pain and tyranny on us; while our co-religionists consider themselves different, they claim, to unify us. This might have been a forced necessity in the past; but today, it's surprising that the traditionalists opt for it voluntarily!

I wish such questions as, "What's your nationality?" or "What's your faith, sect, cult or ideology?" were all eliminated from our global lexicon — along with all discriminatory signs, color marks and symbols! Then, no one would bother over such things. That would be, indeed, Heaven on the Earth, because as the poet said,

"Heaven is where people don't bother one another,
Where there's no nuisance, nor any harassment."

At least, we should try to eliminate the causes of sectarian divisions, particularly our internal meddling. It's no one else's business what I eat or wear, or what color I prefer for my clothes. Those who made such choices a religious requirement don't mean well; rather, they're a bunch of opportunists using religion for their own ends, whether it be on the global stage, or more immediately, in our community.

What does it matter to me, for instance, if my good neighbor likes a certain color or flower, or if she is associated with a certain religion or group? And what is it to her, if I'm fond of a certain other flower or color; or if I believe in a certain scripture; or if today, I read a certain book? It is no one's business but our own.

Throughout the millennia, zealots have used religion as a tool to recruit other followers and to form opposing groups. But today, when we all wish to be members of a global community why should anyone opt for separations and pretentions? The *Talmud* repeats, over and over, that while in the Diaspora, regardless of where you live, you should give precedence to the local government.

Those who want to know my religion, merely intend to impose discrimination; and those who wish to be known as religious, are pretenders.

No one has yet discovered a cure or vaccine for the ill of anti-Semitism. Until they do, the regressors should stop providing the grounds for its spread with their misplaced and useless separatist inclinations and narcissistic tendencies. Being religious, we should remember, has no inherent conflict with thinking globally.

The moment any person or community imagines themselves to be the best and the most perfect of all, that's when they begin to fail.

Wise and knowledgeable advocates of religion render great service to humanity, while ignorant ones, with their misplaced self-importance, are society's worst guides.

Back in Iran, we Iranian Jews didn't have such divisions as exist today. It was the Orthodox Jews of Eastern Europe who created division among our community. They claimed to be doing mitzvots, "rewarding deeds," and to be protecting our interests but really they were acting out of misplaced egotism.

For 2700 years we have followed the road of progress. The modest, unassuming Iranian Jewish culture is much richer and more realistic than the superstition-filled culture of the Orthodox Jews of Eastern Europe.

Those European Jews who achieved greatness in science, politics, or finance, and became reasons for our pride, were among those who chose secular universities instead of Orthodox seminaries. If they had stayed confined to the yeshivot, there would have been no Ben Gurion, no Albert Einstein, none of the thousands of other great Jewish men and women — and certainly, no Independence for the Jewish state.

"The long and winding road to Love is before us.
It's an unpaved road, full of hills and valleys.
What's the downhill? To become the dust of the road.
And what's the pinnacle? None other than self-sacrifice."

It is said that we step into the world with closed eyes and an open mouth; and then spend a lifetime struggling to compensate for this mistake of nature!

Prejudice and arrogance deprive mankind of the opportunity to think reasonably. Indeed, a seemingly educated, yet prejudiced person is more dangerous than an illiterate one just as a narcissistic rich person is worse than a modest poor man.

A man who came in to a large fortune asked a wise man, "Give me advice so that I remain as decent and fair as I was before I came to this fortune." The wise old man ordered him to step toward the window, and look at the outside world. Then he asked the man, "What do you see?" The rich man said, "People who are actively trying to earn a living." The sage then asked him to stand before the mirror. "What do you see now?" he asked. The rich man answered, "Myself..." Then the wise and experienced old man told him, "A single thin layer of silver behind the glass caused you to see nothing but yourself. You should strive not to let layers of gold and silver hinder your view, causing you to see only yourself, neglect others, and become fully isolated from the world."

You, who make such a fuss about who, according to you, is religious and non-religious as a way to create opposition among our own people, should not allow the thin or thick artificial coats of the religion to mask your own false self-importance. Such layers or distinctions do not reflect the best of our religion or way of life. These distinctions are only of use to opportunists such as yourself, eager to find a benefit in our divisions, or as a tool to serve your own self-interest.

One who doesn't add to his knowledge, every day, his knowledge will be of no use.

I address the "newly-religious" people by quoting **Rabbi Ezrahian,** who wisely said that, "The more you become familiar with modern knowledge and science, the better you'll understand the *Torah, Talmud* and *Zohar*. Ignorance of general knowledge causes us not to understand the truth of the Holy Scripture. Don't be content with two or three years of studies in a certain seminary. The *Mishnah* chapters of *Pirkey Avot* say, ***oud la mossif, yassif,*** **that is, whoever**

244

doesn't add to his (knowledge), what he knows (would end) and would be rendered useless.'"

My friends, let's consider on the one hand what our sages have said and on the other, the nonsense that a group of self-proclaimed religious people are promoting. Such nonsense was never a part of Iranian Jewish culture, even though today it's being put forward as the tenets of our religion or the binding principles of a certain sect. **They act like a coat of silver on the back of the glass of religion, reflecting only the regressors' interests in indoctrinating others.**

The best criteria for measuring truth are the power of the ideas being offered. We have had enough of antiquated, narrow-minded, inflexible forced isolation. Let us not see religion used to stymie our youth's advancement. Let us not put them under so much pressure and control, in the name of religion, that they break. Mankind's intellect, when forced to hide under the cover of religion or tradition, loses its shining glory. So much so that when the day comes and they are allowed to speak and write freely, they will have nothing to say but nonsense.

Certainly, you respected reader, will ask, what direct relation is there between becoming religious, and the antiquated way of thinking promoted by the traditionalists? To find the answer, compare two youngsters from your own family, one religious and the other not. You will see for yourself the difference between a rational minded person and a regressor, one who is probably successful and the other not. Thus, you are likely to agree with my point.

It's no service to our youth to waste their time and the irreplaceable opportunities they have in the modern world by having them study golden commentaries (*sic!*) and obsolete issues. Doing so is a sign of intellectual impotence. It's helping them fall into despair and frustration. And it's surely harmful to the philosophy of religion.

Superstition in religion is like poison in food.

Don't let them feed your children with such poisoned food—even though it may be *kosher*! Even *kosher* food can be expired, and thus, poisonous and harmful!

Václav Havel (b. 1936), the Czech thinker, playwright, and a former president of the Czech Republic said, "Where bigotry halts men from thinking, evil emerges, and it takes intellect as his maid."

To understand my point, consider some of the people around you, who were once rather balanced and moderate, but under the influence of religious propaganda changed their ways and attitude. Just look at them and their current condition to see what I mean!

There are many who have no idea what they are talking about.

"I asked him, What's this constant fight over homeland or religion?
He said, 'It's much ado over a meal, or in quest of a bread!'"

I'd like to get your attention to this news clip from our crazy world:

"New Delhi: The Supreme Court of India has decreed that any idol, which after religious rituals, is mounted in a temple as a Hindu god and is being worshipped, has its own legal actuality. This verdict further explains that it's surely not the idol of the Hindu god itself, but people's perception of these sculptures, which has the legal actuality. Thus, the lands and other properties that people endow to these Hindu gods will be legally registered to their names."

"When the beloved doesn't take off her veil,
Why then everyone tell a story of their own imagination?"

Count Axel Oxenstierna (1583-1634), a Chancellor of the world famous Uppsala University of Sweden, said, "You'd be surprised to know that the world is being ruled by so little intellect or understanding."

The spread of these traditionalists doesn't mean that their "flooding springs" have raised the sea level; to the contrary, we should admit that it's our ancestral ship that is being sunk by them, and it's being torn into pieces in the name of "mitzvot"-- rewarding deeds.

Educators in charge! You are the ones responsible for having made our precious youth beg for *mitzvahs*, instead of studying modern science. Every week, we see such embarrassing occurrences as when you compel your adherents to approach strangers, many of them gentiles, asking them to perform "rewarding deeds" that are fully unknown to them. The non-Jews laugh – and we cringe and cry. When you brainwash poor youngsters in your seminaries so much that they become unable to earn a living, let alone defend their country, they are left with no choice but to beg for *mitzvot*.

"You don't attempt to serve Him in return for money,
Because the Master knows how best to take care of His servants."

If the indoctrinated won't listen or change then we should watch over those who still haven't been contaminated. Teachers and educators are to be blamed for spreading nonsense more than the youngsters for believing it. Don't those who train terrorists, and the schools where hatred is being taught, bear as much if not more of the blame than the terrorists themselves? It's one thing to be genuinely religious, and another to pretend to be.

Sigmund Freud, seeing the nonsense attributed to religions, and how the word "imitation" had replaced "adaptation" in the lexicon of the extremists, said, "Religion is a kind of hereditary illness and a brake on civilization!" The actions of extremist advocates of religions have yielded nothing but severe conflicts among us and the world, as well as forced, fabricated observance of rules and traditions.

Until recently, the ancestors of these religious advocates believed a rainbow to be the ladder or gate through which the angels entered and exited our world! They even called any research about the truth of the matter a blasphemy. Have no doubt that the future generation will laugh at many of today's firmly held beliefs.

Let's watch over our children, because miseries can grow in little gardens in which people have cultivated them. Even more sadly, they deny the facts, and plant the same defective seeds again, all in the name of "identity conservation."

Alas, some people have understood from modesty, humility and religiosity, only the mustache and the beard; and because of their long facial hair, they consider themselves pious!

"If I had as much control over my life, as I do over my beard,
I wouldn't let my soul out of my body until the resurrection!"

According to statistics, contemporary humankind considers the 35-year increase in life expectancy to be a direct result of the scientific growth over just the past 100 years.

Was there no religion before then? Religious scriptures, such as the *Halacha* and the writings of different commentators have been around for many centuries, dating back to a time when the average life expectancy was only about 20 to 40 years. However, as time has passed, many commands and laws have proved impractical and obsolete, and thus, politely filed away. Our knowledge has provided us with much scientific fact, some of which literally can help extend or save our life, which sometimes supersedes ancient knowledge. Why then dress up outdated facts in the guise of religion?

Observing the commandments is directly related to the time and place of their practice, except for those people whose interpretive scope seems to be frozen at the times when the commandments were originally offered! Why should we be bound by absurd things like "the product of this or that land" – what land?! The fruit and bread in the baskets before you are each the product of a certain continent, not a particular country or town! Who can tell which city, country or even continent, this apple came from, to be able to practice the laws of *shemita?!* What is this affection for self-deception and pretend "buy and sells"? Do you think so little of God to believe he can't see through your ruses? Let's be honest: To deceive ourselves or others is hypocrisy plain and simple.

Are the religious people of the world able to literally observe all of the religious laws verbatim? Or as the *Holy Torah* explicitly says, should we accept the verdict of the judge of the time, as well? Part of the insecurities of today's world is a result of the efforts of those groups who, in the name of religion, and oblivious to the inevitable progress of modern science, wish to still practice those ancient religious laws literally.

A Jewish sect known as the Karaites, have long wished to observe our religion literally, only based on the *Tanach*, i.e. the Jewish Bible. But have they achieved anything other than scientific, economic and cultural poverty, all due to their rigid ideology?!

If only those who wish to deceive themselves and "remain inside the apple," would stay there! If only the mistaken culture, which imagines a more religious person to be necessarily a better person; would become void and obsolete — then they could find other jobs!

Just look and see what services have been offered to humanity by those whom you call "non-religious" -- services that yourselves benefit from every second of your life. On the other hand, just look around and see what crimes continue to be committed by those who have put on the dress of religion. It's not only religion that makes a better person; but it's the better and more perceptive person who makes his or her religion proud. Most of the valuable or even life-saving discoveries, inventions and scientific advances of our times, the benefits of which we enjoy every minute of our lives, were done by people, many of whom don't even share our religious beliefs.

Indeed, those who use religion as the criteria by which to identify and judge people are the ones who are misguided!

There is much difference between those people, who free of any religious considerations, build nonprofit scientific or defense institutions to provide for the future and the welfare of society, and those, who advocate religion for the so-called benefit of their followers. Look at the list of the names of the benefactors on the walls of hospitals. Do all these generous people, true causes of pride, belong to a single religion? No! They are only humans, and they are only proud of their human identity, and not their religious or traditional identity. They see all humans equally, as deserving, as fellow humans. Yes, there is a big difference between the like of those, who in their time, dug wells at the heart of the desert and built water reservoirs, so that the caravans, whatever their faith or ethnicity, could drink from them—and those who have never done a service, unless there was a witness, a competitor or some self-interest involved!

Consider this true story: Once, a patient was taken to a nonprofit hospital, dedicated by the people of a faith different than his. He needed immediate surgery. Despite the fact that the doctor, who operated on him and saved him from certain death, didn't belong to his faith, either, his one request was that he not receive a transfusion from anyone not of his faith. This strikes me as not only ignorant and prejudiced but ungrateful! This is but one story, and I know more, but there are so many, I can't tell them all.

"I have no fears if the ignorant can't remember me,
But I'd die of sadness if the wise one forgets me."

250

Religion does not make better people, but a decent person can make his religion proud — But surely the so-called religiously observant are not among them! Maintaining the solidarity of families and observing the freedom of other people is much more important than a brand of worship that interferes with the lives of others.

The harm done to society by the regressors and those who follow them blindly, all in the name of God and religion is much worse than the harm caused by a lack of religion. Why do the unambiguous words of *the Ten Commandments*, universally accepted by all people, need any further interpretation? Some people would assert that we are commanded not to alter a word of these commandments. I don't disagree, and I am not for "adding or omitting words" to them. But I believe observing the law literally is wrong and detrimental to the survival of the religion – we need a "living" religion not a dead one – and to do so we need to live the commandments in keeping with our times.

How can it possibly be right to practice the *halacha*, i.e. the extended Jewish religious law, the same way as thousands of years ago, notwithstanding a group of people, who wish to deceive themselves and their God by doing things like those "make-believe trades" at the times of Passover or *shemita*; who wish to gather some robot-like followers around them with their fabricated laws. Anyone who believes that laws are unchangeable has not paid enough attention to Charles Darwin's laws of Evolution – because without it we would still be apes as we were millions of years ago! New scientific findings estimate the age of the universe between 13 to 15 billion years, and the age of our own earth is estimated at about 4.6 billion years. According to this calculation, the age of humankind is no more than a fraction of a second! And yet, we call ourselves "the crown of the creation."

Following the proof of Darwin's theory (1809-1882) of evolution and along with discoveries such as DNA, science has overcome many long-standing religious assumptions, theories and commentaries. As science warns and awakens mankind, human perception, too, evolves and progresses. Those who build their ideas upon a foundation of nonsense and superstition should not be called religious.

In this regard, the story of **Darwin's** theory and the opposition of the **Church** is rather interesting. Darwin was invited to participate in the "1860 Oxford evolution debate," but instead sent his like-minded friend, **Thomas H. Huxley** to present his case. **Bishop Samuel Wilberforce**, the representative of the Church of Oxford ridiculed Huxley and asked whether it was through his grandmother or his grandfather that Huxley considered himself descended from the apes?! To which Huxley famously replied, "I'd rather be descended from an ape than a man who misused his gifts to obscure the truth!"

Consider that Darwin didn't know 99% of what we know today; yet, by sharing the 1% that he knew, he helped establish the growth of the other 99%. Alas, the regressive traditionalists do the opposite, sacrificing that 1% of truth for their 99% of nonsense!

Eventually even the Pope, the representative of God (!), officially accepted Darwin's theory. To become free from the rein of regressive ideas and backward people, can only be achieved by spreading knowledge and acquiring science. Otherwise, those who rise to deceive themselves and others will have no way but being deceived. Let's avoid such people. **Saadi** wrote,

"The one who weaves a straw-rug is a weaver, too,
But he wouldn't be let in a silk factory!
A wise man of a clear mind, wouldn't assign
An ignorant to sensitive tasks."

Yes,

One who loves life and humankind,
He'd step foot in the way of growth.
If there is a ray of God's light in your heart,
Love would come herself to your home."

The history of a nation is the memory of its people. Actions and ideas that are not reasonable or that cause poverty will not last. No one has ever reached the sea by crossing the river instead of sailing down its length -- they only ended up in marshes and swamps! Let us remove from religion that nonsense which is the cause of regression.

You may have forgotten that up until about 65 years ago, religious leaders recommended that a knife be used to draw a line on the ground around someone who had fainted in order to protect that poor person from genies (rather than getting them oxygen)! Rainbows were thought to be an angels' ladder; and when a solar or lunar eclipse took place, religious people were commanded to fast to neutralize this sign of God's wrath!

In this time of intellectual darkness, they lived afraid of genies and fairies. To keep these spirits and the evil eye away, they would resort to brandishing nails and skewers, and took refuge in all sorts of psychic and astrological tricks, such as tarot cards, psychic cups, rolling dice, and many more unspeakable things! Can we possibly claim that such empty and/or despicable deeds should be practiced today just because our ancestors believed in them?

Such nonsense and superstition are not the way to maintain our identity – those who refuse to follow such antiquated practices should not be intimidated by the threat of being labeled non-religious. In the past, when people living in villages migrated to larger cities, they would abandon many rural superstitions. Today, living as we do in highly civilized cultures all over the world, one would expect such rural superstitions to be gone. Yet it is hard to believe that there are those who do just the opposite and not only remain entrenched in their backward mentality but also seek to entrap our children in it, in the name of religion (!).

Until recently, even our European-educated physicians believed that tuberculosis could best be treated in hospitals and sanitariums built in the mountains where the air was "better." Today, like many other wrong ideas of the past, this notion has been refuted: it turns out that mountain air has a much lower concentration of oxygen! Given what we now know, should we just continue with the old ignorant ways, simply because they were traditions?!

You still claim in your sermons and writings that the *khazineh* and *mikveh*, i.e. "traditional water cisterns for ritual bath," are preferred over the modern shower — because it's part of the tradition and was written about in some long-ago commentaries! For you building mikveh is so important, you are willing to sell the synagogue, if necessary, to do so!

Up until recently, our ancestors blamed God when a handicapped child was born — and we protested to Him directly! Today, however, we know better and look for the cause and its cure in our family genes or those of our spouse. This reminds me of yet another superstition, that many marriages between close kin were thought to have been "pre-determined in Heavens!" Today, we take refuge in science which is capable of preventing the misery that can result from the birth of a child with severe deficits.

Let us come to know God through reason and science. Those who preach nonsense in the name of religion believe neither in the power of intellect, nor science or morality. But they do believe in practicing the traditions! Only if they would realize that when our ancestors said, "Two cousin's engagement is made in Heaven!" they meant, "So that they would never get married on the Earth!" Today, in the light of new scientific findings, people have realized that not even the ancient Biblical bans on the marriage of immediately close kin is enough, as we now avoid marrying, in certain circumstances, even distant relatives. Is this, I ask, defying the commandments, or to the contrary, improving on them according to their original intent?

Abraham, the patriarch of all Abrahamian religions, circumcised himself about 3700 years ago, it is said, using a sharp piece of hard stone. But today, should we do circumcision the same way, just because "it's the tradition?!"

When the Jewish people said, *na'asseh ve-nishma,'* i.e. "we act first, then we listen," it was never intended to mean that we wouldn't act better in the future.

Educators in charge! If you still believe in maintaining the traditions, why not use the traditional tools or even the medicine of just 70 years ago, such as the Persian herbals remedies like "shir khesht", "se pestan", or "flous"? When it comes to your health you prefer the best of modern medicine and its drugs. If you believe so strongly in tradition, why not use those old ways instead?

Understanding promotes better action. As it's said, "While the heir of the state is too young, there is no difference between him or the servants, even though he owns the entire property to himself." This notion applies as well to our inherited laws.

Have you noticed that, recently, people leave the hall during a sermon as a sign of protest? As days pass, such judgments will become more common. A Yiddish proverb says, "The silence of the wise is more eloquent than a lecture by an ignorant."

Through history, silence by cowards has led to the annihilation of millions. Brave men and women, on the other hand, continue to shape history.

Mikhail Gorbachev (b. 1931), one of the world's bravest heroes, had a major role in bringing down the Soviet regime. During his historic address to the Soviet parliament during the last months of the regime, he courageously revealed facts about the crimes of **Stalin** (1878-1953), who was responsible for the murder of tens of millions of their compatriots. Suddenly, the page of the parliament handed him a note. Gorbachev read aloud the anonymous note, which said, "Mr. Gorbachev! Given that you had a role in the Stalinist regime, why did you keep your silence back then?!" Gorbachev, from behind the tribune, asked the author of the note to step forward. No one did. He repeated his request two more times, but still no one rose.

Then Gorbachev said, "Dear sir, for the very reason that even today, years after Stalin's death, you can't speak openly. I, too, could not speak out at the time. But today I have a responsibility to speak out, and I stand by my words." As so he did, until that tyrannical regime collapsed.

Let us, at least, be brave enough to remind others of our own shortcomings.

The worse danger is unfounded fear. Let's avoid self-censorship. We shouldn't be afraid of speaking out openly in our strange new land; here, we are fortunate to enjoy freedom of speech, and we should put this freedom to good use.

"I don't ask you to be a sun-loving lizard or a butterfly,
But once you've thought of burning in your love of light,
Do it ever so bravely."

Gorbachev bravely informed the world of the truth and warned everyone who imagined otherwise that their good fortune would not last forever.

"The grace of God would put up with so much of you,
But once it spilled over, shameful things will be revealed."

He told the world about those terrible times when, as a Persian poet wrote,

"The ways of the wise became hidden,
While the work of mad men was spread;
Art became humiliated, while magic found rank;
Truth became hidden, while evil was revealed."

Alas, religion and politics have always been exploited by the speculators of the world.

"God, don't approve of what they've done,
Closing the winery, only to open houses of deceit and hypocrisy!
Hafez, wait and see what happens to that ragged cloak,
When tomorrow angry mobs pull out a silk belt from its underneath!"

Winston Churchill, the British Prime Minister, was among the first political leaders in the world to warn of the dangers of Nazism, as he did in his speech before the British Parliament in 1933. Yet no one listened. Not long after, Germany attacked several countries, including England, setting the world on fire. If America had understood Churchill's warning from the outset, and if **Chamberlain,** the British Prime Minister who preceded Churchill had stood up to Germany instead of bribing Hitler with his policy of appeasement, 40 million human lives would have been spared.

The German philosopher, **Immanuel Kant** (1724-1804) wrote that, "The goal of education is not just to learn facts, but to learn values." Does what the students of fundamentalist schools study in the traditional seminaries give them the tools to make correct decisions for today's world?

Many microbes die at 100 degrees Centigrade, yet some survive at much higher temperature. Bigotry, prejudice, ignorance and narrow-mindedness, like those tough microbes, can survive forever. The major problem with religious prejudice is its endurance. The educators, teachers and other officials of these so-called religious schools, as well as the so-called fundamentalist preachers and all their advocates and supporters, would do well to heed this simple message:

"A wise man would never build a house
Which could collapse by a sneeze.
You weave a web, only to be swept away,
You draw a design, only to be damaged.
You build a foundation, yet loose and defunct,
And when you build a nice design, you draw it on water..."

Depending on religion seems to be a natural human drive. But we shouldn't let bigotry and misplaced passion turn this impulse into hatred toward other people. When a fanatic kills himself and others in the name of religion, it's not just because of that hatred, but also because he wants to end his own feelings of hatred. Religious and factional hostilities have been the deadliest of germs on earth.

It's up to us to begin at the outskirts of hatred, patiently removing pebbles of superstition, in order to succeed some day in eradicating this formidable mountain of hatred.

Let us examine some examples:

There were a handful of Popes who were cruel and tyrannical, taking the lives of others. However the majority have been honorable, caring and sympathetic toward their fellow human beings. Both types of Popes cited identical holy books. This leads me to believe that the difference among them stems not from their religion, but the conscience and piety of each individual Pope. It is not the religious commandments, in of themselves, which contain so many conflicts and contradictions that has determined their actions. The cruelest have gone so far as to set people on fire justifying their actions with their religion — as indeed happened over and over during the Inquisition, in Spain, France and elsewhere. On the one hand, these religious texts say , "Don't murder! Don't rape! Don't steal!" Yet, they permit or even obligate their followers to pillage their neighbors! They say, "Don't lie!" — but allow, encourage and even command their followers to lie to propagate their religion.

Throughout history, zealots have turned commandments from bad into worse, allowing the worst of tragedies to occur. They did so to satiate their own blood-thirsty nature, achieving their malicious goals all in accordance with their religious beliefs. Given the diverging ways in which each religion can interpret the dictates of their faith, any attempt at interfaith dialogue depends on each faith reconciling the contradictions present in their own religion.

Today, under the auspices of the United Nations and other human rights organizations, the Vatican, the Al-Azhar, and our own respected Rabbis, many well-intended interfaith gatherings have been convened to promote dialogue between religions as well as faith-based cooperation to support human rights worldwide. Yet in the end, most of these gatherings end with their representatives back at square one, having achieved almost no results.

The reason is simple: Each religious representative carries a book under his arms that is full of contradictions and rife with declarations against any "other"! The only solution depends on these representatives agreeing to go beyond a literal reading and interpretation of their sacred texts, and adopt a contemporary approach and worldview.

Until then, only the *Holy Torah* (*Deuteronomy*, Ch. 17) commands us to accept the verdict of the judge of our time. "The judge of our time" means the requirements of contemporary civilization.

Can humanity tolerate anymore of the miseries that are attributed to religion?

How often have we heard or read about an evil person who arises in some corner of the world and who, in the name of religion, wishes to set his followers and the world aflame. Even when calm prevails, we know that it is just a pause in a never-ending cycle of religious violence and hatred. This cycle will only be broken only if humanity arrives at religious reconciliation by adjusting our interpretation of the sacred words to our time. This is a necessary pre-condition for any meaningful peace to be achieved.

The horrible social problems and horrendous crimes committed in the name of religion, and even their culprits, are ultimately passing. But religious hostilities, which originate from the discriminatory commands of the religions, remain over time. Even such beasts as **Nero**, **Ghenghis Khan**, **Hitler**, **Eichmann**, **Pol Pot** (1928-1998), and their ilk, left the planet; but religious prejudice and their source books and traditions continue to be the cause of catastrophes and mass murders all over the globe – one day by a beard; another day, by a shaved head.

Thus, the best parts of religions disappear, which reminds me of **Rumi**, who wrote,

*"The flower was plundered, only the thorn remained behind.
They took the treasure, and only the snake was left behind."*

My dear reader,

To remove all signs of unreasonable prejudice, we must begin with ourselves and our families, so that we will not pass along an irrational heritage to the next generation. **Otherwise, the situation will continue until science can fully overcome religious prejudice.**

Science deals with the observable, not the imagined. By contrast, today's misguided religious followers are led by bigotry, prejudice and their belief in the existence of an afterlife to cause rifts among families and communities, causing evil and endangering the lives of the others.

A bigoted religious person imagines that his opposition to other religions is a matter of religious piety and views his doing so on a par with observing any other religious command. Science, on the other hand, at its best, values life, and not just human life, but also the life of animals and plants, and it tries to improve their conditions, devoid of any prejudice.

Throughout the ages, the most fatal social virus has been the handing over of wrong religious beliefs from one generation to the other. We should do our part to prevent this from happening to our future generation. We should consider doing so to be a leak-proof way to preserve of our identity! We need to ask ourselves: which identity is worth preserving, a nonsensical identity or a rational one?

Dear parents and educators, remember that our beliefs determine how we think. The difference between a successful and a hopeless society is the distinction between the rational beliefs of the former versus the irrational beliefs of the latter. Reasonable beliefs lead to making logical decisions. Mankind creates what he believes, and accordingly, leaves behind positive or negative achievements. The explosion of irrational beliefs and their entailed corruption, as we can readily see, has made the world into an unsafe place.

Fanatics pay no attention to the expiration date of beliefs. For them beliefs are frozen in time, never to be changed. They fear thinking differently, and are afraid of those who do so. Fooling ourselves and deceiving our children won't lead to the survival of our religion and society. To the contrary, this can only lead to regression and backwardness.

Throughout the dark ages of ignorance, the world of religion was what they believed in with all its attendant bigotry, magical thinking and superstitions. We can still see the destructive consequences of those old-time ideologies, when someone says, "Whoever doesn't agree with me is against me, though he be my brother or my son!"

A wise man would ask,

"Tell me, what's the nature of fate?
What can we do about a poor destiny?"

While the ignorant thinks that fate is written in stone,

"Mankind plans, but he doesn't know of fate!
No devised plan can stand God's pre-destined will!"

We can understand how a flawed faith could lead to hopelessness, and how it has led many a person away from self-consciousness. Indeed, a bigot is a tool in the hands of a manipulator **because,**

A balanced, moderate benefits from intellect, even as he's devoid of prejudice; while an imbalanced person is all prejudice, no intellect.

Have the bigots ever asked themselves why God left the task of solving the problem of diseases to science and not to the religious clerics?! Could it be that diseases are transferred by microbes and cured by science, rather than by prayers or curses or by shielding against the evil eye or the devil, or by miracles and their like!?

The only prayer that is sometimes effective is a sigh! It's the backlash and punishment for oppression. It's the anger of the oppressed. It's the cry coming from the heart of the wronged innocent. Saadi best portrayed this, when he wrote,

"Sometimes, the fire in a sigh can leave an impact,
Sometimes, a simple look can set someone on fire.
Sometimes, the cry of silence fills the air,
Just from the look in the eyes of an innocent.
The anger and hatred of a poor old woman

Could sometimes bring down a king from his throne.
The painful cries of a distraught man
Can sometimes break the lines of an army.
If you've neglected the burn of the sighs of the people,
Heed that sometimes, an army can burn from the heat of a sigh.
Listen to the humble Saadi's counsel, coming from his heart,
Since sometimes, a blind man can lead the crowd."

Could a large library of prayers and thousands saying prayers ever replace the effectiveness of a single capsule of penicillin? Would they even have any effect? How long should we continue to deceive ourselves and others about prayer vs. medicine? What is the reason for continuing in your ways: because you have seen its positive effect or because those in your family or sect won't allow you to change your ways? Do you truly believe that animal sacrifice as observed in the olden days, was an effective antidote to that time's suffering and oppression? Originally, animal sacrifice was adopted to prevent human sacrifice. But just as we abandoned the cruel traditions of the past, why need we continue with today's artificial replacement? Why not abandon it as well?

When Rumi talks ill of the "rationalists" as having "wooden legs," he's protesting those who only pretend to rely on reason, putting forward some sophistry that upon examination would clearly defy logic and conscience.

Is it merely a coincidence that those societies most steeped in religion are often the most desperate? Poverty and a lack of progressive education, as well as regression, misogyny, stagnation, irrational extremism, and especially, the despicable and unconscionable act of sowing hatred in the minds of children, are just a few examples of its consequences.

Parents have a duty to prevent children's minds from becoming corrupted, anywhere, be it at school or at home.

I have no objection to religious education. But the question is who should teach our children? Should it be teachers with superstitious beliefs who afflict our children with wrong-headed ideas for the rest of their lives? And which textbooks should they study? Books that contain the outdated ideas of long ago commentators? Are these the people we are choosing to lead our children and be our religion's representatives in our stead?!

Which teacher, mullah, or other educator, could ever be more mindful of a child's interests than his parents?

The blame is on you, who, in the name of religion, separate children from their families, and erect false idols before their eyes.

Our religion was established to cast out false idols, not make new ones! Wake up your children, before they fall into a deeper slumber; otherwise, it might be too late. As **Oscar Wilde** (1854-1900) said, "I am not young enough to know everything." But I can remind you this much: Indifference is tantamount to going along with their regression.

"The slumber of the tyrants couldn't have become so deep,
If a loud voice would rise from the breaking of hearts."

Educators in charge: In the old days, seminaries and their teachers represented the greatest available intellectual opportunity. But as they no longer do, why should we continue to support them? Should we do so just to provide jobs for certain rabbis or to serve the interests of a particular group or sect? To hold back our youth from a normal life, in the name of maintaining our Jewish identity, is a disservice to that very identity.

Actually, the best way *not* to know God, and to evade religion altogether, is by studying the books written by the regressors!

264

Teaching those ideas insures a life-time of ignorance, or guarantees that they will question the basic foundations of their faith and flee religion. If God wished mankind to submit blindly to ancient books, He wouldn't have endowed us with the power of reason and argument.

It's easier for the common people to believe a lie which they have heard thousand times, than a truth which they are hearing for the first time. Has society gained anything but misery from repeating and teaching the nonsense of the past?

Not everything in the *Gemarah* is worthy of our veneration. For instance, it says that "The sound of *shofar* distracts and deludes the devil so much, as he won't be able to bring charges against Israel before the court of God." Is this really an essential teaching? We should realize that no good can come from filling our children's heads with such nonsense.

As the famed contemporary poet, **Ms. Mahin Amid** said, let us leave behind us a trace of our good deeds:

"Some day, just a story remains of us in the world,
Only a fuzzy memory of I and thou shall remain.
Everyone wrongly builds for himself an image of the "I",
But what remains of us is not that ego.
Some ashes remain from the flames of the heart,
And some thorns from the garden.
In this ancient house, only a dark ghost remains.
In retrospect, from the good of honest friends,
And from the evil of cruel tyrants,
Only a false, jumbled image would remain.
No one will remember the sadness and the ill of hearts,
No sign of the doctor, nor the medicine, will be left behind; and
Neither, a spark of the flames, nor a sign of the hubbub will remain.
We can't know what will remain of us after we've left.

We don't know the paved road from the pot-holes ahead.
Yet "Negah"(*), this much we can say,
That only a footprint of us shall remain in time.

Adapted from poem in Persian by Mahin (Negah)
Amid

History has many examples of the isolation that ensues from communities trapped in ghettos (both actual and mental). Attempting to revive the past and pursue a program of anti-rationalism is no way to build a future for us, and a life plan that ensures poverty is not sustainable. History can teach us many lessons and expand our world-view, so that we won't repeat our past mistakes.

Those who think that "we have everything because we have the *halacha,*" are woefully mistaken.

Poverty is more than "not having," it's not striving to have more.

History is not just a tale of sorrows. History is an honest broker that by depicting the events of the past, signals a warning about tomorrow to those who are insightful today.

As **Nietzsche** once wrote, whoever does not heed history, has not learned the lesson of life.

The Jewish people, having suffered as much or more than any other nation, should explore what has most hurt the Jewish religion. The answer will not come from prayer but from our history and we should use that knowledge to predict our future dangers.

Whoever has studied history, and done so without bias, must consider each idea (and each person) in a thoughtful manner to see who (and what) is worth admiring and who (and what) should be shunned. That's why that section of the Jewish Bible called *divrey*

266

hayamim, or "The Chronicles", i.e. the "Book of History", is considered holy in Judaism.

If, as I said before, the history of a nation is the memory of its people and if we wish to examine our people's problems, then we must call upon wise men and women to apply their imagination, devoid of religious superstitions, to our present realities. A Persian poem, **Vosoughod-doleh**, says this about history:

"The wise man doesn't blame the mirror,
If an ugly face appears ugly in it.
Your good or bad remains in time, as it is,
History to you is always like that mirror."

The Jewish people, after centuries of wandering, due to forced and expedient migrations, have often found themselves in new places, completely different from their culture, language and traditions. Afraid of losing their identity, Jews often chose isolation thereby depriving themselves of better opportunities in their new environment.

A closed society holds onto its culture and identity and considers it unchanging. An open society considers a dynamic and changing culture to be the key to their society's growth and progress. As the great philanthropist, physician, and Nobel laureate **Albert Schweitzer** (1875-1965) said, the ultimate aim of culture is the moral and spiritual perfection of mankind.

I have no right to pass judgment on others, but like anyone else, I have a right to express my ideas. I agree with the words of the poet,

"To seal lips with silence, when there's need to speak –
It's like hiding your sword behind the shield, when in the battle."

Those who keep silent as regression spreads contribute to the demise of their family and that of society -- whether they know it or not. We need to examine the agendas of the individuals or institutions that we support. Consider the difference between those students who graduate from secular universities seeking intelligence and knowledge as the masters of their own fates, and those who study in the seminaries, lacking any independent thought, and believe their lives to be solely in the hands of God. As it is said so beautifully, **The hand of the artist, who helps himself and contributes to society, is better than the lips that say prayers!**

Live your life so that you deserve praise, not so that you quake after every prayer. We should worship God out of love, not fear. Those who use Hell to scare people are scary indeed! You can't call such fear faith. Human beings are easily misguided and manipulated. Many a historical figure who meant well became evil because of fear-mongering.

"If I try to tell this entire story,
The world will end hundred times over,
Yet the story will not be finished."

The regressive traditionalists refuse to accept the bitter reality of life and the truth of modern science; so instead they offer the sweet promise of heaven and the nonsense of miracles and superstitions. They consider every other group to be regressive; and don't approve of any group other than their own (sometimes even feuding among their own rabbis) – but they save their disdain for us – because they laugh at our people's short memory!

They will pray with each other, for free. But if you need a miracle, they will charge you for their prayers. Is a prayer that can be bought worth anything at all?!

Once upon a time, there was a town where the regressive fanatics spoke of the miracles of one of their prominent religious figures, claiming that his various pairs of shoes would match and line up before him, all by themselves! Some ignorant peasants believed this, and some even claimed that they had witnessed this miracle with their own eyes! As the story circulated, one of the more curious people in the neighborhood decided to ask the cleric's wife whether there was any truth to the story of this miracle. The wife replied, "Honestly, I don't know about the shoes. But this much I can tell you: Every morning, Agha, my husband, looks everywhere and curses the world, 'Where is my damn sock!?'"

A miracle is credible only to those who are ready to accept it as such. Some, to inflate their own prestige, even claim that they "saw it with their own eyes," as if they saw, "that the pair of shoes came together before the Agha's feet!"

Religious people don't realize that the magic of miracles only fosters more magical thinking to the point where truth itself disappears. Those who knew nothing of chemistry, believed it to be a miracle. But when they studied it, they understood it to be a science. In the same way those who study the religious traditionalists will understand them to be hustlers and con men.

If all discoveries had to wait for the imaginary time of a miracle, we'd still be looking to the skies for someone to arrive! Even today, despite the success of science, religious advocacy continues to flourish as a group of speculators go on fishing in muddy waters.

"We are all the captives of our egotism,
And there lies the cause of our divided society!"

In any given society, there are many who wish to be important rather than being useful. To reach the top they use others as ladders and scaffolding. Once they've achieved their goal, they dismantle their human scaffolding and join other groups, lest they lose the right to elitist privileges! They glory in social distinctions based on ridiculous differences in appearance, such as the color, form or texture of a person's hat or scarf, or even their facial hair! In such a regressive culture, they are always looking for ways to separate friend from foe, the people of heaven from those who'll go to hell.

The regressors identify their adherents by their headgear and upon seeing one of their own, they burst into joy. But if a hat was all it took to be pious, any person could put one on their head and claim to be their co-religionist. Indeed, in the 1950's, an Iranian businessman from Tehran's *bazaar*, named Abdol-Hussein, did just that! Born in Isfahan, Abdul-Hussein, a Muslim, had studied in the Jewish school of the city, the local branch of Alliance Israélite Universelle. In 1953 he came to New York to buy some cloth and fabrics for his garment store. He soon learned that most of the people in the garment business were Jewish and wouldn't let others into the game. This crafty man, who had learned the Jewish customs and could read Hebrew from his school days, asked people to recommend a synagogue. Come Saturday morning, he arrived at a Jewish temple and joined the chorus of the worshippers — so that the Jewish businessmen would consider him one of their own!

Yes, pretense, hypocrisy and deception, are as old as religion.

Did Abdol-Hussein become Jewish by simply putting on a *yarmulke* and imitating the Jews? Of course not! He, or the terrorists, who disguise themselves as Orthodox Jews, only to hide a bomb underneath their jacket, is taking advantage of the weaknesses of superficial, narrow-minded people. **I ask you to eliminate such weaknesses.**

It's a sign of utmost short-sightedness to appear in public covered in distinctly different garb — or to choose obscure biblical or religious names just so everyone knows "I'm a religious person!" This also gives our enemies fuel for their prejudices! Where is it written that a Jew has to stand out according to the wishes of our enemies? The answer is negative.

Where in the *Torah* is it written that a Jew should always wear a hat? Why is such exhibitionism necessary? True, some of our enemies forced us to wear a piece of cloth, a yellow star, so that they could discriminate against us and persecute us; but our misguided friends do so voluntarily, as a matter of "faith," so that they can be the targets of prejudice and can themselves discriminate between those they adjudge "religious" and "non-religious"! Let's remind ourselves of what **Saadi** wrote,

"The body of humankind is beautiful because of his soul,
Not just this pretty dress is the sign of humanity."

Voltaire once said that if a silk worm wished to give a name to her cocoon, she would name it "the sky"! How can you tell a 7-year old child that without a piece of cloth on his head, he isn't Jewish? And worse yet, how can you encourage that same child to react with anger to my criticism of this idea. In this way, and so many others, you are sending our children down the wrong path – one that history has shown to be a mistake.

Many of the things we consider to be our points of strength are actually our faults and weaknesses, yet we go on repeating them.

Do you know about the horrible crimes of the 18th century Iranian cleric **Mullah Reyhanollah** who issued a *fatwa* that Iranian Jews had to display a "Jewish patch" on their clothes? Is it any surprise that, years later, in 1933 the cursed Hitler implemented the same despicable order, this time in the supposedly modern country of Germany?

Let us preserve our religion's inner-driven spiritual elements, instead of its outward surface pretentions. **The agreeable commands of the *Holy Torah* don't need any cons or deceptions to enhance their truth or power.**

In 1933, a German Jewish newspaper recommended that all German Jews display the yellow stars as proud Jews. They were fooled, and today, with hindsight we know the true intention of those evil Nazi "law-makers."

Standing out is not the issue. Many from our religion have distinguished themselves by their achievements in medicine, science, law, and public affairs. But being distinguished by your dress code is not an honor. True, there are many ethnic groups that have their own dress code. But the road ahead is not always paved. The one who stands out, be it for the clothes, caps, or religion, is volunteering himself, perhaps unwittingly, to be discriminated against. One day, this could be obligatory; at another time, it could be based on a *mullah's* commentary.

"I've set fire to my own harvest,
So how can I blame my enemies?"

Or as another poet said,

"When you make your own star bleak,
Don't expect heavens to offer you a bright star's blink.
If your tree bends with the fruit of knowledge,
It could bring down the blue celestial wheel."

It's a pity that so many religious followers and their sects would prefer to criticize others instead of improving themselves and their ways; and seek to exploit other's weaknesses by deception for their own enrichment.

It is said that when our fingers are held straight, they appear to be of different sizes but when they're bent, they seem to be of the same size. Likewise, the regressive elements of religion and their adherents at first seem all to be different. But once we examine them more closely, they appear remarkably alike. Each seeks his own pulpit, and all use religion as an excuse for their own intentions.

If only they would leave our poor children alone, giving them a mindset that is pre-historic at best – all in the name of religion!

In the name of religion they are willing to tell any lie. To your face, they are flatterers but behind your back they say, "such nonsense is beneath our dignity!" They lie and pretend and try to hide their hypocrisy as the twin sides to their piety. The Muslim clerics call it *taghieh*, i.e. "an expedient lie", and deem it a "rewarding deed," believing change to be a sin, even though it might bring an improvement!

My friends, a bigot calls any kind of change "non-religious," and agrees with no one but himself.

Once a preacher from the Islamic cult of Sheikhieh offered a sermon in which he stated, "The children of Adam are of two groups: Those who believe in the creator, and all the rest of people, who don't. The latter group are condemned to hell! But those who believe in heavenly religions are in turn of two groups: Muslims, and all the rest. The latter are condemned to hell! The Muslims are of many groups, i.e. the Ja'fari's, and the rest; and the Ja'faris, too, are of two types, i.e. the Akhbaris and the Ossoulis. Except for the Ossoulis, all the rest will go to hell! Even the Ossoulis consist of many groups, among which all, but the Sheikhieh, are condemned to hell! The Sheikhieh are made of the faithful and the rest, the latter group are condemned to hell!" How few, according to this preacher, are in the last group!

Indeed, how few are people of an honest faith.

In every society, there are very few genuine believers who serve others with conscience and kindness, and with no need for witnesses. They don't belong to any cult or other sects, and can't be identified by their head gear or clothes. They are only distinguished by standing in the circle of honest and sincere kindness which is devoid of all deceptions or pretentions.

Many people tell me that writing or talking about such things is useless. I respect them but I don't agree. Let me remind you of the story of a **swallow** who fought against **the fire of Nimrod** with her beak full of water. I humbly yet confidently express my opinion that humanity demands of each and every one of us — you and me, as well as the rest of the humankind, irrespective of our religions or traditions — to accept as a mission and a duty to make an effective contribution to the promotion of love and kindness over hatred. We must place rationalism over extremism, and this lesson needs to be taught and practiced at home, at school, and at the bed side of our children.

Otherwise, one after another, our children will burn, inside and out, from the fire of opposing dualities and conflicts, like the links of a chain, one after the other.

As for the story, it's said that when **Nimrod** threw **Abraham** into the raging flames of the bonfire, Abraham looked up into the skies, and saw a swallow flying back and forth, carrying water in her beak, and splashing it on the fire. Abraham said to the swallow, "You sweet bird, don't you see this mountain of flames? Your small beak can't possibly quench its flames. Why do you tire yourself?" The bird answered, "Yes, I see it, and I know very well that these drops of water are no match for these flames. But everyone has to do something, according to her abilities, to put out the fire." Likewise, I think of my book as a drop of water against the raging flames of fanaticism.

My dear reader, the most misguided people are those who are inflexible and choose bigotry and prejudice, all for the benefit of their ego. To be sure, the followers of different religions and groups are by no means all the same. Hence, society cannot afford to lose the mutual kindness of all these groups. **Today, we have no way but a**

274

combination of tolerance and mutual respect toward the extremists, even as we should seriously prevent any further contamination of our children. We can do the latter by spreading accurate knowledge, while isolating the fanatics.

We should learn from the past, but also leave behind what is stagnating and rotten!

Those who are already lost to brainwashing, are perhaps lost forever. Fortunately, there is a gap between what's being taught in religious schools, on the one hand, and the understanding and knowledge of today's youngsters, on the other. My humble intention is to awaken the teachers, as well as those who have not yet been contaminated with this flaw.

My friends, don't fool yourselves: Your children won't be an exception; and tomorrow might be too late!

A generation can be lost, not through their physical destruction, but by internal strife and regression. First, they divide the community; then the community's productive and useful population declines; and, in the end, once indifference has already replaced logical criticism, the fanatics and their followers rise and take control.

Statistics suggest that the Jewish population worldwide is decreasing. Perhaps this is actually an indication that the wider global population is distancing itself from religion! I would argue that it's a function of the regressor's coming to power and their preaching that many people all over the world are fleeing not only their own religions, but religion in general. Many of those abandoning their religion are actually the children of extremist religious or non-religious. That's because moderate people, especially those who have been well educated, can't be as easily misguided. The extremists, by contrast, lost in their own ignorance, go after recruiting others to their ways even though it could cause their own frustration and destruction, as well as that of others!

Responsible educators,

Today, many universities all over the world, including one in Iran, are presenting their courses in different languages each week so that both professors and students can keep pace with the changing global economy. By graduation each student is familiar with at least four different languages in order to communicate more effectively across nations. Such a graduate is likely to gain as much knowledge as four people, and be a more productive participant at his company or business, and for his family and community than ten people!

In this regard, I'm reminded of some verses by **Rumi:**

"When there's none to the test but facts,
Whoever knows more, he'd have an expanded soul!
Our soul is more vast than an animal's soul,,
Why? Because of the more knowledge it can hold.
Oh, dear heart! Our soul demands knowledge to survive;
Hence, who that knows more has a stronger soul.
Whether our soul knows about good and evil,
Whether it's happy for kindness, or for harms done sheds tears,
Since our head and the essence of our soul contain knowledge,
The one who knows more has more life, more soul.
The world of life, indeed, is itself all about knowledge,
Hence, the one with no life is the one who knows nothing, an empty soul."

I asked a student of a Jewish seminary, who had been studying there for five years, if he could speak modern Hebrew. His answer? No! All he had been doing for those years is reading the ancient Hebrew texts and mouthing the words like a parrot! If you don't believe me, ask for yourself.

During the early years of our immigration, a girl from a low-income family used to work for us. One day, I found her happy. She told me that her brother had got such a high grade in a computer course that he had been hired by the university at a salary of $2500 dollars a month, and thus, they could now cover their daily expenses. A few days later, I met her again, but this time she was crying. Her brother had been told by a fanatic *mullah* that "a brain that can absorb the words of the *Torah* shouldn't learn computer science!"

Should they not be ashamed? Is this nonsense what you call being religious? Are these the words of a faithful follower of our religion? Training our students to be Torah scholars rather than computer experts assures that they will become burdens on our community. He who wasn't taught how to swim won't be able to swim in the oceans of society. Our children deserve better!

Once more, I remind them of **Rumi**:

"Don't waste your eyes on every beggar, as you belong to us.
Don't sell yourself cheap, as you're priceless.
Diamonds such as you can be found in no mine,
A soul like yours can be found nowhere in the world.
This is a world of decay and demise,
While you are an ever-growing living soul."

Alas, *if we take time for granted, we'd end up so ashamed of the outcome of these wasted hours.*

Let's improve upon our great heritage and legacy.

Dear educators in charge;

To preserve religious, ethnic or racial identity doesn't mean sinking into a swamp of nonsense and superstition. We can and should improve upon the legacy that we have inherited.

Our common global human values should be the measure of our worth rather than our appearance, the number of times or ways in which we practice ancient rituals or even the sheer number of our population. Instead let's increase the quality of the knowledge among our youngsters. Let's teach them to think independently rather than promote nonsense via brainwashing. Enslaving a young man's mind with prejudice, blinds his inner vision. Increasing the number of these damaged souls is no indicator of our population's growth.

Increasing the knowledge of our youth has had great benefits, not only for our community but for the world! About 24% of Nobel laureates have been Jewish, which is many times more than the percentage of Jews in the world! This pride of Jewish communities worldwide is a testament to the fact that a better education can compensate for a lower population number.

Now, consider the large families of the religious people, with so many children, especially those who live in Israel. They are mostly burdens to society, and with regard to modern science and information, they are rather illiterate. They don't serve in the army, and they don't produce anything to pay taxes. Is their increase in population truly a benefit to our community? Or are they just an increasing burden on government and society? The same is true for all fundamentalist sects who increase ignorance and poverty and the pockets of their leaders but contribute nothing to society.

What is their practice of "religious observance" really about? I recommend you do what I did, and stay for a few months in one of the so-called ultra-religious settlements. You'll see for yourself how young, transparent, valuable minds corrode, expire and are rendered useless. You'll see how the only ones who profit from this are their leaders and organization, while society ends up providing for their health, maintenance and support.

God has shown us the way, but walking His road is left to us.

Religious commands are constant, but up-to-date knowledge allows us to interpret the commands in ways that help us resolve conflicts. A culture of denial doesn't allow for progress and evolution. To save themselves from drowning in a swamp, wise individuals don't commit suicide; instead, they change directions! Human beings are not solids that remain unchanged, nor vegetables that remain immobile, nor animals with lives limited to eating and sleeping. As long as there is a world, human beings will not stop thinking, doing research, gaining knowledge, and making progress.

If a religious advocate is making the case for his religion, he does so based on tradition and not based on modern rationalism. The whole point of progress is to gain experience, and not return to those times that are better put behind us! Time is the revealer of truths enabling us to adapt religious commands to modern civilization.

A funny story says that three clerics were asked, "At what point can a fetus be considered a human being?" The Christian priest said, "From the moment after conception, when the zygote transforms into the fetus inside the womb, it's considered a human being." Another *mullah* said, "Only from the time of birth." Then a Jewish rabbi disagreed saying, "A fetus is not a full human being, until it has received her doctorate degree!" As we say in Persian, "Not so salty, nor so tasteless," like these traditional seminaries.

Well, this is also another tale of extremes…

Rhazes, the famed 10th century (C.E.) Persian scientist said, "Whenever you run into doubts, take the side of the reason." This echoes **Hillel's** words, who about 2000 years ago said that "Whenever a religious issue was found in conflict with science, side with science." **Fortunately, the *Holy Torah* had the foresight to guide us on this issue:** As we read in *Deuteronomy*, Ch. 17, "If something happens among you that would be hard to judge, refer to the judge of the time, and accept his verdict."

As I noted earlier, there could be no plainer counsel for us to make our religion a living one. Yet so-called religious authorities prefer to live as we did thousands of years ago. Yet even such so-called holy men find more than half of the ancient 613 commandments outdated. The choice is clear: **balanced growth or gradual death.**

The relative success of today's Jewish communities worldwide owes much to the fact that the Jewish people have always considered science to be their refuge. So much so that the Jews are referred to as "The People of the Book"!

Although the religious books and commentaries of the various sages need be accorded respect – the knowledge required for an educated person in today's world is far more extensive, encompassing many other fields. To allow our minds and thoughts to stagnate is equal to regression.

"Oh, thou, the tree! If only you could move around,
You'd never suffer the nail, the saw, nor the cruel blows of the axe."

It's said that someone who exaggerates the merits of a friend is also more likely to gossip and talk ill of him should they become enemies. Misplaced admiration, in the name of religious advocacy has led to false rumors that are very much beneath us.

As the chosen members of humanity, so many of whom have been honored to receive the Nobel Prize, we understand the importance science and education brings to all things, including religion and ethics. The Jewish people are told (*Babylonian Talmud*, 31A), that once someone has died, on the very first night, he or she is asked three questions: Were you honest through life in your relations with other people? Did you try to learn every day? Did you have hope for a better tomorrow? *Honesty, Education, and Hope…*

280

As Victor Hugo once said: Be like a bird that sits on a shaking branch and sings. She feels the trembling of the branch under her feet, but nevertheless, keeps singing — because she is confident in her wings. Time after time, numerous enemies have threatened the Jewish people, but they have never been able to break our wings. The wings and plumage of a young person are his understanding, knowledge and conscience.

Today's greatest problems are the results of the wrong teachings of past generations. If we suffer today it's because we didn't open our eyes, and those of our children, when we had the opportunity. We never told our children that among all religions, there are often cults and sects, who although they follow one common faith, are more contemptuous of each other than any stranger. Why? **Saadi** said,

"Oh, wise man! Wash your hands off that friend,
Who mingles with your enemies!
The true believer in one God, never sways from the path,
Whether you pour gold at his feet,
Or if you put an Indian sword to his neck.
He has no fear of humans, nor sets on them his hope —
And that's the foundation of monotheism, and no other."

Regarding the dangers of intra-religious bigotry, the story of **Teddy Kollek** (1911-2007) is a telling case in point. Kollek, a beloved figure who was called "the father of Modern Jerusalem," was recently disclosed to have been an informer for MI5, the British Intelligence Services who informed on his own comrades during Israel's War of Independence and caused their arrest by the British (See **Classified Case No. 66968**, or the "Scorpion File", a reference to his code name). **Rabbi Ezrahian** had a Persian translation of this story published in *Shofar of New York,* Nos. 316-318.) In the words of **Saadi,**

"Not everything is as good within as it looks without;
Many a nice and delicious cookie, which bears poison inside."

"I'd be a humble servant to anyone,
Who lives free from any belonging,
Under the blue wheel of the skies,"

Teddy Kollek's unforgiveable espionage activities seem to have stemmed from differences of opinion between him and his co-fighters. This reminds me of the story of an Arab *sheikh* and his camel, which may help us better understand Kollek's actions.

Among the primitive Arab tribes, camels were as dear as dogs are among Americans and Europeans, or as cows are among the Malaysian farmers — not to mention Asia's Indians, who go so far as considering the cow to be holy. "In Arab culture the unit of counting for humans, palm trees and camels is the word *nafar*, i.e. 'one *nafar* human', 'three *nafar* camels', etc." This should give us a sense of the reverence the Arabs have for this animal.

One day, an old beloved camel of an Arab *sheikh* died. The depressed *sheikh* saw the camel in his dreams, and asked him, "Have you forgiven me, my dear camel?" The camel told the *sheikh*, "You, Sheikh, made me carry heavy things all my life. You made me wander in dire deserts, with little water or grass, along with various caravans. You took me on long journeys through the desert, during which I had to subsist on whatever little thorny bushes I could find Time after time, you put more weight on my back than I could carry — but I put up with it all. However, I forgive you for all the things you forced on to me except for that day when, in the Hejaz Caravan, you tied my rein to the tail of a donkey, so that it could guide me! That I couldn't bear, so much so that I wanted to kill you."

The message is clear: when anyone, including an extremist, feels he is being led by someone he considers beneath him, he loses patience. He might take out his anger on the one who thinks differently, or send out "secret night pamphlets!" Or still worse, he might call upon strangers to take authority over their friends — as Teddy Kollek did, or as others do, when they go to kiss the hands of the enemy. Still, to make up for his mistakes, Kollek devoted himself to the service of his country and his community. Perhaps in his youth, he never knew or noticed what this Persian poet had said,

"To set bushes on fire between two people, it' not wise,
Because the culprit, caught in between, would be the first to burn ."

Only if someone had told him,

"Don't become arrogant because of your eloquence,
Or for the admiration of the ignorants,
Or after your own imagination."

Miserable is the one who lets others take control of his mind. More miserable are those around him.

Teddy Kollek wasn't against the independence of the State of Israel. He simply disagreed with his co-fighters about how to fight for their cause, so much so that he informed on them to their own mutual enemy, the British.

Likewise, those who disagree with extremist Orthodoxy have no disagreement with the commandments of the *Torah*. They only disagree about how to best interpret and observe the commandments.

However, as the regressive traditionalist lacks anything reasonable to say, he spouts nonsense and venom, causing hatred. By contrast, the rational-minded person chooses reasonable arguments because he knows that kindness is the key to faith and better understanding. As a great man once said, "Even a mother can't love her own child, unless she loved all the children of the world."

Have all the claims of the past preachers been accurate?

My friends, when it comes to prejudice and bigotry, we need to talk openly, publicly and transparently. We need to feel confident based on our merits and achievements that we have the foresight to be a force for change in our community – together with all the other rational people in the world. Only then can mankind achieve an utmost degree of comfort, social welfare and collective success. Consider the words of **Saadi:**

"Until you don't have a condition like ours,
Our condition could be nothing but a myth to you.
Don't compare my burn with another's:
She holds salt in her palms,
While I suffer its sting on my open wounds."

Or as another poet put it,

"You'll have no compassion for my pain, and
Only one who shares my ill can be my friend.
So that I could talk to him every day,
As two wood sticks, who'd be happier to burn
Together, while talking of their wound."

And let us remember,

"We all have our share of blemishes,
So better not mock each other's faults and flaws."

In today's world, it's not enough to learn knowledge from just one language, one religion or one continent. We can't keep our children in the cages of ignorance and oblivion, all in the name of religion! The poisoned weeds of bigotry, prejudice and narrow-mindedness, mixed with deception and hypocrisy, can grow anywhere, among any ethnicity or family, be it in a hut or a castle.

Once an environment is contaminated, everyone is at risk. **Mohammad Reza Shah Pahlavi**, the ousted king of Iran, wrote in his

memoirs about three "miracles" that happened to him: Once, the Imam
of Time, i.e. The Muslims' promised Savior, saved him from typhoid
in his sleep. Second, the Imam saved him from the danger of falling
off a horse on the road to the shrine of Imamzadeh Davood. Third, he
once saw the face of the Imam in a dream. This reminds me of the
following poem,

"If a poor man does a hundred wrongs,
Even his friends wouldn't know,
One in a hundred of his wrongs.
Let a king do one folly,
And it'd be heard by thousands, across lands,
As if the wind was carrying it along."

We witnessed the bitter results of the Shah's attitudes in 1979
when the country was taken over by superstition. Interestingly enough,
his father, **Reza Shah Pahlavi**, didn't hold such beliefs. But his son,
along with his people, caved in to regressions. And as is too often case,
superstition was his undoing: he was forced to flee his country by a
cadre of fanatics even more superstitious than him.

We need to wake up! To quote **Saadi** again,

"A bird won't go to the man who's splashing seeds,
If she sees another bird in the trap.
You too, learn from the suffering of others,
So that others won't take lessons from your life's flap."

**Piety and faith should be the path to beautifying our inner self
for God, not a gimmick proven by how we look to others.** Anyone
so concerned with showing off that he is a religious person, is not
likely to be one. Pretense and imitation are no substitute for true
feeling and understanding.

We need to fight common problems together. Lies are a major problem in our Jewish community — especially those so-called "expedient lies."

I cry out: What expedience?! What consideration?!

Leaving a memorial service, I ran into a friend of mine. He looked unusually sad, so he explained, "A man sat next to me during Mr. X's speech, and kept ridiculing him saying that he was preaching nonsense. But when after his speech, Mr. X sat down next to us, much to my surprise, the man told Mr. X, 'Bravo! That was the best speech I've ever heard!'"

In such an atmosphere, it becomes impossible to know who is lying and who is telling the truth. This despicable behavior does not belong in our community. It's said that **Darius the Great**, King of Iran, prayed to God to save us from three things: *Lies, Famine, and Hypocrisy.* I say, "Amen."

"Perhaps, we could mind our business in silence,
But we could never keep quiet other people's tongues."

No single group or cult has all the answers. Every misstep by religious teachers and advocates, along with what happens at home, can lead our children to a bleak future.

You need to act before some regressive traditionalist arrives at your dinner table — as your child, bride, or groom! To fight malaria, they don't go hunting every mosquito; instead, they identify the source swamps and spray them with pesticides. We should identify the "swamps of fanaticism," -- the schools and centers where regression is being promoted. We should also be careful -- pretending to support these regressive traditionalists out of some respect or nostalgia, can still be taken as approval. They are always looking for any excuse to have the "green light" to recruit more followers. The stability of our families is too important to become contaminated by a corrupt religion. The Iranian Jewish community, in the past, was mostly devoid of such contamination.

Yes, in the words of **Saadi**, *"A father advised his son, 'Oh, thou young man! Heed this from me that anyone who betrays the people of his origin, can't become a cordial person, nor will he succeed."* And yes, we read elsewhere, *"Guard your heritage dear, because a treasure from your ancestors lies in it!"* But "holding this treasure dear" doesn't mean stagnating for the sake of religion!

Over the last thousand years, what success, if any, have humans achieved by re-enacting religious rituals? Why do you continue on the same path? I warn you: If new generations don't choose a different road, they will have nothing ahead of them but re-living the religious, traditional, ideological and sectarian tragedies of the past. Thus, the despicable catastrophes of history will be repeated, *ad infinitum.* Let us take advantage of the opportunities we have, keep our conscience awakened, and fill ourselves with the best of the modern sciences; and let us begin now — tomorrow might be too late.

They asked **Henry Ford** (1863-1947), the great American automobile inventor, the man who put a world in motion, what was the secret to his success? His reply: *I found out one minute before others, and acted 30 seconds before anyone else!* Indeed, we might say this is the rule of thumb for the survival of nations and people.

Hitler, too, at first gave Jews time to leave Germany, but many didn't. Timely understanding, as well as prompt action is the key to success. The extent of our humanity is more important that the degree of their religiosity! Future generations, too, will find drinking clean water to be much better than drinking the dirty water of hatred! Sincerity and peace are greater than hatred, even if the latter comes wrapped in gold.

Given today's many problems we must provide for the welfare of our children and grandchildren by bringing them up as informed and reasonable people. Truth should not be sacrificed for expediency. To postpone things is to deny them!

With the world's population estimated at six billion, it is becoming less and less important to learn local languages. It is up to small communities to join the world chorus so as to better survive and progress. The global future depends on people's behavior and their level of knowledge not on their religion or the extent of their religious observance – isolation is no longer a solution, nor is the self-approval of one's sect a criteria..

We Iranian Jews spent more than 80% of our 3300-year religious history in Iran. During our 2700 years of living in the larger society full of discrimination, we never split ourselves into different schools of religion.

Today, our religious moderate youth, able to exercise freedom of thought, have achieved a higher educational rank and level of knowledge far above that of the students of our traditional seminaries. The dazzling scientific and economic achievements of our youngsters are a cause for pride in the Iranian community. Their success is not simply financial; rather, we can be proud of their knowledge, creativity, merits and nurtured talents and gifts.

I implore you not to drag these innocent minds back to the cages of your traditionalist religious sect. They are like fish that have finally arrived at the ocean, freed at last from millennia of discrimination.

Don't worry about their observance; as the *Talmud* said (123), "Even the *Holy Torah* could be interpreted in 49 ways, and God commanded Moses to make decisions based on the majority's view." Let us value the modern knowledge and talents of our youngsters, so that the world will value them, as well.

288

The late **Chacham Yedidya Shofet**, the former chief rabbi of the Iranian Jewish community, and the father of Rabbi David Shofet, said more than 70 years ago that, "I can hardly wait for the time when the nonsense of the commentators are taken out of the books!" Indeed, this is what many of the modern European and American congregations have already done.

Ever since **Gutenberg** introduced the modern printing press in 1440, the manuscripts of past religious commentators have become frozen in time! Since then, what were essentially the conversations and arguments of that ancient time, based on their limited knowledge, have been printed, reprinted, and distributed for indoctrination, over and over, without any changes, regardless of whether their content is outdated or has become inappropriate.

By contrast, today, we live in a world of constant improvement and innovation, where we discard past contrivances as obsolete for their better iterations – from the telegraph and the telex to chemical and pharmaceutical formulas -- simply because better options become available. No wonder **Mark Twain** famously said, "It ain't those parts of the Bible that I can't understand that bother me; it is the parts that I do understand."

My friends, Let us solve our problems according to reason, and not ignorance. Neither wealth, nor rank, should have precedence over knowledge and wisdom.

The most religious and the most humane person in today's world, in my opinion, who followed his conscience and has done the greatest good, is **Norman Borlaug** (1914-2009), "the father of the Green revolution" who was awarded the 1970 Nobel Peace Prize for his contributions to increasing food supplies. In 1977 he received one of the two highest civilian awards in America, the Presidential Medal of Freedom. Three decades later, he received the other, when he was awarded the Congressional Gold Medal on July 17, 2007. Borlaug saved more than a billion people around the world from starvation and famine by introducing low-cost high-yielding varieties of wheat to such developing countries as Mexico, India and Pakistan, Because of him, many billions more will be saved.

We, the Jewish people, believe that anyone who saves a single life, has saved a world. Borlaug virtually did save a world. And what was his religion? I'd say he was of the same faith as all of the other rational-minded people of the world.

Righteousness is not a matter of how you look, rather it is a matter of what you have done. Religious "good deeds" are often outweighed by the harm caused by their regressive acts.

"The first day that I was handed over to the master,,
He taught wisdom to all others, but made me crazy!"

The *Mishna*, the *Gemarah*, collectively called the *Talmud*, are, to be sure, full of highly instructive matter. But why not cull this material from the nonsense that also appears there? In the *Mishna* tractate called *Berakhot*, which you teach at schools, it's written that "Any religious student who disobeys the orders of the rabbi, is condemned to death!" Fortunately, according to Jewish law, this could only be done by the judgment of a large court, the *Sanhedrin*; and thus, has never actually happened. But you teach that "Becoming a religious person is better than becoming an addict!" As if these are their only two choices!?

Religion and reason should always complement each other, not stand apposite each other. I admit that no religious student has ever been sentenced to death by the Sanhedrin; nor is that likely to ever happen. But why teach such nonsense in the first place? And this is just one example!

Many knowledgeable people see no harm in religion, nor imagine any possible. But during the Pahlavis' time, did anyone imagine that someday such barbaric Islamic laws as maiming, mutilation, amputation and lapidation would be actually done in a country like Iran? Yet, these horrible deeds are being done today. Make no mistake! This is not an exclusive flaw of a single religion; rather, it's a common characteristic of all religions. Anytime extremist followers gain power, they will be brutal in the literal exercise of their written laws and scripture.

Teaching outdated and anachronistic texts and thoughts to our students is dangerous both for them and for the future of society. No one gives his children food or medicine that has expired and might poison or paralyze them. Is Religion any different?

Some self-righteous people place human beings at the center of the universe, believing that without us, creation would be an entity without consciousness, intelligence and foresight. But they fail to acknowledge the destructive power of mankind, who in their short lives, often greedily veer from reason and justice.

Before anything else, human beings should learn how to be human. Even today, mental and physical slavery exists, be it by superstitious ideas or in polygamist *harems*. Historically, no religion emphatically banned slavery; instead, **they just regulated it, and by doing so condoned it! But did it stay?!** Although this despicable tradition continued for many centuries, gradually over time it became abhorrent — in spite of the religions. Slavery is just one example of a practice condoned in the sacred religious texts that has been abandoned. So why not others? If we don't speak out about our religion's shortcomings, there will be a price to pay tomorrow – when our religion lies in ruins, abandoned by its followers.

"It's always the same old tale, this story of sad love,
And yet, I never get tired of hearing it, from just another tongue."

The sad story of our love for truth is just the same. Let's eliminate the nonsense and cast it in the dustbin of abandoned ideas and customs along with the superstitions promoted by our professional prayer-sayers, the extremist religious fanatics.

Professor Gregory S. Paul of the center for religious studies of Creighton University, an American Jesuit institution, is an expert in the theory of Evolution. In a study, Prof. Paul examined 18 developed countries and concluded that religious societies have more social shortcomings and flaws, compared to societies where people make religion a private matter and pay more attention to sports. He also found that a balanced and moderate form of religion doesn't hurt societies.

Today's civilization has arrived to the point where the dark side of many religions has been exposed. As we have witnessed, people who are drawn to those sinister aspects of religion, may even commit crimes in their name. Wherever religion takes over politics in the world, the chance of war increases, a reminder of the centuries-ago Crusades. That's how extremist religions, instead of promoting peace, kindness and calmness, impose hatred and violence both at home and, on a larger scale, on the world.

If only humanity treated religion like sports, a means to improve cooperation and coordination. Indeed, sports has always been the most honorable means for humans to achieve cooperation on the world stage. No athlete or philosopher has murdered a cleric; by contrast, clerics have often murdered philosophers. You only need to read history to see for yourself what criminal atrocities have been committed by these forces of destruction, in the name of religion

Religion has failed to fulfill its essential promise of, peace, friendship and sincere relations between human beings. Sports doesn't say, "A big ball is better"; instead, it says, "The better player is the winner." Thus, sports, at their best, doesn't let discrimination in. An athlete is not in love with his ball to name it "the best"! A lover of sports admires the player, regardless of the ball. If she's a soccer fan, she doesn't consider a tennis fan her enemy! One's understanding of religion is more important than the religion itself and the spirit of sports can even facilitate our understanding of religion.

Success in the world of sports lies in cooperation. The trainer and her athletes learn the most they can from today's failure, so that they could achieve success tomorrow. Regulations in sports are often changed to make the game better. But in the eyes of the fanatic, religion is immutable; so even if one fails thousands of times in practicing a command, he or she has to try it again. Because a fanatic considers change to be a sin, he preaches against it (even if such change would be an improvement).

According to the superficial, extremist religious fanatics, even the outdated and obsolete commands are holy and unchangeable and as a result, in their eyes, they must be observed to preserve the religion; and not practicing such nonsense is a sin! As to what the punishment is for a sin? That, they don't know!

Balance and moderation, promoting kindness in place of hatred, these are the solutions to all our problems. When brainwashing and extremism in religious matters are spread everywhere, even one person could set a world on fire. After all, **Yigal Amir** was a single fanatic who created great havoc by assassinating **Yitzchak Rabin.** Radicals such as him consider lying, oppressing others, breaking up families or even committing crimes to be not only legitimate activities, but also a mitzvah, a "rewarding deed," meant to promote their own religious views. And all because a supposedly higher authority has issued a *fatwa* to this effect!

Today, scientific centers, libraries, and sport arenas, are valuable centers of human interaction and learning where people can go to find what they have been missing, to get comfort, — not the traditional schools of fanatic *mullahs*, or the schools under the control of world's extremists. Millions of students are being nurtured every day, all over the world in extremist schools to be "intelligent nuclear bombs"; yet **the world seems to be in a deep sleep!** Sadly, until these "intelligent nuclear bombs" have "exploded," no one will wake up — and then it will be too late!

"Good and evil are born and raised in our thoughts.
The second shall pass, while the first would be lost."

In the time of **the Shah of Iran**, a disreputable government figure, who had formerly acted as a minister, made himself a candidate for Prime Minister. Someone close to him asked, "How did you dare nominate yourself given your notorious background?!" He simply said, "I am counting on people's forgetfulness!"

Likewise, the influence of the regressive traditionalists deepens every day by relying on people's poor memory. Indeed, we might have already arrived at the bottom of a big hole but they keep digging! We see regretful fathers trying to stay away from these groups, yet their immature youngsters replace them! As they say, "To a bird with broken wings, it doesn't make a difference if he's in the cage or in open air." These youngsters submit to bad conditions for the promise of a fantasized afterlife. They take shelter in constant praying without paying attention to the prayer's meaning.

Descartes said, "I think, therefore I am." In other words, the existence or non-existence of someone who doesn't think is all the same!

We can't expect someone to understand the meaning of things, if like a parrot, he accepts ideas and practices them thoughtlessly. It's a dangerous thing when such thoughtless people get access to speakers or print! Since the ignorant promotes darkness, he can't enlighten anyone else.

If you want to be concerned, just read their books and pamphlets for yourself! Every idea, once accepted, could turn into blind belief. A realistic and reasonable believer, when faced with a flaw in his beliefs, makes an effort and an adjustment to correct the fault. By contrast, there are those who consider any doubt, change or revision, to be a stand against the religion. They refuse to understand that honest debate and inquiry leads to real and enduring truth. They allow no doubt, and threaten curses and damnation and make promises of heaven, to keep their followers blindly under their control. How beautifully **Omar Khayyam** said,

"Putting mud and bricks on the sea, for how long?
I've come to detest both idol-worshippers, and the synagogues.
Who ever said, or where ever was it written, that there'd be a hell?
Who ever went to the hell, or who ever came back from heaven?"

The fanatics want to gain so much control over their followers that they cut off all links between them and the outside world, as well as anyone who doesn't subscribe to their way of living, even their own family members. They do this to keep their followers in the mental cage they've fashioned for them, keeping the reins always in their hands.

"The jewel of intent can't be gained by physical endeavor alone.
It's no more than a fantasy, unless the needed means are available."

***

"Oh, dear hear! Do on your own what you can!
On the path of piety, to bow and imitate is the same as blasphemy!"

***

*"The deeds of the monks made me worship wine!.
Behold that smoke, because of which my letter turned black."*

Human beings are excused for their mistakes; they are even bound
to make errors! But at the same time, it's also possible for men and
books to be corrected, improved — or rejected. To substitute narration
for reasoning is to prepare the ground for cultural ignorance. To close
the doors on doubt and research to those who are eager to learn; to
raise our children as blind followers; to base a religious system on
literal imitation; these won't ever result in anything but being lost.

**One of the secrets of the Jewish survival, especially during the
ages of the Diaspora, has been the Jewish belief in doing good,
according to the commands of our conscience.** Let us pass on this
secret to future generations, so that they too will know that sometimes
a single meal of a rich man can provide one month's supply of food to
a poor family; that to make sad people happy in their hearts is the
greatest of worships. **Rabbi Akiva**, as well as **Hillel**, said that the
famed *Torah* verse (*Leviticus*, 19:18) "Wish for thy neighbor, as you'd
wish for thyself," is the most important command of the entire *Torah*.
This has largely come to be known as the "golden rule of ethics." This
short verse, issued more than 3000 years ago, is the source of all
modern human rights.

In our authentic Persian culture, to pay donation to those in need is
a cause of pride, while someone who is healthy accepting a donation is
considered a pitiful thing, worse than death. Even all of our rabbis in
Iran, by having their own business, followed the three-point basic
conditions of Jewish life: *Torah, Avodah,* and *Gemilot hassadim,* i.e.
"Knowledge, Work, and Helping others without expectation."

For example, I remember that back in Kashan, Iran, **Chacham
Yedidya Shofet** and his father used to be in the business of silk

threads used in weaving carpets and velvets. May the day never come when our children and their grandchildren heed the advice of the religious schools, and set their eyes on the monthly $300 donation, the gift of the chief rabbi (!), as their means of subsistence for themselves, their wives and children.

Unfortunately, there are already some people who have chosen this unfortunate and ignoble path. To be jobless, a burden -- in the name of religion? To what end? Such a life, in the form of "an army of prayer-sayers," has always been beneath the dignity of our culture. We believe,

"Want greatness? Be generous!
Nothing will grow, until you've sown the seeds!"

We feel proud when we donate to and care for those in need because of the voice of our conscience —and not when we end up receiving donations under the fabricated title of a "religious advocate!" We believe that anyone who becomes dependent on donations, by one name or another, will become a burden for the rest of his life. He will suffer a life of deprivation,   spreading empty slogans that have no bearing on and make no contribution to human knowledge. And if they make a living as fundraisers, teachers or preachers of their same failed version of our religion, all they will do is spread the misery in greater numbers to future generations. By solving one problem (earning a living), they create thousands more.

In *Golestan,* **Saadi** told of a king faced with a big problem who pledged to give a bag of golden coins to the pious men, if his prayer was answered. As his wish came true, he asked one of his servants to take the bag of coins and distribute it among the pious men of the city. The servant, being an intelligent man, went around town, then returned the bag to the king, saying, "As hard as I looked, I couldn't find any pious man in town!" The king replied angrily, "As far as I know, there are 400 pious men in this land!" The servant replied, "The pious man won't accept any money un-earned, and the one who accepts such money, is surely not a pious man." The King laughed and told his entourage, "As much as I respect the faithful in God, and as much as this humorous man is full of enmity and denial toward them, we must admit that, to be honest, the truth lies with him!"

If the pious man accepted money for free,
Then you need to look for someone more pious than him."

Because,

"Piety is not in putting on some worn out loin cloth;
Be a pure devout, and wear a velvet dress!
Be righteous in your acts, and put on whatever you wish;
Put a crown on your head, and carry science on your back!"

If someone wants to worship all his life, why others should pay his expenses? **Saadi** said,

"If you expect generous help from a friend,
You're the slave of your own chains, not his."

Greatness is measured by one's intelligence, not one's appearance. Our tradition, culture, and ancestral duty has always been based on respecting religious authorities. But which authority? With what qualifications? With what degree of knowledge — and knowledge of what? Are we going to be content with some caps, hats and long black coats as our indication of wisdom and holiness?! **Saadi** said,

"Though you know they might not heed,
Do your part and give them your advice.
Soon, you'll see those who did the wrong,
Both feet tied in shackles,
Slapping hand on hand in regret,
Asking, 'Why didn't I heed the words of the wise man?'"

My friends,

Humans are the only creature that understands the meaning of past, present and future. We understand that there was something before, and that there will be something after. We also know that a good reputation comes from past actions and not what the future might bring. Mankind understands that to make the most of today, we must reap the benefit of past experiences, and so better decide the future course of things.

In this regard, establishing schools to teach and educate children is one of the most important things we can do. As such, supporting the education of students is a duty, and any person who claims to be of a sound mind cannot and should not disagree with this. A student in need hasn't done anything wrong.

However, we need to collect those books by commentators that are improper and/or out of date, as well we must keep regressive preachers and educators away from schools. We should also insure that any support for such schools stipulates the instruction of modern sciences, as well as moderation and balance in all issues. Otherwise, the generation that is being raised by today's schools of the regressive traditionalists will become a superstitious and hopeless generation. And we will regret that we unwittingly helped cause their desperate situation.

We are a people with a rather distinct culture, something between being ancient and modern; between being a tribe or a people and being cosmopolitan citizens of the world. Time after time, they closed the roads before us; often we missed the caravans of the past; for long, we have wandered among nations. Various strains of our people have grown under the influence of the culture of a different country.

We cannot deny what we have been; neither can we be content with it. The only safe refuge for us is, and will be, following the agreeable commands of the *Holy Torah*, along with modern science and perception.

The stability and endurance of a nation is not only related to their degree of religious commitment... rather, it depends on their level of understanding, the richness of their culture and their moral standing. Naturally, these could lead to a beautiful religious balance. It's said,

"Life is beautiful, oh thou, the connoisseur of beauty!
Only those who think alive can surely arrive at beauty."

To be certain, any religion, including Judaism, can lose a portion of their believers to proselytizing, other cults, or assimilated marriages. But by joining the regressors' darkness of mind and ignorance, everybody will be lost! To quote **Rumi:**

"Put a crow in the company of the parrot,
And the parrot couldn't wait to flee the cage!"

Regressive propagandists and educators use religion as a means to push his own and his group's aims and interests. For instance, they say that the worst of sins is *lashon ha-ra'*, i.e. "ill-talking" or "gossiping" about others! Yet, at their meetings and gatherings at the holiest of places, at in the presence of our dearest of holy books, they will curse a certain minister who has reduced their unemployment salaries; or even commit the ritual of "collective cursing", or _____ _____ *(Pulsa diNora)*!

I ask: Are these the people we want teaching our children?

Can we call such people religious or humane, when they don't sympathize with other people's misfortunes, be it the pain of a minister, who hasn't paid their unemployment salary, or the misery of a pauper on the street ?

Croesus, the king of Lydia (595 B.C.E.-ca. 547 B.C.E.), an ancient kingdom in Asia Minor, according to mythology, asked the Greek philosopher **Solon** (638 B.C.E.-558 B.C.E.), "Have you ever seen anyone happier than me?" Solon smiled and said, "I can only answer your question after your death! That's because even the most fortunate of men can still die more miserably than anyone." In the end, when Croesus was defeated and, according the story, as he was burning in the flames, he remembered the words of the wise man, and uttered, "He was right. I was the most fortunate, yet now, I die the most miserable because of my own mistakes."

Blessed be the pure souls of our ancestors, who always wished the best for everyone — "May you have a good ending." What today's regressors couldn't see in a clean mirror, our wise ancestors could see in a brick! They would say, "You act, and God will bless." Because they believed that no prayer would be effective without the presence of both knowledge and action. If prayers were effective by themselves, then those self-approving, professional prayer-sayers could have improved their own lot. As an old Persian saying goes, "If you were a real doctor, you'd cure your head first!"

"The pious man saw a book, and thought he was a sage!
The egotist stepped on the boat, and thought he was the captain of the ship!"

Doesn't the *Holy Torah* command us not to rejoice at the misery of others, even at the death of our enemy? I don't know why a human being changes into a blood-thirsty beast; why at times of prosperity, he beats the drums of debauchery; and why in times of poverty, he becomes pious, faithful and religious?

"You said, 'Don't do wrong!' So now, heed your words!
Don't shun your own words, when it comes to yourself"

Or as another verse goes,

There's no joy for me in the death of my enemy.
After all, our own life, too, is not everlasting."

The Religious extremists don't understand that the opposite of love is not hatred; the opposite of faith is not blasphemy; the opposite of effort is not indifference or idleness; and the opposite of Orthodoxy is not debauchery! To wish ill for others eventually brings about one's own doom. In the words of the poet,

"One who wishes ill for others won't get anywhere.
He can't bring a single harm to others without bringing hundred upon to himself.
I want your well-being, but you wish my misfortune.
Yet I know that you won't see any good, while no harm will come to me."

Many people, unfairly, view all religious teachers and advocates as a bunch of contemptuous, scornful people. They say,

"In the school of religion, people are of two kinds:
Either, they're hypocrites, or they're played by the deceivers —
And that's no way to the court of God. So you choose:
Either thought and perception, or remaining stuck in this prison."

When a small group follows the wrong path, we are embarrassed by it! **A truly religious person is not one who prays everyday; but a person who prays and *understands*, regardless of the religion or custom.** A person who in his youth doesn't question what he reads or hears; who doesn't do research on his own; that person, in his adulthood, won't arrive at the ripeness of a mature faith. Don't be afraid of the doubts of the youngsters. Instead, be more afraid of those wishing to close opportunities for our youth by preaching words no more credible than their fallible and outdated source.

You pray every day; saying publicly, "God, Protect my tongue from ill-talking, and my lips from hypocrisy, deception and betrayal." Yet you don't realize how your negative words tear apart our community and give fuel to our enemies. Hatred of the sort you dispense can turn millions into beasts, as we saw in Germany where a nation embraced the Nazis.

Einstein preferred "to be on a bicycle and think about God, rather than be in a temple and think about the bicycle!" Yes, it's much better to be a good human being and think humanely, without expecting some imaginary, nonsensical rewards.

In order to receive God's reward in this life or in an afterlife, narrow-minded religious zealots have, over the last several centuries, committed crimes, murders, even massacres. As long as a one-sided view of issues exist, this situation is bound to continue. Let me give you some examples:

In the central Iranian city of Yazd, they used to put a *samovar's* faucet into the mouth of a Bahai infant, to pour hot water in her mouth. In another Iranian city, Kashan, according to *Ferdowsi Magazine*, No. 32, February 1950, our own family doctor, the late **Dr. Soleiman Berjis**, was called over for a house visit. At that house, the family of the supposed patient, murdered this doctor, in the name of their self-righteous, remorseless faith. They murdered him, as a "rewarding good deed" — because he was a Bahai. Each member of the murderous family took turns stabbing him, to have a share in this "rewarding deed."

The shameful history of cruelty and tyranny in the name of religion is full of crimes, born of religiosity, prejudice, bigotry, religious deception and hypocrisy. Such crimes continue to this day with no end in sight. There is no end to the despicable writings attributed to the religious, and no end to hypocrites — each in a different guise, color or flavor; each for a reason; each in his time and place.

Once, a four-year old boy got lost in a crowded place. A kind police officer found the child wandering, hungry and thirsty. He gave him a hug and took him to the police station, to find his parents. But no matter how kind the officer was, the kid continued to cry, louder and louder. The officer gave him candies and toys, all to no avail. At this point, a lady walked over and gave the child a candy bar. The kid calmed down. Then the lady, a total stranger, explained to the perplexed officer, **"The child was crying out of fear from you and your uniform!"**

My address here is to the irrational fanatic extremists, who have placed themselves among the religious people:

Can't you realize that many people are driven away from religion as a result of your very words and deeds, or because they fear you?! They flee, because the way you dress, which is so important to you, makes them afraid – as do the unacceptable words you preach! A wise man scolded a preacher, saying, "As you don't know how to speak, you'd better learn how to keep silent! You well know how to get up there; so you'd better know how to get down, as well!"

Many years ago, I heard of a fanatic *mullah*, who said some nonsense in a memorial ceremony, saying it was from one of the books of commentary. I consulted with the younger brother of the late **Chacham Yedidya**, who confirmed that indeed such wrong-minded ideas are there, adding, "but I have never repeated them." He asked me not to repeat them either. But how, I ask, will future generations know not to repeat such nonsense? Jews were the harbingers of monotheism in the world. So let us be among the first to rid our writings from all types of nonsense and superstition

When superstitions turn into laws and traditions, the entire religion appears to be without reason to friend and foe alike. Judge for yourself whether what you've been saying has been reasonable.

"Find someone better than yourself, and be grateful for the chance. To stay with people just like you will make you miss the train of life."

Just as a spoon-full of spoiled yeast can ruin a ton of flour, just a single word of your nonsense is enough to ruin how the world perceives our religion!

To prevent the coming generations from being misled, first let's remove the preachers of nonsense and superstitious books from our community. No one ever imagined that in such an advanced and sophisticated environment, the regressive traditionalists would find a chance to mislead our children. We can't treat this casually!

Let us not allow the culture of regression to be passed on to our children, like a flawed gene. Otherwise, future generations will be flawed, as well.

We may still be able to correct errors in teaching. But the learning years of youngsters are limited: They can easily be wasted in unacceptable schools, and this loss can never be repaid.

Many benevolent people, impressed by the sight of these schools and their students, commit to support them. But they have no idea what is being taught by the ignorant, dark-minded teachers. They will only realize how misplaced their support has been, the day their beloved child or grandchild comes home repeating the nonsense she just learned at school from her teacher!

Any support to these religious schools should be done on the condition of rejecting this regressive culture, which is so unfitting to ours. We need to do so immediately. Tomorrow might be too late, if today isn't already so! The books of the commentators that they teach from are like an old fishing net: it's torn at some corners, and some lucky fish can still escape. Values don't grow from religious books; they grow from progress and evolution. What is worthless should not be taught. For a young man, what he learns is crucial to his survival, and to his success and failure in the world. It doesn't take much to lead him on a disastrous path.

"Many a good name, that after fifty years,
Brought about its demise by one ugly act."

It's said in a Persian book called *Kherad-nameh* that a wise man ran into someone wearing the clothes of the *mullahs*, but who was saying words beneath the dignity of the dress. The wise man scolded him, "Do one of the two things: Either, say things that fit the dress; or put on something that suits your words!"

"What's the point of being a lover of the essence of God,
If you don't have an understanding of 'being' itself?
Because you are an extension of the Divine light,
So go on seeking the pure and eternal love.
One in love with humanity and life,
Would step foot on the road of growth.
Love means to become liberated from all selfishness,
To become "us", perfect, and human; to become all.
If there's a ray of His light in your heart,
Love would come to your home by herself.
Lovers don't set eyes on the rewards:
For the true lover, the visage and the meaning
Are both one and the same."

Gandhi said that the aim of life is life itself, and that the advantage of those who know more is like the superiority of the living over the dead.

A wise man without piety is like a torch-bearer who's blind!

The famed Iranian literary figure, **Dr. Nafissi**, said, "A bunch of people are throwing sand thinking they could block the sun!" To confine the children in religious schools and make them read and repeat the same old things, over and over, sometimes for a life-time, is the same as throwing dust in the eyes of science.

Would you, who support these schools, send your own children there to be held hostage and forced to read and repeat for a lifetime? If you answer is, as I suspect, negative then why do you consider supporting these schools a "mitzvah"?

The value of one's belief is the same as the value of his motivation for believing.

The extremists are very adept at trapping people in their web of superstition, particularly our naïve and pure-hearted youngsters. The secret to their recruitment technique is that that they prey on the problems that all youngsters have, be the problems physical, emotional, economic, family life, romantic, psychological, or otherwise. They tell their prey that, "You are sinful, and you have to spend your whole life suppressing your needs and making amends!" In essence they identify a problem and provide a solution. Offering a way to suppress concern through mindless prayer, they keep raising the stakes, impelling more ritual, stricter adherence, and requiring their young charges to do their bidding, which they call performing mitzvah, i.e., "good deeds," in the hope of some reward in the afterlife.

What they have done is taken an honorable tradition of doing good deeds, one that is common to all Abrahamian religions, and used it to promote their own version of religion, using a bogus reward to be received in a fantasized afterlife as bait. Their poor followers would do just about anything, no matter how immoral or inhumane it might be, to have their hands on that "reward" — as we have witnessed in our lifetime. I need only mention again the case of **Yigal Amir**, who murdered the peace-loving Prime Minister of Israel, **Yitzchak Rabin**. He, too, sincerely followed religious ceremonies every day. But a faith with no objective morality and conscience, is false, and that is how Amir in his religious frenzy felt empowered to reach for a gun. He didn't have any personal animosity against Rabin — just as **religious people who brainwash people's children, don't have any animosity towards their parents.** To them, Religion is just a tool; otherwise, they have no "bad" intentions.

"What a shame, to bend to tyranny,
Then shake hands with the tyrant!
For a penny, the coward, might stay helpless
Like a deer in the mud;
And if you ask him for a prayer,
He'd sing hundreds for you."

Or as another poet wrote about appreciating life,

"Did you not see what pain endures
A man when pulling a tooth?
Imagine then how hard it'd be,
When life's living his dear body."

"A true lover doesn't boast of piety, every moment that goes;
The real gentleman, instead, shuts his lips and opens his arms."

Religious or traditional beliefs are valuable only when moral value is brought into account as well. For instance, when the *Ten Commandments* pledges that if you respect your parents you'll live longer, it's meant to encourage a moral act.

A faith that is not accompanied by morality is no more than a lie. A person of blind prejudice would consider lies, crimes or even murder, justified as long as he deems it in the interest of his religion — and he would not hesitate to do any of this, if asked to. Indeed, they are already destroying families, far from any humane considerations all for the hope of afterlife rewards. Or in a much more despicable example, they become suicide bombers, exploding themselves to take the lives of others, all in "good faith!"

The faith of a bigot, pitiful as it is, is neither trivial nor harmless. Look at the world and its insecurities to realize what I mean. The value of a person's belief, too, is tangled up with his motivation; does he seek a reward, and so will do the wrong thing, pretend to piety, and cloak superstitions as holy. To believe in morally empty rewards, or to do things in the hope of such a reward, makes people willing to sidestep any scientific or moral imperative — even disrespecting their parents in the process. That is why I, along with other free-spirited people, cry out: "To learn knowledge, to be a better human, and to promote this very idea — these precede adherence to any religion or tradition!" **When the basis of a person's thought is not morality, then any imaginary reward can become fodder for the narrow-minded fanatics.**

Jewish heritage is filled with thousands of "points of light," enough to illuminate the world, yet the traditionalists are fixated on brainwashing people to follow their archaic ways.

In Jewish culture, helping others is considered a moral issue, between mankind and God, not done in hopes of a reward, or acclaim, but in a most quiet way, "As if the right hand gives the gift, without the left hand knowing about it." No human being can claim to have good faith, without observing and practicing the moral ways of life.

"I'd bow before the wise and the sincere men,
Who in their selfless kindness to friends,
Could seem their own enemies."

A person who doesn't like to share his happiness and good fortune with other people, through help and kindness, doesn't deserve to be called human. Our ancestors used to say,

"Advance a little leaf of joy to your own grave!
None shall bring it back from the other side,
So you should send it ahead of yours."

In the Jewish religion, particularly in the *Holy Torah*, there's no talk of Heaven or Hell. Such things come from the regressors who use such concepts for their own ends.

"Whoever said, 'I died for you!', he lied;
I said the truth, that 'I'm alive for you.;"

The various sects and branches of Judaism that differentiate among themselves by how they dress are perpetuating an ugly tradition that has no place in modern society. To place religion as a factor of identity, signified by a person's shoes or cap, shows signs of a myopic mentality. Rationalists don't count religion as an element of identity. They are not looking to judge others or be judged and discriminated against for their appearance. Those who ask about another person's religion, adjust their own behavior according to their audience.

An identity based on appearance is pretentious, and surely nothing to be proud of. As any person could easily imitate their "look" it is without substance, merit and is indefensible.

Several years ago, an Australian Jewish seminary student was killed in New York, all because someone wearing similar garb had run over a neighborhood child. The victim's supporters mistaking the student for the murderer, rejoiced in his death. I hear the words of Solomon, who said, "The worst of people are those who judge too quickly, without knowing the whole truth."

"How long you'll whine, 'Poor me, who's being judged
By some jealous ill-wishers, just looking for my faults!
Sometimes, they rise to pour my blood;
Else, content to sit and wish me ill.'"

310

***

You be good, and you act well,
So that the one with wicked thoughts
Won't find a chance to talk ill of you."

Let's look at the world anew through the glasses of modernity, and let us learn afresh. The goal is to enlighten minds, not to just promote recruiting by some factions and sects who reject everyone but their fellow co-religionists. To them, religion is second to recruiting! They are active where there is a weakness, a problem to be exploited, or a person with a weak will. They set their eyes upon their prey and brainwash him.

Changing their way of life is not a choice but evidence of the harm they've suffered from religion. And when they quote lies, it's not their lie, but their mistake! They believe every lie told them and that passing it on is a "rewarding deed."

Let me tell you a story: A young man left his village for the big city, hoping for a better life only to find himself in more trouble than he ever expected. He took on a difficult job, but he was underpaid. When he broke his arm, his employer fired him. When he became homeless, a seemingly benevolent man took him to his home, only to exploit him even further. After two intolerable years, he decided to write back home, but he was illiterate. So he went to a scribe to have his letter written. When the scribe read back to him what he had just dictated, the young man suddenly burst into an inconsolable cry. Asked why, he replied, "As you were reading back my story, it hit me how truly miserable I am…"

Likewise, years from now, mankind will look back, and realize all the immeasurable harm and destruction caused by religious exploitation; then, humanity will burst into a big cry. Perhaps then, people will embrace science and civilization as mankind's common language — saving our children and sparing everyone from religious, ideological or traditional discrimination.

Will there ever be a more effective vaccine against the fatal virus of contaminated religion than science?

We don't need to read the history of mankind; the misery alone stemming from religious discrimination over the last hundred years would suffice. We should ask ourselves why during the past century, 100 million people, 63 million of which were civilians, were killed. Religion is a painful story which never fails to bring bitter tears to the eyes of the reader. It's strange that religion which meant to ease people's burden in life, has turned into a murderous tool in the hands of bigots. More surprisingly, however, despite the centuries-long atrocities in the name of religion, we have hardly yet begun to fight against this ill. Perhaps, at the dawn of this new millennium, the time has come!?

Life, without the benefit of past experiences, is not worth living.

Let us be mindful of the future of our children. A French writer once wrote,

"Let us write our sorrows in seashore sands;
Let us engrave our joys on mountain rocks."

For example, consider the very valuable command of resting from work for one day per week, which is observed today by the entire world. In this regard, the *Holy Torah* has said that three acts, i.e. "making fire, plowing the soil, and working" are forbidden on the Sabbath. Since then commentators of the Jewish Bible, have turned these 3 prohibitions into 39, just to be on the safe side! But to what end? I ask whether these 36 extra commands, and other similar additions regarding food, clothing, etc., haven't overshadowed the original principle.

312

Considering the issue of *mikveh,* i.e. the "ritual bath" in a water cistern there are 233 commentaries in the *Talmud,* 189 times alone in the *Gemarah.* This ritual, which is supposed to take place in a pool-like *mikveh,* was discussed ages ago, at the time when modern water distribution through pipes, or many other aspects of today's hygiene, were not even imaginable. But is this ritual and its related laws really necessary anymore? These 233 commentaries show an extraordinary attention by the Jews of those times to hygienic issues. But important as they are in historical terms, they have no place in today's world, where people take showers every day and use vitamin-enriched shampoos and other sophisticated products to wash their hair and bodies. And did we forget to mention, we use running water!?

Please note: If there were 4220 commentaries that were written about a matchstick or a cart, we also would have no use for them, as we hardly use matches anymore! A child's words and actions can be a source of pride or shame to their parents and families. Likewise, the words and deeds of the followers of sects and religions, the cited texts and their preachers, could become a cause for pride or shame for the people of that faith all around the world, either uniting them, or else or shattering them into thousands of pieces. There is nothing better than a unified family; and there is no betrayal worse than tearing a family apart. The conflicts among families created, wittingly or unwittingly, by such so-called commentators continue to do just that.

The shortest way to ruin for communities such as ours is to create religious and sectarian divisions among the people, something that we never had within our Iranian Jewish community. For that, the blame falls squarely on you.

Let us reject such preachers of disharmony and send them on their way.

It's not a matter of a particular type of religion or tradition. When all members of a family follow a certain way of life, whatever it might be, they can have their own peace. But when some speculators in the name of *mitzvah*, i.e. a "rewarding deed", but in fact to recruit new members, separate even one member of a 20-member extended family from the majority of his kin, whether they are "religious or non-religious," this is a crime and an insult to humanity. Religion is meant to bring us together not tear us apart – and that is the way it has been for centuries among Iranian Jews, whose ancestors maintained their harmonious uniformity by suffering painful sacrifices. Calling such hypocritical preachers as "religious" comes as an insult to the truly pious people.

It's impossible to be religious before we are better humans, and a better human doesn't act like these people do. One cannot and should not call such preachers "religious"; and we shouldn't wrap up their immoral acts in the cloak of religion.

It would be better for all of society, if the moderate people of faith who hold the respect of the larger society, cooperated to remove the extremists. Because while it's true that not all religious people have a part in destroying families, it's also true that all of those who create conflicts of opinion are called "religious"! While it's true that not all religious people are against the existence of the State of Israel, but those who are, await the arrival of a Savior, and are called "religious." While it's true that not all religious people are the ones who either support our enemies or give them fodder for their anti-Semitism, but all who do, ignore our miraculous success, and are deemed "religious." Ironically, however, they call everyone else extremists, and themselves "moderates"!

They asked Rafael, the great painter, "How did you become a painter?" He replied, "By a kiss of my mother!"

314

False encouragement and respect strengthens the regressors, as he takes it as approval of his wrong deeds.

As **Leo Tolstoy** said, most people are interested in changing everyone but themselves! Those who imagine that they've never made any mistake have never taken a new step.

As **Henry Kissinger** put it, even the wick of the dynamite is not blameless in an explosion. We must cast out this "wick" of prejudice and reject the very idea of regression. Religion can't progress toward perfection by itself. It's everyone's direct responsibility, especially our teachers, to remove the culture of regression, regardless of whatever name it may have assumed. This is necessary, if our community is to remain unified and our religion is to survive. The clean up job begins at home and at schools.

Reading **Thomas H. Maugh II's article,** in the *Los Angeles Times*, November 14th, 2006, about the "latrine practices" of the Essenes, an ancient Jewish sectarian community who lived more than 2000 years ago, was embarrassing (Today, the Essenes are largely associated with the *Dead Seas Scrolls*, which were found in 1947 in caves around Jericho.)

The team of archeologists included **Joe E. Zias** of Hebrew University of Jerusalem who concluded based on archeological and biological evidence that they had found the latrines of that ancient community. They realized that 94% of the people of the sect died before the age of 40, apparently due to their use of an "immersion cistern", i.e. the *mikveh*, for religious reasons, as part of their bathroom practice, resulting in deadly contamination and infections. Let me emphasize that only 6% of the people of this sect reached the age of 40, while archeological evidence shows that about 50% of the people in surrounding areas of the time lived beyond that age. The religious practice of using the *mikveh* was literally killing the Essenes!

I would have liked to write those professors to say that they didn't need to go to so much trouble to research the unhealthy habits of a Jewish sect 2000 years ago. They could have just spoken in person to those who still advocate using the *mikveh* system, today, here is Los Angeles and in Israel! Yes, regression is as old as human folly.

Isn't the use of the *mikveh,* the ritual bath in the cistern filled with rain water, an embarrassment when we live today in a modern, civilized world?! Some argue that "It's such commands that distinguish Jews from other people!" But what are these commands? Should we pursue a practice that was deadly to our people just because in ancient times one ignorant person made the irresponsible comment that "Jews should sell synagogues to build *mikvehs*"?! Such a pity!

I would agree that such practices distinguish the Jewish population -- Yes, thanks to the efforts of the regressors, Jewish people have become so distinguished, that our population, after 3000 years, has sunk below 0.2% of the world population, i.e., below 1 per thousand!

This ritual is just one of many of the nonsense and superstitions propagated by our commentators, past and present that were turned into laws by their sheer mindless repetition and observance over time! Is it not total nonsense to compare the water of modern pools and Jacuzzis — constantly circulated, cleansed, and decontaminated — with the dirty, stagnated water of a ritual bath?!

This is folly. But to even question it is to be considered attacking the Jewish religion itself and all of its culture and civilization. This too, is beyond reason. I have personally seen on many occasions, "religious" people "prescribing" the *mikveh*'s contaminated water as a cure for an incurable patient — even right in the middle of a hospital!? Not only is this beyond reason, it is immoral, and despicable to prey on patients and families in their most desperate moment!

As another example, the coming of a "promised savior" has been the subject of so much exaggeration that we see today even in the cabinet room of a government that a chair has been left empty for their Celestial Savior! Instead, let's allow rational arguments to find a chance to be expressed, heard, and grow. Religious prejudice and bigotry is nothing but a cover over the face of the truth. Let us remove that centuries-long veil, so that it won't be our shameful legacy to the next generation. Let us close the doors of stupefaction, and instead, open the doors of enlightenment. Every day is a new day for a better beginning. Let us wake up those who have remained asleep.

Wise people are those societies who know that **a just reproach is much preferred over a misplaced complement.** Your support or encouragement of regressive traditionalists, whether by your pen or your pocket, wittingly or unwittingly, is hurting our community. Prejudice and bigotry are always accompanied by fantasizing. This dreamer imagines that any action, no matter how unreasonable or despicable, is permitted for the preservation and survival of his religion (!). However,

Only those societies deserve to thrive that have the courage to evolve.

I once heard someone say that some scholars believe that one of the reasons for anti-Semitism is the Jews' insistence on living differently than others.

The regressive traditionalist defends and argues over private and negligible matters so fervently and so clearly out of proportion to the true value of the issue at hand that as a result we all lose sight of the core meaning of the teaching or ritual. A prime example is their focus on rules and regulations regarding food and clothing — what can be eaten or not, what can be worn or not, or the multitude of regulations regarding kitchenware! These have little to do with the original and true intention, meaning and spirit of the prohibitions. What the traditionalists have done is taken commentaries to a humiliating nonsensical vanishing point, where they find ways around regulations to suit them using modern science, while on the other hand ignoring those discoveries that would allow a more rational interpretation of their rules.

When I told one of these fanatical prayer-saying "wacky wobblers" that, "Back in Iran, we didn't have such things!" He replied, "Because back then, we didn't know." To which I replied, "To the contrary, it's today that you don't know!"

By imitating the *ghetto* thinking of the religious theoreticians of Eastern Europe, you ignore the agreeable enlightened ways of your Iranian ancestors – a Jewish community older and wiser, I would argue, than the European Ashkenazi community. You are like the crow, which wished to imitate a partridge's sexy walk, but ended up forgetting her own!

In every generation, interpretations and commentaries would better be based on the scientific methods of that generation……and not on hearsay. Even the *Mishna* prefers the *Babylonian Talmud* over the *Yerushalmi Talmud*, not only because the Babylonian is more recent, but because it better fits the science and perception of its time. Yet the majority of people don't heed such ideas; they are mere spectators to the scene.

In the early 1980's, when Orthodox ideologies first began to penetrate our Iranian Jewish community, religious conflicts began to emerge among us! Around that time, along with the late **Eliahoo Ghodsian**, an exceptionally knowledgeable person on the subjects of the *Torah*, the late **Manoucher Ghodsian**, and **Mr. Ezatollah Delijani**, we went to the Beth Jacob synagogue to meet one of the leaders of Orthodox Judaism, as we hoped to contain the spread of our ideological differences.

After listening to the reasonable arguments of Mr. Ghodsian, the rabbi agreed and said that, "According to the *halacha*, 'the Jewish law', you need to continue your ancestral ways." But do you know what he said *after* hearing about the negative effects of their propagations, which in many cases, had resulted in disrespecting parents against the explicit commandments of the *Torah*? The rabbi said, "It's what it is!"

I have to disagree with the Rabbi. Silence, for what? Those who prevent the publication of criticisms, are knowingly or unknowingly the servants of the regressors. A just criticism is what helps the societies move forward.

Some of the *yeshivot*, the "Jewish seminaries," have become partially awakened by the voices of criticism. They have reduced the so-called religious lessons by a small percentage and replaced them with elective high school courses, calling themselves "universities." This is a positive step, especially since just a few years before even this much was forbidden; and indeed, it's still forbidden in some of the other seminaries. A fanatic once told a friend of mine's two children that, "Doctorate studies are for the gentiles, not for us!" This is a backward mentality, unworthy of our community and of someone who sees himself as a representative of our religion. This way of thinking needs to be thrown where it belongs, in the trash bin of history. Time dictates,

"A moth wouldn't join the sunlight? So what?!
This wouldn't take a single ray away
From the worth of the sunlight!"

Yes, if the moth avoids the sunlight, it's her own loss!

A serious fight against religious regression, I emphasize, shouldn't turn into a fight with the religion in itself. Opposing the regressive and anti-rational rabbis shouldn't make us oppose and fight against all rabbis. The time has come for clerical authorities to consider the best interests of world societies and to find the courage to ban the teaching and practice of regressive ideas.

If they fail to act, this book will serve as but one exclamation of regret, and soon they will be sorry for their mistake, but by then it could be too late. At that time, the unforgiving force of time will reject them albeit with a steep price tag and harsh punishments.

Mark Twain once quipped, and I paraphrase, "Last week, I stated this woman was the ugliest woman I had ever seen. I have since been visited by her sister, and now wish to withdraw that statement." Yes, whenever we study some of the recent nonsense said or written by the regressors, it gives us cause to forgive yesterday's nonsense and those who said them!

I spoke to a religious (!) gentleman about the subject of wills and trust agreements. He said, "Our *rabbi* has said that we shouldn't write such things, because writing a trust means you are inviting the angel of death!"

He is one of those *mullahs* who considers insurance to be illegitimate, and tells people to place the prayers of the *mezuzah* on the door frames — as sufficient insurance! Is it not shameful to hear such nonsense propagated, and even worse, attributed to our religion? It is true that the *akhonds*, too, used to tell people that, "insurance is not legitimate; it's an interference in the act of God." Will there ever be an end to this kind of backward thinking?! But if you don't want to hear such nonsense you shouldn't ask for advice from those desperate fanatics.

Undoubtedly, no writer can keep all of his readers happy.

I ask my dear readers to pay more attention my intentions than my words. It's quite natural if some unkind people purposefully characterize my words unfairly as "non-religious propaganda." But it is my hope that my readers understand that my true intention is to promote rational thinking in the service of preserving our religion — and to prevent the spread of the plague of regression.

In any criticism of the regressive traditionalists, there is a small measure of being embarrassed by their religious beliefs and practices, and there are some critics who have even developed a hatred toward all religions.

It's true that I feel no pride when a nonsense-sayer introduces himself as an advocate of my religion; or when others consider him to be a representative of my religion. I feel sad and ashamed when I hear their nonsense presented in the name of my own religion. I feel sadness and disgust when I see these people breaking up families in the name of religion, and claim that in doing so they are doing a "rewarding good"; and when they are faced with a protest, they play innocent and say, "Who did this? It wasn't me!"

"My beloved shares a breath with a stranger, and it's enough
For my jealous rage to rise and render me dead.
*She laughed and said, 'Oh, **Saadi**! I'm the candle of the public!*
I've no fears, if a moth burned in his love and jealousy for me!'"

I find that these sham-religious leaders have no fear of the cruelty they've imposed — because they don't have a sense of responsibility! They seem to be painfully in need of religion — and earning a living! — thus, they can't understand the pain of others!

"Though I boil, like a barrel of wine, in my heart's flames,
I've sealed my lips — swallowing the blood, and keeping silent!"

The Iranian Jews are a group of people, who after suffering many storms and much famine, left the oldest civilization of the world for its youngest one. From the co-mingling of these two elements, a new enlightened layer of society is taking root in this corner of the world and, perhaps, in the whole world.

Today's educated youngsters consider human intellect, thought, and progressive reason, to be their true religion. They consider anyone who follows these as their co-religionist — not someone who favors inflexibility, ignorance and a rigid way of thinking. Both individuals and societies would disappear altogether from time's memory, if they stagnate and refuse to evolve and reach for greater learning and understanding.

As I argued earlier, should we today accept the idea of "ritual bath" when much improved and healthier substitutes are available, and despite the known harms and dangers of that old practice — only because it has been a tradition?! Should we go on washing the dishes at the edges of a *howz,* "a Persian courtyard pool," or at the brink of some dirty stream, using some ashes, dust or sand, just like our grandmothers — simply because it was the tradition? Or should we wash the clothes on some wooden plates, too — just because they did so in the old days?

Psychologists tell us that when people stick to a certain subject and don't let go of it, it shows their lack of confidence in the subject itself. A sincere believer isn't afraid of adapting to time. The reason behind the regressor's humiliating weakness is that they mix reasonable ideas with unreasonable ones, leaving both friend and foe to argue with them.

322

It's a pity that so many people turn to these self-appointed sect leaders to ask about observing or rejecting these traditions. In vain, they expect a reasonable answer or interpretation – from the same promoters of the most unreasonable traditions and rituals. The resulting disappointment or conflict has been a cause of much pain and embarrassment.

The faith of these people doesn't stem from their knowledge; simply put, it's a legacy of imitation. The thrive on such divisions as Orthodoxy vs. Unorthodoxy which is anathema to our ancestral ways. They separate children from their families and individuals from society. And this is only the beginning of the trouble they cause.

To them, religion is nothing but a means to cast a shadow over people and have them live in the darkness as "good humans," albeit, at the cost of everyone's ignorance!

To be good is such a priceless jewel. It's so valuable that the hypocrites stomp over morality in the name of "rewarding good," just to get their hands on that jewel. But once people realize their true identity, their hypocrisy is all people will know of our religion.

Throughout history, religions have been most damaged not by the anti-religious; rather, religions have been mostly hurt by those who wished to appear good in the name of religion. Over our long history of Diaspora existence, Judaism survived because of the presence of our synagogues. Yet today, they are used as a way to differentiate among our own members and tear us apart, as "religious" or non-religious, rather than bringing us together as a community of Jews.

Regressors even call the 900 modern Jewish congregations of America, with all their benefits and strength, as "*non-kosher,*" despite the presence of the *Torah* in all those congregations — only based on their own nonsensical criteria. Sadly, there are some people naïve enough to believe them!

The usefulness of any belief depends on the extent of the understanding of the believers of that religion or group.

If, as we see today, some people wish to stop synagogues – and on a smaller scale, businesses – from their normal activities, via sophistry and false arguments, or by threats and blackmail, then undoubtedly, the value of the entire religion and its traditions will be questioned, as well. But reality is far from the claims of the regressors. They traffic in irrational beliefs that by their very nature are meant to keep us away from the merits of intelligence and tolerance. Instead, they prefer absolutism, and indulge in hypocritical games of egotism and individualism. They seek all-encompassing power, both individually and collectively. Unfortunately, as peace-loving people we keep silent lest conflicts spread further, and as a result, our community is being led into the hands of anarchy.

"It's not about the withering of a single leaf :
Forests are being destroyed.
These unkind beasts do to people's mind and soul,
What no human would ever do to another."

My friends, due to our immigration, our children moved forward, hundreds of years away from our past. Likewise, we should update our places of prayer, our synagogues, our temples, not only in terms of their physical construction, but also with regard to their content. We've had enough of superficial visions. Only some narrow-minded people would distinguish between different synagogues to wreak conflicts based on imaginary criteria, even though the *Holy Torah* is held inside all of them. Those who promote such conflicts, seek not a temple but a store for their own business. To sigh isn't nearly enough; we need to ask ourselves how we can uproot such notions from our community and our society.

The *Holy Torah* says, "You can pray anywhere and anytime."

Our children need to understand the truth of our commandments so that others can't enslave them with nonsensical arguments.

Awhile back, I attended a memorial service at Sinai Temple, a major synagogue in Los Angeles, for the passing of Mr. M. J.'s mother. The Chacham, at the end of his speech, asked a young rabbi to lead the *arvit*, i.e. the Jewish evening prayer. But that young rabbi told the esteemed Chacham, "I won't do that, because in this synagogue, they use electrical speakers on the Sabbath, and thus, it's not *kosher*!" The Chacham, with a look in his eyes that pitied the young man for his ignorance, uttered the Hebrew sentence I have quoted above, "You can pray anywhere and anytime," and went on conducting the service himself.

Here is a rabbi who stood up for a more rational and compassionate interpretation of our religion – one we must all adopt for our religion to thrive; the rabbi stood up to the ignorance of those backwards elements – whom we need to resist and marginalize. Over the years the rabbis at this temple, as well as their board of directors and its associated school, have been of great service to our community, especially during the early years of our immigration. And their kindness and services will never, ever, be forgotten.

In the Iranian Jewish culture, there was never a distinction between the *Sephardic* (Spanish) and the *Ashkenazi* Jews. Indeed, in the 1940's, when a group of European and Russian Jews fled the Holocaust and took refuge in Iran, the Iranian Jews, themselves living in that environment of poverty, constant worries and discrimination, warmly greeted these war refugees and took care of them. To date, a group of the off-springs of these non-Iranian Jews, who live in Israel, are called "Balade Tehran", i.e. "the Children of Tehran."

Fortunately, conflicts between *Sephardic*, *Mizrahi* and *Ashkenazi* Jews have been resolved by the enlightened attitudes preached by the heads of such temples as Sinai Temple of Los Angeles and other American synagogues. Today marriages between youngsters from these various backgrounds have been facilitated. As they say, "People who pray together, stay together."

I can recall many occasions when **Rabbi Derschwitz**, along with the late **Manoucher Ghodsian**, would come to the airport, offices or hospitals, as early as 5 in the morning, to solve the problems of the immigrants. They opened the doors of their synagogues to the community and offered their services with no reservation.

Rabbi David Wolpe, the current chief rabbi of this synagogue, is considered a pride of the world Jewish community. He is a friend of **Rabbi David Shofet,** and he has been appreciated as one of the most distinguished rabbis among the conservative congregations of America. I encourage you to pay attention to his speeches and writings and compare them to the nonsensical words of the regressive traditionalists. Today, we can proudly say that about a third of the members of the synagogue, as well as the students of the Sinai Akiva, are of Iranian origin, and American and Iranian Jews benefit from each other's company.

Shame on those who pretend to be religious but then cite nonsensical prohibitions such as using electrical speakers on High Holidays – and who do so in ways that are an insult to a truly rational, religious American personality, as well as to our beloved Chacham.

My friends, such malevolent preachers deserve to be cast aside. Let us instead appreciate the wise servants of society, and seat them at the head of the table. As it's said,

"Be grateful for your blessings, and they will grow.
Be ungrateful, and you'll lose all the blessings."

If speakers in a synagogue allow a larger audience and more members to hear the words and prayers of our religion and the sermons of our rabbis, is that not a blessing for which we should be grateful? The regressive traditionalist wants to sit in judgment and lessen our reach and our importance in ways that cause conflict among us. Saying a place is *kosher* or isn't *glatt kosher*, will only drive people from attending religious ceremonies, and weaken our community.

When we can't see anything, we call that "darkness"; and when someone follows some unmeasured thoughts, ideas that haven't been well thought-out, we call him ignorant. We say that he's "in the dark." Normally, mankind is unable to see in two distinct situations — either in extreme darkness, or in extreme light.

The services of the Sinai Temple and the good school of Sinai Akiva, represent "extreme light" which blinds the regressors! So much so that they falsely claim it as "unworthy" --- hoping to promote their own cause and their own "share of the pulpit."

When doctors graduate, they are asked to swear to treat all members of the human society equally, regardless of their religion, color, ethnicity, economic standing, etc. and to respect life at all times: "If I keep this oath faithfully, may I enjoy my life and practice my art, respected by all men and in all times; but if I swerve from it or violate it, may the reverse be my lot."

If only there were a "Hippocratic Oath" for the religious educators! Upon graduation they should swear to avoid anything that leads to hatred and conflict!

It is said that the Mongolian attacks on Iran, during which millions were killed, blinded, or maimed, was the result of the misinterpretation of one single religious verse. As a result, the Iranian people were set back for hundreds of years.

Let us avoid wrongful teachings. We can forgive someone who doesn't know, but we can't forgive a hypocrite who pretends! **Saadi** wrote that,

"An ignorant man in misery is
Better than a non-pious wise man.
Because the former lost the road out of ignorance,
But the latter had both eyes, yet fell into the hole."

They pretend to be religious, and wish to lord their religiosity over all others, but all they accomplish is bringing our community down. To them, repeating the literal words is telling the truth, regardless of whether those words or commands no longer make sense for our times.

Once upon a time people said things like,*" Whoever gave us the teeth, He too shall give us the bread!"* Or if a child contracted small pox, they would immediately attribute it to someone's "evil eye"— or to "fate".

Back then the average life expectancy for our ancestors was about 25-40 years. Today, the average life expectancy for an American is close to 80! Back then, they placed their faith in prayers and believed that their "life is in the hands of God." So, if they were under God's protection, why didn't they live longer?!

God has been good enough to give us the knowledge to improve our life by using science. Shouldn't we thank God by applying the knowledge we've gained?

We can't blame God and religion for human mistakes, sins and regressions. The word "fate," or its Arabic equivalent, *kismet*, i.e. our own Persian *ghesmat*, always appears when people find themselves at a dead-end!

There is no pledge to foster superstition and nonsense as part of our religion, or worse, pass it along to our children. Calling those practice nonsense "religious" is an insult to a reasonable person's intelligence and religion.

My friends, when it comes to a community, what occurs on the surface is often different than what's happening in the depths. We depend on those members of our community who are productive and whose natural or learned abilities are of merit to society as a whole, such as educators. They represent the key to our progress. Educators are our human capital – without them our community would be poor indeed. It is to the teachers, and to the parents in our community that we rely on to foster intellectual growth in individuals and societies.

Let us remember that in most cases, success has been the result of preventing catastrophes. In this wild world, full of problems, especially problems that have originated from religion (!), it's up to you and I to prevent many of today's and tomorrow's miseries.

Wise people solve problems.
The genius prevents them from happening.

There are as many judgments about religion and its achievements, no doubt, as there are religious people in the world. Sadly, since its migration our Iranian Jewish community has become afflicted with intellectual divisiveness, which religious speculators have taken advantage of in order to cause divisions among us.

Perhaps it is human nature that there are those who want to be worshipped, and those who seek out others to worship. To my mind, worshipping an individual is worse than idol-worship — and it was never part of our culture. It is said that after **Alexander the Great's** conquest of Iran, he asked his advisors, "How can I rule the sophisticated people of Persia?" One advisor told him, "Burn their books and kill their wise men." Another, reputed to be **Aristotle**, told him, "There is no need to burn or kill. Among the people of that land, pick those who are less intelligent and more ignorant, and assign them to great tasks; but assign the more intelligent, literate and perceptive members to humble and trivial tasks. The illiterate and idiots will always be grateful to you, even as they will never have the ability to rise. The educated and wise men, however, will either migrate to other places, or else, they will spend the rest of their lives, tired and disappointed, in isolation, at a corner of that vast land."

If we allow a rabbinical position, with all its esteem and responsibilities, to be awarded to an immature and inexperienced youngster, we should not be surprised by the unacceptable or less-than-thoughtful or enlightened things he says. We should be asking: Who decided that they are qualified for their position? Were their own teachers, qualified? To give such a position of importance to a misinformed person is the same as assigning a big task to an ignorant person. And much more dangerous!

I wish that passionate followers of religions, along with educators in charge, would pay attention to this meaningful sentence of *midrash*: "The *Holy Torah* consists of black fire (the words in black ink) and white fire (the space between the lines)." A deep understanding of this phrase and its adoption as one of our guiding principle would help eliminate destructive prejudices and prevent regression from spreading.

We often pray in those moments when we find ourselves powerless before an insoluble problem. It is when we are weakest and most in need that superstition creeps in.

Dear Educators and parents, wouldn't it be better to train our youngsters to use their own incredible powers of intellect to depend on themselves from the early stages of their development than teaching them to solve any crises through prayers and magical thinking? Otherwise, rather than taking responsibility for their actions, they will depend on prayers for their wish fulfillment and will blame their failures on "the evil eye," "fate" or God.

"Fereydoun ordered the Chinese painters,
To sew and draw around his castle.
You wise man, be good to the bad people,
Because good people are good and fortunate as they are."

Antiquarianism and anti-rationalism have never been, and can never be, constructive attitudes for a bright future.

Those young men who have been subject to the regressor's brainwashing are often afflicted by mental paralysis. They spend their days imagining they are fulfilling as many commandments as possible but in reality they are accomplishing very little. Compare that to the moderate young believers who are achieving great things for themselves, their family, their community and the world.

Maimonides said, "[The purpose of what we are commanded in the *Torah* is] to advance compassion, loving kindness, and peace in the world." The *Torah* says in *Leviticus* (19:14), "Don't curse a deaf person, and don't place stones before the path of a blind person." To mislead misinformed youngsters is like placing an eternal stone before their feet.

We should all be vigilant, because tomorrow, it could be your own child's turn.

You are responsible.

***Mitzvot* or "rewarding goods", are meant to make the present world a better place, and not to be held out as a guarantee for a Heavenly afterlife or for fear of Hell.** God calls human beings his own children, saying, "Be good to my children; I will be good to you." A moderate and balanced religious follower is a person who, with or without a head cover or another garb, seeks out modern knowledge, and despises pretense, exhibitionism and propagandizing. He is someone who says to the regressors, "People's faith is no one else's business. Every person is responsible for his or her actions. Enough of interfering in people's affairs and teaching them nonsense!"

A child who learned logic, would never accept nonsense.
But if they indoctrinated him with nonsense, he'd evade logic.

Cecil B. Demille (1881-1959), the famed movie director, was once asked why most of his films, such as *The Ten Commandments,* had a religious theme? He supposedly replied, "What better subject than religion, which has already been publicized for thousands of years?!" Likewise, what better way for the speculators to make an easy living, other than from religion?!

Dear parents and educators,

There are thousands of students at your command. Tomorrow — given their lack of education in scientific, economic, professional or social fields, on the one hand, and the indoctrinated sense of guilt on the other, — will these students, along with their families, become financially independent? Or will they be forced to bring their hands forward in prayers or to collect donations, expecting God to do something?

Is studying religious subjects enough to help them provide for their future?

Rabindranath Tagore (1861-1941), the famed Bengali poet and thinker, wrote,

"Let me not pray to be sheltered from dangers,
But to be fearless in facing them.
Let me not beg for the stilling of my pain,
But for the heart to conquer it.
Let me not look for allies in life's battle-field,

But to my own strength.
Let me not crave in anxious fear to be saved,
But hope for the patience to win my freedom.
Grant me that I may not be a coward,
feeling your mercy in my success alone;
But let me find the grasp of your hand in my failure.
Amen."

Those people, who in the name of religion, propagate regression are raising a generation that doesn't know what it wants, or even what it's supposed to do. **Their only concern is solving their own problems. They never try to elevate themselves to the level of other people. Instead, they bring down the beloved children of the community to their own level.**

My friends, if you want your children to be balanced, moderate and successful in their 30's, then you need begin to talk to them when they are just 3 —as the *Torah* commands says, "Whether you sit at home, walk in the road, rest or rise". You need to begin warning them against all extremism at an early age and make them understand why you are against it.

Maintaining balance brings about success, intelligence and prosperity. Unbalanced mental development is not unlike the disproportionate growth of a human limb; anyone suffering from such a condition is considered to have a handicap. Yes, wherever science and insight exist, there will be balance, too.

"Wisdom sent words to Prosperity:
'Come to me as my comrade.'
Prosperity smiled, 'Why, where I'll be,
You shall have to be there anyway!"

One of the best known ways to hold a debate, i.e. ideological wrestling, goes back to the time of **Socrates** and **Plato** and consists of examining the words, deeds and writings of your opponent, and employing their weaknesses to your advantage.

Please pay attention to the words and writings of the regressors but don't take them lightly or laugh at them. Instead, examine them seriously to realize the depth of the misguidance and ignorance that awaits their students, who are possibly your own children! Here, I repeat a translation of **Rabbi Ezrahian's** words,

"Use your intelligence; and don't be like a robot or a playback device, to automatically repeat whatever you learned in the seminaries, without thinking and pondering for yourselves — thus, humiliating the *Talmud* and the Jewish religion." These are the words of an intelligent, rational chief rabbi. They come from the heart, and thus, will reach other hearts. Rabbis like him will preserve our identity, not the preachers of nonsense.

To reference **Forough Farrokhzad**, this is how some paths die and some paths stay.

Pretending to be asleep to the issues dividing our community doesn't mean that our enemies, too, have fallen asleep in pursuing their agenda.

Today, numerous sects are spending large sums of money and marshalling their resources to impose their dangerous beliefs and goals. Our sects focus on what to wear and how to eat; as if the preservation of our religion depends on diet, clothing, prayers and miracles!? This is surely not the path to piety. Your path leads to failure – failure of your intended goals, and to the **failed students of your traditional schools who are wasting their time!** Today, critiques and protests are being expressed openly against religion in

334

general, and religious people in particular, in a way which wasn't imaginable, even as recently as 25 years ago.

The regressive traditionalists may be successful today in spreading and propagating their beliefs. But every single day of their success means thousands of days of regression for the rest of society.

For humanity, religion has been like clothes, protection from the basic problem of being naked! However, over the course of the millennia, mankind has grown, but our clothes haven't changed. The commentators would like modern mankind to still wear the clothes of our primitive ancestors – regardless of how we may have evolved or changed. But they won't succeed – because the clothes no longer fit! However, the more you support or cooperate with them, the more our religion will have problems. What we need is to make a dress from the same cloth as our religion, one that fits the intelligence, perception and knowledge of our modern youngsters.

We can only consider as religious, those individuals who without personal or group interests, employ the power of religion to expand friendships, family kindness, science and humanity.

There are some Orthodox Jews who consider themselves "more religious" than others, and don't let their children marry other Jewish youngsters who don't meet their definition of Orthodox — (or even, let them sit down together to eat!). And these are the people who claim to be "saving" our religion!

There was never discrimination within the Iranian Jewish community in all its thousands of years of history. You, the traditionalists, are responsible for creating all these unreasonable prohibitions. And you are responsible for tarnishing the image of our religion worldwide. The world doesn't view us as separate sects but as one religion. So we are lumped together, even the hat-wearing, black-coated, long-bearded *mullahs*, who go kissing the hands of our enemies!

In Islamic culture, when a person cannot be held legally responsible for his or her crimes, for reasons of age or insanity, the fine is divided between the closest kin. Likewise, the rational minded and reasonable members of our community have always been paying for the mistakes of these regressors, even wrongly paying their wages or unemployment salaries. Should we continue to make these mistakes, imagining them to be a "rewarding good" although tomorrow they could separate your own children from their parents?

No! A resounding "NO" must be our answer!

They wish us to live in modern *ghettos*, in ways that would make us easy targets. They practically build such *ghettos* in order to be able to walk to their synagogues, or by wearing some so-called religious, traditional clothes that make them stand out in society. Doing so has consistently been a dangerous path to follow – yet they refuse to learn from their mistakes.

Parents and rational educators bear the responsibility of teaching our children to stand up to those who would wish to misguide them. When someone tries to sway them with superstition and nonsense, they need to be able to say "No" with confidence! If they don't they will never think freely or achieve their full intellectual potential.

Religious educators should realize that forcing students to learn by rote does not lead to understanding, and that teachings based on emotion rather than reason are neither stable, nor do they mean that their students have accepted what they've studied or that they've been fully convinced, despite appearances. In contrast, faith is the gradual acceptance of what has been studied.

Saadi said,

"Glass and mirror are found everywhere; hence their cheap value,
Rubies and diamonds? So hard to get! Hence, their high value!"

The times are past when a *mullah* was deemed to understand everything, and people would follow him unquestioningly out of fear! True faith is when people gain knowledge and make their own decisions about faith.

Today, religious texts have become more readily available through translation. We need to study these for ourselves, so that we can better understand better what our religion says and decide for ourselves about the traditionalists' commentators and interpreters.

Dr. Arani once said, "that the river of history is a holy and clear river that pours in the sea of perfection. Let us be, in this holy river, those droplets that arrive at the sea, rather than those which get stuck, and rot in the mud and dirt of the brink."

Our enemies take advantage of the confusing meaning of ancient texts and the writings of the extremists, past and present ...

...and which make our children rebel, evading religion or resisting living a good life. The decrease in our religion's population is testament to this. Let's us remain open-minded.

As **Bernard Shaw** said,

You see things as they are and ask, "Why?"
I dream things as they never were and ask, "Why not?"

Parents will find out how much they know, or don't (!), when their mature children begin to ask them serious questions. Modern knowledge provides us with new answers to old questions, rather than having to rely on incomprehensible so-called religious replies to modern questions!

No nation, people or religion is compelled to practice nonsense and superstitions, or to accept the stated punishments contained in ancient religious books. It's the communities themselves, who encouraged by opportunists, create peer pressure to follow rules they themselves have embroidered. Why should thousands of our most able youngsters be held back, in the name of religion, from making any effort to earn a minimum standard of living or even learning to defend themselves. In some families, these youngsters become even estranged from the kindness of their parents. What meaning can religion have, if it doesn't bring pride to families, unite people and bring them closer? What use does it have, if it doesn't encourage the stability, harmonious unity and survival of families and societies? Just look at the afflicted families around yourself!

There is no difference between the conflict of two brothers of the same religion, who each practice a different variant, and the conflict of two brothers each of whom leads a different way of life. Unresolved differences are the roots of hatred and the spiritual cancer of families and society.

Understanding the religious commandments and maintaining moderation in observing them, are as important as their practice. Understanding the commandments is much more important than just believing in them. A famous Persian proverb states, "Let's say your dad is wise; but what did you gain from his wisdom?"

First, we should prove the inheritance, then claim possession.

The story is told of a man watching a horse race, as one of the horses took over its competition, the man began to boast loudly — in self-admiration. A person next to him asked, "Is she your horse?" He answered, "No, but the bridle is mine!" Are we not just like that, when it comes to feeling that we "own" the legacies of our customs and traditions?

They asked a king, what should we teach your son first: how to write, or how to swim? The king said, "Swimming comes first! If my son needs to write, he can still ask others to do it for him. But if in this whirlwind of life, he finds himself in danger in drowning, no book or person would come to his help."

Today, free-thinking needs to come first – rather than a life-time of stagnation in the cage of religious prejudice and bigotry. Life is not meant to serve religion; to the contrary, it's religion that is here to serve life. Religion is not meant to be the whole of life, and this goes for both "good and bad" religions. Religions are meant to complement and enhance life – to guide people to excellence; and this is true, regardless of the religion. Religious people are those whose belief serves to spread kindness and humanity — and not those, who in the name of religion, provoke children against their parents. They too shall realize the shame of spreading divisiveness, when their own children are taken from them by the ultra-Orthodox *glatt (!)* religious groups!

"Human heart is not made of iron, to be softened on the anvil. Rather, it's like a crystal vase, which once you broke it, forever remains broken."

Jomo Kenyatta (ca. 1894-1978), the first prime minister and generally acknowledged as the founding father of the Kenyan nation, once said, "When the missionaries came to Africa, they had the Bible and we had the land. They taught us to pray with our eyes closed. When we opened them, we had the Bible in our hand, and they had the land." Likewise, after our obligatory immigration, those who rose to guide (!) us, found a job, and the others became their hostages!

They have built a long-standing institution that has always managed to find vulnerable customers. We need to provide accurate information, so others might walk away from this scam.

A regressor is a regressor, no matter what clothes he or she puts on. It's the thoughts and actions of the person, which become causes for pride or shame, and religion is just an excuse.

It's said in *Pirkey Avot* that knowledge brings wisdom, and the wise man is a knowledgeable person. We will not understand reality, it appears, until we become realists.

As **Fyodor Dostoyevsky** (1821-1881) wrote, there is an image of God in human beings, and anyone who can disfigure this image is without his share of human emotions.

Spreading divisions and wreaking fear, first becomes a norm, then a mission. Prejudice and misplaced encouragement can cause even the best of men to forget the ugliness of division. Such people get drunk on a sense of power and control, so much so that they forget the human cost of divisiveness (particularly as between children and parents). Lucky are those who have no contempt at heart and don't know anything but kindness.

The American philosopher and educational reformer, **John Dewey** (1859-1952) wrote, "Education is a social process. Education is growth. Education is, not a preparation for life; education is life itself." In this spirit, are not humanity and kindness, too, religion itself?

Friendship and kindness is not spread by making insults and threats. Zealous propaganda, deceptions, hypocrisy and ruling over others are the gateway to all forms of violations, tyranny, cruelty, and an inability to accept the rights of others. **To be a good and knowledgeable person; only this can give value to a person and his religion.**

The centuries long campaigns of propaganda and massacres for and against religion need to be studied, as ways to understand the reasons for the low Jewish, as well as Zoroastrian, populations worldwide. Consider the following paragraph, for example, which I

340

paraphrase from the Persian magazine *Payvand* (No. 36, 3rd year): "**Comte de Gobineau** wrote that by the end of the **Safavid Dynasty** in Iran, there were [only] about 300,000 Zoroastrian families living in Iran."

During the reign of the Safavids, Zoroastrian persecution and murder increased substantially. Some historians estimated that that at the start of the Safavid's reign, the Zoroastrian population was 600,000 families, or about three million people; by the time **Nasser-e-din Shah Ghajar** became King of Persia, the number of Zoroastrians, without any significant emigration from the country, had dropped to around 8,000 people!

Mr. **Jamshid Pishdadi** has written of the Zoroastrian persecution in Iran, in the Persian magazine *Bidari* (No. 35). Here is an English adaptation of this text prepared for this volume:

"After the **Zand Dynasty**, the condition of Zoroastrians became worse than ever, so much that not more than a handful among them were literate. Their *jaziyeh*, i.e. the "non-Muslim tax" had made them so poor, that at some point, 60 of them in a village, unable to pay this religious tax, and being beaten by clubs of the government officers who demanded the money they didn't have, opted for conversion to Islam. From the **Safavids** onward, the conditions became even worse. They were hated and persecuted by the Muslims, and they often had to work hard labor to make a miserable living. Often, pregnant Zoroastrian women were sent to carry heavy bricks up construction ladders, so that their pregnancy would be aborted. Until 1895, unlike the Muslims, Zoroastrians were not allowed to carry umbrellas, wear glasses or rings, or install bi-partite doors at their homes. They were not allowed to ride donkeys, mules, or horses. On rainy days, they had to avoid touching any Muslim, or they would be beaten nearly dead. They couldn't touch fruits in the market, and when visiting a Muslim home, they had to spread a piece of cloth underneath them, lest they "contaminated" the carpet. The Islamic version of "an eye for an eye" didn't cover the wronged Zoroastrians, as once around 1820, a 16-year old of this faith drank directly from a water reservoir, and a big fight ensued among the Muslims and this people.

"Because of random and fatal invasions into their homes by the Muslim street gangs, they would put yellow turmeric on the cheeks of the girls, to make them look ugly. The Muslims even went after the Zoroastrian dead, stealing what they could from the Zoroastrian sepulchers. Constantly persecuted, often denied the right to buy bread, meat or fruits, they decided to open up stores in their own neighborhoods. They couldn't use public baths, nor drink water from public faucets. The grandmother of this writer's wife [i.e. Mr. Pishdadi's] had a horrible personal experience, when years ago, a few young Muslims cornered her in an alley, took away her walking stick, put a rubber tube around her neck, and pulled her on the ground, to the point of near suffocation. After a month in the hospital, she survived the ordeal, but the culprits got away unscathed, never found.

"Zoroastrian girls were often abducted, and after being violated, they would be forced to convert to Islam. Given that these conversions were handled by major Muslim clerics, it's clear that they had a hand in such atrocities. The world has learned about the suffering of the Jewish people in the hand of Hitler's Germany. Likewise, the world ought to know of the suffering of the Zoroastrians, that millions of them were killed in the hands of the Arabs and Muslim Iranians, and that millions more had to put up with harassments and persecution. Again, what was mentioned was just a fraction of the persecution this people suffered, without mentioning the mountains of murders and massacres that were brought upon them over the centuries. Thus, it seems reasonable if the Iranians try to appease their Zoroastrian compatriots in an annual ceremony and ask for their forgiveness. No one can make up for the tyranny and oppression that they have endured, but this could be a good lesson for the coming generations to treat well people of a different thought.

"May we add that, what the Jewish and Christian peoples, and recently, the Bahais, have seen in that country, in some cases, is on par with what the Zoroastrians suffered." – and we might add, if not more.

As for the Jewish population of Iran, according to the late **Prof. Amnon Netzer** (*Padyavand,* P. 55*)*, toward the middle of the 12th century C.E., i.e. just about 800 years ago, there were about 600,000 Jews living in 50 Iranian cities (some claim that during the **Sassanid Dynasty,** about 1750 years ago, the number was even higher). Even if we assume the average life expectancy then to be 40 years of age, today's population should be exponentially larger than it is.

This explains why religion, in the general sense of the world, hasn't served humanity well. Indeed, contrary to religious claims, Religion has brought great harm to humanity by spreading prejudice — a malice that continues to this date. Humans have not reached that liberating point, at which according to a Persian poet, "he could only see God." Instead, mankind has continued to focus on appearances and superficial differences. There are many who believe that the tree of truth has only one branch, the one which they have seized; for this reason, they can't see any of the other branches! But each and every leaf in nature holds a message, and it demands listening ears and healthy minds to hear their story.

The founders of these two ancient religions, i.e. Judaism and Zoroastrianism, deprived of the right to propagate their religion, wished to make these separate lakes of their communities survive independently — independent from the larger society! But the fact that any water at all has remained in these once vast oceans, with no new water coming in, after thousands years of drought, natural or man-made, can only be described as a miracle. We might ask, they suffered so much, when they didn't proselytize almost at all; how much more they could have suffered, if they did try to spread their religion?

Wherever they have lived, the Jewish people have been a *de facto* social barometer. From the beginning, Jews did not seek to convert others because they felt no need to advertise or impose their way on others. So why today do certain groups use sophistry to force their ideas on others in the community?! Back in Iran, there were no signs of the kind of commercial religious speculators that we see here, and we all lived under a single umbrella.

In recent years, due to their large families, the so-called religious population has increased. However, no one seems to taking note of the numbers of people who are giving up on religion altogether. By analogy, some might look at current statistics and conclude that the divorce rate is declining, but consider that in California, marriage rates have dropped 30%! Statistics don't lie; they simply put the facts before us. But they can be manipulated. In this case consider that real reason divorce rates seem to be declining is that "there hasn't been any marriage to be divorced!"

It's said that **King Abbas, the Safavid** ruler, asked his minister, "How is the economic situation of our land this year?" The minister said, "Thanks God, it's good enough that all of shoe-menders have been able to go on a pilgrimage to *Mecca*!" The king said, "You idiot! If people were in a good financial shape, the shoe-*makers* would have gone to the Mecca, not the shoe-*menders*! People can't afford new shoes, so they keep mending them. Go on, find out where the problem is, so that we can find a solution."

So as you see, a proper indicator, despite its simplicity, can express the condition of the system in its entirety.

In studying the increase in the religious population, we need to consider the issue from many different angles. Can we call a brainwashed person "religious," even if he believes that someone can't be Jewish if he doesn't have a piece of cloth on his head? The number of religious adherents will increase, that is until the truth about them is disseminated, and then people will flee in droves – but, unfortunately, they may flee religion altogether.

Gandhi said,

To be arrogant about one's knowledge is the worst form of ignorance.

A community's survival depends on keeping pace with other world civilizations, not in being in awe of their own beliefs and sealing themselves off from others. If knowledge and religion are not tied together, both become paralyzed, and the communities suffer as a result. A prejudiced person is someone who never understood the philosophy of religion.

Indeed, mankind's animosity toward one another throughout history has its roots in the self-importance, egotism, and absolutism of religious believers whose cults and traditions have sprung from these religions. Meanwhile, the distinguished people, "the chosen people," have been those who were wiser and acted even more wisely.

Whenever one religion has held power over another, it has brought nothing but tyranny, cruelty, oppression and corruption — for itself, its followers, as well as for others.

What is it that makes a bigot violate another's rights – is it religious absolutism or human selfishness – or both? By contrast freedom of thought can make a balanced and moderate person out of anyone.

It's well known that delusions of grandeur and arrogance have their roots in ignorance. And indifference leads to the growth of regression. To quote **Saadi**,

"The wise man neither assumes arrogance,
Nor the humility that would lower his worth.
He would neither overestimate his value,
Nor would he yield in altogether to pitiful humiliation."

Society must teach our children that bigotry and prejudice are mankind's most horrifying illness. Throughout history, religion has been the source of many tragedies and catastrophes; and there is no reason to think that this has stopped. However, it is rumor and gossip that often ignites such catastrophes. Gossip to a catastrophe is like yeast to bread!

What happened in New York on September 11, 2001, despicable as that act was, could only have been committed by people whose minds were filled with spurious theories, and false claims fueled by twisted rumors and promises of rewards in an imagined afterlife. Someone who is brainwashed to kill himself and others for some "greater purpose," some self-inflated notion of grandeur, is like the donkey that throws himself off the cliff, so that its master would die along! Despite this, let us not forget that this young man was once a child, who years ago in classrooms and at home, at the bench or at the dinner table, heard hate-filled stories! He was drawn into a web of revenge and as a result, the world saw a flood of human death, along with millions of tons of concrete and steel, all burning up in flames, all coming down from the collapse of the World Trade Center. Yet, in the end, it wasn't the planes or the explosion of jet fuel that triggered that day's events; rather, it was the vanishing point of what religious hatred and intolerance can wreak on society.

On September 11, 2001, mankind was forced to acknowledge that in the 21rst Century hatred has gone global! The United Nations and the leaders of the developed countries should now realize that the true frontiers of fighting terrorism are where hatred is being promoted, i.e. the extremist schools of religions, be they poor or rich — with the poor people "fighting" under the control of prejudiced, bigoted rich people. To fight this war, we should correct the culture and the teachings of such schools, and we should banish, once and for all, the promulgators of hatred and their related books. Otherwise, this endless, vicious cycle of fear, hatred and destruction will continue, generation after generation, in the name of religion.

Bertrand Russell, the great English philosopher said, "Society is a lamb that deserves the government of wolves."

Allowing extremist schools to flourish and the number of their students to grow is not only negligent, it's dangerous. Inevitably it leads to war. Sixty years ago, it was in Europe; today, it's in Iraq, Afghanistan and tens of other countries, each inflamed by some form of religious conflict.

Instead of spending trillions of dollars to make weapons and kill indiscriminately, we should root out these lairs of corruption and ban those textbooks that are being used in extremist religious schools all over the world. Fighting extremists on the war front will make no difference if we don't target the schools that are producing more and more brain-washed radicals.

May the day never come when today's benevolent citizens become tomorrow's guilt-ridden group, filled with remorse over what they allowed to occur. The irony is that religion which wishes to provide for the welfare and happiness of mankind has more often than not been the source of conflicts providing a way for opportunists to exploit prejudice and hatred to cause humanity harm!

Around 65 years ago, in one of the sections of the famous central *bazaar* of Tehran, the population of mice increased substantially to the point that the businessmen became alarmed. An old man from a village went to them and said, "Give me a few empty vases, and I will uproot all the mice for you." And he did just that! How? The old man threw several mice into each of those vases, and let them be with no food or water for awhile. As time passed, the stronger mice ate the weaker ones. He freed the killer mice in the *bazaar* who then proceeded to eat all the baby mice.

One could argue that we followed a similar plan by training unbridled violent rebels to fight the Communists in Afghanistan, who with time turned against their very hosts. Is it not our responsibility to attack these problems or should we wait for the Savior to rescue us?!

Goethe said, "Everyone hears only what he understands."

Hafez said,

*"Don't blame me for growing
By myself, in this lawn,
I grow only
The way they grow me."*

Dear parents,

Students need to be exposed to modern knowledge before they become contaminated by outdated notions. A higher education, social interactions with both members of his community and those from other communities, are the experiences each student deserves. As I said earlier: **No bird ever learned to fly inside a cage.** A human brain is like a parachute; it can only save someone if it's opened. A youngster whose brain religion has closed to reason – his fall is inevitable.

Dear parents, you need to be aware of what they are teaching in our schools. It's not only the ancient commentaries which are so out-of-step with our times and border on the comical; worse, it's the regressive readings of the teachers, citing scriptures and commentaries to enforce a severely limited worldview and an unproductive way of life. The day may come that you find your children, or bride or groom, have become contaminated with such prejudice and bigotry that their minds can no longer be changed. Instead, they will be insistent on changing you! All the while, the educators will tell you, "Don't worry about secondary things! *May the big barrel of the wine be intact, even if a small cup fell and shattered into pieces!*"

When **Prof. Chaim Weizmann** (1874-1952) and **David Ben Gurion** asked **Prof. Albert Einstein** to be candidate for president of the newly-founded State of Israel, Einstein rejected their offer saying that he could be of more service if he remained with science.

Science is the force that discredited yesterday's anti-Semites. Monumental scientific figures such as Pasteur, Fleming, Einstein, Salk, Koch, etc., brought the forces marshaled against progress to their knees. The medical cures they and their colleagues discovered vastly improved our world in a way these anti-humanists can't ignore.

We now find ourselves faced with a society, a world, so vastly different from the one we once knew. Consider, for example, the balance and moderation evident in the religious beliefs of Iranian Jewish families and their unity with other people as compared to other religious groups. The Iranian immigration hasn't been just a matter of moving from one place to another. We also traveled from one time to another. We bear a duty to put behind us the nonsense and superstitions of the past, to have an outlook that is beyond religion and in synch with modern times. We must treasure those qualities of moderation and balance that assured our survival and bonded us as a community and reject those directives that seek to break families apart.

Moderation gives balance. It doesn't say, "I'm the only one who is right." Instead, it prefers "We" over "I." It doesn't burn, but it warms. It's not a forced imposition, but it's a thoughtful pause. It's not fate, but wise solutions. It's not dumbing down but curiosity and research. It doesn't create hatred but spreads love and kindness.

"Nicer than the voice of love, I never found a souvenir
That could stay and endure, under this turning blue dome."

Moderation goes with kindness, and it favors the guidance of human intelligence. As such, it leads to harmonious thought, devoid of agitation.

Religious leaders, concerned about the dangers of modern life as expressed in popular culture and advertising such as a variety of cults, promiscuity, homosexuality, gangs, addictions, etc., would prefer our children be blinded by their extremist beliefs! And although they are right to be concerned about popular culture, should we not also be concerned about religious extremism? Shouldn't we instead have our children choose those religious beliefs that lead to pride and not toward nonsense and superstition.

Should we encourage our children to believe, for instance, a religious (!) teacher who tells a 12-year old boy, "every time you shake hands with a woman, 20 years will be deducted from your life-time!" What will this child's feelings be toward other women when he grows up, from his wife to his sister or even his mother?

Or consider, the rabbi who advised people at a recent dinner that, "Anyone who eats raw green vegetables, which are possibly polluted with some tiny little insects, he or she would be subject to 37 whips in the afterlife!" Isn't it a shame to call such people "rabbis"? Seventy years ago, back in Iran, when more than 80% of our forefathers were illiterate, our mothers and grandmothers would disinfect green vegetables by washing them with permanganate.

Before you give money to these religious leaders and institutions, please talk to them. See if they are truly concerned with the preservation and support of the Jewish people, or only themselves. Please listen to what ideas they are preaching, and make sure you want to support them.

One of the controversial areas of religion is the concept of "the soul." To a scientific-minded person the soul is nothing more than a manifestation of the hereditary intellectual and moral principles largely embedded in our DNA. Someone who lacks intellectual and mental capacities is referred to as "soul-less." We can see a true "séance" with clear eyes in the actions, behavior, moods and attitudes, even the appearances of the survivors of a deceased person – as their genetic inheritors not because of the deceptive practices of some psychics! These genetic traits are our eternal soul that emerges in the next generations, and according to the Hebrew term *gil-gool,* i.e. "re-incarnation", we can see it in the body and spirit of the future generations — generating love, or wreaking hatred.

A regressor believes that his own soul and the souls of his like-minded fellows are above all others! This is the attitude that informs his teaching ignorance and weaving nonsense!

According to modern scientific findings, people who don't like others because of their sense of self-importance actually hate themselves! As it's been said,

"The scorpion stings, not because of contempt,
But because it's a requirement of its nature."

And this is the very scorpion, when faced with a dead-end, unable to sting another or escape, surprisingly enough, kills itself.

In the city of Kashan in Iran, scorpions abounded. People would place a fatal scorpion at the center of a lead tray, surrounded by cotton balls, drenched in kerosene or alcohol. Once they set the cotton balls on fire, the scorpion, seeing itself besieged by flames, unable to find a way to escape, would sting its own brain with its venom. This is the same creature that comes into the world by tearing the sack of its mother.

I am reminded of a recent event in the democratic country of Denmark. It seemed that a group of immigrant children were the cause of an outbreak of lice in the schools that was so bad that the government distributed anti-lice disinfectant powder to schools' parents. But some Danish parents refused to use this lethal powder because they didn't want to encourage their children to kill animals. Instead the government was forced to distribute some small vacuum cleaners among the parents, to extract the lice alive from the hair of their children, by suction.

Compare this attitude regarding the treatment of animals to the way animals are treated in most Middle Eastern countries to understand the difference between the civilized moderate citizens of a country such as Denmark, and those countries where brutal murders, massacres, executions, and lapidations (i.e. "stoning"), are practiced and for which religion is often blamed.

One day, the advocates of hatred will finally understand that all such atrocities are the products of the seeds of hatred sown during childhood. In some rituals a child's pet lamb is slaughtered before their eyes; or a beautiful bird is killed and swung over their heads, its feathers plucked, in order "to fend off evil." They seek to compensate for a wrong by doing another wrong. The impact of such inhumane rituals on children and their development is horrendous. Whether it makes them sad, mad, or brutal, it's not hard to imagine the horrible impact such scenes have on children. What could possibly come out of such brutal acts? We all have memories of such inhumane behavior.

The Korean neighbor of a friend of mine told him, "You Middle Eastern people commit a sin; you sacrifice an animal as redemption for the sin; then you resume doing more sins!" Indeed, the way others perceive the behavior of any community is part of the more or less bitter realities of that society. The annual tale of the ritual sacrificing of chickens and rooster is nothing but a shame and embarrassment for all of us.

If only these religious hypocrites and impostors could solve the problem of their daily bread with a vacuum cleaner!

One the best articles I ever read about the Middle East, said (I am paraphrasing), "**Muhammad Reza Shah Pahlavi,** the last king of Iran, was the cleverest of all men in history, because he succeeded in making his people appear to the world as he wished!"

His father, the late **Reza Shah Pahlavi**, once said, "**Sometimes it's necessary to force happiness onto an ignorant bunch!**"

Do we need to be forced to keep in step with modern civilization? For a long time, the slaughtering of animals, even for religious customs, has been forbidden by many European countries, including the Netherlands. This was a very wise and good decision.

The Syrian born psychologist, **Dr. Vafa Sultan** (b. 1958), recently displayed an Islamic religious tractate on Aljazeera TV which stated that "If a man were praying, and a dog, a pig, or a woman (*sic!*) passed close by him, his prayer would become void!"

Do we need to support religious rules which discriminate against women? The Persian poet **Parvin E'tessami** (1907-1941) wrote in one of her poems,

"Piety is in the purity of intention, not in one's clean clothes;
So many an impure, who's clad in a clean cloak.
A burnt out wood stick can't light our path, as a candle would;
We need to turn on a torch, which can still shed light.
You don't waste the jewel of time with such reckless deeds;
There's a high price to pay for this priceless jewel."

The majority of problems in the world today stem from the extremist schools of religion. To waste our children's time in the so-called religious classrooms, teaching them long out-of-date lessons, is like trying to benefit from the light of a burnt-out piece of lumber! To illuminate the road ahead, let's light a shining torch for our children, not a burnt-out candle.

Let us lead our children towards a rational, scientific approach that includes religion, instead of filling their heads with religious nonsense and superstition! We can't blame our ancestors for the way they observed their religion. The blame is on people today, who, thanks to their misplaced financial support, enable the observance of ancient customs and rituals and who in their ignorance of the true intent of these religious zealots bring great harm to our community.

False faith is much worse than an atomic bomb. Just look at those suicide bombers who are acclaimed by the zealots for their piety in murdering others. What sort of faith is this? What sort of God? The God of kindness and love, or the God of anger and cruelty? This is where reason and human intellect no longer rule; instead, provoked emotions, devoid of all foresight, take over.

"A wise man is not one who asks for a higher rank;
Instead, he'd be thinking of the end of things."

We must warn the leaders of regressive religious sects that not all commentaries are wise or reasonable and not all interpretations are sound by today's standards.

"How long your eyes make love to the design of the vase?
Let go of the surface, and look for the water inside!
So many shells of human body, all over the world,
And all alive, so that life could go on;
But not inside every shell one could find a pearl.

Open your eyes! Look inside of each!
And see if there, one could be found!"

Prejudice is a means to exploit others and to commit cruelties. It begins by lying in the name of religion; It grows by people's tolerance, even as they are deceived; And it continues in the name of "rewarding deeds." Finally it gets to the point where all reason is put aside and it is considered a sin not to practice some nonsense ritual.

Even if your intention is good, that doesn't mean your way isn't wrong. The path of the religious fanatics allows opportunists to take control for their own purposes, and empowers them to mislead everybody else by disrespecting any other person, government or nation who thinks differently than they do. They do so by claiming that another's food, cloth or way of life is *har_m,* i.e. *non-kosher,* and sinful — yet the money of those very people is quite respectfully welcome!

"It's a wonder, indeed, that after all that poison
Which brushed over the eyes of this garden,
There's remained still a bountiful of
Petals and colorful jasmines."

Albert Einstein told us *not to be ashamed of our old clothes, but of our old thoughts.*

Today's miracles are the everyday miracles of science, and not the ugly, despicable words of fanatic religious advocates. The success of any community requires its scientists and we will not produce any by keeping our elite youngsters captives at the traditional religious seminaries. If you have been successful in your life, is it because you stayed within a cage, or because you broke free? Did members of the Jewish community achieve those things they are proud of in religious schools or by being graduates of secular schools?

Our Persian Jewish community has never had any internal ideological conflicts. For 2700 years, our community has observed the *Ten Commandments*, as well as such prominent commands, as "Wish for thy neighbor, as you'd wish for thyself" without believing they only apply to a "person of your color, religion, gender, or race." The Jewish people have acknowledged our fellow Jews from other communities such as the dark-skinned Ethiopian Jews who rejoined the larger Jewish community after 3000 years! Neither color, nor race, nor religion, should matter to a free-minded person. The only thing that matters is to be human.

The world's extremists thrive with their gifts of causing divisions and creating conflict. In their propaganda, they appeal to youngsters' emotions.

Dear instructors, educators, preachers, religious advocates, and anyone else who's in charge of the religious schools and seminaries:

On what basis do you choose your textbooks? Is your criteria teaching tradition or knowledge? Any book or article that doesn't help our students improve their future and their future quality of life, is not worthy of being taught. Teaching our students the most current scientific thinking is indeed a "rewarding deed." However teaching them ignorant superstitions such as the *mechitza* or "the partition between sexes in the synagogue"; *blekh* or "tin plate"; religious scarf covering the head, or the superstitious wigs, etc., is not.

Teaching foolishness leads to people leaving religion altogether, far more than mixed or unhappy marriages. Your teaching nonsense is more responsible for the decline in the population of our religion than anything else. Even though you may claim that as the Orthodox have large families, and that your numbers are increasing; it is your example that is driving the more moderate members of our religion away from observance, support of and self-identification with our community.

How you chose to interpret and observe our traditions is critical to our future survival. Not all the readings, and especially the mistaken commentaries and interpretations of the past, are acceptable. I bring an example from **Saadi** that I will try to render in English:

"A Hindu said sarcastically, 'Oh, dudes, are there two Gods?'
Damn be anyone who says that there is only one God!'"

They scolded Saadi, "Oh, thou Saadi! Why did you blaspheme as such?!" He said, "I did not; you read it wrong, and you interpreted it erroneously!"

Here is the correct rendition:
A Hindu said sarcastically, 'Oh, dudes, are there two Gods?
Damn be anyone who says that! There is only one God!,"

With a single punctuation mark, the entire meaning of the phrase changes, and a blasphemy becomes praise of God! So too with the way we teach our religion. We need to open minds, not close them.

Einstein used the following analogy to describe the limitations of human perception: Imagine nature to be like a lion who's shown us nothing but its tail. What we know of this tail of nature is very much like what a flea could know of a lion by squatting on its tail.

My friends, In the words of a Persian poet,

"Our story, good and bad, will all be recorded.
Time has a page, a book, an office and a court."

Rumi has portrayed the case of a wise man with foresight in one of his most wonderful stories of the *Mathnavi*, a summary of which I find most useful to our discussion. He wrote,

A wise man was riding his horse in the plains, when he noticed a snake crawling into the open mouth of a man in deep slumber. Although he

rushed to the rescue, he was too late to catch the snake by the tail. Thus, he devised another plan.

He awakened the sleeping man with heavy blows of the whip. The startled man jumped to his feet, and began to implore the horseman to stop beating him. But the horseman didn't heed his pleas, and instead, drove him toward an apple tree. Then, as he kept slicing the air with whiplashes, he forced the poor man to pick some rotten apples from the ground, and eat more and more of the stinky fruit. The man cried, swore, pleaded, begged for mercy, but these led to no avail.

"Cursed be the moment when we met!
What did I do to deserve you?
Are you an angel of death?!", he asked.

This went on for awhile, until he could have no more apples, at which point, the horseman made him run, as fast as he could, across the meadow — and he did just that, tired as he was, until the rotten apple began to ferment inside his stomach. Night was falling, when finally, fatigue and fermentation made the poor man vomit whatever he had swallowed, now sour and reeking of a horrible stench. And behold, there emerged the cursed snake! Then the man realized the wisdom behind the horseman's inexplicable cruelty, and began to thank him for having saved his life. The wise horseman said,

"If I had told you the secret, you'd die of fear!
That's the nature of wise men's enmity:
Even their poison is a medicine.
In contrast, the friendship of the ignorant people
Can only bring suffering and darkness."

The hostility of the regressors is not based on reason; rather, it's based on emotion. Rational thought serves them not at all. The venomous snakes of prejudice and creating divisions among our

358

people are what the religious opportunists push into the open mouths of our people.

We need to condition our support for these religious schools on their agreement to teach our children modern science. Our children need to be taught religion and study religious texts and the commentaries of the rabbis of the past, but they must be placed in the context of their history, their time and the environment in which they were written. Knowledge must be passed along to the next generation, not superstition.

Those schools and instructors that are fully sealed against all contemporary thought are not worthy of our support. To the contrary, we must seek to isolate them from affecting our community. Such groups are fearful of their followers becoming awakened and informed.

I warn parents that to compromise over such fundamental issues as children's education is an irredeemable act of cruelty toward present and future generations. For too long superstitions have taken precedence over the commandments.

Communities can't let a certain group of people take control of our schools, only to have them quash science and promote superstition...

A school or university is the proper place to teach science, not to promote prejudice. The good or ill prospects of a nation, a country, a town or a family, can be gauged by the progress and knowledge of their children. I read this very awakening truth that according to statistics —— a Japanese university student has four times the knowledge of an American student; and on average, a Chinese person has ten times the savings of his corresponding member in American society (adjusted for their cost of living).

Based on these facts, we don't need a psychic to predict the future of these countries. For the largest countries in today's world, such as the United States, the indication of their wealth and power resides neither with their military nor in their financial centers but in their universities. This is true as well for our community – but is our future dependent on our students in secular universities or those in religious seminaries? Those who recommend or teach the lessons of such traditional schools are, in reality, not our friends. A school shouldn't become a toy in the hands of some opportunists eager to separate youngsters from their families and set them apart from the world and modern civilization.

When a child's mind is contaminated with hatred and superstitions from an early age by his parents, and when these ills are only intensified at school by the teachers and the books they use, we can be assured of his future as a pawn in the traditionalist's game. We can count on him to contaminate his own children in turn, and like the domino effect, to spread the seeds of hatred. Just look at the world, and see for yourself that it's already happening.

As things stand now, these children will never be fully cured. By contrast the child who receives a proper higher education can become a productive member of society What's needed is more informed parents and instructors to develop moral sensitivity and responsibility in our children.

Absolutism — or narcissism — only yields conflict and hatred. If only the self-proclaimed advocates of religion would allow space for people to sit next to each other; if only they would hold hands in walking the difficult path of life; if only they would teach everyone that:

All people, despite all differences, regardless of race, color of the skin, religion, sect, and the like, are equal in essence, and equally deserving of respect.

Jean-Jacques Rousseau (1712-1778), the French philosopher, said that, if we know all humans, then our love toward other human beings wouldn't know any borders or religions. Likewise, the followers of religions would also see no borders between lands and no differences between human beings. The true heroes of society are those individuals who try to make the world a better place to live.

When **Pope John Paul II**, the leader of the Roman Catholic world, died the world united in mourning his passing. Even a hard-headed Communist like **Fidel Castro** (b.1926) announced three days of mourning in Cuba! Even in Islamic Iran, in the *Husseinieh Ershad*, one of the major religious-cultural centers of the country, they convened a memorial service for him! The world understood that Pope John Paul II had been baptized in the pure ocean of kindness and compassion, and not in the dirty pool of bigotry, narrow-mindedness, and prejudice.

As recently as 1956, I can recall personally seeing a sign in a restaurant in Tennessee that read, "No dogs or negroes allowed!" By contrast, today, African-Americans hold the highest positions in the land. Yes, change can occur, if we have good teachers.

Unfortunately, the world's extremist religious leaders continue to propagandize without even the slightest regard for human values. In their view, anyone who is more extremist, more fanatical, or more superstitious, is more "religious" than others. One should have reminded them of the words of the Persian poet **Ferdowsi:**

"Those with immature thoughts:
Their words aren't worth listening."

The future will not judge our generation by the degree of our religious observance or avoidance but by whether the humane values of our time have been passed along successfully to the next generation.

The regressors in our society have so far succeeded thanks to the naïveté of the ill-informed people. As a Persian poet, **Sa'eb Tabrizi** (1601/02-1677) wrote,

"Once, a pious man took me to a mosque,
So that I'd repent;
I went and I repented that I'd never again
Go to any place without thinking!"

A candle doesn't lose anything, even if it lights all other candles of the world.

Alliance Israélite Universelle was a bright candle in the dark nights of Iran, which continues to shine to this day.

During the 19th century, our ancestors in Iran, living in a most discriminatory atmosphere, severely impoverished, both economically and scientifically, wrote to the Jews of France for assistance. The Jewish Association of France wrote back, saying that what the Iranian Jews needed was to give their children a proper education.

The Iranians responded that, "We are in need now, *today!*" only to receive the same reply — educate your children, so that others would need *you*. The French didn't tell them what to eat or not, when to wear a scarf or a cap, or how to pray! Instead, they told them to educate their children.

On July 12th, 1873, the Iranian Qajar king, **Nasser al-din Shah** (1831-1936), on a visit to Paris, met with a delegation of French Jews, led by **Monsieur Adolphe Crémieux** (1796-1880), the founding president famed Alliance Israélite Universelle who was at the time a member of the French Assembly.

In the presence of **Mirza Hussein Khan Sepah-Salar**, a member of the king's entourage, the delegation of French Jews asked the king of Qajar to allow Alliance Israélite Universelle to begin building its schools in Iran. Much to everyone's satisfaction, the king of Persia agreed.

Obtaining this permission has a long and sweet story of its own, which is unfortunately outside the scope of this volume. Once the royal permission was granted, given the state of life in those days, it took them about 25 years to find, secure and prepare the locations for the schools, and to train the needed faculty to be sent to Iran. It was not until 1898 that the first Alliance school was opened in Tehran, "in the European style," as they used to say. This was followed by a second school in Hamedan (1900), a third one in Isfahan (1901), the fourth in Shiraz (1903), and the fifth in Kermanshah (1904). Over time, they gradually founded more new branches in other cities with a sizeable Jewish population, such as Nahavand, Sanandaj, Bijar, Boroujerd, Yazd, Kashan, etc.

According to the Persian book by **Ms. Nategh**, *"The Cultural Report of the Foreigners in Iran,"* these were, at one time, up to 23 locations throughout Iran. In 1925, they were able to send the first group of the graduates of Alliance Israélite of Isfahan to Europe.

In 1898, at the opening ceremony of the first Alliance Israélite Universelle in Tehran, or as the Iranians would later know them more commonly as "Alliance Francaise" or "Etteh_d", **Monsieur Joseph**

Cases, the representative of the institution in Iran, said, and I paraphrase,

"By opening the Alliance schools in Iran, civilization will begin to flow into the country, as it already has in Turkey and in Morocco."

Beginning in 1873, those truly courageous, brave and civilized French Jews, men and women, non-religious or secular, yet believers, of the Alliance Israélite Universelle and their associates helped and saved numerous people out of poverty. **At that time, the leaders of Alliance didn't send religious books or instructors from Paris!** Instead, they worked hard for 25 years, studying the circumstances and building the grounds for the enormous task ahead. They fought hard for this goal, even against Russian, British, American and German governments, governments which supported the Christian missionary schools as a means to control the areas under the influence of the French language.

Finally, in 1898, they sent the very first group of teachers, men and women, in modern garbs, with no religious cover or veils, well-learned in the European civilization of the time. They travelled on horses, mules and donkeys, on carts or *kajaveh's,* i.e. "camel panniers", passing through thousands of miles of unsafe desert and mountain roads, until they reached us. Is this not an excellent example of this writer's claims having been realized? Is this not proof enough of my assertions?

The Alliance didn't create prejudice or bigotry and never told us that a non-Jew wouldn't be accepted in the Alliance schools. As a result, many of the government figures, in the early years of the **Pahlavi** period, received their education in the Alliance schools.

In past generations, not only Jews, but also Iranian Muslims, as well as many other Middle Eastern and North African countries (Morocco in 1862, and Baghdad in 1864), got a true sense of

364

contemporary civilization through a modern education. If it were not
for Alliance, not only our ancestors, but also we **would have had to
continue learning some *mullah-type* stories in the traditional
religious or secular schools,** adding more misinformation each day.

To give some comfort to ourselves, we might have ended up
saying,

"It's no sorrow if our plumage was tragically burnt:
We're content that our ashes can no more be set to flames!"

One of the reasons behind the relative success of the Iranian
Jewish community during the **Pahlavi Dynasty** (1925-1979) was that
we benefitted from the knowledge of the many generations of Alliance
graduates in Iran. Many of us and many Iranian Muslims are indebted
to the kindness of the Alliance Israélite Universelle, which came to our
aid in those times of religious discrimination and severe poverty, both
social, economic and cultural poverty. Indeed, if Alliance Israélite had
not acted to educate our children in those times, and if the wise leaders
of the majority of our community had not welcomed the aid of
Alliance, we wouldn't have been what we are today!

In the meantime, the story of a student from my hometown, the late
Dr. Jahanshah Saleh (b. 1904) is of utmost interest. Dr. Saleh
received his elementary education at Alliance Israélite school of the
city of Kashan, where he also learned French and English. During the
Pahlavi Dynasty, he went on to become a Senator in the Iranian
parliament, one of the most prominent presidents of Tehran
University, and a Minister of Health as well as a Minister of Culture.

The Etteh_d school of the city of Kashan – later renamed by its
original French, "Alliance" – was founded in 1904 by the late **Agha
Yeghuti-El** and his wife **Sara**, who had no children. (In Jewish
culture, Yeghuti-El is another name for Moses). The school had a
capacity for 500 students. But this was not to be an easy task.

Unfortunately, throughout history, the fanatics have always tried to keep life inside children stagnate, because they believe that the children would otherwise run away! When Agha Yeghuti-El opened the school, a bunch of myopic *mullahs* made the parents pledge that their children would not learn the foreign language, i.e. French! In such a climate, Agha Yeghuti-El was forced to devise a plan. Therefore, he decided to hire those traditional instructors to teach at the school. Soon, those who had called for a ban on the Alliance schools, found themselves teaching in its classrooms! The opposition ceased.

Yes, we can know people from what they do. Agha Yeghuti-El was much ahead of his time. **If today's societies, too, don't have such leaders, rabbis, and teachers, ahead of their time and above their place, then some desperate hunters would catch the astray members of the community, and take their prey to the cages of fanaticism and regression.**

Fortunately, over the past few years, after one hundred years since the opening of the original Alliance in Kashan, a project was initiated to appreciate the services of the founder of the school, and to commemorate and preserve his name for posterity. Accordingly, thanks to the efforts of some of the former students of that school, now in their 60's or 70's, a center has been established in the name of **Agha Yeghuti-El and Sara Kashani**. The center includes a synagogue, library, classrooms, and a beautiful hall for festivities, and it's near completion. As for the school in Kashan, it still stands there after more than 100 years. Recently, with financial help from **Lord David Alliance** (b. 1932), another of the former students of that elementary school, the building was renovated and has been reopened.

There is a saying that, "Fish grows from the head, not the tail!" Societies, grow and progress, or fall into their demise, by the heads of their societies. We were fortunate that the majority of our religious leaders in those days were not like some of those that we see today, who keep talking nonsense and call themselves leaders. They greeted Alliance Israélite whole-heartedly.

Only the *mullahs* of two Iranian cities of those times, i.e. the Eastern city of **Mash-had**, and the south-central city of **Yazd**, didn't welcome the Alliance. One said, "There is no point for poor kids to become literate and educated!" Another said, "These guys have come from the foreign countries to drive us out of our faith and religion!" But throughout the history of human civilization, productive changes have occurred when two different, contrasting cultured have faced each other.

I read a book in Persian by the skilled writer and scholar, **Ms. Homa Nategh,** called "The Cultural Report of Foreigners in Iran" (*Karnameyeh Farhangi Farangi dar Iran)*, with much enthusiasm and pleasure. By the end of this book, I realized that as early as the 1860's, Alliance Israélite Universelle had also been involved in founding the schools of **Tabriz** in the European style (!), namely the Roshdieh, Loghmanieh and Eh-san schools. I also learned that at some point, of the 654 students of the Alliance Israelite school in the city of **Hamedan**, only 173 students had been Jewish (Hamedan used to host a large Jewish population, and has a shrine that's widely believed to be the mausoleum of **Esther** and **Mordecai**, i.e. the central characters of the story of *Purim* . **I highly recommend studying this book to all my friends.**

In writing the book, **Ms. Nategh** has closely examined some of the Alliance's old documents in Paris, as well as pertinent correspondence with the French Foreign Ministry. On page 11 of the book, she writes, and I paraphrase,

"Studying the history of Alliance Israélite schools and Iranian Jews, in the 19th century and early 20th century Iran, casts much light on one of the most obscure corners of the social history of Iran. In retrospect, we might say that in regards to anti-Semitism and Jewish persecution in Iran, the Iranians proved themselves to be much more honorable, compared to the foreigners, especially the British. Because during the early years of the **Mozaffar al-Din Shah Qajar** (1853-1907), when these schools began to be established, the biggest sabotages and the greatest hostilities came not from the Iranian government, nor the Iranian political figures, nor even the Iranian clerics, but they came from the British Ambassador **Arthur Harding**, and the British consul in Iran. To shut down the nascent Alliance Israélite schools, the English went so far as to threaten the Iranian government. They took it as far as creating rebellions and violent clashes, so far as organizing the commoners and the hooligans to protest against these schools in the cities of **Isfahan** and **Shiraz**!"

(The British corruption, conspiracies, sabotage and bribery, had come to a point that even the intellectual members of the **Qajar** government had become frustrated with them. These included a very knowledgeable Qajar Prime Minister, who fighting against the imperialism, said in a derogatory language,

"Oh, you Englishman!
May your body become paralyzed!
And may your London become as destroyed
As our own desolate village of Sanglaj!")

On p. 12, Ms. Nategh continues that, "In those years, none of the European governments were willing to give their support to the Alliance schools and the helpless Iranian Jews."

"Thus, it's highly surprising that the reporters, historians, and writers of memoires of the Constitutional Period of Iranian history, have forgotten about the history of Alliance schools in Iran, despite the fact, that they housed more students than all other Iranian schools; that many Iranians, both those involved in education, as well as government figures and businessmen, were members of its committee; that today, many of its high school graduates are considered among the greatest of Persian poets, writers and translators of Iran."

Recently, a child of one of those students donated millions of dollars to charities, including a $30 Million donation to the University of Southern California. It's safe to assert that no other foreign entity ever did what Alliance Israélite did for Iran. As Haji Agha, an Iranian neighbor of ours put it, "In those times, if any engine broke, they'd say, 'Call an Armenian guy to fix it!'" and if a letter arrived from abroad, they'd say, 'Call a Jewish boy to read it!"

Science and culture have the ability to provide for mankind's future, not religion, skull caps and hats, or facial hair...

The Persian poet **Sa'eb** wrote,

"If anyone could play the drum
Of wisdom on his turban,
The dome of the King's Mosque
Would've been the wisest among men!"

Let us learn from our bitter past experiences that judging people by their religion or the level of their religious observance only leads to pain. Religion is a private human matter, not a means to identify individual or collective good.

Pre-historic man had a brain that was about twice as large as a chimp's but it functioned five times faster and more accurately. Primitive man exited the Stone Age through his intellectual growth and evolved as a person. He and she learned how to fight heat, cold and darkness by finding shelter, putting on clothes, or lighting fire. He learned the secrets of plants and seeds and so, developed agriculture.

She learned how to domesticate animals and raise cattle. He invented the wheel so they could move about faster and with greater ease for longer distances. This evolution continued to this day when human beings are creative and productive creatures. Yet, with every day that passes, we must acknowledge that we're just at the beginning of the path of progress.

Naturally, people have different powers of perception and intellectual growth. Some who are endowed with more spiritual and physical talents and abilities became leaders and used the laws of fear and revenge to control their followers. They devised inhumane punishments for those who stood against them. At some point, they made religion into a means of earning a living, so much so, that the book of *Jeremiah* (23:16) warned:

"Thus saith the Lord of hosts: Hearken not unto the words of the prophets that prophesy unto you — they lead you unto vanity. They speak a vision of their own heart, and not out of the mouth of the Lord."

People have often accepted whatever was said to them just because it was attributed to religion. When there was no rational basis for their arguments, they reached for the tool of "miracles." They recognized no law other than the law of religion.

For ages, superstitions continued to be accepted as facts or truth. This was the case until some learned and wise groups, though the ways of enlightened religions, adopted rational and humane principles such as the *Ten Commandments* to guide them. They realized that a criminal or his religion cannot shoulder the entire blame for religious folly. Parents, teachers, schools, and in general, the whole society, all have their share of guilt and ought to be blamed for any mistakes committed by an individual in the name of his religion. As individuals and as a society, as we progress, we try to move away from pitting us one against the other.

Each religion, and its self-proclaimed advocates, offers it own path for the welfare of its believers and to improve the human condition. Yet it's surprising that today some groups believe that their students might have a better life by banishing modern knowledge and sciences from their school curricula! They omit that knowledge that might enlighten their students and instead hire ignorant, dark-minded instructors to teach nonsensical theories about the Savior, as well as Hell and Heaven. At its core, all they are teaching is unquestioned obedience.

Dear educators,

My humble message is this: "Don't confuse prejudice with faith: Prejudice and bigotry are the results of fear and unreal emotions, while faith originates from reason and rational arguments."

In ancient times of ignorance and lawlessness, the sages were forced to teach their followers by rote emulation and by appealing to their superstitions and fears. The wisdom, values and ethics that they had to impart were packaged in ritual and fueled by their own limited knowledge and worldview. As the world has become more sophisticated, we need to prune those ideas and practices that are illogical, impractical and nonsensical in order that our core values and ethics are not lost.

Those who wish to dominate others to evil ends find no better tool than a cruel and inflexible religion. Having followers that unthinkingly imitate their every ritual and obey every command make them easy targets for being defrauded and manipulated.

I'm reminded of a poem by the Qajar era Persian poet, **Yaghma Jandaghi** (1782-1859), about a certain Persian diplomatic figure of the time, **Mirza Aghassi** (1783-1848), the prime minister of **Mohammad Shah Qajar** (1808-1848). It seems that **Mirza Aghassi** spent the entire budget of the country, more or less, on two things: building *ghan_ts* — i.e. an ancient Persian irrigation system of connected wells — and making weapons, guns and cannons. Jandaghi wrote,

> *"**The Haji** didn't left a penny through the whole kingdom,*
> *As almost all was spent on building* ghan_ts *and cannons!*
> *But neither the farm of the friend got a drop of that water,*
> *Nor the house of the foe is a bit scared of those cannons!"*

The net result of the religious traditionalists' behavior and propagandizing is that there will be no one who remains "religious" in the true sense of the word: having alienated those who would do the religion honor and increasing the numbers of those whose actions are deceptive rather religious. Furthermore, their actions will only result in the net decline of our population.

In a world in which cats and dogs no longer fight, it's a pity that divisiveness has yet to cease among religious factions.

My intention in writing these pages is to study why we are being torn apart; and if in the process we uncover some faults and problems among us, they are only being exposed so that we may find solutions. It is in this spirit of seeking answers that I hope my readers will overlook the shortcomings of this book and this writer.

As the poet wrote,

"Many a time I said it, and many a time I'll say again,
That I, madly in love, don't search this road on my own."

***

"Scores of arrows I sent at all directions,
So that one would manage to do the job."

Even if a single person benefits from these lines, I will feel as if I've fulfilled my mission.

My friends,

About 25 years ago, we were warned that the regressive traditionalists would one day show up at all of our family meals in the form of our children, brides, grooms, sisters, brothers, and other family members. We need only compare today's number of families which have been afflicted with this problem to their number in those earlier days: The sharp rise is staggering.

Unfortunately, the propagators have been able to exploit the unconscious fear of nonsense and superstition in our community and in society as a whole. Unless rational people speak out and stand up against their propaganda, the invisible power of this fear will find its way to everyone's home.

When we remain silent in the face of a wrong, it only emboldens the perpetrators who take our silence as our approval.

Those trafficking in extremism will use any means, and make any alliance that serves their goals. Consider the connections between God-less Communists such as Cuba's **Fidel Castro**, and the supposedly God-knowing militant religious extremists. Such unholy alliances exist in all societies, or even families, albeit in different forms. Once a religious person or an ideologue becomes unreasonable, he or she would accept any story, no matter how illogical it is, irrespective of his or her faith in God, or the lack of it! Such a person imagines that the aims justify the means, even as human lives are "sacrificed" (!), or families are destroyed.

The only thing that matters to a regressor is recruiting more and more followers.

More than a thousand years ago, the great Persian poet **Ferdowsi** predicted that famous religious people would join in with the most renowned God-less people. They would kiss the hands of their long-time archenemies, in such a way that,

"A new race would emerge
From the peasant, the Turk and the Arab,
Yet it'll be neither the peasant, nor the Turk, nor the Arab.
Words turn into nothing but empty games, before their acts.
They'd hide all treasures beneath cloaks,
While they'd try and give away
People's lives and harvest to the foe.
They'd spill blood for their ways,
And ugliness would befall the visage of the world.
They'd seek others' harm to their own end,
And they'd bring in religion, only to help and justify it all."

Indeed, true watchfulness comes with a sense of responsibility and action that fulfills one's duties. Misplaced silence is a sign of irresponsibility.

The German philosopher **Immanuel Kant** (1724-1804), wrote that ***the greatest human virtue is to fulfill our duty for the sake of duty.***

It is not the traditionalists' ill-conceived ideas and false beliefs per se that are the problem. It is that in the face of indifference the regressors would impose their ways and will on us: in order to "glorify the name of God", they even ask the non-Jewish merchants in their neighborhoods to close their stores on the Sabbath! Or they close roads and public cinemas for the Sabbath, as they do in Jerusalem.

374

Modern psychology tells us that the moral value of a person depends on the number of duties he undertakes and fulfills.

Confucius (551-429 B.C.E.) said that a wise man would not use duty and responsibility as a means to serve his interests, gain a profit, or make a living. Indeed, the act of fulfilling a responsibility is the very reason for him to go on living. **The happiness and good fortune of a society are the rewards of the timely fulfillment of duties by its members.** It's this sense of responsibility that connects human beings together, much like the links in a chain. **Religion doesn't constitute the whole of life, so let's not interrupt all life in the name of religion.**

The harmful impact of "brain-drain" on communities is simply irreparable. Just consider the intelligence we lose to a cloistered unproductive life, and the many intelligent and productive people who flee religion altogether – both as a response to extremist religious practice.

Hannah Arendt (1906-1975) said that revolutions do not bring down the system; rather, it's the collapse of the system that brings about the revolution. Indeed, the bankruptcy of our deeds as a whole is one of the main reasons for the declining Jewish population.

Karl Popper (1902-1994) said that society was like a house: for it to stay clean, you need to keep sweeping!

The inflexible and narrow-minded claimants of religions, past and present, instead of cleaning up the house of religion, have been hoarding ancient, unusable tools — and saying that they are the basis of preserving and spreading the religion! Nothing is more destructive than coming to realize that someone or something, in whom or which we truly believed, has been deceiving us all along.

I wish you well but I warn you and our community of the dangers of your ways.

Dr. **Albert Szent-Györgyi** (1893-1986), the Hungarian scientist known for his discovery of vitamin C, for which he was awarded the 1973 Nobel prize in Physiology or Medicine said,

"Any race or species that cannot adapt to its environment is doomed to extinction."

The Jewish population is decreasing, not because we are adapting to our modern environment as the traditionalists preach, but rather because our religion is not adapting.

"Turn back from the thought of division, so that you become a whole: Since once the devil leaves, the angel of God would arrive."

Moses Mendelssohn (1729-1786), the great Jewish philosopher of the Reform Movement, said, **"My religion recognizes no obligation to resolve doubt other than through rational means; and it commands no mere faith in eternal truths."** In other words, you can't analyze faith, and our religion proceeds through rational questioning not dogmatic faith and blind ritual.

Religion was dealt a severe blow when emulation replaced understanding, and religion itself became a means to earn a living. When pretending means more than believing, and when standing out is how you equate being religious, religion loses its value – and invites discrimination and bigotry.

Enough of forcing people to do things by spreading fear! Put an end to identifying people based on their religion, way of life, dress or head gear! The Jewish people have suffered long enough for following this very path.

The Biblical commentator, **Rashi** (1040-1105) wrote, "Better worship out of love than out of fear." By no means, can it be taken as an act of religious practice to throw people into a big well, lest they might fall into a small puddle!

A poet once wrote, taking on the voice of God,

"We look at the inside, and the condition,
Not the outside, and the surface hubbub."

According to a video series I saw, **today's China has more exceptional students than the entire population of the United States, since that country managed progress from its ancient culture.**

Meanwhile, for "religious" reasons, bright students who might excel in various fields of learning and various professions are kept in a virtual cage, forced to parse the meaning of ancient prayers and commentaries. You are not only impoverishing them but our entire community and depriving future generations of their potential contributions to society.

What good has ever come out of making our youngsters assume the looks, attitudes and mentalities of our ancestors in ancient times?

Erich Fromm (1900-1980) wrote that, "The history of man is a graveyard of great cultures that came to catastrophic ends because of their incapacity for planned, rational, voluntary reaction to challenge."

Breaking up families lays the groundwork for destroying society at large. There is a vast difference — like the difference between heaven and earth, or day and night — or between a fire from afar, and the suffering of those who are standing at the center of the fire as their families are destroyed before their eyes. It's said in the Jewish culture, from the voice of God,

Better my name be washed away with water, than a family be broken up.

In Jewish culture, the family is referred to as the Holy Temple. You bear the blame for destroying many families in the name of promoting your version of religion. Perhaps this wasn't your intention but regression is the cause, and those who support it are to be held responsible, whether they acted knowingly or unknowingly.

Back in Iran, neither we nor our ancestors had such customs or divisive dictates. They say, "A healthy mind is found in a healthy body." Likewise, a healthy society is one with rational ideas, customs, and ways of life. Let us help our youngsters have a rational understanding of religious commandments and laws rather than letting them become part of a parrot-like, imitative culture.

The day will come when the world's Jewish society finally realizes the reasons behind international anti-Semitism and finds regression and the regressors within our own community with their isolationist attitudes to blame.

"These two things drove me to sin:
An unfulfilled fortune, and an imperfect intellect.
If you make me into a religious man, I deserve it.
And if you forgive me, it'd be better than revenge."

The *lives* of our ancestors had little in common with today's *living*. A Jewish mother used to be carried away with joy when her children and husband returned home, so much so that she would forget her hunger — because she thought more of *life*, than of *living*.

The Chinese under Mao, starved near a billion people in the greatest ghetto ever created. They said, in good faith, that "because we have Mao's book, we have everything we need!" Yet China today has progressed in ways unimaginable 50 years ago.

378

My friends, we have seen with our own eyes that societies which can change have proved they can succeed. They will survive and progress. But those, who stagnate mentally, who try to remain where they are, will eventually join the vanished peoples of history.

The *Talmud*, in a section on friendship and social interaction, says, _____ __ _____ — "Chavrota O Mitota", i.e. "Either Friendship or Death;" either being with the world, or meeting our demise.

The *Talmud* equates, rather unequivocally, the misfortune of not having a friend, a companion, a social life, with death and demise. For a wise man lives among the daily events not in an isolated world made up of sectarian and religious discrimination.

Dear instructors of religious schools: My address is to you.

When so much Jewish knowledge is wise, why continue to teach outdated nonsensical superstitions and include them in everything you write as if the whole religion depended on it. Why? Why not blind us with the brilliant contemporary applications of the *Talmud*, i.e. the *Gemarah and Mishnah*?

Indeed, **when a teacher himself is a fanatic, how can he guide any other person?**

"One's pain can't be cured by whining about it.
One's mouth won't taste sweet by talking about honey.
Stomping doesn't make the pain go away, and
This bed-ridden patient can't thus rise from the bed.
This I know, that if the first line of our freedom isn't
Written in the words of science, it'll never grow legible."

Much of the nonsense that these narrow-minded people call "our religious laws" is too embarrassing and foolish to repeat. Just read their books to find out how misinformation is used by their sages against us, and how vintage wines are made into sour vinegars. Yet, you keep yielding more vinegar, and you have your followers distribute them! Just read your own translations to see who is to blame. How long should we go on hiding our heads in the sand, in denial or indifference?

The amount of technical information in the world doubles each year. Today, on average, what a person learns within a day is more than what an eighteenth century person would learn in an entire year. Yet, to date, you've continued to teach the books of certain superstitious *mullahs* in the name of religion! If the intellectual atmosphere in traditional schools is confined to religion, nothing significant or worthwhile will be left for the world.

A regressor takes advantage of even a just criticism, claiming it as an insult to his religion, in order to protect his own interests and justify his position.

Our very humanity commands us to treat every person with kindness. No person or position is deemed holy, but we accord respect to those whose actions merit it. For some groups pretending some ignorant person is important is no more than a way to gather customers.

Once, a great man said, "Never act in such a way that would please the followers of hypocrisy but hurt those who tread the path of truth! If you do so, you'll fall out with both!"

Heraclitus (540-480 B.C.E.) wrote that, "The secret of Happiness is Freedom, and the secret of Freedom, Courage." **Religiosity or piety is found in the light of reason, true faith and loyalty, not because of a hat, a cloak, or a prayer composed of flattering admiration!**

There is a vast difference between a passionate believer of a religion ("an ideologue") who is emotionally wedded to the idea that their religion is without fault and their leaders should be followed without question and a logical, rational person, who's in quest of an ideal ("an idealist") for whom religion is imperfect but which he seeks for its spiritual, communal, and even traditional value. The ideologue considers all kinds of change to be a sin; while the idealist is open to all reasonable ideas, regardless of their source. An idealist **would be ready to change directions and choose a better path, if he realizes that indeed, he's been wrong; an ideologue thinks change, no matter how reasonable, to be a sin.**

I once talked to the father of a religious young man. Previously, he had encouraged his child to follow this path; but now, he regretted having done so. He said, "I told him to observe Sabbath, to rest one day per week; but I had no idea that his discussions of the *mikveh,* the *kosher* kitchen, etc., would lead to his rejecting his mother and me as 'deniers!'"

Speak to parents who've been afflicted by this plague, before your own children become contaminated. This same father continued, sadly, "They told me if your child becomes religious, he wouldn't become addicted, wouldn't join the gangs, and if he adopts a certain appearance, he would avoid all things wrong! But then, I watched him become addicted in a different way." Not only did the other children in his extended family not come to any harm but, to the contrary, they became high academic performers, successful financial achievers, people of good reputation, owning their own homes and businesses while remaining proud members of their religion. This only increased his regrets.

Meanwhile, his observant son and his fellow fanatics have many children, that are poorly supervised, and that have become a financial burden to their grandparents. "They take solace that through lives are devoted to God," he said, "who, frankly, has no need for admiration from them or you or me; and who tells us at every stage of life, *'You act, and I give you the blessings.'"*

My friends,

The great Greek philosopher **Plato** (428-348 B.C.E.) wrote that, sensations are mere appearances: passing, temporary, unstable, ephemeral. Only a deep understanding of things shall remain.

Things that we feel with our five senses, i.e. what we see, hear, touch, taste or smell, these do not last. But one's understanding of the meaning of issues is what transcends the momentary – and our understanding has to do with a person's perception and the degree of their intellectual sophistication.

Clothes themselves have no heat but they keep a body warm. The religious commandments, too, have no heat in and of themselves; it's how individuals perceive, understand and observe them that gives them life. Hence, the same verse can influence one person to be a terrorist; while another person, with a different understanding of the same texts can be inspired to be a moderate believer and a paragon of society.

The actions of the prejudiced members of religions demonstrate how destructive the ideas of religious leaders_, past and present_, can be. Fortunate is the one who deems doing good a moral duty, and doesn't do so out of the bogus fear of an imaginary hell or the idea of "sin."

"Oh, brother! A story's like a cup,
And the meaning therein like a seed.
A wise man takes out the seed of meaning, and
He doesn't heed the container, even if it's talked about."

Reason and belief, faith and morality: They all complement each other; they're all necessary. An unscrupulous believer would tie a suicide belt around his waist in the name of God; while another believer sees service to others as a moral duty and would never allow an act of terror.

To support their nonsense the regressors cite like-minded commentators; and when anyone complains, they say the dissenter is not religious! But let's make sure they know that such tricks don't work anymore.

A prejudiced person allows other people no rights of their own to complain or protest, nor to reveal any shortcomings or faults and flaws in their system of belief!

The mullahs and self-appointed religious tyrants who worship in a manner so contrary to our ancestral ways, will broach no dissent. But it is our duty to speak out and to stand up against them, with all due respect.

Friends often ask me, "What made you decide to spend years of your life on writing a book, and to spend such large sums of money to get your words out, just so that people could hear them?"

My intense desire to serve people has led me to spend much time and heavy expense to publish my thoughts. Knowing I couldn't change everything, I decided to begin removing the mountain of nonsense and superstitions by taking out the pebbles at the mountain skirts. Thus, page by page, argument by argument, quotation by quotation, I too gradually became an author.

My journey began in 2003, when I was very disappointed by a group of Orthodox rabbis. This convinced me to write a long and detailed letter to them, in English, which was subsequently published in the *Shofar of New York*. Soon after, I received a call from **Mr. Yousef Shaheri**, the founder and editor of that magazine, telling me that **Rabbi Yamin Levy**, who held a high position at Yeshiva University, wished to talk to me.

I prepared myself for harsh criticism and perhaps even a serious protest! Instead when Rabbi Yamin called the next day, he said, "Mr. Gabay, We've decided to publish your letter, as it is, in the magazine of Yeshiva University. For this, we need your approval!"

I agreed but admitted I was surprised: "You and your institution are Orthodox. How is it that you approve of this letter?!" "What you wrote," he replied, "isn't against the truth." This gave me great encouragement.

Over the course of many years, through many sleepless nights and by much effort, that single letter turned into a voluminous book in Persian, *Lahaz_ti Bar_ye Tafakkor*, or "Moments of Contemplation" — and subsequently, the present volume which is an abridged English adaptation of it. Obviously, not all of Orthodoxy is as inflexible as we sometimes believe. Like any other sect, some Orthodox Jews are pragmatic while others remain lost in a fantasy world. Unfortunately, our Iranian Jewish community has been for the most part in the latter group!

A writer finds inspiration when he has to something to say and a pain to talk about. He shares his experience with others, hoping that by doing so he might untie one of society's knots. This, without a doubt, makes him rather vulnerable, particularly in a society such as ours, where few people would be willing to leave records in the hands of unkind people. Thus, the writer gives himself the courage to fearlessly relate what he thinks with sincerity, supporting his case with pertinent documents, evidence and proof.

Writing these pages has taught me a similar lesson. I could no longer sit on the sidelines and watch families be broken apart, one after the other. Hence, I took pen in hand and began to write.

384

Abraham Lincoln, the great American president, advised, "To be kind to others through sharing our sorrows and joys; to try comforting people and healing their anguish and wounds; these would ease our own pain, even as they make us forget our sorrows."

Likewise, if I hadn't introduced my ideas and thoughts to the larger society, perhaps few would know me at all –which may for the best!

The mind of a regressor works very much like an eye's pupil: The more light you shine on it, the tighter it gets!

Successful people rise to their feet when everyone else has given up. They hold the pen and write, without fear of criticism, when others are afraid of writing about reality. They tend to think of hardships as facts of life. If the river-bed was devoid of all rocks, the sweet music of the water would not be heard. Thousands of promises don't make a fraction of the deep impression that a good piece of writing does.

It isn't an insult when someone reveals disturbing facts; or points out the mistakes of a particular person; or says that certain sayings are longer meaningful for our times. To judge or condemn a particular rabbi is not an insult to the religion, but rather a way to protect the reputation and defend the work of all other virtuous, honest rabbis. Indeed, the Holy *Torah* teaches that not even the prophets were devoid of errors!

There's a difference between telling the truth and insulting others. Obviously, no one would have anything to do with me, or the likes of me, if I had kept my thoughts to myself. But once anyone offers his ideas, he should prepare himself for hurting others, getting hurt, and all sorts of criticisms. **Only an unwritten assignment has no errors in it!** When something is written, it's quite natural for it to have mistakes, especially in the eyes of those whose interests have been threatened by it! A famous author once wrote: If a writer didn't make mistakes in his writings, then what else could he do?!

A good piece of writing is like a jar of honey, prepared by the efforts of thousands of bees, to sweeten the mouth of the reader. Sadly, a non-rational person is allergic to this honey! What a brave few are they, who might even pledge their lives to serve humanity, yet don't want to have anything to do with religion! Let us find out how we could benefit more from civilized advocates of our religious commandments.

A great person once said, **"Religion is harmful, but necessary."** It's harmful, because all religions are absolutists; they deny each other, and thus, they create opposing conflicts. But it's necessary, because mankind has not yet arrived at that degree of civilization where we can do without the benefits of the community, ethics, morals and good deeds that religion commands of us. But will such religious absolutism always be necessary?

You don't need to live for another hundred years to see the future. The visionary French science fiction author, **Jules Verne** (1828-1905), who was way ahead of his time, vividly depicted in his novels a future in which our humanity guides us.

For a rational and free-minded person, it's our conscience that takes precedence over all other beliefs. The vaccine of conscience compensates for the harms of extremism.

Dr. Jonas Salk (1914-1995), whose discovery of the first polio vaccine saved millions of people from this dreadful disease, was a free-thinking Jewish doctor. His dedication to humanity was such that he even tested the vaccine first on himself, as no volunteers could be found for the experiments! Later, when asked about his refusal to hold on to the exclusive legal rights to his discovery, he explained that, the honor of the discovery belonged not just to him, but to all humanity. Billions of people have so far benefitted from this discovery.

Such ideas can only grow in free environments, in "open societies," far from considerations such as a person's religion, ideology, tradition, sect, color, or gender. Then all is done solely in the name of humanity.

The Jewish people's intense and unquenchable thirst for freedom, much like the principles on which the United States was founded, has always been about extending social rights and liberties to everyone and eliminating all forms of arbitrary discrimination. To paraphrase the great contemporary Iranian humorist, **Mr. Hadi Khorsandi**, "The sound of truth is like the *smell* of garlic!" As long as the "*scent* of garlic" comes from the open mouth of a legitimate majority, there's no problem. But if any other person's mouth, i.e. a minority, "reeks of the *stench* of the garlic, then "all hell breaks loose"! This is especially true for those societies "which have never had any garlic." Then, even on the basis of some absurd criteria as the color of someone's eyes or the shape of his eyebrows (!), people are accused of having "*stinking* mouths!"

Certainly, in the years to come, the multi-million population of rational Iranian immigrants will find a strong voice in this debate. As a minority group within open societies, they will bring in a rare understanding of the harms of "never having tasted garlic!" as well as a loving appreciation of the pleasures of free-thinking. This is bound to make them among the most serious advocates and promulgators of human rights and liberty.

In many ways, this will be similar to what happened on this very land just a few centuries ago, when a group of free-spirited, rational immigrants, devoid of any religious bias, managed to bring about the independence of the United States of America. By extension, in the far future, the immigrant population of the world will give birth to the founders of a global body of government. This is natural **because it's an immigrant who experiences cosmopolitanism first hand.**

We should hope the globalization of humanity erases all excuses for conflicts and divisions in the name of religion, tradition, ideology, sect, country, or the like. If so, anyone's country will be the very place where he or she lives, even as his or her national or ethnic identities are preserved.

Does the world truly understand the myriad dangers of a generation that has been brought up by prejudice in the religious schools? What will happen to the world, when these millions grow up?

Will humanity wake up any time soon? For far too long these plagues have pervaded the world, in the name of religion. Countless families, indeed much of the whole world, continue to walk the path of annihilation in the name of various faiths or ideologies. For far too long we've been divided into "the friendly sect" versus "the enemy."

Up until now, the United Nations has been an organization that waits for wars to begin, so that it can step in to play the role of mediator! Instead, wouldn't it be better to give this institution the kind of power that would enable it to prevent wars by identifying their roots long in advance?

If only the United Nation's Security Council would identify the explosive power of bigotry and prejudice as the reason for our lack of global security! Security is not maintained by mere soldiers, weapons, and wealth! **If only they realized that it's misplaced prejudice that puts those weapons to work!** Over the last millennia it is religious and sectarian discrimination, that appears in every corner of the world, regardless of which religion, and that leads inevitably to sectarian violence and war. Wherever students are taught fanaticism, violence follows. A few decades ago, it was the religious schools of Europe, including Germany; then it was the turn of Afghanistan; today it's Pakistan; tomorrow it might be Ireland or England; the day after tomorrow it could be Saudi Arabia, Yemen, and …. even if they put out the fire of this malice in one corner, it emerges soon in another.

Let us identify the roots of this problem, and cast out those religious extremists and fanatics from our homes and schools and close down the so-called religious schools. This would curtail the growth and spread of fanatic prejudice mixed with hatred and the source of destructive domestic and foreign wars.

We shouldn't underestimate religious, traditional, ideological, or sectarian prejudice and bigotry, such as the divisions of Orthodox versus non-Orthodox in our own community.

Our forefathers deemed insignificant those insulting discriminations by the grocery man on the corner of our street. Yet, little did we know that the children of those bigots, raised in a culture of evil, would someday rise to leadership positions and make the shameful attitudes of their fathers a matter of national policy. Let us learn our lesson!

It is a parents' duty to uproot all types of prejudice, bigotry, nonsense and superstition from their homes, in order to protect the happiness of their children.

Today's huge tree was once no more than a tiny seed. We need to beware of allowing our children to adopt even the smallest of religious superstitions. Who would accept that "being superstitious" means "being more religious"?

Václav Havel (b. 1936), the famous playwright and former president of the Czech Republic, said, "The measure of civilization, for both men and governments, is how humanely they treat the minorities among them."

How is it that anti-Semitism still exists, even in places where no Jews live? Anti-Semites have even gone as far as to call the pride of Persian history, **Cyrus the Great** (600 / 576 -530 B.C.E.), a Zionist! Why? Because 2500 years ago he codified human rights and by doing so granted rights to the Jewish people! Could **Blaise Pascal** (1623-1662) have been right, when he wrote, "Envy toward a person is an admission of the superiority of that person."

Hereditary anti-Semitism, like today's anti-Americanism, calls to my mind a verse from *Nahj al-Balagheh*, the second most important book to Shiite Muslims, which reads, "Avoid the evil of someone to whom you have done only good."

The hostility of many anti-Semites, as well as anti-Americans, run counter to the many contributions (intellectual, moral, ethical, legal – even their books) and the many kindnesses of the American people as well as the Jews throughout history. Is their twisted reaction some false sense of inferiority toward those who've offered positive examples? Are they just seeking someone to blame for their own failings? Since they can't imagine themselves indebted to another person, for their literacy, knowledge, science, or at times, their very faith or even life, they fight one another, and engage in anti-Semitism. In some cases, some countries have refused to accept aid of the most basic sort because of their bigotry even following a natural catastrophe.

Let's be clear on this point: The world is indebted to America. It was America that made global science and popularized industrial technology and the internet. Yet, an ignorant bunch continues to remain ungrateful.

Alas, human beings have as much potential to become misled as they have to be ennobled — particularly when it comes to the message of a given text. The truly great men of religion, however, have always been among the great teachers of morality. They knew that **it's up to humans to adapt their books and their religious understanding to the realities of their time — and not the other way around!**

I was in the presence of a literary figure, and asked him: **What does "faith" mean, and what about "religion"?** He said, **"Faith means 'perception, vision and insight', while Religion means 'the path, the way of life.' And it's a person's perception of things that decides his path."**

The roots of faith and religion run deep to the core of our very being – to that part that cries out for something to rely on. Yet the nature of that religious belief and its observance varies from person to person. Some people are deep and principled, while others are superficial. The spectrum runs the gamut from those who find themselves anywhere in between, to others who seem to be at the extremes.

Similarly there is a great amount of independent thinking regarding religious observance. There are those who rely on others to read for them (!), think for them (!) and offer a way of life for them (!) — all so that they can be good imitators! These followers, who tend to consider themselves more religious, have for centuries sought themselves a *mullah* –leader, *gha'ed*, etc. – to emulate. And when such leaders aren't available to them, they create one so that they can remain followers! For them, the key to solving all of the world's problems is found in the words and ideas of past generations — in the *halacha*, or "the Jewish law" — as it's endorsed by their current representatives.

They don't wish to accept that **a law or an issue, even if there is any truth in it, can be discredited in three ways: Exaggeration, Oblivion, and Wrongful Defense.** They wrongly imagine that by exaggerating the mistaken words of the religious sages, they elevate the status of those words. **The more illogical the words** attributed to the religion are, the more doubt attached to the other more authentic and reasonable beliefs.

Rumi wrote,

"This tale asks for much detail,
Yet I fear divulging ancient ciphers.
Since many a myopic & ossified mind
Who'd read into it hundreds of ill tales."

Some commentaries which are being taught are no doubt valuable. However the sophistication of today's students is not the same as it was when those verses were written.

Preserving the flawed culture of the *ghettos* doesn't contribute to the survival of Judaism — it's simply a continuation of a narrow-minded mentality born of captivity.

Freedom without discipline, and discipline without freedom, are equally destructive. It's balance and moderation that provide the grounds for growth. To interfere in other people's lives and to create conflict within families is not an exercise of religious liberty, but a violation of others' freedoms.

I ask you to remove those books that contain nonsense and superstition as well as those propagators of regression, from our schools, communities, and society.

These regressors stand out in sharp contrast to the very progressive ways of our forefathers. They've brought us little but backwardness and divisiveness. We should insist that they teach the *Torah* according to today's reasonable translations, and not according to some *mullah's* commentaries. Translations are how the world came to learn about the greatness of such Persian figures as **Avicenna, Omar Khayyam,** or **Rumi**. A German proverb says, *A clean mirror is more eloquent than thousand pictures imagined.* Let's wipe our mirrors clean.

392

In ancient times, people were largely worried about the ruinous attacks of wild, primitive tribes on civilized communities. (Think of the Vandals in Europe, or the Mongols in Asia, if you wish!) – but today, although people may be more learned, we should fear the attacks of those with impure motives.

"Both silver and gold come from stones,
Yet you can't find them both in all stones.
Soheil, the star of south, shines on the whole world:
Somewhere, it gives rise to a stinking leather sac,
Elsewhere, it turns out a scented leather pouch."

As we have seen recently, even science can be used to evil ends, turning fanatics into bomb delivery systems and causing destruction. In the fourth volume of *Mathnavi*, **Rumi** writes,

"Teaching science and technique to a man of bad essence:
It's like placing a sword into the hands of the bandits!
Better put a knife in the palm of a drunken slave,
Than let science come into an ignorant's grip."

The West is deeply asleep, dreaming about human rights, oblivious to the fact that it's training its own enemies. The words of **Rumi** ring in my ear,

"A high place does to an ignorant
What shame would never do to a lion.
Once an ignorant climbs the throne, carrying a crown,
The whole desert swarms with snakes, and with scorpions."

Mohamed Atta was the terrorist in control of the first plane that crashed into the World Trade Center in New York on September 11, 2001. When receiving flying lessons in the United States, this Egyptian born man told his American trainer, "Just teach me how to fly. Don't worry about how to land!" Sadly, the flight trainer didn't grasp the true meaning of his words.

Alas,

"Either the world never knew of loyalty,
Or else, it's not to be found in our days.
No one learned the science of arrow from me,
Who at the end, didn't aim it back at me."

**The flight trainer didn't realize that he was in the presence of a
man who had lost the capacity to remain human.** Saadi wrote,

"Compassion and gracious bravery are what define humanity;
So don't think that being human is all about this monstrous design.
If a man is devoid of all wisdom and virtue,
What difference then between him and a drawing on the wall?"

Mohamed Atta, too, considered himself very religious, as he, in
good faith and with sincerity, prayed five times a day. But his
dangerous faith was not combined with morality and conscience. That
he hadn't learned. What a different person he would have become, if
instead of hatred, he had been taught kindness and compassion. Again,
I am reminded of the words of **Saadi**:

"In the eyes of the wise,
Better a pregnant women give birth
To a snake, than bring to the world
Some unruly child."

Mohamed Atta didn't learn love and kindness from his parents,
teachers and *mullahs*; instead, he was filled with prejudice by the
preachers of hatred.

While we could never control all the families in the world, we can
turn to our governments and social institutions to rein in our schools to
make sure children everywhere are taught kindness and not hatred.
Rather than procuring more and more arms and weapons, let's prevent
the seeds of hatred from being conceived at our schools.

"A chicken's barely hatched the egg,
When it already asks for its food!
Lo the humankind, who shows no signs
Of intellect or the power of recognition."

Religious extremism is a kind of illness. To cure such sickness we shouldn't scold the patient but instead keep them from those who make them ill. The very same "ill makers" who are produced and nurtured by the indifference of the majority!

Every day, billions of dollars are being spent on teaching children but no one seems to be concerned with the misinformation they receive. Governments, the United Nations, and human rights organizations need to take notice and supervise what's being taught at schools all over the world. Then, teaching hatred, in the name of religion or ideology, would be prevented. Otherwise, this vicious cycle will go on forever, and every day, a new Mohammed Atta or **Yigal Amir** will emerge somewhere in the world, destruction-bent.

4000 years ago, the Chinese emperors built the Great Wall of China. Today, countries such as America, Israel, Saudi Arabia, Yemen, and Chechnya, have been building their own versions of partition walls. Altogether, more than thirty countries have built impenetrable partitions all over the world, instead of bridges of friendship. These walls are intended to ward off dangers and calm its residents' insecurities, most of which are ultimately rooted in religious and sectarian differences.

The material used in building these walls might have changed but the reasons behind them remain the same. In ancient China and Egypt, they used to leave human corpses between the bricks. Today, they've been replaced by round poles of steel!

No longer can you build and maintain impenetrable walls around your homes. No dam ever stood permanently against the percolation of all corruption. If anything, corruption grows more readily inside closed communities.

If the myopic, extremist, Orthodox Jews had held a majority in the past, there would have never been a Jewish state – the same state that today allows them to live by government subsidies! No doubt they would have continued to live in ghettos, awaiting the coming of the Savior, and looking for "miracles" – much as they still live in certain neighborhoods, villages and cities, always in walking distance to their own brand of synagogue!

Religion should never be allowed to become a way to earn an income, a means to be exploited by opportunists, or a tool in the hands of a sincere yet ignorant group. The fight by religious schools against modernism and against all innovative learning can only lead civilized society backwards. Only those societies that are equipped with the tools of civilization and modern science and are capable of adapting themselves to their times shall stand out — will become "the chosen ones," if you wish.

I'm reminded of a couplet by the founding father of modern Persian poetry, **Nima Yooshij** (1896-1960), who wrote,

"I've upset a whole people with my poetry!
I've stirred and mixed both their good and the bad!
Myself sitting aside, goggling at the scene,
For I've poured water into the ants nest!"

If you ask them, exactly which sentence in a text is untrue, they are rendered speechless, because they simply don't know. Writing in a pure and polite language is an art; otherwise, just any artless person could insult others with a contaminated pen. A frail will with a feeble logic would only yield vacuous words and insults. In contrast, a strong will with a sound logic would produce action and courtesy. The regressors should realize that no one can survive by denying or even destroying reality.

"Don't begin to speak before
You've contemplated your words for a pause.
Say something worthwhile then, and never mind
If your audience has had to wait for a bit more."

In any society, the efforts of teachers and authors could produce positive results, if they are backed by courtesy and good counsel, and not by prejudice and bigotry. It's not enough to ask, "Who's right?" You should also see what's in the interest of our children, today and tomorrow.

"Scold me, as much as you wish,
But the darkness of my skin you can't wash!"

Sending our children into the wells of regression, trusting their lives with the rotten ropes of irrational commentaries, all in the name of religion, would leave us with nothing but regret. Sooner or later, we'd end up repeating, "Only if we'd kept our children safe from the regressors…"

Once upon a time, in the darkness of the night, a thief broke into a house. But no matter how hard he searched, he couldn't find anything worthwhile to steal. All he saw was a *tonbak* (a Persian drum), lying in one corner of the room, and a man and a woman lying next to each other in a deep sleep! Then he remembered that this was the same poor couple who made a living by performing together around town, with the wife dancing to the drumming of her husband. He hit on the drum to wake them up. The startled couple jumped up and the thief who still had a bit of a heart and some remnants of a conscience, told the man, "I won't hurt you two. Just please, play something and have your wife dance for me. I'll enjoy watching for a few minutes; then I'll go." Thus, the husband began to play with trembling hands, hours past midnight, while his wife was forced to dance.

A few songs and some beautiful steps later, the thief thanked them and left their home for good. At that point, the man began beating his wife, telling her, "I had to do this to save our lives, and to keep the drum, the means of our livelihood! I *had* to play, and you *had* to dance!" As she was crying, the woman implored, "Then why do you beat me?!" The husband replied, "Did you have to dance so well, so seductively for a thief!"

The story of the thief with a conscience reminds me of **Mirza Reza Kermani** (1848-1897), the man who assassinated **Nasser al-din Shah**, the king of Qajar. His grandson, **Parviz Khatibi** (1923-1993), a renowned writer and poet, wrote a biography of the **Mirza** in which he recounts the Mirza saying, "One day, in one of the gardens around the city, I found a chance to kill the King. As it happens, on that same day, some Jewish families had gathered there for a picnic, as well. I realized that if I killed the King on that day, everyone would blame it on the Jews, and there would be a massacre. So, I decided to postpone my assassination."

Here was a man, clearly with a heart, with remnants of a good conscience evident in his thought and deed. Yet, in some ways, like that thief who did some wrong out of poverty, the Mirza too was going to do something horrible out of his beliefs. Eventually, he did assassinate the King, and as punishment he was executed.

Neither Mirza Reza, showing compassion for the Jews in Iran nor the thief, moved by the performing couple's poverty, opted for moderation. They were both captive of their own fixations, which robbed them of the moral wisdom to do otherwise.

To my point, although many of our nonsensical traditions originated in earlier times and in strange lands but I can't forgive the regressors, those opportunists and speculators, from making a living off of them.

Avicenna wrote, "If we make one mistake, and offer one thousand reasons and excuses to pretend that it is right, then we've just made one thousand and one mistakes!" The regressors would have us believe in their "miracles" even if it runs counter to human knowledge. **"Miracles" are for the most part unexpected events often inexplicable due to the inadequacies of human perception.** Imagine if each of the past century's great inventors had instead claimed to have performed a "miracle," they would have had millions of followers!

"Miracles" are just traps to ensnare unsuspecting youngsters. **Yet, even if we allow the regressors the benefit of the doubt that their misinterpretations and ill counsel are given without malicious intent, it makes no difference because we still suffer the consequences.**

Alchemy, one of mankind's earlier attempts at a miracle, never managed to turn a single milligram of copper into gold. However, it did lead to the great science of chemistry which changed our world.

The French philosopher **Denis Diderot** (1713-1784) said that if you take away the fear of hell from a zealot Christian, you've taken away all his beliefs!

Likewise, if you take away the belief in miracle from a regressor, nothing will be left for him to say. Miracles are the hole through which the regressor escapes from truth and misguides immature followers.

Regardless of their particular religion or sect, speak with a traditionalist and you'll see that whenever they can't understand something, or make others understand it with a rational argument, they immediately take refuge in some superstition or the claim of a miracle, or the nonsense of "ciphers" — *"Here, A means this, and B means that!"*

Today's true miracles are not the words of this or that so-called religious sage. Today's miracles are the product of science and technology — the wonder of Internet being simply one of the most recent and most important of these scientific miracles. Nowadays, we can send sound, image, or text, within a blink of an eye, to anywhere in the world — and lo and behold, with no wires! Let us enter the wide world of the Web to forget the miracles that have no rational or philosophical basis; and let us actively try to eliminate bothersome superstitions, even if they have a traditional basis.

Preventing students from access to the Internet, TV or other media, in the name of religion, is not a service, but an irreparable disservice. Not only it's a regressive step, but also it gives rise to a "forbidden fruit" complex:

"The harder to get, the hotter human's desire for it!"

We need to remind children of the possible dangers and harms of technology, based on scientific and rational arguments, devoid of superstitions. Not even water, electricity, or the air itself, are without danger! Should we stop using electricity, as well, because of the risk of electrocution?! I have heard that some of the religious schools make parents pledge that they won't have radio, TV, or Internet connections at home! Are we Luddites? Should we raise children blind so that they won't see things that are deemed inappropriate? Or should we educate them about the dangers and provide accurate information so they can make the right decisions for themselves? Humans are inquisitive and curious creatures and the human child even more so. In the end, he'll find what you try to keep away from him.

In every community, there are people who by their facial make up, hairstyle or other aspect of their appearance, whether it is by

wearing a particular dress or putting on some colorful hats, wish to compensate for their psychological needs, in any way possible. Such people often make up stories attributed to religion and tell anecdotes about miracles that have supposedly happened to them or to others! **Sadly, they turn the sweetest of wines, i.e. our holy commandments, into the sourest of vinegars — impossible to drink, and useless for cooking. Such people try to make the coal white, by the force of the soap of a miracle!**

They do so because they know very well that a human being, wandering, bewildered, lost and confused, and in total ignorance is susceptible to such manipulation. A person who is willing to put reason aside in the search for religious comfort, is readily attracted to any such nonsense and hangs onto it because of his insecurities. He accepts claims of miracles, and he is more than willing to take part in imitation and emulation. By then, he is so vulnerable, that he could **accept even the most irrational of formulas. This typically ends in absolute acquiescence and mental and intellectual paralysis. Soon, he'd begin to defend matters and beliefs that, until yesterday, he had been opposing feverishly, and not feel any conflict at all about doing so!**

Educators in charge: Children are like sheets of white paper: Their value and significance depends always on what is being written on them. Once any nonsense has been written on these papers, it can't be erased.

Nothing is stronger than an idea whose time has come. And nothing is weaker than those thoughts whose time has expired. Passing ideas on to others that are long past their expiration date is an act of cruelty against our own offspring. We can forgive our ancestors who didn't know better, but had they removed those nonsensical and superstitious ideas then, we would be living in a better world.

It's said that there's a candlelight within our being, and another in our hands that moves ahead of us. The candlelight in our hands could be extinguished at any moment, or flicker when we hit any object on our way, or dance and thin out with every blow of the wind. But the candlelight within our being should never be affected by the winds of outside propaganda and advertisements. This candle, which we might call "our identity," controls our thought, intellect and being. We need to actively preserve this light. Otherwise,

"Time could bring out thousands of designs; but
None would be like the one in the mirror of our imagination"

Let us remember the story of the peasant who said that *"My horse, once he got used to working without food, passed away!"*

To get used to the nonsense of the regressive traditionalists, and to put up or coexist with them is a *de facto* acceptance of their idiocy and nonsense. By contrast, science is never content with any idea as the final answer.

Science has always been willing to destroy today the very building it erected yesterday, only to build a new, better edifice in its place. The secret to the progress of science is in destroying what no longer works and building something better in its place. Likewise, the secret to the endurance and survival of religion is to adapt to changing times. **It's the duty of each and every member of our community to replace the millennia-old culture of imitation with rational thinking and to substitute adherence to human intellect for adherence to people.**

We need to teach our children to revise those superstitious beliefs that have been inherited from past generations and throw away those that are worthless, before they are passed on to the next generation. Doing so would close the gap between the free-thinkers and the regressors, and allow mutual trust and rational understanding to

402

emerge among all groups. If our forefathers had done this in their time, we wouldn't have the ongoing dangers of regression.

"The religion that a clergy receives by virtue of the rank,
It's bound to grow corrupt over time.
Once religion set foot on the head of reason,
It'll be captured and distorted by the narrative.
One group goes after opening shops of faith,
One sect seeks profit through the road of deception.
Every mistake becomes a decree from Heaven,
The religion now limited to its tear-jerking tales!
Then, an iron stone would cure a terminally ill!
A wooden palm would make thousands of miracles!
Religion without wisdom, knowledge and science,
Would never be sheltered against superstitions!"

The enthusiasm for research among our youngsters who have a command of modern knowledge, will bring about such change – even in the face of the speculative bigots, who are waiting for the Savior to arrive.

I came across an anecdote in a Persian newspaper, which I find rather pertinent to our discussion (even though I am not sure of its historical truth): One day, the late **Shah** of Iran went to visit a small island in the north-western side of Iran. His chief of hunting, a German, explaining that this island had the best conditions for hunting said, "Your highness, if we bring animals from all over the world to this island, in just ten years we'll have the best royal hunting field imaginable." The Shah agreed.

Ten years passed, and the king went to visit the island, again joined by his chief of hunting. Excited at the sight of the bountiful herd, the King jumped on his horse, and began the hunt. He shot one reindeer, then another and then a third. But he was disappointed that the animals didn't even attempt to flee – shooting them was like shooting chickens in a backyard. His hunting chief examined the animals and concluded that being in a habitat without their natural enemies had made them lazy. The hunting chief asked the Shah for two years to improve the situation. They reintroduced wild animals to the island so that the law of nature would correct the situation. Soon, a few tame animals perished but before long, the rest learned to flee! Thus, the solution proved successful.

Indeed, the practical, the real, experience of life isn't taught at traditional religious schools. That's why their students tie their hopes to miracles, begging to do and to collect more and more "rewarding good deeds."

In 1875, there took place a debate in America between a teacher and a priest. The question was whether some day, human beings could fly. The priest, **Bishop Milton Wright** (1828-1917), stubbornly and angrily reacted to the question, as he exclaimed, "Blasphemy! Utter blasphemy! God intends only his angels to fly." As strange as life can be, this seemingly prejudiced, ossified priest, had two sons, named **Orville** and **Wilbur**, who 28 years later, became the first humans to invent and to fly a modern designed airplane!

Yes, the famed Wright Brothers, the inventors of the modern airplane, were the sons of that very clergyman, Reverend Wright, who stubbornly believed that his religion dictated that flying was a miracle and the exclusive realm of the angels of God!

Ridiculous as this sounds today, alas, there are still people who claim that, "*This* is our miracle: Anyone who votes for us, will enjoy a longer life, and shall reserve a place for himself in Heaven!" Even more sadly, there are others who believe their nonsense, and "get coins as reward!"

404

According to statistics provided by Cambridge (Source: Zuckerman, Phil; Cambridge University Press, Cambridge UK, 2005), the number of atheists and those in doubt (agnostics) have risen to 64% in Japan; 81% in Vietnam; and in France, Germany, England, Sweden, Netherlands, the Czech Republic and Belgium, to above 40%. But sadly enough, anti-religiosity, in the sense of anti-Humanism, i.e. the hostility of man against man, which also includes anti-Semitism, continues to date. Hopefully, humanity will realize someday that the only way to control the wild aspects of mankind's nature is to promote a love of other people – in other words, promoting that golden rule of morality, **Wish for thy neighbor as you'd wish for thyself.**

During an interview, **Oriana Fallaci**, the famed Italian journalist, asked **Golda Meir** (1898-1978), the Israeli Prime Minister, whether she was a religious person? Golda Meir replied, and I paraphrase, "No, I've never been religious, even in my youth. I believe in kindness toward other human beings, and in my infinite love toward humanity, not in religion." She asked **Indira Gandhi** (1917-1984), the Prime Minister of India, the same question and she got a similar answer, "I believe in humanity and not in gods." I ask, whether loving humankind and humanity is not the same as that well-known command of the *Holy Torah*, "Wish for thy neighbor, as you'd wish for thyself."

The French poet **Jean la Fontaine** (1621-1695) said, "It's no use running; to set out on time is the main point." Many of the informed members of all societies tell themselves that it's better to stay silent and not make a fuss – whether they do so out of fear or misplaced caution, I can't say. I have chosen another path: to joyfully hold a pen in hand, writing out my ideas, and leaving no doubt about my thoughts! I believe that it's better to write, just as it is to set out on time. Otherwise, in retrospect, one might have regrets, saying "I meant to say something!"

A rational, passionate and loving author extends his life, on paper, through writing —because, as the saying goes, until a lover has not seen the colorful locks of his beloved, he can't make a rainbow from the waves of her hair. Likewise, until a writer has not suffered from the subjects of his discussion, until he has gained enough experience, he can't speak about sufferings; because whoever wishes to talk about love has to have been in love.

This author has had his share of watching those who offer religion for sale. That's how I could weave this cloth, this book, out of the threads of my experience; that's how I could plant a scion from these seeds; that's why I was moved to leave, for the coming generations, a record of those experiences, and some notes and ideas, which are as broad as the thought of rational-minded people.

One poet's verses fully resonates with how I feel,

"With all likelihood, we won't be here, but the book will.
Some day, perhaps, there'll be left of us no signs, no name.
Before we existed, there were no effects, no problems.
But now that we wrote, even after we leave, the book shall stay."

Einstein has a famous quote about miracles, "There are only two ways to live your life: One is as though nothing is a miracle; the other is as though everything is a miracle." Let us not force our children to examine the books of the *mullahs*, like some archeologists, looking for some treasure! Let us enrichen them with our modern scientific treasures, containing the miracles found in the textbooks and classrooms of the universities.

I once asked an American Orthodox Jewish couple, "When did you choose to become Orthodox Jews? As far as I know, neither of your families believed in or practiced such a way of life?" They said that they had chosen this path about 20 years before. I asked, "Why did you choose this road?" The husband said, "I have two sister-in-laws, both of whom married gentiles and had no sense of *any* religion left in their homes. For me, this was like a warning sign and I chose this road to preserve my identity."

After speaking to this couple, as well as some of our own Iranian followers of the Orthodox way of life and their supporters, I realized that they see Orthodoxy as the key to preserving their own Jewish identity as well as the survival of Judaism. Accordingly, for them any words attributed to this religious sector, good or bad, appear as a commandment. When faced by some nonsense, in which they never believed, in which perhaps they still don't believe, they don't accord it much weight but accept it, or even defend it, for the sake of the greater cause of identity preservation!

As regards preserving our Jewish identity and maintaining our ancestral traditions, I share these groups' concerns. However, doing so does not require that we accept the nonsense and superstition of the regressors. Regression presents itself as a form of self-preservation but is a formula for diminishing our present and ruining our future.

Be assured that if we continue like this, both groups will lose out. Some will be lost to anti-rationalism, others to inappropriate marriages, and still others will flee the religion entirely Our Jewish population will grow thinner by the day. The regressors may take refuge in prayers and miracles, but these won't help.

The wise members of any society remain among the living, Even though they might have passed away.

Near the end of his life, the American President, **Thomas Jefferson** designed his own gravestone and prepared the text to be engraved on it. His gravestone reads, without any mention of his title of President, as follows,

"Here Was Buried

Thomas Jefferson

Author Of The

Declaration

Of

American Independence

Of The

Statute Of Virginia

For

Religious Freedom

And Father Of The

University Of Virginia."

This very civilized and exalted president, took out a pair of scissors and cut out any reference to miracles in his copy of the Bible, and told everyone, **"This is my Holy Bible!"** which is preserved to this day in a museum.

No one called him a heretic, no one accused him of blasphemy, and no one offended him out of ignorance! The civilized and rational-minded people of the world regard him in the highest esteem.

Gandhi said, "Our birth and death might not be in our own hands, but it's largely left to us how to live.

In the near future, the regressors' nonsense will come to afflict our community and the larger society as well as our social institutions and organizations. We will lose more rationally minded people and find those in the business of religion prospering through the kindness of those whose ignorance or benevolence has been taken advantage of.

Unfortunately, there are some successful middle-aged people, with good intentions, who although they would never send their own children to such religious schools, nonetheless give financial, material, and intellectual support to the regressors – whether out of nostalgia or a false notion of identity preservation. Only when their own children fall under the regressor's spell will they regret their actions; but then, it will be too late!

There are many people, who would accept as truth any tradition or belief, no matter how irrational, just because their parents or ancestors believed in them. Regardless of whether the true meaning of those ideas or traditions is outdated, or worse yet, reprehensible, they will defend them.

The poet **Khalil Gibran** (1883-1931) wrote, "**Pity the nation divided into fragments, each fragment deeming itself a nation.**" The regressor's aim is to recruit ever more members for his own faction, and this is against our ancestral way of life. The outcome of this approach is divisiveness and separations, even banning marriage between different sects of the same religion! **Nietzsche** said, and I paraphrase, "In order not to be an idol-worshiper, breaking the idols isn't enough: You should have also abandoned the practice of worshipping idols."

Those who help the regressors, unknowingly bring about separations, and practically encourage them. These sects rarely even approve of their own colleagues, **and each one of them seeks a pulpit of his own, and his share of followers!** They lie, and call any writing against their own beliefs as "anti-religious" just to prevent their friends and followers from becoming informed.

They don't want to understand that even the greatest scientists, inventors and discoverers of history, didn't have any idea about 99% of our current knowledge. Yet, that 1% became the basis of future discoveries and inventions, based on their original findings. Likewise, if mankind will preserve just 1%, of the core inspiration, fundamental morals, values and tenets of religion and abandon all of the unessential accumulated elements that are not supported by contemporary knowledge and science, religion will achieve its full potential good to mankind. Religion itself isn't a dynamic and transformable entity, but human beings are, ready to evolve on the road of progress.

Religious sectarianism chews on the unity of societies, as termites do to buildings.

I once read a very informative scientific study, which is related to the discussion of tradition in general and includes the "tradition" of anti-Semitism, or in its broader form, anti-humanism – the animosity of one human being against another – that are rooted in religious, tribal, ethnic, regional, or other causes. I find it most appropriate to study for our discussion:

HOW A PARADIGM IS FORMED

A group of scientists placed 5 monkeys in a cage; and in the middle, a ladder with bananas on the top. Every time a monkey went up the ladder, the scientists soaked the rest of the monkeys

with cold water. After a while, every time any monkey went up the ladder, the others would beat him or her up. After some time, no monkey dared go up the ladder, no matter how strong the temptation was.

Scientists then decided to substitute one of the monkeys. The first thing this new monkey did was to go up the ladder to get the banana. Immediately the other monkeys beat him up. After several beatings, the new member learned not to climb the ladder even though he never knew why. After some time, a second monkey was replaced, and the same occurred. This time, even the first substitute monkey participated on the beating for the second monkey, even though he had been absent from the first phase of the experiment, when the water was being poured on the animals. Soon, a third monkey was replaced; again, the new monkey tried to climb the ladder, and again, she was beat up by other monkeys. The same happened when the fourth monkey was replaced by a new member. Finally the fifth monkey was replaced, as well, with the same result.

At this point, there was a group of 5 monkeys left, none of whom had ever received a cold shower, who nonetheless continued to beat up any monkey who attempted to climb the ladder!

If it were possible to ask the monkeys why they beat up all those who attempted to go up the ladder, I bet their answer would be, "I don't know – that's how things are done around here!" Does it sound familiar?

Coming back to the study of the monkeys, wouldn't you think that such mindless imitations can also be true for humans? This study makes us realize how improper behaviors and ideas are mindlessly imitated, generation after generation, without ever knowing why.

For instance, some people think that just because their parents hated a certain religion, ideology or tradition, they too should hate those things. Are most people even aware when they repeat the despicable acts of the past and present? The answer is, "No." **Imitating traditions, habits, and fomenting ugly ideas, such as anti-Semitism, regression, etc., become "naturalized" and sustained once they are clad in the ugly dress of religion, as well.** When such things are taught in religious schools all over the world, they are passed on from generation to generation.

"Only two things are infinite: The universe and human stupidity. And I am not so sure about the former." Albert Einstein

The seeds of hatred are conceived in the classrooms of religious extremists; then they grow at homes, within families; and consequently, are inherited by the following generations. As a Persian poet once wrote,

"People became annihilated because of their imitation. May this ill of Imitation be cursed hundreds of times."

Were all of the religious and social sages of the world truly wise, or all-knowing?! Is everything ever said and written always reasonable?

A Spanish Marrano Jew who witnessed the expulsion of Jews and Muslims from Spain in 1492, recorded a tragic account in his memoirs:

A sailor noticed a group of expelled Jews, hopelessly wandering at the brink of the sea. He invited them all on his ship, and the ship sailed away from the shore. After a few days, the ship returned, albeit without its passengers. The Marrano man asked the sailor, "Where did you take them?" The sailor replied, "I dropped all of them in a dire, desolate island, with no inhabitants, no water or greens, at the middle of nowhere, at the heart of the sea; then I

returned all by myself!" The Marrano asked, "Did you know them?" The sailor's reply was negative. "Did you have any specific animosity toward them?" Again the answer was no. "Then why did you do such a cruel crime?" The sailor simply answered, "Because they were Jews."

What reason could there be for this sailor's attitude other than the seeds of religious hatred, planted in his mind when he was a child?

Wikipedia states that, **Marranos**— or **secret Jews**, also known as **Anusim** — were **Sephardic** Jews — i.e. Jewish residents of the **Iberian Peninsula** — who were forced to adopt Christianity under threat of expulsion. They continued, however, to practice Judaism secretly; thus, preserving their Jewish identity. The term **marrano** in Spanish meant "pigs," and stemmed from the ritual prohibition against eating pork, a prohibition practiced by both Jews and Muslims. In Spanish, the term acquired the meaning of "swine" or "filthy." In contemporary Spanish, it is no longer associated with Jews. You can read more about this group at www.Wikipedia.org.

It's said that the animosity of man towards each other, which also includes anti-Semitism as a subset, has its roots in slavery, human worship and the absolutism of religions. History has shown us that every so often, in some corner of the world, under orders from a mad man, millions of people commit acts of cruelty that seem beyond reason and not in keeping with their history or culture. The most obvious case in point is the German people during World War Two.

The German soldier is the most obedient of all soldiers, and their actions caused the death of more than 40 million people in WWII. Similarly, the result of the blind obedience of Japanese soldiers was the massacre of millions of innocent Chinese. The outcome of the blind obedience of other groups of soldiers was erecting *minarets,* or towers, made by human skulls in Iran. Unfortunately, the story goes on and on….

Did the soldiers, the mercenaries, or other people who carried out such crimes, have any obligation to commit these acts? Or else, did they commit these crimes because of their environment? Did the individuals who carried out these acts merely give in to their natural temptations?

Once, when a spouse did something stupid, she explained to me, "My spouse asked me to!" "But you knew it was wrong," I said. "So why did you do it?" She answered: "When I married, on my wedding night, I promised to fulfill my spouse's wishes!" This may be a loyal spouse, but it is also an example of a human-looking robot that still lives in the age of slavery. This sort of slavery also commonly occurs in the name of religion, ideology, faction or cult.

Do humans deserve the exalted rank of the "highest among the creation"? Not according to history, in light of the many cruelties devoid of conscience committed by mankind over the ages in the name of religion.

Human folly is older than history. For more than 500 years we have known that **Christopher Columbus** (1451-1506) mistakenly called the inhabitants of the new-found continent "Indians," because he believed he had reached India! Yet despite all we know, like that monkey who beat others for no reason even in the absence of the original shower, we continue to call these native Americans, "Indians"!

When false chronic hatred and hostilities are passed on to children as a legacy, these traits replicate, intensify, reproduce and imitate, like a bad gene; and the tragedy is that they are taught in the so-called religious schools of all faiths.

Those who lure and entrap youngsters have no power themselves. They exploit the power of religion! They have done so for thousands of years and will continue to do so until science and knowledge can put an end to it. Our ancestors didn't have the means and conditions to bring about such change. Today, however, our knowledge is such that we have a duty to discard destructive prejudices and bias and make the regressors fully understand the truth of the way things are, even if their common response to most progressive entreaties is to say, "We already have everything we need!"

Times have changed. Absolutism, as well as blind obedience, as well as a *fatwa* from an individual are no longer the rules by which the majority lives. Today, it's not the ideas of a single person that dominates our lives, but the opinions of the majority.

My friends,

Religion is important and in the case of children, it's even more important to keep religion from becoming corrupted.

To confine our children like subdued captives, isolating them in religious schools and seminaries for the rest of their lives is no behavior for our times. There is a famous prayer, known today as *The Serenity Prayer*, thought to have been originally composed by **Reinhold Niebuhr** (1892-1971):

God grant me the serenity,
To accept the things I cannot change;
Courage to change the things I can;
And wisdom to know the difference.

In other words, may we have the wisdom and understanding not to expect the world and the people in it to act according to my wishes.

If today, I use my words to try and get your attention, it is not because I consider myself to be an authority on these subjects. Rather, it's because after hearing so much nonsense attributed to our religion, I feel personally responsible to speak out and tell everyone that these beliefs not only don't represent our religion, they are not even a part of modern civilization!

The French Prime Minister and President, **George Pompidou** (1911-1974), once said, "Any place could come down in ruins for any of these three reasons: War, Earthquakes, or The Counsel of Ignorants."

To follow someone's *fatwa* is not rational at all. A wise man, observing the mistakes of others, corrects himself.

They asked a tree, "Why don't you speak?" It said, "My fruits speak for me!" Just look at the outcome of the regressor's divisive acts. Isn't that answer enough?

"The effects of our deeds will be the signs
Which will remain of us in the world.
After we're gone, they'll see us in our effects."

*****

"One who neglects the future,
Shall look a servant before
The coming generations."

Those who promote superstitions don't realize that their focus on trivia will prevent young people from fulfilling great things. Religion was offered to the world to remove human ignorance, so that mankind could shed light, and not to take people into the darkness in the name of religion.

"He pretends loyalty, love and passion;
But he's nothing more than a con man,
Selling barley and claiming it to be wheat."

Being ignorant about understanding religion is like the story of a blind person who told his friend, "I know darkness, but I don't know the color white." His friend replied, "White is like a white swan, which gracefully swims on the surface of the lake." The blind man asked, "What is a swan?" His friend raised his arm and bent his wrist, imitating the shape of the swan's neck, and replied, "A white swan is like this." The blind man touched his friend's hand carefully, then said, "Now, I understand what the color white is!" Many people's understanding of religion doesn't fare much better.

The difference between religious indoctrination during the Inquisition in Europe, as opposed to the East, has been this: In the West, the intellectuals eventually rose up until the Church was finally defeated, and science was victorious. But in the East, under the pretense of preserving religion, they continued to close their eyes to reality.

Indeed, religion is not a problem to be solved, but a gift to be enjoyed.

"These subjects were possible to be told, only to this point.
Henceforth, whatever follows, will be of a hidden nature.
This word is like milk in the breast:
It won't flow without being sucked."

Dear educators in charge,

You say that during your lessons, whenever you get to the "inappropriate" sections, the unreasonable parts of religious literature, you try to "pass by them" as quickly as possible! This reminds me of the English saying which states, "**Law of Probability**: The probability of being watched is directly proportional to the stupidity of your act!" Rather than "passing them by" we should acknowledge that there are many outdated "inappropriate" rules, rituals, traditions, texts, and commentaries that we should drop once and for all.

"Drown must yourself in a sea of love's wine;
You can't get drunk with a single drop.
You, a mortal drop, become immortal instead, by merging with the sea,
As the difference between a sea and a drop is vast, as the sea."

The first step to know God is self-knowledge. The 13th century C.E. Persian poet, Sufi and Philosopher, **Baba Afzal Kashani** wrote,

"Thou who seekest God: Come to! Know thyself!
Ask thyself for God, since God isn't apart from thee!
First, know thyself, thence, learn of God;
Then thou'll come to admit the self-standing deity of God."

The foam will vanish, but the ocean shall stay. Religious interpretations which do not fit our time, shall pass, too; but the immortal Commandments of the *Torah* shall stay.

Scuba diving experts tell us that after a certain depth, 100 meters or so, a diver can lose his sense of direction and swim down rather than up – and drown.

We need to watch our children to make sure they don't dive deeply into a sea of superstitions, lose their way and drown. Let us save those who have not yet sunk too far. Because those who have already sunk below the danger zone, are already gone forever.

For more than 100 years, the French daily newspaper, *Le Figaro*, has been featuring the words of **Beaumarchais** (1732-1799) as its front page motto, *"Sans la liberté de blâmer, il n'est point d'éloge flatteur."* That is, "Without the freedom to criticize, there is no true praise". The American intellectual, **Walter Lippmann** (1889-1974), too, said, "When everyone thinks alike, no one thinks very much." Let us not be afraid of just criticism. As the poet wrote,

"Air-headed men heat up by
The first empty word!
A soft breeze could bring out
The howls in a field of straws."

Bertrand Russell said, "We can sacrifice anything for humankind, except humanity itself."

Let us hate "sin" and not the "sinner." Let us look for the causes rather than hiding them. This author's intent is to recognize the reasons behind these ills in our community, so we can take action and bring about effective remedies. Covering-up, negligence, oblivion, or indifference helps no one. We can't hang or "execute" a thought; neither can we confine it to a prison. But we can rectify misapprehensions via thinking correctly.

There will always be those honest but naïve individuals, who rely on ancient texts, quotes, to recommend irrational thoughts believing that "since they are not telling a lie, they must be telling the truth." They may be quoting accurately, but that doesn't mean what they are saying is true. In the words of the Persian poet **Sa'eb**,

"In the book of love, full innocence
Is itself not fully clear of sins.
Joseph goes to the prison,
Out of the purity of his deeds."

With regard to the Holocaust it's been said that, "To forget a tragedy is a preface to the next tragedy." To repeat a mistake, too, is an introduction to repeating the next mistakes.

"Better avoid one, who gives you no peace.
Better not waste life, conversing with him.

Solitude's thousands times better over a company,
Who'd give you, over and over, the pain of the heart."

Once, the famed Canadian physician, and historian, **Dr. William Osler** (1849-1919) was testing a student of medicine. During final exams, he asked a student how much medicine he would prescribe for a patient diagnosed with a certain illness. The student thought for a moment and said, "Twenty-four grams, professor." Four minutes later, the student came back to his professor to correct himself, "Oh, Professor; I'm so sorry. I made a mistake. Please let me answer the question again." Osler looked at his watch and said, "Oh, there's no further use. The patient died three minutes ago, as a result of your over-dose!"

Let's hope the day never comes when we find out that our original religious and ethnic unity already died "three minutes ago" — because of the propagation of fanatical ideas; or because of our community's silence in the face of such propagation. Many mistakes are like poison; their danger is only revealed when it's too late for any cure.

You, who've lost your way in the name of religion, look around: Your children won't be exempt!

Wealth decorates the house; but it's virtue that beautifies the host. Let us bring up our children as wise and virtuous people, and not as raw, immature religious fanatics. No teacher is a friend who wishes to hold our child's hand at the mountain's base, only to leave her alone and uninformed at the mountain top.

As **Einstein** said, Let us not forget the sea for the temptation of a drop. Let us not tarnish the Commandments based on some misguided commentaries.

"When we can fix an ill by talking,
So why should we hold back on
Repeating, 'Why? Why?!'"

The Hebrew command, *Zakhor*, "Remember!" is repeated 169 times in the *Holy Torah*. To gain experience, *Remember!* To fulfill your duties, *Remember!* To exercise justice, *Remember!* To avoid repeating past mistakes, *Remember!* To put the experience in use, *Remember!*

Every single day, throughout our life, there is much we need to remember so that we can succeed, be saved and liberated.

As **Einstein** said, "The pursuit of knowledge for its own sake, an almost fanatical love of justice, and the desire for personal independence — these are features of the Jewish tradition which make me thank my lucky stars that I belong to it."

A Chinese proverb says, "Seeking to satisfy only our senses would starve our intellect."

One of the greatest of all European philosophers, **Immanuel Kant** wrote, "Enlightenment is man's leaving his self-caused immaturity. Immaturity is the incapacity to use one's intelligence without the guidance of another." In other words, enlightenment is when we grow and become intellectually independent.

Zakhor! Let us remember. Whenever intelligent and rational arguments begin to go limp, religion will go astray. The Persian poet **Farrokhi Yazdi** (1887-1939) wrote,

"Hearts' thumping sound's grown, bit by bit, into groans.
Wait 'til these whispers fortify, when they turn into roars and cries."

Zakhor! Let us remember that we cannot suddenly erase all prejudice, discrimination and conflict from the world. But if we continue to repeat our past, we will experience more not less of these problems.

Zakhor! Let us remember that those who do not learn from the events of the past, from history, are condemned to re-live those events and experiences. We should never sacrifice free-thinking for nonsense and superstitions and call it "religious observance." **Hafez** wrote,

"We've already tried our luck in this town.
Now it's time to pull out our cloth,
And leave out of this desolate land."

Let us build families so balanced that their children won't be misguided by an extreme lack of religion, or paralyzed by an excess of it.

As the Chinese proverb states, "The Western doctor looks at the illness, not the patient." We need to heed the patient as well as the illness. Our people are abundant in quality but diminishing in quantity, so much so that we can't risk letting some members lead our community astray in the name of religion.

The Biblical story of Cain and Abel makes clear that animosity toward one another, even among brothers, is part of human nature. Misguided people have often used religion to exploit that animosity, making easy prey of minorities. This evil has been imitated and passed on from generation to generation among humans, no better than what we saw among the monkeys.

It was not because of religion that mankind left the Stone Age behind but thanks to his rational, practical efforts. Man grew more organized and prospered with the help of science and the development of ethics.

The human desire for constant improvement, our aspiration to perfection, is rooted in our very DNA and the structure of our brain. Any human not willing to step out his self-made cage is just being a child. We can't stop progress, so **let's not postpone it!**

Many things that once seemed impossible or fantasies, such as flying, space travel, smartphones and internet communication, are now

readily available for us to enjoy. Each day reminds us of how little we
know and how much progress remains to be made!

Sir Isaac Newton once said, "I do not know what I may appear to
the world, but to myself I seem to have been only like a boy playing on
the seashore, diverting myself now and then by finding a smoother
pebble or a prettier shell than ordinary, whilst the great ocean of truth
lay all undiscovered before me." If anything, this description fits most
people.

It's said that there have three great innovations in **the last
thousand years of human history.** The first was agriculture; the
second was the industrial revolution. **As for the third, the Internet,
mankind is just starting to uncover its potential and its impact.**

Recently, 163 years after their invention, the giant telegraph
devices and instruments invented and developed my **Samuel Morse**
(1791-1872), which were considered a miracle when first used, were
consigned to a **history museum!**

Today, there is an international movement to protect the
environment from pollution. Likewise, we need a global movement to
prevent the further pollution of the human mind by religious
extremism.

History is also the record of what has been written. We are the
agents charged with recording this history. Each day that passes by
may bring a new chapter, recording a quake that shook our history.
Days shall pass; voices will disappear; moments will fly by; but it's
only recorded words and texts that shall remain. If we don't say, if we
don't write, and if we don't act, we will be held responsible.

The British philosopher, **David Hume** (1711-1776) said,

"A wise man proportions his belief to the evidence."

There are those who despite knowing that many of their beliefs have no basis in fact, still promote them to earn themselves power, or to paint themselves as "holier than thou." They traffic in prejudice, bias and bigotry, oblivious to the powder keg they are igniting. They remain oblivious to the fact that, **until the thoughts and ideas of human societies have not blossomed like flowers, communities won't turn into beautiful gardens.**

Belief or "faith" are topics of interest to a great many. Yet the regressors insist on claiming that religious observance is their exclusive property! That they are more "faithful" and that the more extremist they are, the more so-called Jewish — or Muslim, or Catholic, etc. — they are. It's as if they've made advance reservations in Heaven!

If only we were truly moral, we could build real heaven here on earth, instead of fantasizing about it!

A professor and his students were engaged in a discussion:

"Does the Devil exist? Did God create the Devil?" the university professor challenged his students. No answer.

"Did God create everything that exists?" the Professor asked. One student responded, "Yes." The professor asked again, "So God created everything, right?" Again the student replied, "Yes, He did so, Sir." The professor continued, "If God created *everything*, then it follows that he created the Devil, as well. Because the Devil, the *Satan* if you will, exists. So, according to the rule that 'we are manifest in our deeds', God is the Devil, as well."

The student sat down calmly and didn't say any more. The professor sat down, content with himself.

Then another student raised his hand, and asked, "Professor, could I ask you a question?" "Certainly!" the professor replied. He rose and asked, "Does 'cold' exist?" The professor said, "Of course it does! What kind of a question is that?!" Other students laughed at the young man's question. Yet the young man continued, "But Sir, according to the laws of physics, what we refer to as 'cold' is in fact the absence of heat."

Then he asked, "Professor, does 'darkness' exist?" The professor replied, "Of course it does." The student responded, "No, there is no 'darkness' either. Darkness is a word to used to designate the absence of light."

Finally, the student asked the professor, "So Sir, does the Devil exist?" This time, the professor wasn't as sure as he'd been before. Still, he hesitantly replied, "Yes, as I said before, we see the Devil every day. He could be seen every day in examples of inhumane behavior of humankind toward one another. He exists in the countless crimes and acts of violence, which take place around the world. These don't signify anything but the Devil."

The student, however, replied, "No, Sir. You are wrong. There exists no Devil, or at least, it doesn't exist as a real type, or as an independent entity. We can simply consider the 'devil' to be the absence of God, just like 'cold' and 'darkness." His classmates gave him a unanimous ovation.

That student's name was Albert Einstein.

Similarly, bigotry is "evidenced" by the absence of proper understanding; ignorance "emerges" in the absence of reason and intellect! And hatred and discrimination are their illegitimate children!

"Benefits of the sea would be immense, were it not for the fear of the waves.
Company of the rose would be pleasant, were it not for the agony of

the thorns.
Last night, I was proudly strolling in the garden of communion with
my beloved.
Now, parted with reason, away from the beloved, I twist and turn, like
a snake."

The world is much more dangerous than our educators imagine. In such a wild, wild world, we need to promote kindness and unity to prepare society's children to fight against all types of "devils" in the world. If we don't they may, thanks to your efforts and with your naive supporters, be pushed into begging for prayers and imaginary "good deeds," forever mental captives trapped in seminaries, schools and restrictive communities – all to be considered by your standards sufficiently "religious." Is this really the aim of religion, and what's best for the future of our community?

Today, we don't even drink water the way those ancient people whom you so frequently quote, did!

Up until recent times, when a patient was dying because of clotted heart arteries, they'd bring a *mullah* to her bedside to recite prayers, and sacrifice a lamb, to fend off the "evil eye"! Today, is there any ignorance greater than wasting even a minute to get such a patient to a hospital?

The longest of journeys begins by taking the smallest of steps. Likewise, to remove regression and discrimination, between men and women, let us begin by rejecting and removing the smallest of nonsense and superstitions currently in circulation.

"Wiping out *superstitions*" and "rejecting the *superstitious*" does not mean "wiping out religion." We have no objection or issue with our religion or the Commandments. My words are addressed to the religious traditionalist regressors over their nonsensical rules and prohibitions, which they claim to be religious commands and which they enforce every day and everywhere by taking advantage of other people's ignorance or indifference, to benefit themselves!

How will future generations judge us?

Christianity flourished in Europe once Religion was made separate from the State, and citizens were encouraged to rely as much on the pen and science, as they once had on religion, allowing them **to rapidly grow and advance** — and yes, even exploit to their own advantage others' centuries of backwardness. They began to think instead of imitate.

The legacy of the wise men is the rationalism of those whom they leave behind. In contrast, the legacy of ignorant people is the regression of their heirs.

The regressors wish to lead our children backwards in time and lock them in a darkroom, in the name of religion, to keep from the explosion of news and information that is advancing further, day by day.

Today, in the age of the internet, control and censorship has become increasingly impossible. Whatever it is that the regressors are attempting to keep from their captive students, is reaching them much more intensely, every second, from backchannels, which are outside of our control. We have arrived at the age of the end of censorship. Accordingly, it would be better if teachers and parents discuss reality with their children, and place them in the context of today's world.

The interpretations of religious subjects are of such a variety, contrast, and so full of contradictions, that understanding them is like interpreting dreams! No scholars or persons see them exactly the same way. Yet the "care-takers of religions" claim repeatedly that "you don't understand, but we do!"

The extremists' interpretations, commentaries, words and deeds which are so far away from our true culture are exploited by these religious opportunists. The Jewish extremists use partial truths to advance their cause; while the enemies of the Jewish religion rely on many of those same partial truths to use Judaism as their scapegoat, publishing anti-Semitic tracts in the hundreds of thousands, attributing to the religion those same bigoted misinterpretations that many of us feel do not represent our beliefs.

But the commandments of the *Holy Torah* are like the constitution of the Jewish civilization, while the traditions, commentaries and interpretations are its codes of conduct, regulations and caveats, which could be changed for our times.

Do you know the story of the man in love with a blind girl? To realize his beloved's dream of seeing, he gave his eyes to her, as a gift, secretly and anonymously. However, when the girl regained her sight and saw that her husband was without eyes, she pushed him away. He cried out, "Leave me, if you want. But please take care of the eyes that I gave you as a gift…" **At this moment, the woman realized that it was her husband's love for her that enabled her to see with his eyes.**

I tell this story because I wish to address those ungrateful people, who with their words, funds, or weapons attack the Jewish people:

"Please, do your best to take care of the eyes that the Jewish people gave you as a gift. **Denying that would be equal to denying everyone's power to see.** If you are proud of your own books and laws, then look to their source and know that your pride stems from a common pride in our shared beliefs, values and ethics. It is the Jewish people, who over thousands of years, tolerating unspeakable suffering and hardship, has been able to fight on, in order to introduce monotheism to the world. The Jewish people did so by putting an end to such despicable practices as human sacrifice, the worship of animals, idols, or the deification of individual human beings; claims of wizardry, and the occult. This fight has often cost them their lives, as well as thousands of years of hatred and enmity.

"**Shirin and Farhad**" are a kind of ancient Persian "Romeo and Juliet." According to the legend, Farhad spent years of his life building a monument, known as **Bistoon** or **Bisotun**, for his beloved Shirin. Yet a poet wrote,

"It was love, which engraved Bistoon,
Yet it was Farhad, who took on the fame.
It was the nightingale that suffered for the flower,
Yet it was the wind who took the petals away."

There would have been no Holy Book without the knowledge of God. You will realize the services of the Jewish people to the world when you read carefully about the outcome of the cults and ideologies of the past hundred years such as the Godless Communists, to the cruel and zealot human-worshippers, such as the Nazis, Maoists, and their ilk. The Jewish people still fight against those people whose thoughts and deeds promote superstition and slavery.

The history of the Jewish people reminds one of the sage who was asked, "Thou the wise man, please tell us why they put the ring on the left hand, while the right hand has so many virtues?" He replied, "Haven't you heard that the virtuous men are always the most deprived?!"

The Jewish people, consistently discriminated against, have always been the right hand of history as the harbingers and announcers of monotheism, and promoters of knowledge, science and freedom.

The **pessimists** complain of the wind; the **optimists** wait impatiently for it to change direction; the **realists** adapt themselves to it! **It's human beings, who adjust their religious understanding to incorporate the knowledge, science and the realities of their time; otherwise, the books don't change.**

Neither we, nor other societies, can change the direction of the winds. But to survive, to stay, we could adjust the mainsail of our boat to the wind.

No religion, cult or ideology has all the answers. If we wish to rid our religion of those parts that no longer conform to modern times or current knowledge, we can't turn to those whose own cults invented many of these erroneous practices; or to those who use them to promote their sects or to those teachers and preachers who owe their own high position, inflated self-importance and living to these practices.

Religion is not an "all or nothing," or a "black and white" situation. We need to fear "brain-drain," having intelligent men and women leave the circle of faith, because they find the beliefs, rituals and practices so irrational and impractical.

There is a saying: Don't be afraid of someone who has a library; but be afraid of someone who has only one book and imagines that all the knowledge of the world is contained therein! Such a person is like the man who brought home a bucket of sea water and claimed, "Look everyone! I brought you the sea"! It's also very much like the story of those who claim, "Since we have the *Halacha*, the religious laws, we have everything!"

Today, accredited universities the world over are revising and republishing their textbooks every three to six months, and textbooks from past semesters are taken out of circulation. In addition, students often receive daily updates to remain current with the cutting edge advances in their field of study. More often than not, by the time the "latest" developments become available in print, rapid progress in research has already rendered that information obsolete. In such an era, can we really consider the textbooks in religious schools eternal?

True death occurs when useful learning is stopped.

"Oh, you, who have no knowledge of
The burnt and the one who could burn!
You pay attention: Love is not acquired!
Rather, it has to come by itself."

Dear educators in charge,

You cannot decide to fall in love; rather, true love should capture you and your students through intellect and reason. A fantasizing and superstitious lover, in love with some figment of his or her imagination, is not a lover, but a nuisance. Let us not be deceived by appearances.

"Seeds of loyalty and hatred
Would manifest in this vast farmland,
When the time of harvest arrives..."

Thanksgiving is a very nice American tradition, a day for families to celebrate together and be grateful. The Jews, too, have a weekly festivity of "thanksgiving," that is Friday nights or the eve of Sabbath. Yet some Jewish factions, under order from their leaders, their *mullahs*, won't allow their followers to have dinner with their families, because they don't allow them to drive on the Sabbath, and their family home is too far away to walk to. Is not using a vehicle truly a "religious observance"? Is it rational or moral? I say to such children,

"Don't take for granted this conversation,
Since once we've left behind

This camp on the crossroads,
We won't find another chance to meet."

Neither parents, nor the opportunities to meet with the elders of their family, will last forever.

"Wake up now, 'cause someday, you'll get enough sleep — under
The mud — With no company, friend, partner, or caring comrade!
Be warned, and don't tell this secret to anyone:
The tulip, once withered, won't ever blossom again."

The traditionalist fanatic sects are filled with nonsensical declarations. One such "authority" even claimed that, "A tree could be counted as part of the *minyan* — i.e. the quorum of 10 adult Jews needed to say public prayers — but a woman can't!" We cannot allow this irrational culture born of the *ghettos* to grow in our own community. And let us not wait for others to take the first steps to rectify the situation. Instead, let us begin in our homes.

"Life is the warmth of hearts Intertwined.
'Til there's no intellect, all doors are closed."

We can turn back the clocks, but we can't stop time. Let us teach our youngsters that we should be determined in our belief in religion; but that we should be resilient, and follow our conscience when it comes to practicing its related commands. Otherwise, the belief and its practice will become obsolete.

The problem is not a lack of faith. The problem is a faith devoid of morality and wisdom, which leads to extremism on both sides, a kind of "bipolar extremism." As **Ferdowsi** wrote,

"Our full-hearted salute goes to the man,
Whose fabric's woven of justice and wisdom."

We should *have* faith — and not force or impose it in a way that's only for show, or that's hypocritical or pretentious.

The best way to damage a good cause is to defend it in the wrong way.

Napoleon said, "Science and history, on the one hand, and religion, on the other, are the arch-enemies of each other." The more literate and knowledgeable a person is, the less likely they are to be swayed by the regressors.

There are many wise men and women in the world committed to morality and to helping others who have cut themselves loose of world's religions. Such people know piety, religious observance, even "religiosity" as they give their whole to others. Are they the truly religious, or is it those who in the name of religion, stomp over morality?

I have witnessed one of these so-called religious persons asking for a huge amount of money to "cure" one of their supporters who had become ill by praying for him! Using their religion in immoral ways, taking advantage of the sick, and bringing the patient no benefit other than disappointment, is this being "religious"?

In informed societies, people gain power and respect from their understanding, and not from their ranks, positions, wealth — or the exercise of their religious beliefs.

Benjamin Franklin once wrote, "Tart words make no friends; a spoonful of honey will catch more flies than a gallon of vinegar." Indeed, a single logical word is much more instructive than thousands of seditious books.

Today, educated youngsters who listen to religious sermons are often more informed than the speaker! They accept that human intellect is more efficient than propaganda and that greater knowledge will lead to better understanding.

The French author **François de La Rochefoucauld** (1613-1680) wrote, "A healthy intellect is a precious commodity which God has bestowed upon very few people. Yet few people consider themselves deprived of it…"

The courageous and proud Jewish people of the Iranian city of Mash-had, as well as the early Marrano Jews of Spain abandoned those commands which they could not observe under the regime then in power; and yet, they succeeded in preserving their Jewish heritage. Did they preserve a legacy of nonsense and superstition, or rather, the essence of their dynamic Jewish civilization?

They continued to honor their religion. One small example is told about a couple in Mash-had, in1800 C.E., whose wedding vows were being offered in Arabic. The bride and groom were bitterly crying as their unusually Arabic names were being recited. Meanwhile, the dowry from poor parents, offered to the groom, was a volume of the word of God — a copy of the *Holy Torah*, a gift from the Iranian city of Hamedan — and not the void and nonsensical claims of some people today.

Here is a question that the regressors don't answer: What happens if someone doesn't wear a skullcap or a hat or prays in a synagogue that has electrical loudspeakers? Is there any punishment or consequence whatever?

Religion cannot remain stagnant. Otherwise like a fetid pond, all its living creatures, such as its trout, will die. Instead its fish need to flow to the sea joining part in a much larger environment. Today, the successful youngsters in our communities are like those trout. They have grown up in dynamic rivers and joined the ocean following the laws of nature that demand either a balanced growth, or a gradual demise.

History has taught mankind that if we cannot predict the moment an earthquake will occur, at least we understand the conditions which make such an upheaval possible. We used to think that floods and storms originated from the skies and the mountains. But after the tragic Tsunami event of 2004 of East-Asia, we realized that such catastrophic events could also originate at the bottom of the oceans, from the movement of miles-long layers of the earth at the depths of the sea. Perhaps the only other comparable event in our recorded history took place on 31st of June, 365 C.E., in the coasts of Greece. Thus, we saw that, after 1640 years, such tectonic movements, as they occurred on December 26th, 2004, in the Indian Ocean, could cause a massive body of water to travel 400 miles per hour toward the shores. In a short amount of time, the immense power of the Tsunami was able to destroy thousands of miles of land.

Like the Tsunami, which was a single tragic event, **Stalin**, a single man, killed about 20 million people of his own compatriots, the citizens of his own country, during his cruel reign. Stalin, of course was not the only murderous tyrant in history. Others such as **Genghis Khan**, **Mao**, and **Hitler,** each in their own turn, were mass murderers -- all in the name of ideologies, religion, sects, or cults. Experience has shown us that in this crazy world, fanatical dictators will emerge, often greeted warmly by the most ignorant members of society.

Unfortunately, the greatest lesson of history is that human beings don't learn from their own history.

If Einstein, Edison or Pasteur came back to life, they would be surprised to find that some students disagree with some of their findings, but for the great part they would be shocked to see how far research has come in extending and expanding on their ideas. This is

the same attitude we should have towards the religious sages of old –
thanking them for the contributions they made to their time, and
showing them how we have evolved.

**How sorry we should feel for those, who in order to provide for
some false interests, or some presumed "rewarding good deed" (!)
turn toward the past, without being aware that by doing this they
have turned their backs on the future!** This reminds me of the
northern Iranian province of Geylan, where chickens are kept and
raised under baskets, so they grow fat! Do you expect that to fulfill a
"rewarding good deed" we should take youngsters of poor financial
standing as captives of the seminaries? Because captivity is good, of
course, for the neighbor, "the others," but not for us?!

**No! No one here is opposed to education or educational
support.** But our assistance should stipulate eradicating regression.
Otherwise, we are nothing more than accomplices in promoting
backwardness in our community. We should provide for others what
we wish for our own children – with good reason, as those children
may one day become our son or daughters-in-law or our grandchildren
or their spouses – as happened to this humble writer.

You, who support the regressors do so from the goodness of your
heart but must realize that doing so assures the continuity and
expansion of the regressor's mission, even as it ruins the lives of our
youth and intrudes on the personal lives of the families in our
community. You give your support unconditionally – but it is in your
power to require that these centers of learning teach modern
knowledge and science and stop propagating regression.

Generosity and Forgiveness, For a Better Life, Not For Pity and Stagnation!

I have no desire to attack individuals. My goal is to inform others and to oppose the destructive plague of prejudice and bigotry. My many years of bitter and poisonous experience in such matters forces me to conclude that the manner in which so-called religious people propagate and teach their ideas leads to divisiveness and the regression of the entire society.

Just compare the *useful* knowledge of a graduate of a religious school against that of a university graduate. One group spends years of their precious lives in traditional schools within the so-called religious culture. While the other spends time in accredited modern universities. Although the former might be better at citing obscure Rabbinic quotations, the latter group is the one you would bet on to assure the survival and progress of our youngsters. The latter is more likely to achieve financial independence and contribute to the welfare of the community; the former is more likely to lead our community to stagnation, frustration, and scientific, economic and cultural poverty.

When **Einstein's** theories were first being considered by the world's scientific society, Einstein predicted, "If my theory of relativity is proven successful, Germany will claim me as a German and France will declare that I am a citizen of the world. Should my theory prove untrue, France will say that I am a German and Germany will declare **that I am a Jew!"**

When Judaism first introduced Monotheism to the world more than 3300 years ago, the fortune-tellers, animal-worshippers, and the wizards and "medicine men," along with the idol-worshippers **considered this new religion and the people who first heralded it, as their competition.** Unfortunately, even today, with all the monotheistic faiths in the world, with all their shared monotheistic beliefs, there are still people who view Jews or even the Jewish religion as their competition. This is all the more ironic, since many of these other religions share so much in common with Judaism. If anything, it's their own pride that they rely on! Anytime and anywhere that they need a scapegoat, they blame all the problems of the world on the Jewish people; this is how they "reward" us for offering monotheism to humanity, and closing down the shops of wizardry and their like.

People of my age will soon retire from an active social life. Hence, the duty falls upon you, the successful and highly worthy middle-aged members of our community for choosing the way of balance and moderation, which agrees with the ways of your fathers. At the same time you must keep step with time by studying both the ways of extremists and the experiences of the past.

The regressors are nothing without the financial support of others. It is up to you and your generation to dictate to them the way of moderation and balance, and save the present and future society from chaos, conflicts and division. The regressors would try to win you over by nonsense and emotion, not logic! Falling under their influence will not only do you harm but imagine the harm to your brainwashed religious children. If you don't believe me, you will realize this when one day, your own brainwashed children will not accept even yourself.

There should be no support for teaching nonsense and superstition. By conditioning your support, we can remove the culture of regression from our religious schools. It is up to you to find practical ways to achieve your good intentions. No children should go astray, under any name. **No balanced, moderate person opposes learning knowledge and science, or supporting students.** If we remove the regressors and their misguided teachings from the schools; then you'll see our community united again.

438

No student should remain beholden to superstition, or dress in a given manner just because of superstitious belief or because he or she has a lack of financial means. Don't be manipulated by the demagogues or those who pretend to be innocent and victimized. Only with courage and bravery can we make amends for past and present mistakes. Change will occur but not merely by tying our hopes to *ha-Shem*, i.e. God, and constantly repeating some old ways…We need to act!

"You talked of the vices of wine, now speak of its virtues, too.
Don't deny truth and wisdom, for the sake of a bunch of commoners."

You say that, "The teachers and heads of these religious schools mean well." While I agree with you, I reply nonetheless that, "**Since their beliefs are filled with misinterpretations, wrong advice and bad decisions, their good intentions don't yield results that differ from evil intentions."**

"My dear, Good words aren't the sole condition of goodness;
If you already speak right, you need to complement it with good deeds.
To mend a ruined building, you need to bring in
Not only good material, but an expert constructor."

The principals and instructors of these schools are themselves graduates of the school of regression. Ever since they were children, they've been captives of the same propagators and believers of nonsense and superstition. In such religious schools, those who have had a traditional schooling are given priority in employment. Could we expect a willow tree to bear apples; then how is it that you take care of the willow, and hope for the fruit?!

They say that the prophets have brought us news of the very far future, but history brings us the news of the past. How could societies build their future, if they follow the advice of those who claim, "We already have everything!" — as those fanatics say with regard to the *halacha*, the religious law? To know the causes of past hardships and sufferings, and how they relate to our today's and tomorrow's life — this is fundamental to providing a better life for our children. Could we pass through such storms by relying solely only on religion, in a world that has everything but justice? **Alas, not learning from experience is a big pain; what suffering it is to know but not to will – and what a misery it is to be a bigot and persist in prejudice.** Indeed, the mistaken theory that states, "We have the book, so we have everything!" is not something unique or without precedence. On page 33 of *Akhb_r-ol-Hakam_t*, published in Egypt, and page 33 of *Mo'ajjem-ol-boldan*, we read,

"After the Arab invasion of Iran and other lands, whatever scientific books and keepsakes had remained, were burnt or thrown in the water. During the conquest of Egypt, when **Amr ibn al-_s** (ca. 583-664 C.E.) got his hand on the scientific treasures of Alexandria, he asked for orders from **Omar ibn al-Khatt_b** (ca. 586-644 C.E.), the second *khalifa*, as what to do with the books. The *khalifa* replied, 'If they contain words in agreement with God's Book, they can be spared; but if they contain anything against God's book, there is no need to keep them: have them destroyed.' Once Ibn al-As got the news, he began to distribute the books among the baths of Alexandria. It's said that these books provided the heating fuel of the baths for six months!"

The same thing happened when they attacked Iran, or Persia. **Sa'd ibn Abi Waqq_s** (ca. 590-664 C.E.) asked Omar ibn al-Khattab as what to do with the books of the Persian libraries, and he wrote back, "Throw them all into the water. Either, they contain guidance, in which case we don't need them, because God has already guided us with a better book; or else, they are causes for misguidance, in which case, God has made us devoid of needing them." As a result, today, no one, no power or authority, can determine the material and spiritual value of those treasures.

Alas, the ill of blindness from prejudice has still no cure, and sometimes, the blind become guides to the blind. And sadly, people often ignore the dangers that poses.

"They're calling you from
The top of the throne (of skies)!
I wonder what has
Fallen into this trap hole..."

Only God knows. Perhaps, there were hundreds of others like **Avicenna**, whose name and any sign of them were lost, once those books were burnt.

Today, when human rights has become a matter of politics, we can hear the footsteps of discrimination among religions, even calls for a continuation of the Crusades! Society's leaders have their heads buried in the sand in total denial. They don't wish to see that the regressors are, in fact, human rights abusers!

In our religion, we mourn the passing of an individual for seven days; but we will be punished for seven generations for the mistakes of our religious educators. The superstitious myths and legends of religions are full of fantasies and fictions that were invented when a *mullah* was like "a myopic man, deemed to have the best vision in a town of the blind!" Why do you go on teaching materials that have no relevance or significance to today's and tomorrow's generation? We have so many valuable commandments; so why don't you focus on them, instead?

To reach the light, societies first have to know the darkness. And if they truly wish to know what it is that keeps humans healthy, or makes them ill, they should learn from experience. The pages of history are vastly heavier with accounts of human barbarism than with stories of civilized behavior. We need only look to how quickly we arrive at the biblical account of Cain and Abel, wherein one man's hand was stained with the blood of his brother, whom he murdered, some supposedly 5000 years ago when both were the sole owners of the world! But Why?

Who was there? Who recorded this event? On what paper? By what handwriting? With what literacy?! Where was it kept all that time? How, contrary to the good intention behind the writing of it, i.e. leaving a record of it as a moral fable, did it became an example for "brother-killings" among the "grandchildren" of the forefathers of monotheistic religions. For thousands of years, such crimes have been repeated, each day, in every corner of the world, and each time under a different name and for different interests. Alas, there has been no Abraham, no help, no savior, to neutralize such prejudice mixed with hatred. No one has stood up to tell everyone, "The goal of these stories was the moral of the story; the reasonable conclusions made by their audience; to help you become better people. The rest is nothing!"

Yesterday's anti-Semite has grown to become today's anti-Humanist committed to his beliefs, and not to the truth. This is the nature of prejudice and has nothing to do with a particular religion or ideology. After all, the man who assassinated Yitzchak Rabin, the prime minister of Israel, was a so-called religious Jewish fanatic whose faith lacked a sense of morality. Such faith as his, has delivered no benefits, no solutions, and only pain for society.

Indeed, all terrorists in history have fully believed in their faith. It's quite alright to raise children as faithful, with deep beliefs. But belief in what? Believing in conscience, or believing in a lack of conscience? Was not the person who assassinated **Mahatma Gandhi** a religious Hindu, too? In 1914, **Gavrilo Princip** assassinated **Archduke Franz Ferdinand of Austria,** in Sarajevo igniting World War I, causing the death of tens of millions of innocent people. And as you might have guessed, Gavrilo, too, was a fanatic, a so-called Christian religious man.

Human society, today, is paying the price for its past silence in the face of anti-Semitism; the expulsion of Jews and Muslims from Spain in 1492 C.E.; and also, in the face of all other brutal violations of human rights, such as the massacre of 1.5 million Armenians by the Turkish forces; the massacre of 800,000 members of the Tutsi ethnic group of Rwanda in the hands of the Hutu tribes; or the recent genocide of the Christians in Darfur, Sudan; etc.

Never, in any part of the world, could anyone make people into better humans by spreading prejudice and bigotry. They have only succeeded in fostering discrimination and division.

Today, the germ of anti-Humanism, the hostility toward other human beings, has risen against itself and humanity, as it was with the case of the tyrants of history who would save the last bullet for their own heads! The best remedy against human hostility, and the best way to prevent its spread, is neither prayers nor fasting, but the free-thinking spread of kindness. For this battle we need to be armed with knowledge, science, and other accurate information.

God shall wish them humiliated, those who choose bigotry over science, and who bring about the downfall of their children by irrational teachings, both at home and at school. Narrow-mindedness and prejudice, and the propagation of hatred in the name of a group or religion, is much more harmful than having no religion at all. Yes, we should practice our religion, but out of love for it, not out of fear of Hell, or by treating others with cruelty, in the hope of going to Heaven! Just look at the afflicted families around you! Anyone who wishes to show off his or her piety and religiosity to others, is not truly a religious person, but a hypocrite exhibitionist. Indeed, as the walking stick is a necessity for the blind, so are pretention and prejudice necessary for the ignorant who sacrifice their faith, as well as others' to superstition.

Ferdowsi wrote,

"You should think of a Demon as a bad person,
Someone who has no sense of gratitude toward God.
Whoever abandoned the way of humanity,
Count him as a Demon, and not among humans."

There is a very interesting **French proverb**, which states, "The happiness of a people has an inverse relation to the length of its history." In other words, the longer the history of a nation, the more problems a nation will have. The accumulation of traditions over the course of a long history brings with it prejudice, bigotry and small-mindedness often expressed as nationalism. This hampers the society decreasing its culture and civilization and its ability to innovate and create.

The so-called extremist "sages," who propagate such nonsense stand out even more, under this theory, as a force retarding society and its progress. We should all remember that the roads to God are as many in number as there are individual human beings. It's up to each and every one of us to find his or her own path.

The *Psalms* put it so beautifully, that *God has not revealed himself in His full force; rather, He appears to each person according to his or her capacity.*

As the British philosopher **Bertrand Russell** wrote, and I paraphrase, I don't understand how, in an increasingly smaller world, with an increasingly larger population, people stay so distant from each other, like strangers. This is the same world, which is predicted to change into a few continent-nations, including the United States, Europe, Asia and Africa, to be followed by a single global government, in the distant future.

Look at India. In the 15th century, in the city of Ahmad Abad, in the province of Gujarat, there used to be a temple that belonged to the

Hindus. Later on, that temple was destroyed in the hands of the Muslims, and a mosque was built in its place, called the **Babri Mosque**. This place has changed hands a few times, until recently, when there were rumors of building a temple there again. Once the rumor was out, within a short time, around 3000 people were killed over the ensuing tensions, including numerous people who were burnt alive.

Look at Europe. Throughout centuries, they killed and massacred millions of their own subjects and citizens, over conquering land, expanding their borders, or over religious and ideological differences. Finally, at least for now, 27 countries have ratified a pact of unity to form the European Union. To prevent any unwelcome, damaging religious tension, they agreed not to mention the name of God in the entire document! These member countries have one parliament, one defense minister, one foreign minister, one law, one currency, and a common border! Pity those poor millions, who killed and were killed over the centuries, encouraged by the popes, kings, knights, priest, dictators, and the mad men of history!

If only those who died, and those who expedited their death, could rise now and see, who was the victor and who was defeated? What tradition or ideology? What border, name, or religion? What ethnicity? What color? These 27 European countries, the founders of the regional-global governments, accept qualified members much as an Olympic or international sport clubs! Everyone is trying to elbow their way in for membership! Even the half-European Turkey and the Middle Eastern country of Israel say, "We are members, too!"

That doesn't mean there are no more extremists, and no more violence. Examples abound. Some are "fighting" for the independence (!) of the Basque area of Spain; some are "fighting" over religious causes in Ireland — and none of them can take off their dark glasses, and realize that the *caravan* and the travelers have long passed, and left them behind!

As I write these lines, the leaders of the European Parliament, i.e. the third most populated "country" in the world, with a population of about 500 million people, as a first step, hired more than 4500 translators, so that they could understand each other! Mutual understanding is the first step towards mutual respect. Today most religious followers don't even understand the language of their own religion – much less the language of other religions. How then can we expect those followers to respect, let alone love each other or even understand each other?

I asked a student of a religious seminary, belonging to my own religion, a high-ranking student of a *yeshiva* who presumably had studied there for many years, "Do you know the Hebrew language?" He answered, "No!" Don't believe me? Ask for yourself!

It's said that, **For the world to go toward evil, it's enough that the righteous people sit around and do nothing!**

According to the laws of nature, our eyes age and occasionally we need to change or upgrade our spectacles, getting stronger prescriptions, or perhaps have an operation to improve our vision. If not, we might even become blind. Spectacles have been used for several centuries but it was only in 1925, that modern eyeglasses were offered to the world. Most people need glasses by middle age. Given how many people wear glasses today, imagine how past generations were limited and how difficult it was for some to read, no less acquire knowledge. By contrast, today even in kindergarten children wear glasses.

Similarly our interpretation of the holy commandments, scripture, and rituals needs adjustment as our religion moves into its middle age. A better lens on our tradition and our practices will help us see,

446

understand and practice our religion better. Just as wearing glasses is no insult to the wearer, so too preserving the rational commandments, customs and traditions of any religion or ideological group does not mean refuting or rejecting all other groups.

Future generations, no doubt, will talk about our times the way we remember the Stone Age. They will wonder why people who despite owning millions of acres of land, sent each other's youngsters to their doom — fighting over a fist-size plot of mud, sand, brick or stone? Can't a synagogue, mosque, church or temple, which is erected in our time, be considered sacred and holy; while what was created in the past ages is considered a historical world treasure? Thousands of synagogues, churches, mosques, and other holy religious places of religions have been destroyed over the years by the Communists, Nazis, or the fanatic members of various religions.

Until the 13th century C.E., the monumental Christian cathedral of Córdoba, Spain was a Muslim mosque; the **Hagia Sophia** mosque of **Istanbul**, Turkey, was originally built as a Christian church and mosaic images of Jesus still cover the walls. Is not the life of a single person worth this whole world? **The great philosopher, Plato, had an answer worth considering:**

They asked **Plato**, "How did you live?' He answered, "I came into the world by an urgent force and despite my will; I lived in bewilderment; and now, I leave this world, contrary to my will. This much has become known to me, that nothing is ever known."

Or as Omar Khayyam said in the Rubyat:

"At first, I was compelled to live by an act of creation.
Years of life add none to it but bewilderment.
We survived, reluctantly, never told what this was all about –
The intention behind this coming, being, and leaving..."

… just as the survival of no one temple depends on the destruction of another place of worship. The Indian spiritual leader, **Gautama Buddha** (died ca. 400 B.C.E.) said, "All that we are is the result of what we have thought. The mind is everything. What we think we become."

Let us teach this to our children so they won't allow others to lead them down the wrong road in the name of religion, ideology or tradition. There is no religion or ideology above humanity.

We can't prohibit a person from holding an irrational belief. But this is no reason for a person to think his beliefs represent the absolute truth; or to deem anyone who disagrees with him as his opposition and enemy; or as reason to interfere in the affairs of others to the cost of breaking up families; and to hate others in the name of "rewarding good deeds." There is no difference between the dark-minded, ignorant persons of one particular group and those of another group.

Dear fundamentalist religious educators: Instead of always calling your innocent, oppressed students "sinners," teach them to focus on their responsibilities. You would have them spend their time confessing to sins – when most of what you find offensive is no affront and no breach to the practice of our religion or to our religious identity. In the past, wizardry and magic, miracle and prayers were the basic and primary means of promoting religion, and inducing the average person with an "understanding" of superstitions, e.g. demonstrating for an illiterate crowd a "picture of a snake" instead of the word "snake".

Fortunately, today's world is vastly different. Please don't take the silence of rational minded people as approval for your ways. Instead those free thinking people who remain silent cry when extremist educated groups become a community's leaders.

Immanuel Kant wrote that mankind has two standards by which to measure truth; one is his intellect, and the next, the intellect of others, who look at the same problem from a different point of view. **All societies have to learn that tolerating other people's rational and logical ideas is part of being civilized.**

We need to have beliefs to live. But the problem begins when absolutism sets in and a person thinks their beliefs to be the ultimate, infallible truth.

The past is where memories belong; the future, is where hopes reside. Presently, however, we must make a continuous effort to better understand our duties and responsibilities. No statement is absolute. Everything must be understood in context and interpreted according to our time.

The greatest tragedies in human history have been rooted in the absolutism of religions.

Dear School Officials: You should be teaching our students that we are all responsible for the safety and comfort of each other. It's said that to have Knowledge is better than to have Wealth and Riches. But in truth, *not* having Wealth is worse than *not* having Knowledge – in the same way that extremist religiosity is worse than having no religion.

Laws, customs and traditions differ greatly from one religion or even one community to another – some that are praiseworthy among one are despicable to another. **For Example:** I was once talking to some East Asian friends. My friend from the Philippines, told me that it was customary for a guest in a Filipino house to signal that a meal was delicious by belching loudly. My Chinese friend countered that in a Chinese home to show that one is enjoying one's soup, one must slurp loudly. As for my Indian friend, he explained that in a number of religious cults there, when someone dies, the dead body is burned and if by chance while doing so the head explodes this is taken as an omen that the deceased's sins have been absolved and forgiven.

Thus, we see that there is no absolute good or bad. Absolutism requires a one-sided, mono-dimensional view that is suffused with dogmatism, rigid-mindedness, mental ossification, and corruption. Absolute-minded extremists brainwash their followers to turn knowledge into superstition, philosophy into nonsense, and art into pretention and exhibitionism. I have heard such nonsense peddlers announce that "All illnesses are the messengers of God!" and proclaim that the attack of a swarm of locusts, these 'angels of God' is a punishment for our sins!

Saadi asked a wise man, "Whom did you learn from so much knowledge and wisdom?" The man replied, "From the blind, who don't take a step, before they have examined the ground before them with the stick."

There is no end to man's cruelty to man and the lengths to which inhumane behavior can be prized by those in the thrall of an absolutist ideology. For example, in 1942 in the city of Berlin, the German government gave a prize of honor to **Rudolf Hoess, the Auschwitz commandant,** who had murdered **430,000** innocent people in a mere 56 days. And for this, the German nation applauded him!

Given the present situation, it's enough for a cruel tyrant to gain power, small or giant, in any time, position or place, to be able to manifest his inherent bestiality.

Even the most rational minded among us cannot deny the hold religion has on people. Instead what we can do, what we must do, is goad the religious to be vigilant against absolutism, and stalwart against extremism, to embrace a rational-minded contemporary approach to religion blocking the opportunists who target people's life or well-being.

The criminals of history, such as **Hitler, Mussolini** and their henchmen would have never been able to commit the atrocities they did, without convincing their followers of the absolute importance of their mission, holding them in near religious fervor for the commission of genocide. All that cruelty was perpetrated, as everyone knows, while the Church kept silent.

Nietzsche wrote that, "In order not to be an idol-worshiper, it's not enough for you to have just broken the idols; rather, you should have abandoned the act of worshipping the idols altogether." Post-Renaissance Europeans may have given up idols, but they didn't abandon religious hatred rooted in holy books and scripture. That's because no political party, nor any dictatorship, has been able to reach its shameful aims, without gaining access to the invisible power of religion, tradition or ideology.

Consider God's Command to Adam and Eve, in the early chapters of *Genesis*, forbidding them to eat from the fruit of the "Tree of Knowledge" and prohibiting them from having the ability to distinguish between good and evil. Was it meant to keep rebellious, "brother-killing" in a state of ignorance — the human being, who has such a strong passion for inquiring, doing research, playing around, experimenting, building and destroying? Do you think that humanity was punished because we were accused of eating the forbidden fruit and because our eyes were opened?!

Abraham, the father of all monotheistic religions, was coerced into "*almost* sacrificing his beloved son, only to be replaced by a ram" — in order to stop human beings from sacrificing their fellow humans! He did so, hoping to make primitive people understand not to sacrifice their own children based on nonsensical religious ideas and superstitions! He did so, as if to say, "For the time being, sacrifice animals, until the day you realize that there is no need for these sort of sacrifices: To find favor in the eyes of God, to be loved by Him, you just need to be a better human being."

Alas, however, even today, the extremists of different groups go on committing one sin in the name of religion, in order to compensate for another. As a poet wrote, *"If the listener isn't capable of understanding what's being said, you can't blame it on the rhetorical power of the speaker!"*

Human beings throughout history have created pecking orders, inventing social classifications making one person "better" than another, so that whoever did not belong to the aristocracy, for example, would be considered worthless and expendable. We can see the remnants of this in India, among the "elite Hindu castes" versus the "impure tribes." This is while humanity commands us, "Anyone standing tall has the right to look down at another person, only when he's bent down to give that person a helping hand."

Anti-Semitism means "animosity toward the Semite race," which includes both Jews as well as Arabs. But it has never been applied that way, and remains a one way hate-filled street of calumny against the Jews. Arabs all over the world continue everyday to ignore this "animosity toward itself," shouting propaganda against "the Jews." They praise anti-Semitism, so much so that during World War Two their grand *mufti* – the one who issues *fatwas* – was vocal in his embrace of Hitler and his anti-Semitic policies.

Dear Educators,

Mankind's creativity has been his most important tool and weapon for survival, and his primary means of progress. When an appropriate environment does not exist in religious schools to nurture the creativity of our youngsters; when the need for adaptability, resilience, and accepting change, is ignored; when by relying on religious absolutist

452

mindsets, the inherent potentials of the students is not unleashed; then these student's lives are diminished, their horizons limited, the potential and future restricted.

Aristotle wrote so meaningfully that, "Injustice is experienced where there are more laws than are needed.

One of the problems that you have created is to indiscriminately teach conflicting interpretations of outdated rules, prohibitions and commandments by a variety of religious commentators, spanning several centuries, many of which, over time, such as the absurd number of Sabbath laws, have become religious laws -- wrongly.

Instead of arguing about what you can and can't do on the Sabbath, why not prepare students for real life by teaching them modern knowledge! As harsh as it may sound, prayers did not save the lives of the six million innocent Jews murdered in the Holocaust.

Napoleon Bonaparte warned us, "to be afraid of those who pretend to agree with us, but don't have the courage to tell us about their disagreements." Only some wrongful people, who play both sides, would pretend constructive criticism to be an attack on religion itself.

Criticism of a religion should only make it stronger. It would be a better world if religious people sought to improve their own religions rather than look down or hate the followers of other religions, or the followers of different factions of their own religion. To date, religion has not been able to bring peace and reconciliation even among the followers of the same book! How then can we expect religion as a whole to do any good?

I ask those who think their prayers are answered, to pray for us, but also pray for raising understanding and awareness of those commandments that are within the knowledge and the capabilities of today's human beings.

Many of today's modern human illnesses are like the side-effects of the drugs that people have been using to cure themselves. Likewise, we have seen that the consequences of religious extremism are often far worse than the benefits of religious belief. It's the absolutist who considers anyone thinking differently than him to be an enemy. This is how fanatics can be persuaded in the name of religion to murder a political leader who seeks peace, attack innocents in public places such as buses, crowded markets and office buildings, and to commit suicide in the process of murdering others.

A high ranking religious leader considered his people to be so backward that during the elections season, he announced, **"Whoever votes for my party, that person would secure a place for himself in Heaven!"**

For such "religious leaders" to say such nonsense for personal gain is not so surprising. **What's truly sad, however, is the people who and give financial assistance and material support to the likes of them!** Or go to the likes of him for religious advice on how to observe the religion!

In every society, religion has been exploited to attract the attention of simple-minded people, and thus bring financial rewards and greater power to the exploiters. Religion is so powerful that any deceptive person can spread the traps of "religiosity" in order to capture some prey; and so that with the help of this bait, he could capture more and more of these "innocent doves."

In my opinion, however religious observance is like playing the piano: You need to learn how to play the instrument based on certain rules; and it requires a certain discipline and practice – but after that --- those who play by rote neither enjoy themselves, nor give pleasure to the listener. Instead to truly experience the beauty of what the piano and the music it can produce offers, the player must "forget" those absolute rules, act beyond "the score," listen, even "play by ear," and create music that is personal, meaningful and that gives pleasure to the player and the listener alike.

The Jewish people, throughout history, have been able to solve many problems, except the problem of their low population number. Today, we have re-gained our freedom as a people – yet, the culture of captivity, the *ghetto* mentality lingers on. Even amid our new-found freedom, some still feel that living as if we were still in the ghetto will preserve our identity and maintain our religion, and this what they preach. All over the world, inappropriate words in the name of religion would make many people dare question God and the religion itself, and cause many to leave religion altogether.

The leaders of these groups are the children of either *religious* extremists, or *non-religious* extremists – and not the children of moderate people. And *you* are to be blamed!

The annual decrease in Jewish population worldwide attests to the fact that such people, even if they stay within their religion, would be no more than some feeble, unstable, shallow followers! They are, as the Persian saying goes, "feeble like yogurt" or *kashki*?! And what they preach – or peddle, as the case may be, are *harfe moft*, i.e. "worthless things"? Indeed, there are many people who keep saying "worthless things," but they would never do this "without worth," i.e. for free!

It's said that once upon a time in Iran, there was an *akhond*, who was known as **Akhond Mullah Kashki!** The town's deputy, who respected the man very much, saw him one day in a sad mood. Asked why, the *akhond* said, **"I am sad over this title of *Kashki*!"** The deputy thus issued an order, announcing that thenceforth, whoever called that *akhond* as "Mullah Kashki" would receive 100 floggings! Instead, everyone had to begin calling him Akho**nd Mullah Fazel**, i.e.

"the Knowledgeable and Wise man"! Awhile later, the deputy found the *akhond* again in a sad mood. "Why, aren't people already calling you Mullah Fazel?" The *akhond* replied, **"Yes, but they now pronounce 'Mullah Fazel' in a tone and accent that means the same as 'Mullah Kashki!'"**

"By the way of repentance, one could escape
The wrath of God, but not the tongues of people!"

Trying to make people religious via some myths and childish stories will never make them become truly wise and *fazel*. Their faith would be *kashki*, and they would go on reiterating some "worthless, free words"! And where does this expression *harfe moft*, or literally "free letters", or "worthless words", come from?

It's said that during the Qajar Dynasty, when **Mokhber od-Dowleh** brought the **Morse Telegraph** system to Iran, people didn't believe in the service and wouldn't use it, even though it cost very little. He reduced the price to even fewer coins, but people refused to use it. Then one day, everyone saw a big sign above the gate of the telegraph office, which read, "Sending Telegraphs Free up to 20 Letters!" At this point, crowds of people, their greed aroused by the lure of the "free 20 letters" – i.e. those *harfe moft*! – poured into the office! After receiving their replies, they began to believe in the miracle of the telegraph. Then, a few days later, they saw a new sign, **"Harfe Moft No More Accepted!"**

Ever since, the two expressions, *kashki* and *harfe moft*, have entered the glossary of Persian idioms, and anyone who says something nonsensical and worthless is said to be offering "free letters!" These expressions are used as much when talking of politics and religions, as when speaking about someone's mother-in-law!

You may be able to capture a few youngsters by brainwashing. You may break pens or refuse to print this or that article, such as an

456

essay that disagrees with regression, either because you support the regressors or out of some baseless fear. You can even try to shut people's mouth. But no one can break the pen of history! No one can forever silence the voice of history!

Religious extremism will only stop when the regressors, faced with serious opposition from the rest of the community, begin to teach more accurate, useful knowledge. Then they'd realize that religious observance is not the exclusive property of one single person or group; and that being religious doesn't mean being an extremist. The goal of religion should be to make us better people, not more religiously observant ones.

If ancestral knowledge is combined with modern insight, it would moderate our understanding of religion. We should add the filter of science, reason and conscience, and not merely rely on teaching myths. Children need to have some exalted human beings as their examples and models, because human beings learn by seeing and watching, more than by reading or hearing.

It is neither religion or "non-religiosity" that threatens society. Rather, what put societies at risk and destabilizes them from inside, is a one-sided view of things; an inability to adapt to modern times; promoting gossip and "ill-talking"; and the tragedy of teaching hatred at schools and in the home.

As **Omar Khayyam** put it,

"One people pondering about faith and religion,
Another wondering between doubt and certainty –
When a harbinger jumps out of the ambush, calling out,
"Oh, you ignorant bunch! The path is neither this, nor that way!"

As a first step, the regressors might better keep silent; as **Saadi** put it,

"When you are deprived of wisdom and virtues,
Better keep your tongue confined in the mouth!
Humankind is betrayed by his tongue,
As an empty walnut is betrayed by its lightness."

To those who keep repeating some nonsense in the name of religion, I say, *Once the pearl is found, what else do you need the sea for?* When you have the principle commandments of the *Torah*, what need do you have for useless commentaries?

"You trusted the words of the hypocrite,
And you broke your promise to the friend.
Now, look back and see, from whom did you break,
And to whom were you joined…"

"Until certain of the truth of the words, don't utter them.
And what wouldn't beget a nice reply, just don't say it."

Sadly, there are too many ridiculous examples of "religious" nonsense circulated by the regressors – rules about everything and truly, rules about nothing! About them, I would say,

"If I'm wearing this modest cloak,
It's not out of extreme of piety:
Rather, I'm putting on a cover
Over hundreds of hidden flaws!

The Jewish people have learned the hard way, through many years of suffering, that even though falling down is inevitable, we must pick ourselves up and move forward. Staying in a state of descent, and remaining isolated, is tantamount to being destroyed. Our success has always rested on our resilience, adaptability, and our readiness to accept change; as well as in building trust by connecting to the world. If we follow the regressors and remain in our self-made cage; or even worse, if we keep our children confined in the traditional schools; then we will regress far

458

backwards and that will be tragic, for us, for them and for our
community.

We'd rather accept religion
Not only as a legacy or heritage,
But as a changing, adaptable gift,
That constantly evolves and improves.

No good ever came from blind imitation, emulation, absolutism, or
antique-worshipping.

There was a time when humans were sacrificed, whether to please
the idols, or "the gods of sun or moon" or just to bring a smile to the
face of a Roman emperor, such as Nero. However, in time, harbingers
of morality forced all society to change.

Such appeals to kindness by the harbingers of morality, whose
pioneer was **Hillel HaZaken**, are a spark of progressive evolution.
More than 2000 years ago, by substituting "prayers" for "sacrifice" all
of the extended commands, laws and regulations of the *Torah*
regarding animal sacrifices were abandoned.

We are often told that the Jewish book of laws, the Torah contains
613 commandments, but why not praise people for the commandments
they observe, rather than chastise them for the ones they don't? Given
that many of the commandments are no longer observed, such as those
related to animal sacrifice, why this obsessive insistence that others be
followed literally, or more extensively than originally commanded
(such as the Sabbath prohibitions)? The regressors only do so to keep
their followers in their thrall and to increase their own power,
importance, and to gather the funds to support themselves.

Rabbi Yedidia Ezrahian, a well-informed and qualified authority, wrote in an article in the trusted Persian magazine *Payam* (No. 537, P. 20), "Sacrificing Chickens and Roosters Is an Act of Idol-Worshippers" about this present version of "sacrificing animals": **"Let us join together and take away this opportunity from the hands of the hustlers,"** he wrote, **"who by advertising about making such 'sacrifices' tarnish the reputation of our community."**

In support of Rabbi Ezrahian's opinion, we must add that fraudulent men have existed in all societies, all over the world. During the Inquisition in 15th century Europe, hustler priests sold shares of Heaven with the approval of the Pope! One man, angry at this hypocrisy, went directly to the Pope and purchased 100% of the shares of Hell for a large sum of money! The next day, he announced, "I have bought Hell in its entirety, and I am not going to let anyone in – ever! **Don't waste your money on buying shares of Heaven out of fear of the Hell, pouring your precious money into the pockets of the cheaters!"** And thus, the "store" of these religious hustlers was shut down!

"The stomach is a handcuff, and it's like shackles around the feet. One who's slave to the stomach, would worship God less."

In the past, Persian people used to call edible gelatin (what we call "jello") as *larzanak*, i.e. "the trembling thing." **Someone told his friend, "Eat some *larzanak*; it gives you strength."** The man replied, "If This *larzanak* shakes with every move how could it possibly keep me upright?!"

I am continually surprised by the power of brainwashing and the ability of hustlers to impose empty, void and feeble thoughts on others. It never ceases to amaze me how seekers are impressed by such hustles and how they are lured in the hope of gaining greater power over their lives – when in reality they are doing just the

460

opposite in submitting themselves to these religious taskmasters. Many have suggested that the philosophy of accepting religion lies in our sense of fear of the unknown.

Zoologist and founder of ethnology, **Dr. Konrad Lorenz** (1903-1989) wrote, "There are four major instincts that govern the behavior of all animals: **Hunger, Fear, Lust** and **Aggression." If** mankind took refuge in religion, out of the fear of the unknown then perhaps his aggression provoked by religion has to do with his fear of losing this imagined shelter.

The self-proclaimed caretakers of religions, too, by exploiting this **fear of the unknown**, have tried to scare people with such unknowns as Heaven and Hell, trying to ward off plagues and "the evil eye," or with "stinging words", sacrifices, talismans, and the like. They would have us believe that religion will remove many of the unknowns in life — just as **Mozaffar ad-Din Shah** (1853-1907), the Iranian king of **Qajar** did, who would hide himself under the cloak of a religious *mullah* called **Seyyed Bahreyni** whenever a lightning and thunder occurred!

If only we'd had the cooperation of religious educators over the last centuries to tackle the social ills they once endorsed, such as slavery. But over and over again, it is civil society and not religion that has passed those laws that keep us current and that promote a greater ethical and moral stance – such as American civil rights legislation. It is my hope that the day will come when alienation and divisiveness are banished from all societies. Then we'll have a springtime, devoid of any hatred, beautifully ornamented with morality, albeit at a high price. This day will surely come, it is the inevitable step on the path of the unstoppable, uncontrollable, progressive evolution of humankind. Let's hope for that day, the foundations of which are upon us today!

Knowledge of God was offered to humanity to prevent "Godlessness" and to combat the human lack of conscience. It was meant to be a means to an end, giving man a description of goodness, good deeds, compassion and forgiveness. In a way, man has accepted the worship of God, to have a scale against which to describe Godlessness and a lack of conscience. Alas, however, the dogmatic absolutism of religions has itself proved be a cause for unconscientious acts, sometimes commanding one group of followers to fight against the other! This includes Anti-Semitism, and other forms of bigotry by one group against another.

The double-standard of religious commandments, based on discriminating between "us" and "the outsiders," exists in many different forms, and has been invariably horrific. For example, all religious books command, "Thou Shall Not Murder!" — Yet, the history of religion, and the pages of religious scripture, are filled with horrible stories of killings, massacres, murders, all considered "worthy" and "legitimate."

The religious books say, "Do not lie!"— But it's considered alright to lie in order to propagate the religion itself!

They command, "Do not steal!" — But it's alright to pillage!

Who is this stranger, this alien, this "other"? — Whoever thinks differently than us.

Who is to tell the difference between the two? — Apparently only the very executive members of these religions — someone both setting the criteria and making the judgment!

Thus, there's little wonder that for centuries blood has been dripping from the pages of the world's religious, sectarian or ideological books. They have sanctioned a world in which opportunists can label a person as an "outsider"—anyone, anytime, rather capriciously, including their own co-religionists.

The conditional enforcement of commandments and ethics has created a climate in which no rule need be followed, no moral lived by – unless their mullah approves. As such they don't see the world as it is, only as to the agenda of their leaders. If inside they truly applied the morals and ethics of their religion to all people and followed a religion of ensuring basic human rights, the world would calm down, and the coming generations, perhaps as early as our grandchildren, could finally begin to live in peace and comfort.

How long should the mistakes of history be repeated; How many human lives should be lost or wasted, or like the sands at the seashore be moved around by ruthless storms — Until humanity is finally placed on the progressive path of civilization; and until mankind realizes that humanity consists of "loving our fellow humans unconditionally." Let us all come together to nurture this idea, so that the shameful tradition of passing judgment based on religion is finally uprooted.

Drawing lines among people along religious differences has been a staple of the culture of "religion-centered" groups. For too long they have fooled people by selling such arbitrary differences to them in the name of "providing for their happiness." But true happiness lies in eliminating this very damaging mentality. If we are to uproot this harmful arbitrary form of discrimination we should begin first by decontaminating our own minds, then our homes, and our families. This would eventually lead to the decontamination of the entire society from this dangerous mentality, and it would render the future generations forever free of the harms of religious discrimination.

As the saying goes, "If everyone keeps their door fronts clean, the whole town would always be clean."

Virtually all people around the world agree that happiness is the principle foundation of life. Yet, what they can't seem to agree upon is how to get there.

Einstein said, "No law could be better than those who practice it." In the hands of ignorant people, the best of religious command, or secular laws, is no different than the worst of laws!

As for Judaism, today: Considering the multitude of contrasting traditions, differences or even conflicts, which may be observed between our communities scattered all around the world, it becomes evident that Judaism is not merely a religion. Indeed, Judaism is part of the world's culture and civilization.

Rabbi Mordecai Kaplan (1881-1983), the co-founder of **Reconstructionist Judaism**, in his important essay, titled "On the Need for a University of Judaism," set the grounds for the establishment of a university of the same name. He saw Judaism as an evolving civilization, and he proposed the theory that Judaism is composed of three elements:

1) Jewish religion,

2) Jewish Civilization,

3) Jewish philosophy and mysticism.

What makes it possible for us to reach to this level of civilization is neither religious observance, nor a lack of religion. Rather, it's a proper understanding of the morals, ethics and values underpinning the religion such as the *Ten Commandments*, or the golden rule of morality, i.e. "Wish for thy neighbor as you'd wish for thyself." The wealth of knowledge and science of our civilization is much more enduring than mere blind, absolutist, dogmatic beliefs; and we must recognize that the deceived extremist members of the religions weaken our religion not strengthen it.

464

"A cage is still a cage, even if it's as vast as the world.
Were there no medicine, even the doctor would die of the disease.
Oh, dear heart! Once set on the path of quest, just think of the road,
Because such a horizon would never have an end in sight."

To echo **Émile Zola**'s famous phrase, *J'Accuse!* **I Accuse!** The harm that the regressors are bringing upon society is much greater than the dubious positive results they claim to be aiming for.

Religion can be thought of as certain individual's collective way of life. Considering that there are no limits on the variety of beliefs and ideas or religions, and there is no possibility to say "Yes" to all of them, human intellect, reason, dictates that we follow its essence, "conscience." Religion is meant to make us see the folly of evil ways and to counsel us to act in a moral and ethical manner.

Rational followers of different religions join in unison to call any cruel oppressor "someone without a conscience." Once we study a variety of schools, we would realize that the majority of the people of the world consider faith to be something useful, or even necessary, for the psychological dependence of mankind. While we agree with this, we also observe countless religious people throughout history, whose faith has been empty and devoid of human conscience. Such people have been committing the worst of cruelties and crimes against humanity. That's because "faith" alone is never enough! Faith is only an unbridled flame. If it's not brought under the command of human conscience and morality, it will get out of control, and lead to corruption.

The propagation of superstition so weakens religion that a reasonable person cannot help but cry out loud against it.

"Ever happened to you, while asleep,
When you wished to shout, but could not?
When you wished to call on your co-travelers,

If only for a moment, on top of the lungs, but could not?
I'm that very man in that deep sleep,
Whose voice no one hears.
I've opened mouth to call out to the friend,
But no voice seems to emerge with the shout…"

When youngsters submit fully to regression in the name of "becoming religious," it is often out of yearning to be more moral and to lead a more structured proscribed life, safe from modern challenges – yet by doing so they are doing both themselves and the religion a disservice.

It is possible to be modern and be religious; to study the ancient texts and learn from the commentaries, but to do so as part of the modern world with knowledge of the most current thinking with regard to science, technology, arts and culture. The student educated in such a balanced and moderate fashion, with a foot in each world, the modern and the ancient, the secular and the religious, will find himself a more complete person and more prepared to face whatever challenge may emerge. No criticism of himself or his religion will trouble his self-assurance and deter from his road to success. He will know the satisfaction of working in the world, supporting his family, and being at peace with his family and his fellow man.

On this path, each person should do his or her part, and contribute his or her share. No one might have remembered this author, if he had kept his thoughts secretly hidden inside his mind! It's much better to express constructive criticism and useful thoughts than keep them to yourself.

Otherwise, those youths who find themselves a prisoner of the narrow minded religious leaders and their institutions will find themselves paralyzed by their own bigotry, prejudice, fanaticism,

466

dogmatism and regression. Whoever steps into this swamp will sink deeper into the marsh with each passing minute.

Dear reader, beware -- for your children too will be no exception.

If the present generation doesn't stop the growth and spread of regression, future generations will encounter a new crop of children and *mullahs,* who'll be even more dogmatic and rigid-minded than those of today.

Today, speculators and opportunists are leading our youngsters backwards. The true reason that those who imprison them do so, is that it pays their rent – this is the reprehensible way that they earn their living for themselves and their children.

However it need not be so: one can be religious, without suffering from an ossified mind. One can be religious and not fight modernism. One can be religious and follow modern science at the same time. One can be a free-thinking person, and remain faithful — and continue to evolve and progress. But wherever change and adaptation are deemed to be sins, progressive evolution toward civilization will be blocked from occurring.

"Utopia" will never be achieved until we remove the borders of hatred, long drawn between different religions and sects as well as obliterating the geographic boundaries between nations.

Jeremiah said,

"The days are coming, says the Lord, when I will make a new covenant with the house of Israel and the house of Judah." [Book of Jeremiah, 31:31]

The Christian Church gave these words a certain meaning – but that doesn't mean we can't see another meaning in them. Could we not take "the new covenant" to mean "keeping step with our time," in order to practice the commandments in sync with the innovations and demands of our time?

Books and ideologies, too, have a lifetime. If they don't keep in step with the times, they will fade away. One of the secrets of the survival of *the Holy Torah* – and the strength of Judaism in general – has been its resilience. As we said before, 80 percent of today's spoken Hebrew is different from the original Hebrew language; and no doubt, it will continue to change. If this language hadn't changed, it would have eventually died.

There is a difference between "maturation" and "growth," on the one hand, and "getting old" on the other. Those who "don't grow" "die" long before they have actually "gotten old."

Religion does not make you and me more valuable. To the contrary, it's up to us, to make our religion worthwhile. Those who imagine themselves or their sect to be the only worthy God-worshippers are ignorant of history. Neither do they understand the meaning of the 10th Commandment, "Thou shall not covet…", i.e. don't be jealous of others — and don't make yourself the subject of jealousy. Do not covet another religion or its hold on others. Coveting creates hostilities against religion; and hostilities related to religion.

"How good it is to be freed from the cage of one's self,
Beginning to see not just ourselves, but others, too."

To illustrate the point, compare the communication between universities or other scientific centers of the world — which is transparent and devoid of prejudice — versus the relationship between those religious figures — who typically suffer from inflated self-importance! Doing so makes one realize that,

"Fire is not that flame which would make the candle laugh!
True fire is what is set to the harvest.
Until the locks of the hair of words

Are combed with pens,
No one could ever remove the mask off of the
*Face of a thought, as **Hafez** does. "*

Centuries ago, it was written that **Jeremiah** (29:5-7) "Encourages and approves of the social and cultural co-mingling of the Jews with the world."

The contemporary Iranian scholar, **Ms. Nahid Pirnazar,** reminded us (*Shofar of Los Angeles*, No. 158, P. 34), that it's said in the Biblical books of *Psalms, Job* and *Ecclesiastes* that, "God founded the world on the basis of reason and intellect. And the absolute truth is hidden, as it awaits being uncovered by human beings. It's in such a school that human beings could reach their aims and ideals, by appreciating the value of an education which is combined with logic and intellect."

I repeat: Mankind will have peace and comfort when he has reached that level of civilization where the differences of opinions based on religion no longer exist; and when religion is no longer allowed to create such double-standards as "Us vs. Others", as in "Death is bad, unless it's for the others!"

The greatest threat to today's world is the issue of religion. We cannot eliminate it; neither should we follow it passively and blindly. We must bring religion into balance, and that can be done beginning with, and through, your family and mine.

"If everyone cleans up their door front, the whole town would always be clean." We need to wipe away any smears of religious hatred from our children's to make secure our children's future happiness.

As **Saadi** put it,

"Oh brother, speak now while you can,
And utter sweet words of happiness.

For once the angel of death arrives,
You'll be compelled to withdraw the tongue."

We should not accept religion just as an unalterable legacy but as an entity entrusted to us that has the potential to evolve. Let us think of the future of our children and accompany them on the path of progressive evolution.

We should never allow our serious fight against regression to turn into a grudge against religion that might harm our ancestral values. Instead of cursing and swearing at the darkness, we'd better light candles of reason to help us see the right way and pray for the human will to follow the correct path. Human will combined with modern intellect and insight can drive enormous change.

We should all work towards the victory of love and truth over lies and hypocrisy, regardless of anyone's particular brand of religion, ideology or tradition. We need to teach the world's children that the more resilient they are and the more they love each other, the happier they will be.

Our children need to follow religion to learn the eternal values and morals that make us a civilization. However a regressor uses religion and *mitzvah*, i.e. "rewarding good deeds", as an excuse to achieve his own aims. This is while the 16th century Persian scientist, **Hakim Sheikh Bahai** (1547-1621 _ C.E._) once wisely wrote,

"You may fast every day,
You may pray every night,
Visit Mecca every year,
Or walk barefooted into temples,
Do all the imperatives,
And avoid all the prohibitions —
Yet I swear to God,
None of these would be nearly

As good to anyone
As opening a closed door
On a hopeless man…"

Let us raise our children as informed people. The most dangerous weapon in the world is a man without conscience, not just someone who's religious, or has no religion. As we can see, religion is like fire: Contained within boundaries of moderation, it gives us warmth and energy. A contained fire is most useful; a raging fire wreaks havoc and destruction.

Jewish culture and civilization is more responsible for the survival of Judaism for thousands of years than the sayings or writings of many of the promoters of the religion.

The true face of the many religious leaders, past and present is evidenced by the sad state of religion today. Otherwise,

"All these fights, all this ado, are spurred
By nothing but shortsightedness.
Look with pure eyes, and you'd realize that
Ka'aba and the Wine-house are indeed one and the same…"

We can't ignore that some religious writings are outdated, make no sense, or worse yet are dangerous. Before we say that we believe in a religious commentary let's make sure that we really understand what it is saying – regardless of which religion is proclaiming it. Hiding behind equivocal, multi-serving or sarcastic interpretations or commentaries that are like "excuses worse than the sin" cannot cover up the truth. As a Persian proverb goes, about someone who insisted that he didn't have a rooster with him, "Should I believe your swearing, or the tail feathers of the rooster sticking out of your cloak!"

It's not about a particular type or brand of religion. The most obvious difference between free-thinking people and regressors is that rational people respect religion as a private matter and consider it only *part* of their overall human, national and ethnic, identity. But the "care-takers" of religion for their own ulterior motives seek to form a rigid-minded, dogmatic community of families that stand out from the rest of society.

The problem with the seditious groups lies here: rational people don't disseminate any propaganda, and don't interfere at all in other families' beliefs or way of life. The regressors, meanwhile, take advantage of rational people's indifference and silence, and even benefit from their material and financial support. The regressors wreak nuisance all over the world, even directly interfering in the private affairs of other families, as part of their mission to attract more and more recruits.

BEWARE: If the free-thinkers continue their silence and indifference, the regressors will succeed in their aims. As a result, the mainstream part of the religion will be marginalized while the overall population of followers will decrease.

What then is the solution? We need to prevent those acts of meddling and interfering; maintain balance and moderation; and take the initiative ourselves to make the necessary changes.

Anyone, wherever he or she stands, should take a step forward! The whole progress of the world starts just here...

It's said that the people of the city of Tous asked the famous Persian *Sufi*, **Sheikh Abusa'id Abolkhayr** (967-1049 C.E.), to deliver a sermon one day to the town's people. In the *Sufi* temple known in Persian as *khan-ghah*, they raised a platform for him to speak from. The day arrived, and a huge crowd showed up in the *khan-ghah,* so much so that there was no space left, and still, people kept trying to enter the place. The *sheikh* was ready to speak, when a man standing outside the *khan-ghah* pushed his head inside, and shouted, "May God bless anyone who would take a step forward from where he's standing!"

When the *sheikh* heard this, he said, "Whatever I wished to say, and whatever all other *sheikhs* and sages have said, their essence, and their conclusion, was expressed in the words of this man: '*May God bless the one, who takes one step forward from where he stands...*' Having said that, the *sheikh* descended from the platform and left, content with his sermon.

Religion won't evolve toward perfection on its own. In the opinion of this author, it's up to us to make progress happen. We'd better study, do research, observe past and present religious misfortunes and equipped with this information, step forward. While, at the same time, we should not allow anyone to make our children regress back to the ages of antiquity, in the name of religion.

"Everyone understood the said statement
According to his own intellectual capacity.
*But in the absence of the Sage (of intellect), you **Hafez***
Would excuse us for not offering a better explication!"

Dear Mothers,

Inform your children accurately, and raise their awareness as much as possible. As they say, "Teach your children how to swim, and you would no more be afraid of your neighbor's pool."

The most critical responsibility in today's society is to protect children's minds from becoming contaminated and corrupted; and to promote love and kindness instead of hatred – a task in which mothers play a crucial role.

It's been said that mothers give milk to Tomorrow, to the future teachers of the world. Mothers need to encourage their children to be free-thinking people, and not to be afraid of expressing their opinions.

Once upon a time we lived in an undeveloped land, where censorship and backwardness were the accepted way and where self-censorship was rampant – these traditions are not worthy of preserving. Today we must not be afraid to criticize and to do so to improve our understanding and our way of life – that is the path to preserving our religion and having our children and our children's children progress in the world.

Conclusion

Dear Friends,

To resolve a problem, it's quite natural to examine its roots and causes.

The world's religions and the many leaders promulgating a narrow one sided worldview have caused much of the world's tragedies. Out of mankind's 3425 years of documented history, only a meager 268 years have been devoid of any wars – and we daringly assert that religious and mono-maniac views have been the primary cause.

We might not readily see the roots of a huge tree as they are buried deep beneath the soil. Likewise, even to date, the world, including our own small Jewish community, does not see the dangerous growth of a highly contagious disease – the kind of one-dimensional religious mentality that is the source of so much conflict in the world.

Such ill will is spread via brain-washing and through modern public media. The fanatical forces of regression abuse, exploit and take advantage civil societies' freedom, laws and human rights and then turn them against the civilized world.

Although mankind's greatest advantage is their ability to pass on their experiences to subsequent generations, we have not learned from our past mistakes. The world of religion is in dire need of a major revolution, a renaissance, an awakening, a rebirth, on both international and local levels; a change with an impact much stronger than the 19th century enlightenment in Europe. We must begin by renouncing all absolutist and one-dimensional ways of thinking, particularly among the followers of religions as well as the fanatical members of other ideological schools.

Such a major change will not take place until we heed that famous proverb which states: **Everyone should begin by sweeping clean their house-fronts, so that the whole city would become clean.**

When the great **Israeli Prime Minister David Ben-Gurion** was asked whether he was a Communist, a Socialist, or a Religious person, he answered: "I will act in whatever way is in society's best interest at the time."

When so-called religious people bring many children into the world, children that will become a burden to their families, to the government and to their society, are they acting in society's best interest, I ask, or merely their own? Are they doing "good" or "evil"?

Such people imagine themselves to be free of all "considerations" and "calculations," but they are like farmers, seeding their ideas among our youth, irrigating the land with prayers! We must speak out against them. Otherwise, someday, such very people could end up sitting at our dinner table, as members of our families.

A **holy man** spoke at his death-bed of *tikkun olam* ("repairing the world") and how changing the world begins by changing ourselves. "When I was a child," he said, "I wished to change the world. Then I grew up a bit, and I thought, 'The world is way too big for me! I'd better begin by changing the people of my town.' As a teenager, I realized that the town was still too big an undertaking; so I thought, 'Maybe I should just change my neighborhood.' By the time I was middle-aged, I thought, 'I should start changing things in my own family.' But now, at the end of my life, I realize that I should have started with myself in the first place, '**Because if I had begun with myself, I'd be able then to change my family, my neighborhood, my town and even my country, to the extent of my abilities."**

Today, each one of us, by ourselves, and by using the Internet can promote free-thinking and rational thought to drive away from our schools and our community the narrow-minded one-dimensional absolutist mindset of the regressors. We need to let the next generation understand that preserving one's own beliefs doesn't depend on repudiating others. It's only the single-minded absolutist who says: **"Only my way! Only my book! Only my belief! All things else are worthless!"**

Each person's own knowledge and intellectual insight determines their value. No religion or belief confers any value on its own. Rather, it's the thoughts and deeds of the followers of a religion that endows their religion and beliefs with value, investing them with credit.

Jules Renard said, "An absolutist mindset is like an hourglass; it fills the heart, even as it empties the brain." Let us have faith in ourselves.

Rational religious thought is like a sun that would melt the despicable snows of religious and sectarian discrimination. Many of the world's scientific theories and revolutions were initially called "blasphemies" by the religious establishment. But today we have the Internet so that we might research the truth of any claims and so that each one of us can share his or her thoughts and opinions with others freely, without any censor.

Tim Berners-Lee, a little known scientist, along with his colleagues at CERN, the European Particle Physics Laboratories, invented the World Wide Web in March 1989, in order to facilitate the exchange of ideas between the world's scientists. At the time, he never imagined that this unprecedented breakthrough would spread all over the world at such a rapid rate; that it would transform our world so deeply that the end of the change it has brought about is not even in sight.

Let us not take this unprecedented and unique global tool for granted. Let us appreciate this amazing gift, which is available to all of us for free. It's up to us to do our best to prevent discrimination and hatred, be it domestic or foreign, local or global, from being passed on to the next generation. This is our duty, our responsibility, and our mission.

The Persian poet **Saeb** wrote,

> *"Blasphemy and religion will both end up in one place!*
> *It's just one dream, with a variety of interpretations."*

"Interpretation" has long been a source of conflict among religions – often within the same religion. Consider that Christianity, a religion that claims to promote kindness among people, has sprouted into at least 34 different sects, each of which has its own dedicated place of worship. All Christians follow the same prophet; yet as a result of absolutist mindsets, these various sects have long been busy shedding each other's blood! And even worse, the absolutist mindset had led to the silence of such figures as the Pope during the massacre of the Armenian Catholics; and the silence of the church concerning the murder of the Jews during the Holocaust.

God is meant for the unity of mankind, not as a tool for those who wish to wreak havoc. Absolutism inevitably leads to bigotry and prejudice, and in turn to violence, divisiveness and hatred.

Speaking of sects, Islam too has been divided into seven major sects, while Judaism features at least eight. Buddhism, Hinduism, even the Bahai faith, each have spawned several factions, each of which shout the same words:

Only my way! Only my book! And: Only my God!

This is the inevitable outcome of absolutist mindsets and religious one-dimensional worldviews.

Mahatma Gandhi said, "My pain is not just one. Rather, it's the death of a people who deem poverty as contentment, and incompetence as patience; and who with a smile on their face, imagine these plagues to be their fate and a result of Divine wisdom."

The global problem of religion, including within our community, is a challenge that is passed from generation to generation. How do certain religions proclaim that practicing superstition and promoting falsehood is a sin, yet they not only tolerate bogus thought and pseudo-science but call promoting them "rewarding good deeds." These groups keep turning the wheel of ignorance, passing on such miseries to the next generation in the name of "preserving our identity." But as **Steven Weinberg,** American physicist and a Nobel Laureate said, *"With or without religion, you would have good people doing good things and evil people doing evil things. But for good people to do evil things, that takes religion."*

Let me quote **Shakespeare**'s words, to effect, "I have a Divine spark in my chest, named Conscience." Let us consider this holy flame burning inside mankind's chest as "God's representative" on Earth. Let us support a religion that follows human conscience and reason along with such universal laws as "The Ten Commandments," to overcome all kinds of divisions, prejudices and discrimination.

Socrates once wrote, "Justice is lacking most where there are too many laws." If we seek a civil world, we must maintain moderation and balance, promote rational belief and the rule of law. However, following immutable and irrational rules, regulations and rituals that have passed their expiration date will only lead civilization to its demise and the ruin of religion.

We are not responsible for others' perceptions of us, but we are responsible for allowing others to behave in ways that reflects poorly on us; all the more so when they do so with malicious intent and we keep silent out of indifference.

The future is not something that mankind will automatically inherit. Rather, the future will be what we make it to be. **"We" and "You" must formulate our "response" to future generations.** It's time to begin -- with ourselves and our families. Individual apathy and silence in the face of such a colossal atrocity would be tantamount to a crime. Collective apathy and silence would amount to avoid fulfilling our responsibilities. The only sure road to failure, to repeating the mistakes of the past, and suffering the consequences, over and over, is one thing: Making no effort at removing the causes behind the problems.

Let us come together. Let us find the causes behind our age-old miseries. Let us uproot those phony religious, traditional or ideological obstacles, which have plagued mankind for too long. Let us hope for a better tomorrow, free of regression, fanaticism, blind imitation, and superstition. Let us build a better world, for ourselves, and let us pass on the best of our experiences to future generations. Let us start this change, beginning with ourselves, our families, our schools and our children. Let us hope for a world devoid of superstitions, a world which will be governed by reason and conscience. And let us do our best to bring it about.

Norman "Nourollah" Gabay
November 2010, Los Angeles

Afterword

I admit that these pages have many shortcomings. However, I feel the responsibility to communicate my message, as clearly as possible, so that everyone will understand the dangers facing our community and what we must do.

I am neither a religious authority nor an expert on any aspect of religion, religious history or religious observance. However I am someone who has seen many people go astray because of religion in general and certain extremist religious elements in our community, in particular. It is my responsibility to speak about the problems I see, their possible causes and the possible solutions to these dangers.

To me, the duty of doing this outweighs the inevitable agreement or disagreement of others. Although there may even be some unkind, biased people, who would partially quote these writings, taking my statements out of context, I ask that you consider my comments in their full context. If you understand my words, and my intention, then I have succeeded, regardless of whether you agree or not with the opinions stated herein. It is my belief that our lives are not just a number we reach, but rather the collection of experiences, acts and deeds, and the memorabilia that we leave behind, such as this volume – these are the kind of things that will remain after us, and by which the future will judge us.

Ferdowsi wrote,

"The world endures, and we leave,
Nothing remains of people, but
Some words and stories — and a name.
The only thing right for me is
To die with a good repute.
I need a good name; otherwise,
This body was always meant to leave..."

The warning contained in the following epic poem speaks to my concerns:

"A group of people, with help from hypocrisy,
Have erected a mountain of deception,
And a tower of seditious conspiracy,
Inside the womb of this mother of Faith –
Reproducing fetuses of ignorance, to be
Spread all around the world.
Their thoughts are contaminated and corrupt,
Yet they shout claims of faith, all rising from deception.

Now, it's you and the honor of the father's identity!
Now, it's you and the honor of the mother's love!
Now, it's you and the safeguarding of the legacy of love –
And of peace among all members of humankind!
Now, it's you and the answer of history…

It's now time for us to break
The links of the chain of ignorance, inside
The magic hat of religious propagation!
And alongside those, whose faith is placed in reason,
In step with those, who tread the path of evolution,
Uncover the veils of deceit
Off of the face of history…"

Dr. Jamshid Amoozegar (b. 1923 C.E.), a former Iranian Minister during the last years of the Pahlavi Dynasty, once said, "A good speech should be like a mini-skirt: Just long enough to cover the subject, but not too long to become boring!"

In the end, it is not for me to say how much space the thoughts in this volume need to be fully expressed. There have been many who wrote tens of volumes to criticize or oppose a thought or a system. But so far, you've just had this single volume from this humble writer.

"This story has more to it, but it's locked inside.
The windows have closed, and it won't get out.
The rest of this story would thus flow directly, with no words,
Into the heart of anyone, who bears inside the light of life."

And finally,

"The story of our "goods and bads" —
This shall remain forever on record.
After all, life has
A pen, a book, a registrar,
And an archive to hold the books…"

Let's discuss the contents of these collected thoughts, mediations and arguments, the warnings given and the suggestions made, with our wise and knowledgeable friends and our dear children. Let us speak to them, in their own language trusting that by further exploring and discussing the subjects therein, we may strengthen our families and improve our community. Indeed, hundreds of claims and thousands of promises would not have the deep constructive effect of one single positive act — and I say this in full humility, even as I remember the words of the poet, who said,

"It wouldn't be easy to take a drop of water to the ocean,
Or to take the dry thorn bushes of the desert to a garden of flowers.
But what can I do about it — when the ants have the habit of
Carrying the leg of a locust to the court of Solomon…"

Thank you.

Truly Yours,
Norman N. Gabay, a.k.a. "Babanouri"
Los Angeles, Winter 2011

For the time being, to leave your comments, or receive copies of the book, please visit the following site: www.BabaNouri.com or email invitationtoreason@hotmail.com

The proceeds from this book will go to Bikur Cholim Hospital.

Translator: Payman Akhlaghi

Editor: Tom Teicholz

484

Short Biography of Norman Gabay
The Author

Norman Gabay was born in 1929 in the City of Kashan, Iran to a traditional Jewish family. He attended Alliance Israelit Etehad Kashan primary school and upon completing sixth grade in 1941, was sent by his parents to Tehran for a practical education in business. There, while attending night school he went to work for an import/export business where he remained for seven years until 1948 when he established his own import/export and manufacturing business.

In 1953 he married Ms. Mahboubeh and two years later Kamran, the first of three children was born. In 1955 Norman went to New York to open a purchasing office, which provided the eventual inspiration to immigrate to the United States.

In 1971 he brought his children to the United States so they can have a better education, and subsequently received alien resident status for the entire family. In 1979, three months before the Iranian revolution, Norman Gabay and his family moved to the United States. After the revolution, the Islamic government seized all his assets. Upon his arrival in the United States, the family migrated to Southern California where, with the help of his sons, he started a real estate development company which continues to thrive as of this date.

Mr. Gabay belongs to a generation of Jews born in Iran during the 20's and 30's which overcame a culture of discrimination and persecution and took advantage of a window in Iranian history to foster an atmosphere of tolerance. This generation would be the core of the initial migration to United States. It was during the early years of this migration that Norman felt that the community was transforming from a very tolerant communal society to a highly polarized and broken community that was straying from their 2500 year old Iranian Jewish tradition. He felt it is his obligation to share his insight by publishing articles in community publications to make the community aware of this potentially destructive behavior which he continues to do to this day.

Currently, Norman Gabay is semi-retired and mostly he spends his time studying, writing, and traveling to different countries. He is one of the founding members of the Magbit foundation, which provides financial support to more than 10,000 students in six universities where he continues to serve as the chairman of the board of trustees. He also served as the vice-president of the board of trustees of the Iranian-American Jewish Federation and served as an advisor of the Center for Oral History and a long time member of Sinai Temple.